Fodor's UpCLOSE

PARIS

the complete guide, thoroughly up-to-date

SAVVY TRAVELING: WHERE TO SPEND, HOW TO SAVE

packed with details that will make your trip

CULTURAL TIPS: ESSENTIAL LOCAL DO'S AND TABOOS

must-see sights, on and off the beaten path

INSIDER SECRETS: WHAT'S HIP AND WHAT TO SKIP

the buzz on restaurants, the lowdown on lodgings

FIND YOUR WAY WITH CLEAR AND EASY-TO-USE MAPS

Previously published as *The Berkeley Guide to Paris*

FODOR'S TRAVEL PUBLICATIONS, INC.

NEW YORK • TORONTO • LONDON • SYDNEY • AUCKLAND

www.fodors.com/

FODOR'S UPCLOSE™ PARIS

EDITOR: Natasha Lesser

Editorial Contributors: Kim Conniff, Simon Hewitt, Suzanne Rowan Kelleher, Alexander Lobrano, Ian Phillips

Editorial Production: Laura Kidder, Tracy Patruno

Maps: David Lindroth, *cartographer*; Bob Blake, *map editor*

Design: Fabrizio La Rocca, *creative director*; Allison Saltzman, *cover and text design*; Jolie Novak, *photo editor*

Production/Manufacturing: Robert B. Shields

Cover Art: Moirenc/DIAF

CONTENTS

I.   BASICS *1*

2. EXPLORING PARIS 34

7. ILE-DE-FRANCE *160*

FRENCH GLOSSARY *176*

INDEX *182*

TRAVELING
UPCLOSE

S tay in a turn-of-the-century hotel. Try a hostel. Shop for a picnic. Have lunch on a hilltop park bench. Take the métro. Prowl the flea markets. Go up the Eiffel Tower. Memorize the symphony of the streets. And if you want to experience the heart and soul of Paris, whatever you do, don't spend too much money.

The deep and rich experience of Paris that every true traveler yearns for is one of the things in life that money can't buy. In fact, if you have it, don't use it. Traveling lavishly is the surest way to turn yourself into a sideline traveler. Restaurants with white-glove service are great—sometimes—but they're usually not the best place to find the perfect pâté. Doormen at plush hotels have their place, but not when your look-alike room could be anywhere from Dusseldorf to Detroit. Better to stay in a more intimate place that truly gives you the atmosphere you traveled so far to experience. Don't just stand and watch—jump into the spirit of what's around you.

If you want to see Paris up close and savor the essence of the city and its people in all their charming, stylish, sometimes infuriatingly arrogant glory, this book is for you. We'll show you the local culture, the offbeat sights, the bars and cafés where tourists rarely tread, and small, family-run hotels and other hostelries where you'll meet fellow travelers—places where the locals would send their friends. And because you'll probably want to see the famous places if you haven't already been there, we give you tips on losing the crowds, plus the quirky and obscure facts you want as well as the basics everyone needs.

OUR GANG

Who are we? We're artists and poets, slackers and straight arrows, and travel writers and journalists, who in our less hedonistic moments report on local news and spin out an occasional opinion piece. What we share is a certain footloose spirit and a passion for the City of Light, which we celebrate in this guidebook. Shamelessly, we've revealed all of our favorite places and our deepest, darkest travel secrets, all so that you can learn from our past mistakes and experience the best part of Paris to the fullest. If you can't take your best friend on the road or if your best friend is hopeless with directions, stick with us.

KIMBERLY CONNIFF • Following a hedonistic spring in Provence in 1991, Kimberly had an overwhelming itch for all things francophone. Five years later, she decided to tame her feisty bohemian dreams and move to Paris, jobless but ready to break into journalism in the cultural capital. She managed to find enough freelance work to keep her afloat, including reporting on Paris for the UpCLOSE guide. She has since moved to the world's other capital city, New York, to continue her career in journalism.

SIMON HEWITT • Simon headed to Paris straight from studying French and Art History at Oxford. It was a return to base: his grandmother was French, as are his wife and daughter. He recently moved to Versailles to gain a different perspective on life in and around the French capital. When not contemplating the Sacre-Coeur's aesthetic fallout or the Sun King's bigger-than-life Baroque home, his thoughts often turn to cricket—he is captain of the French national team.

SUZANNE ROWAN KELLEHER • Suzanne traded bagels for croissants five years ago when she moved from New York to Paris. A wayfarer by nature, Suzanne is a travel writer who knows how to find deals in Paris, from the perfect little top-floor garret to designer dresses at discount. She has good news about shopping and lodging in the city, reporting that France's recession has forced Paris to become increasingly value-oriented.

NATASHA LESSER • Natasha, the editor, spent a year in Paris that passed far too quickly. During that time she explored many a boulevard and back rue of this great capital and ate quite a few chocolate croissants. In the process of working on this book, she had to restrain herself numerous times from taking all the writer's good advice to heart and getting on a plane for Paris. Luckily, she stayed at her desk in New York long enough to pass their good advice on to you.

ALEXANDER LOBRANO • Alexander has lived in Paris 12 years, after eating his way through Boston, New York, and London. He writes a weekly dining column for *Paris Time Out* and has reported on French food and restaurants for many British and American publications. Alexander can tell you where to splurge on a great French meal that won't leave you franc-less, find one of the finest falafels in Paris, or enjoy a simple but unforgettable picnic of bread and cheese.

IAN PHILLIPS • Ian originally moved from Britain to Paris by mistake. He had applied for a job in the Mediterranean, following his dream of sailing yachts on the Mediterranean, but ended up taking bateaux-mouches down the Seine in Paris instead. Still, he very swiftly found his way around the French capital—in his first three years in the city, he lived in 13 apartments. Finally he found his footing as a freelance journalist, writing on culture and fashion for publications in Paris, London, and New York.

A SEND-OFF

Always call ahead. We knock ourselves out to check all the facts, but everything changes all the time, in ways that none of us can ever fully anticipate. Whenever you're making a special trip to a special place, as opposed to merely wandering, always call ahead. Trust us on this.

And then, if something doesn't go quite right—as inevitably happens with even the best-laid plans—stay cool. Missed your train? Stuck in the airport? Use the time to study the people. Strike up a conversation with a stranger. Study the newsstands or flip through the local press. Take a walk. Find the silver lining in the clouds, whatever it is. And do send us a postcard to tell us what went wrong and what went right. You can e-mail us at editors@fodors.com (specify the name of the book on the subject line), or write the Paris editor at Fodor's upCLOSE, 201 East 50th Street, New York, NY 10022. We'll put your ideas to good use and let other travelers benefit from your experiences. In the mean time, bon voyage!

INTRODUCTION

To understand what Paris is all about, you need to understand the city's brooms. Over a decade ago, Paris decided to remake itself as the cleanest metropolis in the world. The city didn't want American-style urban renewal (this was tried unsuccessfully in the '60s and '70s), nor did it want to turn deteriorated neighborhoods into cutesy historical districts (that's Disney's domain). The idea was to keep Paris looking the same—only cleaner—so some bureaucrat decided to institute the regular sweeping of every street in Paris by hand. Of course, to do this they needed the perfect broom. After a painstaking search for the most efficient street-cleaning broom, a committee of urban undersecretaries settled on a traditional peasant mōdel, like the ones made out of a bunch of twigs bound to a big stick. Of course, rather than use actual sticks and twigs, they came up with a durable plastic that could be cast in stick and twig molds. The plastic brooms look like their ancestors in almost every way—except for their fluorescent green color. Like the lime-green brooms used to sweep its streets, Paris is a strange concoction of tradition and high technology, of highly developed aesthetics and slightly screwy social conditions (observe the migrant workers pushing said peasant brooms).

Former president François Mitterrand was the man responsible for this project and other major changes in the Parisian landscape. His Grands Travaux (literally Big Projects, like the Pyramides du Louvre and La Défense) established him as one of the great builders in French history, along with Philippe August, Louis XIV, and Napoléon III. Even though the Grands Travaux are funded nationally, nearly all have been undertaken in Paris. Of course, this is no coincidence: To many, Paris *is* France. New president Jacques Chirac, however, is more intent on trimming the national budget than initiating new projects. The *fonctionnaire* (government worker) strikes that ripped through Paris in 1995 were a reaction to drastic cutbacks in social programs once taken for granted. If Chirac's shearing continues, the neon brooms and other urban renewal projects may someday elicit the same nostalgia as the original stick and twig ones they were based on.

Paradoxically, Paris is simultaneously a forum for politicians and self-appointed guardians of French tradition, as well as a magnet drawing poets, philosophers, and social butterflies. When the government outlawed the commercial use of non-French (i.e., English) words in 1993, an odd coalition of merchants, academics, and journalists came together to protest—and the law was soon ruled unconstitutional. And, while keepers of the cultural flame try to preserve all that they hold dear, they can't keep modernity from encroaching on this city, one of the great urban centers of Europe. These contradictory forces explain how the frumpiest, run-down neighborhood bistro will swipe your credit card through a hand-held computer, instantly debiting your account thousands of miles away for 1,000F of wine.

Paris's tension between tradition and modernity, though, is not always apparent as you walk down the street. The city usually seems as carefully orchestrated as ever: Students spiff up to see and be seen, and 85-year-old matrons do the shopping in smart little day suits—even Paris's parks, last bastions of nature, are planned down to the last blade of grass. But when you see a suited-up businessman *bavarder* (chatting) with an Algerian street-sweeper leaning on his broom in front of an Internet café, you'll suddenly realize that Paris is a city of sometimes startling contradictions.

PARIS ARRONDISSEMENTS

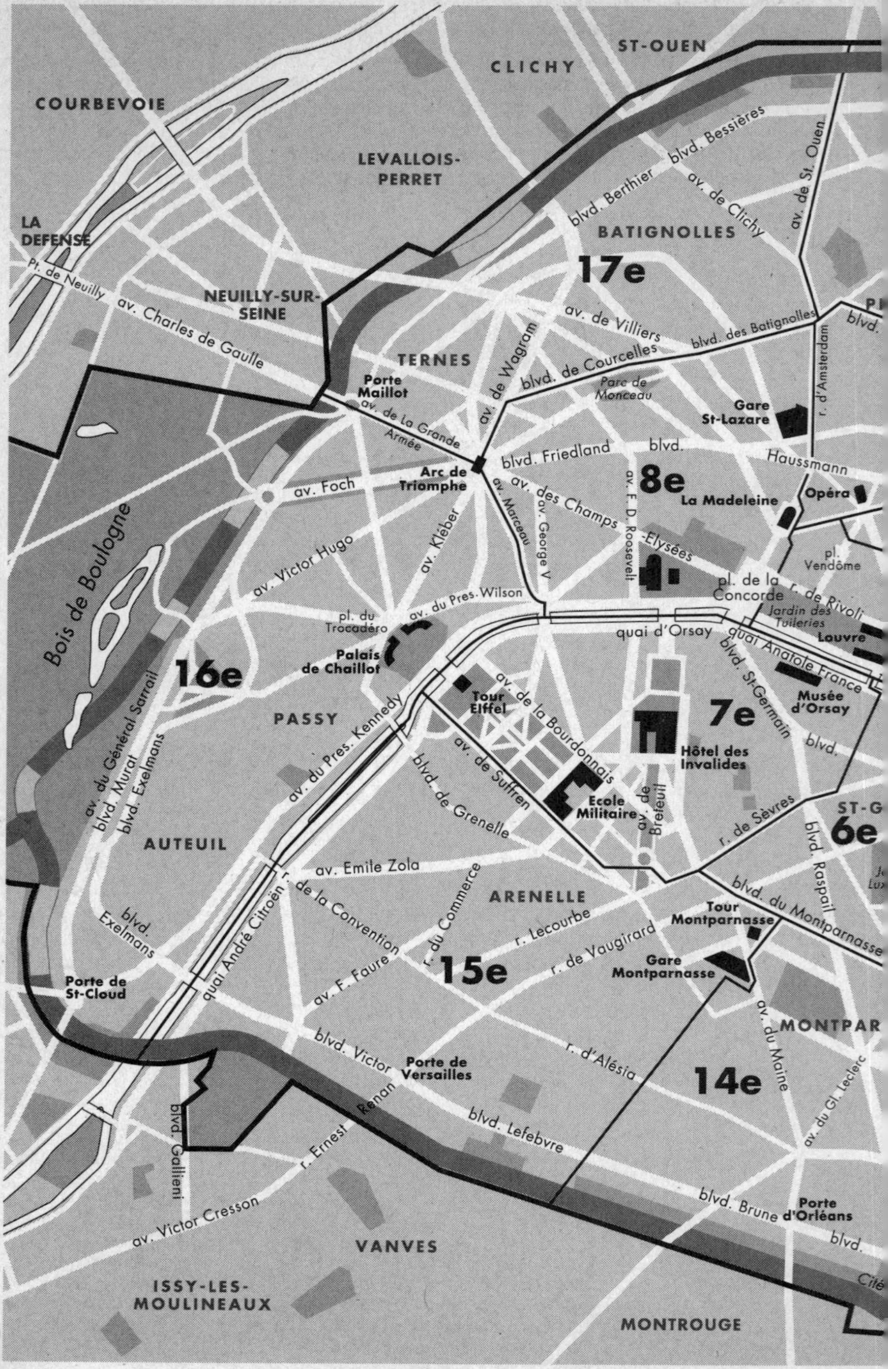

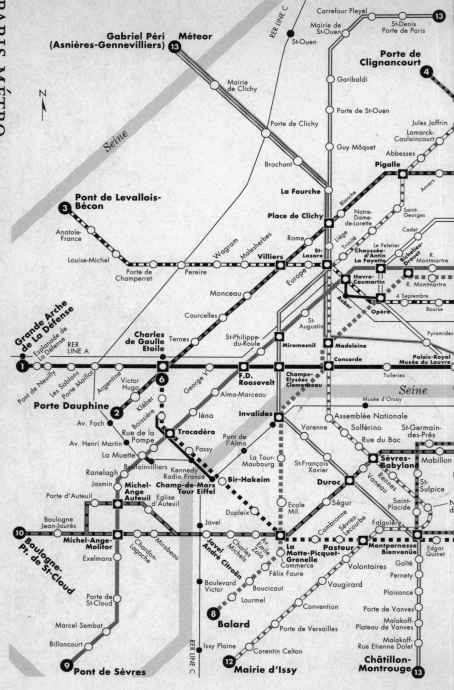

PARIS MÉTRO

PARIS MÉTRO

FORGET TO PACK ENOUGH MONEY?

MoneyGram^{SM} can help you, NOW!

- Your money arrives in just minutes to any of our 3,300 locations throughout Europe

- Customer Service Representatives available 24 hours a day who can inform you where the closest MoneyGram^{SM} money transfer location is.

So, if the money you need to see Europe has seen its last days, call us and we'll direct you to a MoneyGram^{SM} Agent close to you.

France
05-905311

BASICS

contacts and savvy tips to make your trip hassle-free

I

f you've ever traveled with anyone before, you know that there are two types of people in the world—the planners and the nonplanners. Travel brings out the worst in both groups. Left to their own devices, the planners will have you goose-stepping from attraction to attraction on a cultural blitzkrieg, while the nonplanners will invariably miss the flight, the bus, and maybe even the point. This chapter offers you a middle ground; we hope it provides enough information to help you plan your trip to Paris without nailing you down. Keep flexible and remember that the most hair-pulling situations turn into the best travel stories back home.

AIR TRAVEL

MAJOR AIRLINE OR LOW-COST CARRIER?

You'll probably choose a flight based on price, but there are other issues to consider. Major airlines offer the greatest number of departures; smaller airlines—including regional, low-cost and no-frill airlines—usually have a more limited number of flights daily. Major airlines have frequent-flyer partners, which allow you to credit mileage earned on one airline to your account with another. Low-cost airlines offer a definite price advantage and fewer restrictions, such as advance-purchase requirements. Safety-wise, low-cost carriers as a group have a good history, but if you've gotten a great deal on an airline you've never heard of before, **check the safety record before booking** any low-cost carrier; call the Federal Aviation Administration's Consumer Hotline (*see* Airline Complaints, *below*).

MAJOR AIRLINES • From the U.S.: **Air France** (tel. 800/237–2747) to Charles de Gaulle. **American Airlines** (tel. 800/433–7300) to Charles de Gaulle, Orly. **Continental** (tel. 800/231–0856) to Charles de Gaulle. **Delta** (tel. 800/241–4141) to Charles de Gaulle. **Northwest** (tel. 800/225–2525) to Charles de Gaulle. **TWA** (tel. 800/892–4141) to Charles de Gaulle. **United** (tel. 800/538–2929) to Charles de Gaulle. **USAirways** (tel. 800/428–4322) to Charles de Gaulle. From Canada: **Air Canada** (tel. 800/361–8620 in Québec or 800/268–7240 in Ontario). **Canadian Airlines** (tel. 800/426–7000). From the U.K.: **Air France** (tel. 0181/742–6600). **British Airways** (tel. 0345/222–111). **British Midland** (tel. 0181/754–7321 or 0345/554–554). **Air U.K.** (tel. 0345/666–777). From Down Under: **Qantas** (tel. 02/957–0111). **Continental** (tel. 02/693–5266 in Sydney or 09/379–5682 in Auckland).

OFFICES IN PARIS • **Air Canada** (tel. 01−44−50−20−20). **Air France** (tel. 01−44−08−22−22).
American Airlines (tel. 01−69−32−73−07). **British Airways** (tel. 08−02−80−29−02). **Continental** (tel.
01−42−99−09−09). **Delta** (tel. 01−47−68−92−92). **Northwest** (tel. 01−42−66−90−00). **United** (tel.
01−41−40−30−30).

GET THE LOWEST FARE

Flexibility is the key to getting a serious bargain on airfare. If you can play around with your departure
date, destination, and return date, you will probably save money. Ask which days of the week are the
cheapest to fly on—weekends are often the most expensive. Even the time of day you fly can make a big
difference in the cost of your ticket. The least-expensive airfares to Paris are priced for round-trip travel.
Major airlines usually require that you **book in advance and buy the ticket within 24 hours,** and you
may have to **stay over a Saturday night.** It's smart to **call a number of airlines and travel agencies, and
when you are quoted a good price, book it on the spot**—the same fare may not be available on the
same flight the next day.

Travel agents, especially those who specialize in finding the lowest fares (*see* Discounts & Deals, Travel
Agencies, and Students, *below*), can be especially helpful when booking a plane ticket. And don't be
afraid to call 1-800 numbers. When you're quoted a price, **ask the travel agent if the price is likely to
get any lower.** Good agents know the seasonal fluctuations of airfares and can usually anticipate a sale
or fare war. However, waiting can be risky: The fare could go *up* as seats become scarce, and you may
wait so long that your preferred flight sells out. A wait-and-see strategy works best if your plans are flexible, but if you must arrive and depart on certain dates, don't delay.

Airlines generally allow you to change your return date for a fee $25−$50. If you don't use your ticket
you can apply the cost toward the purchase of a new ticket, again for a small charge. However, most
low-fare tickets are nonrefundable. To get the lowest airfare, **check different routes.** If you can't get a
cheap flight into Paris, look into other destinations. Flying into Brussels is convenient; the airport is connected to the train station and the train trip to Paris costs about 290F second class and takes about
three hours. Amsterdam and Frankfurt are also good bets. One-way second-class train tickets cost 399F
and 467F respectively. Also look into discounts available through student- and budget-travel organizations (*see* Students *and* Travel Agencies, *below*).

To save money on round-trip flights originating in the United Kingdom, **look into an APEX or Super-PEX
ticket.** APEX tickets must be booked in advance and have certain restrictions. Super-PEX tickets can be
purchased at the airport on the day of departure—subject to availability.

CHECK WITH CONSOLIDATORS

Consolidators, also known as bucket shops, buy tickets for scheduled flights at reduced rates from the
airlines then sell them at prices that beat the best fare available directly from the airlines, usually without advance restrictions. Sometimes you can even get your money back if you need to return the ticket.
Carefully read the fine print detailing penalties for changes and cancellations, **confirm your consolida-
tor reservation with the airline,** and be sure to check restrictions, refund possibilities, and payment
conditions.

CONSOLIDATORS • **Airfare Busters** (5100 Westheimer, Suite 550, Houston, TX 77056, tel. 713/
961−5109 or 800/232−8783, fax 713/961−3385). **Globe Travel** (507 5th Ave., Suite 606, New York, NY
10017, tel. 212/843−9885 or 800/969−4562, fax 212/843−9889). **United States Air Consolidators
Association** (925 L St., Suite 220, Sacramento, CA 95814, tel. 916/441−4166, fax 916/441−3520).
UniTravel (1177 N. Warson Rd., St. Louis, MO 63132, tel. 314/569−2501 or 800/325−2222, fax 314/
569−2503). **Up & Away Travel** (347 5th Ave., Suite 202, New York, NY 10016, tel. 212/889−2345 or
800/275−8001, fax 212/889−2350).

CONSIDER A CHARTER

Charters usually have the lowest fares but are not always dependable. Departures are infrequent and
seldom on time, check-in can be chaos, schedules are often weird, and flights can be delayed for up to
48 hours or can be canceled for any reason up to 10 days before you're scheduled to leave. Moreover,
itineraries and prices can change after you've booked your flight, so you must **be very careful to choose
a legitimate charter carrier.** Don't commit to a charter operator that doesn't follow proper booking pro-
cedures. Be especially careful when buying a charter ticket. Read the fine print regarding refund policies. If you can't pay with a credit card, **make your check payable to a charter carrier's escrow account**

(unless you're dealing with a travel agent, in which case his or her check should be made payable to the escrow account). The name of the bank should be in the charter contract.

CHARTER CARRIERS • DER Tours (Box 1606, Des Plains, IL 60017, tel. 800/782–2424). **Martin-Air** (tel. 800/627–8462). **Tower Air** (tel. 800/34–TOWER). **Travel CUTS** (187 College St., Toronto, Ont. M5T 1P7, tel. 416/979–2406). **Council Travel** and **STA** (*see* Students, *below*) also offer exclusively negotiated discount airfares on scheduled airlines.

GO AS A COURIER

Courier flights are simple: You sign a contract with a courier service to baby-sit their packages (often without ever laying eyes on them, let alone hands), and the courier company pays half or more of your airfare. On the day of departure, you arrive at the airport a few hours early, meet someone who hands you a ticket and customs forms, and off you go. After you land, you simply clear customs with the courier luggage, and deliver it to a waiting agent.

It's cheap and easy, but there are restrictions: Flights are usually booked only a week or two in advance—often only a few days in advance—and you are allowed carry-on luggage only, because the courier uses your checked luggage allowance to transport the shipment. You must return within one to four weeks, and times and destinations are limited. If you plan to travel with a companion, you'll probably have to travel a day apart. And you may be asked to pay a deposit, to be refunded after you have completed your assignment.

COURIER CONTACTS • Discount Travel International (169 W. 81st St., New York, NY 10024, tel. 212/362–3636, fax 212/362–3236). **Now Voyager** (tel. 212/431–1616, fax 212/334–5243).

ENJOY THE FLIGHT

Get to the gate and **check in as early as possible** (at least two hours before your flight) for security reasons and also to avoid being bumped from your flight, especially during peak periods. You'll be required to show your passport or another form of photo ID.

To make your flight more comfortable, especially if you're tall, **request an emergency-aisle seat**; tell them you don't want to sit in the row in front of the emergency aisle or in front of a bulkhead, where seats may not recline. If you don't like airline food, you can **ask for special meals**—vegetarian, low-cholesterol, or kosher, for example—when booking. Some carriers have prohibited smoking throughout their systems; others allow smoking only on certain routes or even certain departures from that route, so **contact your carrier regarding its smoking policy.**

COMPLAIN IF NECESSARY

If your baggage goes astray or your flight goes awry, complain right away. Most carriers require that you file a claim immediately.

AIRLINE COMPLAINTS • U.S. Department of Transportation **Aviation Consumer Protection Division** (C-75, Washington, DC 20590, tel. 202/366–2220). **Federal Aviation Administration (FAA) Consumer Hotline** (tel. 800/322–7873).

AIRPORTS & TRANSFERS

Paris's main airports lie a fair distance outside town—Charles de Gaulle (also called Roissy) is 26 km (16 mi) northeast, and Orly 16 km (10 mi) south—but transportation to both is extensive. If you plan to fly out of Paris, arrive at the airport a full two hours before departure time; you'll probably encounter long lines at the ticket counters and baggage check and complete indifference from airline employees if you're about to miss your flight. Both airports have currency exchange desks and 24-hour cash exchange machines.

AIRPORT INFORMATION • Charles de Gaulle (tel. 01–48–62–22–80, 24 hours a day). **Orly** (tel. 01–49–75–15–15, 6 AM–11:30 PM).

TRANSFERS

You can get to both airports on **Air France buses** that depart for Paris every 12–15 minutes between 6 AM and 11 PM. The bus from Charles de Gaulle (55F) stops at the Air France office at Porte Maillot (17e, tel. 44–09–51–00; métro Porte Maillot), not far from the Arc de Triomphe; the one from Orly (40F) runs to the Hôtel des Invalides (Esplanade des Invalides, 7e, tel. 01–43–17–20–20; métro Latour-Mabourg

RUES WITH A VIEW: SCENIC BUS RIDES

There are several bus lines that you can ride for a good, cheap tour of Paris, sans irritating commentary. Some are traveled by buses with small balconies at the rear, though the proximity to gusts of carbon monoxide is less than pleasant.

NO. 29: The interesting section of the route stretches from Gare St-Lazare, past the Opéra and Pompidou Center, and through the heart of the Marais, crossing place des Vosges before ending up at the Bastille. This is one of the few lines primarily running through small neighborhood streets, and it has an open back.

NO. 69: Get on at the Champ de Mars (the park right by the Eiffel Tower) and ride through parts of the Quartier Latin, across the bridge to the Right Bank near the Louvre, by the Hôtel de Ville (City Hall), and out to the Bastille area.

NO. 72: River lovers will appreciate this line. It follows the Seine from the Hôtel de Ville west past the Louvre, Trocadéro, and most of the big-name Right Bank sights. You also get good views of the Left Bank, including the Eiffel Tower.

MONTMARTROBUS: If you want to see all of Montmartre without facing the hills "à pied" (on foot), pick up this bus at Pigalle for a winding tour of the area, including a pass under the Sacré Coeur. No special ticket is needed.

or Varenne). The trip takes about 40 minutes from Charles de Gaulle and 20 minutes from Orly, depending on traffic. A **taxi** from the airport is expensive; it costs about 200F to get to the center of Paris from Charles de Gaulle and 160F from Orly. If you have a lot of stuff and want to take the Air France bus or public transportation into Paris and then catch a cab to wherever you're staying, keep in mind that it costs an extra 10F per bag.

CHARLES DE GAULLE/ROISSY • If you're trying to catch a plane out of Paris, your safest bet is to connect with **RER B** from any métro or RER station to Roissy Aéroport Charles de Gaulle, since you won't have to worry about traffic, which can delay the buses for up to an hour. Look at the posters in the train to determine if you need to get off at terminal (*aerogare*) 1 or 2. A free *navette* (shuttle bus) takes you between the airport gates and the RER station in both directions. Tickets to the airport cost 48F; trains leave about every 10 minutes and the ride itself takes around 45 minutes. Trains start running at 5:30 AM toward the airport and at 6:30 AM toward town; either way they keep going until nearly midnight.

The **ROISSYBUS,** run by the RATP, is also easy and convenient, though traffic can thwart the projected 45-minute ride time. It costs 40F, and it takes you straight from your terminal to métro Opéra every 15 minutes from 5:45 AM to 11 PM.

ORLY • Orly has two terminals—Orly-Ouest and Orly-Sud—make sure you know which one you want. **RER C** to Orly plus a free shuttle brings you to the airport for 30F in about 30 minutes between 5:50 AM and 10:25 PM; trains in the other direction run 5:30 AM–11:30 PM. Trains in either direction leave about every 10 minutes. For 50F, you can take the **RER B** to Antony and grab the **Orlyval shuttle** to the airport. For 30F, the RATP-run **ORLYBUS** links the terminals with Métro Denfert-Rochereau, just south of the Quartier Latin. Look for the emblem on the side of the shuttle.

BICYCLING

It's not uncommon to see hardy souls with baguettes in their backpacks pedaling their way through Paris's treacherous traffic—**bicycling is one of the more efficient ways to get around the city,** especially if you manage to emerge with your baguette intact. Your lungs, however, might not be so lucky: Many French bikers have started wearing masks to protect themselves from the pollution.

BIKE RENTALS • Paris-Vélo (2 rue du Fer-à-Moulin, 5e, tel. 01–43–37–59–22, métro Censier-Daubenton; open Mon.–Sat. 10–12:30 and 2–7) rents bikes for 80F per day, 160F for two days and one night, and 520F per week, with a 2,000F deposit. It accepts MasterCard and Visa.

BOAT TRAVEL

In summer, hordes of Bateaux-Mouches creep and down the river, offering commentary in five languages and shining floodlights on the buildings at night. The lights show off the monuments to their best advantage, but they make people living (and kissing) along the river very unhappy. Dress warmly enough to ride on the upper deck, and you might avoid the crush below. Board the boat for a 40F, 1¼-hour tour at the Pont de l'Alma. From April to September, a less touristy alternative is Bateaux Parisiens, a small boat that runs between Pont de la Bourdonnais at the Eiffel Tower and the Hôtel de Ville on a one-hour tour for 40F during the day and 50F at night. The boats begin running daily at 10 AM and leave about every 30 minutes until 9 PM. Another option is the Bateaux Bus, with stops all along the Seine, beginning at the Eiffel Tower; watch for signs. The whole trip is 60F; smaller distances cost less.

BOAT COMPANIES • Bateaux-Mouches (Pont de l'Alma, tel. 01–40–76–99–99). **Bateaux Parisiens** (Pont de la Bourdonnais, tel. 01–44–11–33–55).

BUS TRAVEL

IN PARIS

Taking **the bus offers the distinct advantage of letting you see where you're going,** how you're getting there, and anything interesting along the way. However, **during rush hour the bus offers the distinct disadvantage of getting you there very slowly.** Métro tickets are accepted on the buses. Theoretically you need one to three tickets, depending on how far you're going, but it is highly unlikely anyone's going to check up on how many you use. In fact, even a used métro ticket will fly on most buses if you're subtle and don't mind a slight risk factor. If you're caught, though, you'll have to pay a 100F fine. Stamp your ticket in the machine at the front of the bus. If you have a Carte Orange, though, don't ever stamp it, or it will become invalid—just flash it to the driver.

There are maps of the bus system at most bus stops; all 63 bus lines run Monday through Saturday from 6:30 AM to 8:30 PM, with limited service until 12:30 AM and all day on Sunday. A handy little service, the **Noctambus runs 10 lines throughout the night,** every hour on the half hour between 1:30 AM and 5:30 AM; all lines start at métro Châtelet, leaving from just in front of the Hôtel de Ville. Stops served by the Noctambus have a yellow-and-black owl symbol on them. Technically, a single ride gobbles up four tickets, though rarely does anyone pay all four; a monthly or weekly Carte Orange works on Noctambuses, too. For a map of the night-bus routes, ask for a "Grand Plan de Paris" at any métro station; the Noctambus lines are drawn in the corner.

From mid-April through September, on Sundays and holidays from noon until 9, the **RATP runs a bus line called the Balabus, which hits all major sights in the city** and takes about an hour one-way. Buses start at the La Défense or Gare de Lyon métro stations; you can get it at all bus stops with the sign BB-BALABUS. The full ride costs three normal tickets, though again you can probably get away with stamping just one.

INTERNATIONAL ROUTES

Eurolines, Paris's lone bus company, provides international service only. If you take a bus into Paris, it will most likely drop you off at the Eurolines office close to Métro Gallieni. Some of its most popular routes are to London (9 hrs, 260F), Barcelona (15 hrs, 530F), and Berlin (12 hrs, 490F). The company's international buses also arrive and depart from Avignon, Bordeaux, Lille, Lyon, Toulouse, and Tours. Unfortunately, Eurail passes don't get you any discount.

BUS COMPANY • Eurolines (28 av. du Général-de-Gaulle, Bagnolet, tel. 01–49–72–51–51, métro Gallieni; open daily 9 AM–11 PM. 55 rue St-Jacques, 5e, tel. 01–43–54–11–99, métro Cluny–La Sorbonne; open daily 9 AM–7 PM).

BUSINESS HOURS

Most **museums are closed one day a week** (usually Monday or Tuesday) and on national holidays (*see* Holidays, *below*). Normal opening times are from 9:30 AM to 5 or 6 PM, occasionally with a long lunch break between noon and 2. Large stores stay open without a lunch break from 9 or 9:30 AM until 6 or 7 PM. Smaller shops often open an hour or so earlier and close a few hours later, sometimes with a lengthy lunch break in between. Banks are open weekdays (and sometimes Saturdays) roughly 9:30–4:30. Most banks, but not all, take a one-hour to 90-minute lunch break. For the most part, **stores (large and small), food shops (except for convenient corner stores), and government offices are generally closed on Sunday.**

CAR RENTAL

Although renting a car is more expensive in France than in the U.S., several agencies have pretty reasonable rates. However, it is rare to find a car with automatic transmission in France, so **make sure you know how to drive a stick-shift before you go.** The cheapest cars are very small stick-shifts and go for around 300F per day or 1,000F–1,500F a week. Some agencies include mileage in the cost, while others may charge you extra once you reach a certain number of kilometers. Rates in Paris begin at $60 a day and $196 a week for an economy car with air conditioning, a manual transmission, and unlimited mileage. This does not include tax on car rentals, which is 20.6%. Also, keep in mind that gas is unbelievably expensive (*see* Driving, *below*). Many agencies require that you be at least 23 years old and have a credit card in order to rent a car.

MAJOR AGENCIES • **Avis** (tel. 800/331–1084, 800/879–2847 in Canada). **Budget** (tel. 800/527–0700, 0800/181181 in the U.K.). **Dollar** (tel. 800/800–4000; 0990/565656 in the U.K., where it is known as Eurodollar). **Hertz** (tel. 800/654–3001, 800/263–0600 in Canada, 0345/555888 in the U.K.). **National InterRent** (tel. 800/227–3876; 0345/222525 in the U.K., where it is known as Europcar InterRent).

BEWARE SURCHARGES

No matter who you rent from, remember to ask about required deposits, cancellation penalties, holiday schedules, and drop-off charges if you're planning to pick up the car in one city and leave it in another. Note, too, that some rental agencies charge extra if you return the car before the time specified on your contract. To avoid a hefty refueling fee, fill the tank just before you turn in the car, but be aware that gas stations near the rental outlet may overcharge.

CUT COSTS

To get the best deal, book through a travel agent who is willing to shop around or **call a number of different car rental agencies.** Make rental arrangements before leaving home; **you can generally get a much better rate at home than in France.** Look for guaranteed exchange rates, which protect you against a falling dollar. With your rate locked in, you won't pay more even if the price goes up in the local currency. Be sure to **look into wholesalers,** companies that do not own fleets but rent in bulk from those that do and often offer better rates than traditional car-rental operations. Prices are best during off-peak periods. Rentals booked through wholesalers must be paid for before you leave the United States.

RENTAL WHOLESALERS • **Auto Europe** (tel. 207/842–2000 or 800/223–5555, fax 800–235–6321). **DER Travel Services** (9501 W. Devon Ave., Rosemont, IL 60018, tel. 800/782–2424, fax 800/282–7474 for information or 800/860–9944 for brochures). **Europe by Car** (tel. 212/581–3040 or 800/223–1516, fax 212/246–1458). The **Kemwel Group** (tel. 914/835–5555 or 800/678–0678, fax 914/835–5126). **Renault Eurodrive** (tel. 800/221–1052 from eastern U.S.; tel. 800/477–7716 from western U.S.; and tel. 800/777–7131 from FL and Puerto Rico; www.eurodrive.net) leases cars for a 17-day minimum that includes all taxes, insurance, and unlimited mileage.

MEET THE REQUIREMENTS

In France **you can use your own driver's license** for short stays. If you're staying longer, an International Driver's Permit (IDP) is a good idea, however; it's available from the American Automobile Association ($10) or the Canadian Automobile Association, or, in the United Kingdom, from the Automobile Association or Royal Automobile Club. The IDP will cost you $10 and two passport-size photos. Nonmembers must pay cash. Some offices can issue an IDP on the spot in about 15 minutes, but be sure to call ahead; during the busy season IDPs can take a week or more. For information about rules of the road, *see* Driving, *below*.

AUTO CLUBS • In the U.S., **American Automobile Association** (tel. 800/564–6222). In the U.K., **Automobile Association** (AA, tel. 0990/500–600), **Royal Automobile Club** (RAC, tel. 0990/722–722 for membership, 0345/121–345 for insurance).

NEED INSURANCE?

When driving a rented car you are generally responsible for any damage to or loss of the vehicle. Before you rent, **see what coverage you already have** under the terms of your personal auto-insurance policy and credit cards. Collision policies that car-rental companies sell for European rentals typically do not cover stolen vehicles. Before you buy additional coverage for theft, find out if your credit card or personal auto insurance will cover the loss.

THE CHANNEL TUNNEL

Since the early 1800s, visionaries have dreamed of building a tunnel between France and England. But endless obstacles have stood in the way. The Channel itself wasn't the problem; the chalk on the Channel floor is actually quite firm and amenable to tunneling. Still, bureaucratic fumbling and money problems delayed the opening of the tunnel considerably. At last it's complete. Now, short of flying, the "Chunnel" is the fastest way to cross the English Channel: 35 minutes from Folkestone to Calais, 60 minutes from motorway to motorway, or three hours from London's Waterloo Station to Paris's Gare du Nord. Passenger trains through the Chunnel are operated by Eurostar. One-way Eurostar tickets cost 250F–450F, though you can get cheaper rates with rail pass discounts if you stay over a Saturday night or if you are under age 26. Though you can't drive through it, you can put your car on the train known as Le Shuttle. One-way Le Shuttle tickets go for 490F (395F if bought 15 days in advance). However, prices fluctuate depending on time of day, week, and year, so be sure to check prices before you make your plans.

CAR TRANSPORT • **Le Shuttle** (tel. 800/388–3876 in the U.S.; 0990/353535 in the U.K.; 01–47–42–50–00 in Paris).

EUROSTAR • In the U.S., **BritRail Travel** (tel. 800/677–8585), **Rail Europe** (tel. 800/942–4866). In the U.K., **Eurostar** (tel. 0345/881881), **InterCity Europe** (Victoria Station, London, tel. 0171/834–2345, 0171/828–0892 for credit-card bookings). In Paris, **Eurostar** (tel. 08–36–35–35–39) tickets can be purchased at Gare du Nord or reserved at any train station in the city.

CONSUMER PROTECTION

Whenever possible, when you're shelling out money for those big items (plane tickets, car, hotel, new duds, etc.), **pay with a major credit card** so you can cancel payment if there's a problem, provided that you can provide documentation. If you're doing business with a particular company for the first time, **contact your local Better Business Bureau and the attorney general's offices** in your state and the company's home state, as well. Have any complaints been filed? Finally, if you're buying a package, always **consider travel insurance** that includes default coverage (*see* Insurance, *below*).

LOCAL BBBS • **Council of Better Business Bureaus** (4200 Wilson Blvd., Suite 800, Arlington, VA 22203, tel. 703/276–0100, fax 703/525–8277).

CUSTOMS & DUTIES

When shopping, **keep receipts** for all of your purchases. Upon reentering the country, **be ready to show customs officials what you've bought.** It's best to have everything in one easily accessible place—and don't wrap gifts. If you feel a duty is incorrect, appeal the assessment. If you object to the way your clearance was handled, get the inspector's badge number. In either case, first ask to see a supervisor, then write to the port director at the address listed on your receipt. Send a copy of the receipt and other appropriate documentation. If you still don't get satisfaction you can take your case to customs headquarters in Washington.

ENTERING AUSTRALIA

If you're 18 or older, you may bring back A$400 worth of souvenirs and gifts, including jewelry. Your duty-free allowance also includes 250 cigarettes or 250 grams of tobacco and 1,125ml of alcohol, including wine, beer, or spirits. Residents under 18 may bring back A$200 worth of goods.

RESOURCES • Australian Customs Service (Regional Director, Box 8, Sydney, NSW 2001, tel. 02/9213–2000, fax 02/9213–4000).

ENTERING CANADA

If you've been out of Canada for at least seven days you may bring in C$500 worth of goods duty-free. If you've been away for fewer than seven days but more than 48 hours, the duty-free allowance drops to C$200; if your trip lasts 24–48 hours, the allowance is C$50. You may not pool allowances with family members. Goods claimed under the C$500 exemption may follow you by mail; those claimed under the lesser exemptions must accompany you.

Alcohol and tobacco products may be included in the seven-day and 48-hour exemptions but not in the 24-hour exemption. If you meet the age requirements of the province or territory through which you reenter Canada you may bring in, duty-free, 1.14 liters (40 imperial ounces) of wine or liquor or 24 12-ounce cans or bottles of beer or ale. If you are 16 or older you may bring in, duty-free, 200 cigarettes and 50 cigars; these items must accompany you.

You may send an unlimited number of gifts worth up to C$60 each duty-free to Canada. Label the package UNSOLICITED GIFT—VALUE UNDER $60. Alcohol and tobacco are excluded.

RESOURCES • Revenue Canada (2265 St. Laurent Blvd. S, Ottawa, Ontario K1G 4K3, tel. 613/993–0534, 800/461–9999 in Canada).

ENTERING FRANCE

Going through customs in Paris is usually pretty painless. The officials will check your passport but probably won't touch your luggage unless you look shady or their dogs have caught a whiff of something interesting in your bags.

If you're coming from outside the European Union, you may import duty free: (1) 200 cigarettes or 100 cigarillos or 50 cigars or 250 grams of tobacco (twice that if you live outside Europe); (2) 2 liters of wine and, in addition, (a) 1 liter of alcohol over 22% volume (most spirits) or (b) 2 liters of alcohol under 22% volume (fortified or sparkling wine) or (c) 2 more liters of table wine; (3) 50 milliliters of perfume and 250 milliliters of toilet water; (4) 200 grams of coffee, 100 grams of tea; and (5) other goods to the value of 300F (100F for those under 15).

If you're arriving from a European Union country, you may be required to declare all goods and prove that anything over the standard limit is for personal consumption. Since January 1993, however, there is no longer any limit or customs tariff imposed on goods carried within the European Union (EU).

Any amount of French or foreign currency may be brought into France, but foreign currencies converted into francs may be reconverted into a foreign currency only up to the equivalent of 5,000F.

ENTERING NEW ZEALAND

Although greeted with a "Haere Mai" ("Welcome to New Zealand"), homeward-bound travelers with goods to declare must present themselves for inspection. If you're 17 or older, you may bring back NZ$700 worth of souvenirs and gifts. Your duty-free allowance also includes 200 cigarettes or 250 grams of tobacco or 50 cigars or a combo of all three up to 250 grams; 4.5 liters of wine or beer and one 1,125-ml bottle of spirits.

RESOURCES • New Zealand Customs (Custom House, 50 Anzac Ave., Box 29, Auckland, New Zealand, tel. 09/359–6655, fax 09/309–2978).

ENTERING THE U.K.

If your journey was wholly within European Union (EU) countries, you needn't pass through customs when you return to the United Kingdom. If you plan to bring back large quantities of alcohol or tobacco, check on EU limits beforehand.

RESOURCES • HM Customs and Excise (Dorset House, Stamford St., London SE1 9NG, tel. 0171/202–4227).

ENTERING THE U.S.

Like most government organizations, the U.S. Customs Service enforces a number of mysterious rules: When you return to the United States, you have to declare all items you bought abroad, but you won't have to pay duty unless you come home with more than $400 worth of foreign goods—as long as you've been out of the country for at least 48 hours and haven't already used the $400 allowance or any part of it in the past 30 days. For purchases between $400 and $1,000, you have to pay a 10% duty. You also have to pay tax if you exceed your duty-free allowances: one liter of alcohol or wine, 100 non-Cuban cigars (sorry, Fidel) or 200 cigarettes or 2 kilograms of tobacco, and one bottle of perfume. Prohibited: meat products, seeds, plants, and fruits.

You may bring back 1 liter of alcohol duty-free, providing you're at least 21. In addition, regardless of your age, you are allowed 200 cigarettes and 100 non-Cuban cigars. (At press time, a federal rule restricting tobacco access to persons 18 years and older did not apply to importation.) Antiques, which the U.S. Customs Service defines as objects more than 100 years old, enter duty-free, as do original works of art done entirely by hand, including paintings, drawings, and sculptures.

You may also send packages home duty-free: up to $200 worth of goods for your own use, with a limit of one parcel per addressee per day (and no alcohol or tobacco products or perfume worth more than $5); label the package PERSONAL USE, and attach a list of its contents and their retail value. Do not label the package UNSOLICITED GIFT, or your duty-free exemption will drop to $100. Mailed items do not affect your duty-free allowance on your return.

RESOURCES • U.S. Customs Service (Inquiries, Box 7407, Washington, DC 20044, tel. 202/927–6724; complaints, Commissioner's Office, 1301 Constitution Ave. NW, Washington, DC 20229; registration of equipment, Resource Management, 1301 Constitution Ave. NW, Washington DC, 20229, tel. 202/927–0540).

DISABILITIES & ACCESSIBILITY

ACCESS IN PARIS

Although Paris has spent a lot of money rebuilding itself during the past decade, only recently was a law passed requiring that new buildings be wheelchair accessible. You'll still find very few buildings that are barrier-free, though some monuments, hotels, and museums—especially those constructed in the last decade—are equipped with ramps, elevators, and special toilet facilities. Most hotels in Paris, however, are in buildings that are hundreds of years old and unsuited to guests with impaired mobility. In general, more expensive or chain hotels are better equipped. Contact the Association des Paralysés de France for a list of wheelchair-accessible accommodations. For more information, **get a hold of the excellent, government-published, free booklet (in French),** *Touristes Quand Même;* it details, region by region, which tourist attractions and transportation systems are accessible to people with disabilities. The booklet is available from tourist offices and from the Comité National Français de Liaison pour la Réadaptation des Handicapés. The tourist office also sells *Paris, Ile-de-France pour Tous* (60F), a reasonably complete guide book for travelers with disabilities.

RESOURCES • Association des Paralysés de France (17 blvd. Auguste-Blanqui, 13e, tel. 01–40–78–69–00). **Comité National Français de Liaison pour la Réadaptation des Handicapés** (236 bis rue de Tolbiac, 13e, tel. 01–53–80–66–66).

GETTING AROUND IN PARIS

Taxi drivers are required by law to assist travelers with disabilities in and out of their vehicles. Unfortunately, most of Paris's métro lines (like the bus system) are unfortunately inaccessible to travelers with disabilities, but the RER is slightly more accessible. The following Paris RER stations have elevators: Auber (direction Charles de Gaulle–Etoile only), Châtelet, Cité Universitaire (direction south only), La Défense, Denfert-Rochereau, Gare de Lyon, Gare du Nord, St-Michel (elevator on side street rue Xavier-Privas), and Vincennes. Some of these may require escalator use as well, however, and you may have to push a call button for assistance. Charles de Gaulle–Etoile has escalators only, but they'll take you all the way to the street if you use one of the Champs-Elysées exits. Nation has an escalator for direction Marne-la-Vallée (toward Disneyland Paris, where the station is accessible). Port Royal has escalator access for direction Gentilly and access for exits only from direction Châtelet. For more details, **ask the Régie Autonome des Transports Parisiens (RATP) for its brochure on accessibility.**

The SNCF, France's rail service, has cars on some trains that are equipped for travelers with disabilities, and passengers using wheelchairs can be escorted on and off trains. All places for those with wheelchairs are now in no-smoking cars. You need to **contact SNCF in Paris to request wheelchair assistance in advance** and for tickets; for more wheelchair access information, **try the SNCF Accessibilité Service.** Many trains and train stations in Western Europe are wheelchair accessible, though many in more remote locations are not. The *Guide du Voyageur à Mobilité Réduite,* available free at all train stations in Paris, is a comprehensive list of the services offered by every station in France.

RATP RESOURCES • Régie Autonome des Transports Parisiens (RATP; pl. de la Madeleine, 8e, tel. 01–40–46–42–17).

SNCF RESOURCES • SNCF (tel. 08–36–35–35–35). **SNCF Accessibilité Service** (toll-free in France only, tel. 0–800–15–47–53).

TIPS & HINTS

When discussing accessibility with a reservationist or a tour operator, **ask hard questions.** Are there any stairs, inside *or* out? Are there grab bars next to the toilet *and* in the shower/tub? How wide is the door-way to the room? To the bathroom? When possible, **opt for newer accommodations,** which are more likely to have been designed with access in mind. Older buildings may have more limited facilities. Be sure to **discuss your needs before booking.**

COMPLAINTS • **Disability Rights Section** (U.S. Department of Justice, Box 66738, Washington, DC 20035–6738, tel. 202/514–0301 or 800/514–0301, fax 202/307–1198, TTY 202/514–0383 or 800/514–0383) for general complaints. **Aviation Consumer Protection Division** (*see* Air Travel, *above*) for airline-related problems. **Civil Rights Office** (U.S. Department of Transportation, Departmental Office of Civil Rights, S-30, 400 7th St. SW, Room 10215, Washington, DC, 20590, tel. 202/366–4648) for prob-lems with surface transportation.

TRAVEL AGENCIES

Some agencies specialize in travel arrangements for individuals with disabilities. **BEST BETS** • **Access Adventures** (206 Chestnut Ridge Rd., Rochester, NY 14624, tel. 716/889–9096), run by a former physical-rehabilitation counselor. **Flying Wheels Travel** (143 W. Bridge St., Box 382, Owatonna, MN 55060, tel. 507/451–5005 or 800/535–6790, fax 507/451–1685), specializing in European cruises and tours. **Hinsdale Travel Service** (201 E. Ogden Ave., Suite 100, Hinsdale, IL 60521, tel. 630/325–1335), which offers advice from wheelchair traveler Janice Perkins. **Wheelchair Journeys** (16979 Redmond Way, Redmond, WA 98052, tel. 206/885–2210 or 800/313–4751), for gen-eral travel arrangements.

DISCOUNTS & DEALS

While your travel plans are still in the fantasy stage, start studying the travel sections of major Sunday newspapers: You'll often find listings for good packages and incredibly cheap flights. Surfing on the Internet can also give you some good ideas. Travel agents are another obvious resource; the computer networks to which they have access show the lowest fares before they're even advertised. Agencies on or near college campuses, accustomed to dealing with budget travelers, can also be especially helpful (*see* Students, *below*).

Always **compare all your options before making a choice.** A plane ticket bought with a promotional coupon may not be cheaper than the least expensive fare from a discount ticket agency. (For more on getting a deal on airfares, *see* Air Travel, Get the Lowest Fare, *above*.) When evaluating a package, keep in mind that what you get is just as important as what you save. Just because something is cheap doesn't mean it's a bargain.

CREDIT CARDS & AUTO CLUBS

When you use your credit card to make travel purchases you may get free travel-accident insurance, col-lision-damage insurance, and medical or legal help, depending on the card and the bank that issued it. So **check your credit card's travel-benefits policy.** If you are a member of the American Automobile Association (AAA) or an oil-company-sponsored road-assistance plan, **always ask hotel or car-rental reservationists about auto-club discounts.** Some clubs offer additional discounts on admission to attrac-tions. And don't forget that auto-club membership entitles you to free maps and trip-planning services.

DISCOUNTS BY PHONE

Don't hesitate to **check out "1-800" discount reservations services,** which use their buying power to get a better price on airline tickets, hotels, and even car rentals. When booking a room, always **call the hotel's local toll-free number** (if one is available) rather than the central reservations number—you'll often get a better price. Always ask about special packages.

CHEAP AIRLINE TICKETS • Tel. 800/FLY–4–LESS.

CHEAP HOTEL ROOMS • **Hotels Plus** (tel. 800/235–0909). **Hotel Reservations Network** (HRN; tel. 800/964–6835). **International Marketing & Travel Concepts** (IMTC; tel. 800/790–4682). **Steigenberger Reservation Service** (tel. 800/223–5652).

SAVE ON COMBOS

Packages and guided tours can both save you money, but don't confuse the two. When you buy a package your travel remains independent, just as though you had planned and booked the trip yourself. Fly/drive packages, which combine airfare and car rental, are often a good deal. In Paris, ask the tourist office about hotel packages (especially off-season). These often include tickets to major museum exhibits and other special events you'd be going to anyway. If you **buy a rail/drive pass** you'll save on train tickets and car rentals (*see* Train Travel, *below*).

DRIVING

Getting around Paris by car is a very bad idea—dealing with the traffic and the parking situation will just give you a big headache. But if you're planning to cruise the countryside, having a car gives you the ultimate travel freedom. Keep in mind, however, that gas is very expensive in France (about 6F per liter for regular unleaded, 6F10 for super unleaded). If you do decide to park in Paris, meters and ticket machines (pay and display) are common: Make sure you **have a supply of 1-, 2-, and 5-franc coins.** Parking is free during August in most of Paris, but be sure to **always check the signs before you park,** as rules vary.

Many small cars in France use diesel (gazole) instead of gas. The pumps are easy to confuse, and a mistake can wreck your engine.

Using **your own driver's license in France is acceptable,** though you may want to consider getting an International Driver's Permit (*see* Car Rental, *above*). When driving in France, note that the driver on your right has the right of way—and will take it. You must **wear your seat belt,** and children under 12 may not travel in the front seat. Speed limits are 130 kph (80 mph) on expressways, 110 kph (70 mph) on divided highways, 90 kph (55 mph) on other roads, 50 kph (30 mph) in towns. French drivers break these limits and police dish out hefty on-the-spot fines with equal abandon.

ROADSIDE ASSISTANCE • The **French Automobile Club National** (ACN; 5 rue Auber, 75009 Paris, tel. 01–44–51–53–99, fax 01–49–24–93–99) charges a small fee for roadside breakdown service and 24-hour towing. FYI, *remorquer* means "to tow," while the noun form is *la remorque.* If you're an AAA member, you can get reimbursed for ACN charges when you get home.

ELECTRICITY

Before tossing a blow-dryer into your bag, consider that European electrical outlets pump out 220 volts, enough to fry American appliances. So **you'll want a converter** that matches the outlet's current and the wattage of your hair dryer (which still may blow). You'll also want an adapter to plug it in; wall outlets in Paris take Continental-type plugs, with two round prongs.

You can get by with just the adapter if you bring a dual-voltage appliance, available from travel gear catalogs (*see* Travel Gear, *below*). Don't use 110-volt outlets, marked FOR SHAVERS ONLY, for high-wattage appliances (like your blow-dryer). Most laptops operate equally well on 110 and 220 volts and need only an adapter.

EMBASSIES

Your embassy can help you if your passport has been stolen or lost, or if you need any other kind of international-level assistance.

EMBASSIES • **Australia** (4 rue Jean-Rey, 15e, tel. 01–40–59–33–00, 01–40–59–33–01 in emergencies; métro Bir-Hakeim; open weekdays 9–5:30). **Canada** (35 av. Montaigne, 8e, tel. 01–44–43–29–16; métro Franklin D. Roosevelt; open weekdays 8:30–11). **Ireland** (4 rue Rude, 16e, tel. 01–45–00–20–87; métro Charles de Gaulle–Etoile; open weekdays 9:30–noon). **New Zealand** (7 ter rue Léonard-de-Vinci, 16e, tel. 01–45–00–24–11; métro Victor Hugo; open weekdays 9–1 and 2–5:30. **United Kingdom** (35 rue Faubourg St-Honoré , 8e, tel. 01–44–51–31–00; métro Madeleine;

open weekdays 9:30-12:30 and 2:30–5). **United States** (2 rue St-Florentin, 1er, tel. 01–43–12–22–22 métro Concorde; open weekdays 9–4).

EMERGENCIES

As in any big city, if you encounter trouble in the streets of Paris, the best thing to do is **yell for help** *(au secours!)* and attract as much attention as possible. There are a number of hot lines you can call if you or one of your companions is ill, but not all of them speak English. In case you lose your French with your cool, here are a few phrases to keep you going: *urgence* (emergency), *samu* (ambulance), *pompiers* (firemen), *poste de police* (police station), *médecin* (doctor), *médicament* (medicine), and *hôpital* (hospital).

EMERGENCY NUMBERS • Police (tel. 17). **Ambulance** (tel. 15). **Fire department** (tel. 18).

HOT LINES • ** Hot lines for **suicide prevention (tel. 01–46–66–66–66) and the **poison center** (Centre Anti-Poison, tel. 01–40–37–04–04) are available for emergencies, but there's no guarantee the staff will speak English. **SOS Viol** (tel. 08–00–05–95–95) is a rape crisis hot line; they answer calls weekdays 10–6. Women who have been assaulted should call **SOS Femmes Battues** (14 rue Mendelssohn, 20e, tel. 01–43–48–20–40, métro Porte Montreuil). There are no doctors on call at English-speaking **SOS Help** (tel. 01–47–23–80–80), but between 3 PM and 11 PM they can help you with medical referrals. For **AIDS** information, call tel. 0–800–80–04–08–00.

DOCTORS & HOSPITALS

About 45 minutes outside the city center, the **American Hospital operates a 24-hour emergency service.** Just like American hospitals, it is very expensive. A consultation with a doctor costs 500F. If you're American and lucky enough to have Blue Cross/Blue Shield (carry your card with you), they should cover the cost at the time of your visit. Otherwise, you have to pay up front and hope to be reimbursed by your insurance company when you return to the U.S. EU citizens also have to pay first but can be reimbursed while still in France if they have form E-111, available at some of the bigger post offices.

Also about 45 minutes outside the city, in Levallois, the **Hôpital Anglais (English Hospital), also known as the Hôpital Britannique, has 24-hour emergency service** and two British doctors on duty. Consultations vary between 150F–220F, depending on which doctor you get. Here again, Americans have to pay up front and get reimbursed at home; EU citizens pay up front and can be reimbursed through form E-111. Most of the staff speaks no English.

DOCTORS • ** In emergencies, information for **doctors (tel. 01–47–07–77–77) and **dentists** (SOS Dentaire, tel. 01–43–37–51–00) is available, but there's no guarantee the staff will speak English. In a pinch, the **American embassy** (*see* Embassies, *above*) has a list of English-speaking doctors.

HOSPITALS • American Hospital (63 blvd. Victor-Hugo, Neuilly-sur-Seine, tel. 01–46–41–25–25; take Métro to Pont de Neuilly, then follow blvd. du Château 15 min). **English Hospital** (3 rue Barbès, Levallois, tel. 01–46–39–22–22, métro Anatole-France).

PHARMACIES

Besides basic over-the-counter medication, pharmacies (identifiable by green neon crosses) provide all sorts of useful health and beauty aids. If you're looking for homeopathic medicines, try the pharmacies homéopathiques. Most pharmacies close at 7 or 8 PM, but the commissariat de police in every city has a list of the *pharmacies de garde,* the pharmacists on call for the evening. This is an emergency-only service, and you may have to go to (as opposed to just call) the commissariat in order to get the name. These 24-hour pharmacies are also sometimes listed in newspapers or posted on the doors of closed pharmacies.

LATE-NIGHT PHARMACIES • Pharmacie Dhéry (84 av. des Champs-Elysées, 8e, tel. 01–45–62–02–41, métro George V) is open 24 hours. Three pharmacies open until midnight are: **Caillaud** (6 blvd. des Capucines, 9e, tel. 01–42–65–88–29, métro Opéra). **Cariglioli** (10 blvd. Sépastopol, 4e, tel. 01–42–72–03–23, métro Châtelet). **La Nation** (13 pl. de la Nation, 11e, tel. 01–43–73–24–03, métro Nation).

ENGLISH-LANGUAGE PUBLICATIONS

The **Free Voice**, a free monthly paper available at English-language bookstores, some restaurants, and the American Church (*see* Visitor Information, *below*), provides an outlet for English-language comment upon Parisian life and lists upcoming events for the Anglophone community. *France-USA Contacts* (known as *FUSAC*) is another free biweekly publication, which has classified listings in English and French for apartment rentals, goods for sale, work exchange, and language classes; it's available at English-language bookstores, some restaurants, and the CIEE office on place de l'Odéon. Most newsstands carry the *International Herald-Tribune,* as well as international versions of *Time* and *Newsweek. Boulevard Magazine* is a glossy magazine for high-brow tourists and well-to-do expats that also has a lot of information on what's going on in Paris.

Pariscope (3F), a comprehensive listing of weekly events in Paris (theater, film, concerts, restaurant and bar picks, etc.) that comes out ever Wednesday, has an English-language section called "Time Out." The English version can be slow on the update, so cross-check with the French-language listings. For more information on English-language bookstores in Paris, *see* Chapter 6, Shopping.

FERRY TRAVEL

Lots of ferry and Hovercraft companies transport travelers and their cars across the Channel. With the arrival of the Channel Tunnel, **many ferry companies are slashing their prices.** Calais is becoming the Channel-crossing hub; only Hoverspeed still sends speedy Seacats between Boulogne and Folkestone (mid-April–September only). From Calais, Sealink and P&O Ferries make the 1½-hour ferry trip to Dover all year long for 200F–300F round-trip without a car, 650F–1,050F with a car. Hoverspeed sends Hovercraft over in half the time and charges 295F–330F round-trip, 650F with a car.

Ferry companies are working hard to compete with the Chunnel, and P&O Ferries occasionally offers round trips for 20F. The catch is that you have to complete your trip within 48 hours—but how they force you to use the return portion of your ticket is unclear.

Driving distances from the French ports to Paris are as follows: from Calais, 290 km (180 mi); from Boulogne, 243 km (151 mi); from Dieppe, 193 km (120 mi); from Dunkerque, 257 km (160 mi). The fastest routes to Paris from each port are via the N43, A26, and A1 from Calais and the Channel Tunnel; via the N1 from Boulogne; via the N15 from Le Havre; via the D915 and N1 from Dieppe; and via the A25 and A1 from Dunkerque.

FERRY COMPANIES • Hoverspeed (tel. 01–40–25–22–00 in France; International Hoverport, Marine Parade, Dover CT17 9TG, 01304/240241 in the U.K.). **P&O European Ferries** (tel. 01–44–51–00–51 in France; Channel House, Channel View Rd., Dover, Kent CT17 9TJ, 0181/575–8555 in the U.K.). **Sealink** (tel. 01–44–94–40–40 in France; Charter House, Park St., Ashford, Kent TN24 8EX, 01233/646801 in the U.K.).

GAY & LESBIAN TRAVEL

The gay scene is alive and well in Paris, although it's fairly concentrated in the bars and clubs of the Marais. Lesbian spots are harder to find. Fewer hate crimes are committed against gays in France than in the United States and the United Kingdom, but once you leave Paris, a less-than-warm welcome may await you in the more conservative provinces.

For the most detailed information about gay life in Paris **look for local publications.** The ultimate source of information and places to go for gay men in Paris is *Guide Illico,* sold monthly for 9F at newsstands throughout Paris and available free at many gay restaurants and bars. Unfortunately, it's all in French. Publications Illico also put out *Double Face,* a free monthly supplement to gay life, and *Trixx* (35F), a collection of enticing photos. The *Guide Gai,* available for 50F from **Les Mots à la Bouche** (*see* Bookstores, *in* Chapter 6), lists popular gay hangouts in the city. The English-language version of *Paris Scene* costs 60F. For a large selection of gay magazines and other publications, check out Paris's **Le Kiosque des Amis.**

GAY- AND LESBIAN-FRIENDLY TRAVEL AGENCIES • Advance Damron (1 Greenway Plaza, Suite 800, Houston, TX 77046, tel. 713/682–2002 or 800/695–0880, fax 713/888–1010). **Club Travel** (8739 Santa Monica Blvd., West Hollywood, CA 90069, tel. 310/358–2200 or 800/429–8747, fax 310/358–2222). **Islanders/Kennedy Travel** (183 W. 10th St., New York, NY 10014, tel. 212/242–3222 or 800/988–1181, fax 212/929–8530). **Now Voyager** (4406 18th St., San Francisco, CA 94114, tel. 415/626–1169 or 800/255–6951, fax 415/626–8626). **Yellowbrick Road** (1500 W. Balmoral Ave.,

Chicago, IL 60640, tel. 773/561–1800 or 800/642–2488, fax 773/561–4497). **Skylink Women's Travel** (3577 Moorland Ave., Santa Rosa, CA 95407, tel. 707/585–8355 or 800/225–5759, fax 707/584–5637), serving lesbian travelers.

LOCAL RESOURCES • Act Up–Paris has weekly meetings in the 6th arrondissement; call for more information (45 rue Sedaine, 11e, tel. 01–48–06–13–89). **Centre Gai et Lesbien** (3 rue Keller, 11e, tel. 01–43–57–21–47) has information on upcoming events, support groups, speakers, and lists of gay-friendly establishments in Paris. **Le Kiosque des Amis** (29 blvd. des Italiens, 2e, tel. 01–42–65–00–94, métro Opéra). **Maison des Femmes** (8 cité Proust, 11e, tel. 01–43–48–24–91) has lesbian-specific information and support.

HEALTH

There are few serious health risks associated with travel in France. Many travelers do suffer from mild diarrhea and nausea during their travels, but it's more often caused by stress and changes in diet than any nasty bacteria. In general, get plenty of rest, watch out for sun exposure, eat balanced meals—do we sound like your mother yet?

It's a good idea to **bring a basic first-aid kit** with bandages, antiseptic, cortisone cream, tweezers, a thermometer in a sturdy case, an antacid such as Alka-Seltzer, something for diarrhea (Pepto Bismol or Imodium), and, of course, aspirin. If you're prone to motion sickness, take along some Dramamine, and **bring any prescription medicine that you may need.** French pharmacies all have well-trained staffs ready to dispense medicine, but they don't necessarily speak English, and they won't let you just grab something off a shelf. Learn the generic names of your favorite drugs if you insist on something familiar to stop your headache or unstuff your nose, or get your doctor to write a note with the generic name of your medicine in case of emergencies. For emergency information, *see* Emergencies, *above.*

HITCHING

While hitchhiking out of Paris is virtually impossible from the city center, a couple of organized carpool systems do exist. Allostop Provoya hooks up willing drivers with paying passengers. You simply call Allostop and see what they have available. The price runs 20 centimes per kilometer plus a 30F charge for trips under 200 km (124 mi), 70F for over 500 km (310 mi). Some sample prices for trips from Paris are: Marseille (223F), Montpellier (221F), Grenoble (183F), and Geneva (179F). Anyone is welcome to use this service, but if your French is rusty, **make sure you've made your destination clear**—you might end up in Barcelona instead of Marseille.

BEST BET • Allostop Provoya (8 rue Rochambeau, 9e, tel. 01–53–20–42–42, métro Cadet or Poissonière) is open weekdays 9–7:30, Saturday 9–1 and 2–6.

HOLIDAYS

Although only a small percentage of the population still treks to church on Sunday, the calendar reflects France's Catholic heritage. If a holiday falls on a Tuesday or Thursday, many businesses *font le pont* (make the bridge) and close on that Monday or Friday as well. Here's a quick list of major holidays:

New Year's Day (January 1); **Easter Monday** (April 13, 1998; April 5, 1999); **Labor Day** (May 1); **World War II Armistice Day and Ascension Day** (May 8); **Pentecost Monday** (May 24, 1998; June 1, 1999); **Bastille Day** (July 14); **Assumption** (August 15); **All Saints' Day** (November 1); **World War I Armistice** (November 11); **Christmas** (December 25).

INSURANCE

Many private health-insurance policies do not cover you outside the United States. If yours is among them, **consider buying supplemental medical coverage,** available through several private organizations. Make sure you're covered, especially if you are pregnant or have a preexisting medical condition. Organizations such as STA Travel and the Council on International Educational Exchange (*see* Students, *below*) include health-and-accident coverage when you get a student ID. Citizens of the U.K. can buy an annual travel-insurance policy valid for most vacations during the year in which it's purchased.

TRAVEL INSURERS • In the U.S., **Access America** (6600 W. Broad St., Richmond, VA 23230, tel. 804/285–3300 or 800/284–8300), **Carefree Travel Insurance** (Box 9366, 100 Garden City Plaza, Garden City, NY 11530, tel. 516/294–0220 or 800/323–3149), **Travel Guard International** (1145 Clark St., Stevens Point, WI 54481, tel. 715/345–0505 or 800/826–1300), **Travel Insured International** (Box 280568, East Hartford, CT 06128–0568, tel. 860/528–7663 or 800/243–3174). In Canada, **Mutual of Omaha** (Travel Division, 500 University Ave., Toronto, Ontario M5G 1V8, tel. 416/598–4083, 800/268–8825 in Canada). In the U.K., **Association of British Insurers** (51 Gresham St., London EC2V 7HQ, tel. 0171/600–3333).

LAUNDRY

If your socks have a life all their own and people move away from you as you board the métro, you need a *laverie* (laundromat). You'll have to shell out 22F to clean one load of laundry. Dryers cost about 5F for 8 minutes. Most laundromats will also dispense soap for 2F. Make sure you **come with handfuls of 10F and 2F coins** because there are rarely change machines.

You shouldn't have any problem finding a laundromat near you, but here are a few Laverie Libre Service to get you started: 9 rue de Jouy, 4e, métro St-Paul; 212 rue St-Jacques, 5e, métro Maubert-Mutualité; 28 rue des Trois-Frères, 18e, métro Abbesses; 2 rue du Lappe, 11e, métro Bastille; 28 rue Beaubourg, 3e, métro Arts-et-Métiers; 113 rue Monge, 5e, métro Censier-Daubenton; 27 rue Vieille du Temple, 4e, métro Hôtel de Ville.

LIBRARIES

Paris has a plethora of academic and cultural resources for you to take advantage of.

AMERICAN LIBRARY

Here you'll find the largest collection of English-language books in Paris, with more than 80,000 volumes. A single day's admittance costs 70F, but if you want to take books out, you have to sign up for the year (570F) or the summer (260F). *10 rue du Général-Camou, 7e, tel. 01–45–51–46–82. Métro: Ecole Militaire or Alma-Marceau. Open Tues.–Sat. 10–7; shorter hrs in Aug.*

BIBLIOTHEQUE FORNEY

Housed in the 17th-century Hôtel de Sens, this library has the best collection of art and architecture materials in Paris. Books and periodicals are accessible for free, but to check out materials you need a picture ID and proof that you've lived in Paris for at least three months. *1 rue du Fiquier, 4e, tel. 01–42–78–14–60. Métro: Pont Marie or St-Paul. Open Tues.–Fri. 1:30–8, Sat. 10–8.*

BIBLIOTHEQUE FRANÇOIS-MITTERRAND

This 5.2-billion-franc home for the Bibliothèque Nationale's collection celebrated its grand opening in 1997. The massive library—its 395 km (245 mi) of shelves make it one of the largest in the world—is a tribute to urban renewal in the Tolbiac district. Four buildings designed as giant open books enclose a vast rectangular park. Most of the books from the Richelieu branch of the Bibliothèque Nationale will be moved here. *Quai François Muriac, 13e, tel. 01–53–79–59–79. Métro: Quai de la Gare.*

BIBLIOTHEQUE NATIONALE DE FRANCE

The Richelieu location of the Bibliothèque Nationale de France traces its origin to 1368, when Charles V first founded a library in the Louvre. François I expanded the collection in 1537 when he ordered publishers to send him a copy of every book they published—this brought in more books and allowed the king to keep a close eye on what was being written. A seat in this megalibrary's splendid 19th-century reading room is by far the most coveted study space in all of France. The intelligentsia of the world vie for access to what is considered to be the largest library collection ever, housed both here and in the new Bibliothèque François Mitterrand: 10 million books, 1.5 million photographs, 1.5 million music manuscripts, 1.1 million discs and videos, 650,000 maps, 350,000 manuscripts, and 350,000 periodicals, plus collections stored elsewhere. To get in, you need to present a letter of accreditation from a university stating that you are either a professor or a graduate student in your third year of a Ph.D. program. The unaccredited can merely peek in and look around. *58 rue Richelieu, 2e, tel. 01–47–03–81–26. Métro: Bourse. Main reading room open daily 10–6.*

BIBLIOTHEQUE PUBLIQUE D'INFORMATIONS (BPI)

At the Centre Pompidou's (*see* Major Attractions *in* Chapter 2) BPI you can access 3,000 periodicals (including foreign presses), 14,000 records and CDs (with listening stations), 2,000 films on video (with monitors), 400,000 books (many in English), and an extensive CD-ROM library. Expect to wait in line at the entrance and navigate your way through hundreds of people to find a table. Books aren't reshelved during the day, so if you come in the evening you'll have a hard time finding what you need. *31 rue St-Merri, on pl. Igor-Stravinsky, 4e, tel. 01–44–78–44. Open Mon. and Wed.–Fri. noon–10, weekends 10–10.*

BIBLIOTHEQUE STE-GENEVIEVE

Founded when the library of the now-demolished Eglise Ste-Geneviève was nationalized during the Revolution, the Bibliothèque Ste-Geneviève has a collection spanning all disciplines, with an emphasis on 19th- and 20th-century documents. The library is free to students from any university (even non-French) and to anyone over 18 or with a high school degree. A day pass provides you with limited access, but there is no borrowing. *10 pl. du Panthéon, 5e, tel. 01–44–41–97–97. Métro: Maubert-Mutualité. Open Mon.–Sat. 10–10; closed Aug. 1–15.*

BRITISH CULTURAL CENTER

The British center has a large, sunny reference library and occasionally hosts art expos and lectures. Although the events are usually free, you have to pay 30F a day (Brits are allowed in free) or 250F a year to access the library. *9–11 rue Constantine, 7e, tel. 01–49–55–73–00. Métro: Invalides. Open weekdays 11–6 (Wed. until 7).*

CENTRE DE DOCUMENTATION JUIVE CONTEMPORAINE

Above the Mémorial du Martyr Juif Inconnu, this center is the best resource for Jewish studies in town. Technically, there's a 30F fee per day or 150F annual membership, but if you just want to use it for a short time they're usually pretty lax about collecting. *17 rue Geoffroy-l'Asnier, 4e, tel. 01–42–77–44–72. Métro: Pont Marie or St-Paul. Open Mon.–Thurs. 2–6.*

INSTITUT DU MONDE ARABE

This modern architectural wonder (*see* Major Attractions *in* Chapter 2) is the center of Arabic studies in France. Its library has 50,000 volumes and 1,000 periodicals in Arabic, French, and English. The stacks and reading room are open to the public, but only a small number of volumes can be checked out. *1 rue Fossés-St-Bernard, 5e, tel. 01–40–51–38–38. Métro: Jussieu or Cardinal Lemoine. Open Tues.–Sat. 1–8.*

MUNICIPAL LIBRARIES

Every arrondissement in Paris has its own municipal library, complete with study space, a satisfactory collection of books and periodicals, and some English-language titles. You need proof of residence to get a free library card and borrow books. Call the main office for the library nearest you. *6 rue François Miron, 4e, tel. 01–44–78–80–50, Métro: St-Paul.*

PAVILLON DE L'ARSENAL

The library of the Centre d'Urbanisme et d'Architecture de la Ville de Paris (*see* Museums, French History and Culture, *in* Chapter 2) has a fine collection of French- and English-language books and periodicals, but its collection of 70,000 photographs and images of Paris is truly spectacular. *21 blvd. Morland, 4e, tel. 01–42–76–33–97. Métro: Sully-Morland. Open Tues.–Fri. 2–6.*

LOST & FOUND

The entire city shares one lost-and-found office, and this is it. They won't give information over the telephone; you have to trek over to see if you can find your belongings among the Louis Vuitton bags.
WHERE TO GO • Service des Objets Trouvés (Lost & Found Service; 36 rue des Morillons, 15e, tel. 01–55–76–20–20, métro Convention; open weekdays 8:30–5).

MAIL

You can **identify post offices by the yellow signs with blue letters that say LA POSTE.** Mailboxes are yellow, with one slot for letters to Paris and one for AUTRES destinations (everywhere else). Both airmail letters and postcards to the United States and Canada cost 4F40 for 20 grams. Letters to the United Kingdom cost 3F. Postcards sent to most European countries cost 3F, 5F20 to Australia and New Zealand. Buy stamps in post offices if you really like standing in line. Otherwise, head to one of Paris's ubiquitous *tabacs* (tobacco shops) and say "J'aimerais des timbres" (I'd like some stamps). Mail generally takes 5–7 days to make its way from France to the United States, about half that to reach Britain, and 10 days to two weeks to reach Australia.

POST OFFICES

Many post offices not only have mail service but also have telephone, telegram, Minitel (*see* Telephones, *below*), photocopy, and *poste restante* (general delivery mail) services. Paris's central post office, the Hôtel des Postes, is open 24 hours. During regular business hours (weekdays 8–7, Saturday 8–noon) you can also use the fax machines and exchange money. All post offices in Paris accept general delivery mail, but your mail will end up at the main post office if the sender fails to specify a branch. Have your mail addressed to: Last name (in capital letters), first name, Poste Restante, 75001 Paris. Bring your passport with you to pick it up.

WHERE TO GO • Main post office (52 rue du Louvre, at rue Etienne-Marcel, 1er, tel. 01–40–28–20–00, métro Sentier). The **Champs-Elysées** office (near rond point des Champs-Elysées, 71 av. des Champs-Elysées, 8e, tel. 01–44–13–66–00, métro Franklin D. Roosevelt; open Mon.–Sat. 8 AM–7 PM, Sun. 10–7) has extended hours for mail, telegram, and telephone services.

To figure out the zip code of any point in Paris, just tack the arrondissement number onto the digits 750. For example, for the fifth arrondissement, 5e (cinquième), the five-digit zip code would be 75005—turning 5 into 05.

MEDIA

NEWSPAPERS & MAGAZINES

The French press has something for everyone, from gossip-thirsty voyeurs to super-conservative right-wingers. The following are a few of the more popular choices.

Le Monde is an eminently respectable centrist daily with good arts and books supplements. Famous philosophers often write dense articles—sometimes stridently nationalist—for the front page. The Paris daily *Le Figaro* has been around since 1866. It leans to the right a little more than the others, and its business section is very reputable. Jean-Paul Sartre was the first editor of *Libération,* a witty, slangy weekly paper that is one of the best and most accessible. The slant is to the left but is becoming less so. Looking for something a little further to the left? Affiliated with the French Communist Party, *L'Humanité* is still being published, though with a little ideological confusion. You have to be very up on your French slang to understand the satirical weekly *Le Canard Enchaîné,* which has funny cartoons and investigates the latest political scandals with biting humor. *L'Equipe* is both a daily newspaper and weekly magazine for sports buffs.

Weekly magazines include the extremely popular *Le Nouvel Observateur,* with middle-of-the-road articles on politics à la *Time* or *Newsweek. L'Evenement de Jeudi* also tackles politics but specializes in in-depth special reports on anything from the veracity of the Bible to an intimate look at Picasso's lovers. *L'Express* is less fun, more businesslike, and conservative, and *Le Point* tends to lean even a little more to the right than *L'Express.* For those dying for celebrity gossip and scandal, check out *Paris-Match* or *VSD,* where you can read up on celebrities and royal families.

RADIO

France radio has an eclectic mix of music, with more variety than you'd expect. Some to check out are **Fréquence Gaie** (94.4), aimed at the gay community; **Fréquence Juive** (94.8), for Jewish listeners; and **France Maghreb** (94.2), which targets Paris's North African community. Don't let that dial slow-down near teeny-bopper favorites **Fun Radio** (101.9) and **NRG** (101.3).

Africa No. 1 (107.5) is generally upbeat, playing mostly West and Saharan African tunes. **FIP** (105.1) spins an arbitrary mix of classical, contemporary French favorites, and jazz. **France Infos** (105.5) is a nonstop news station. For classical music, listen to **France Musique** (91.7 and 92.1). The best of all the rock stations, **Ouï Rock You** (102.3), is also the most "alternative." **Radio Montmartre** (102.7) plays mostly traditional French tunes. **Radio Nova** (101.5) has a fresh, flavorful mix of world music, contemporary jazz, and weekend techno.

TELEVISION

French television can be a shock, especially if you expected programs created, say, in France. French television offers only six *chaînes* (channels). Frequently you'll see dubbed versions of American originals such as *Les Drôles de Dames* (roughly translated as "those crazy ladies," otherwise known as *Charlie's Angels*) and the newer fad, *Urgences* (*ER*). In the mornings and evenings, most channels have the news. Channels One through Three form the network core; Channel Four is the cable station. If your French slang and political savvy is up to par, you'll enjoy Channel Four's *Guignols de l'Info* (7:50 PM–8:05 PM), a puppet show that lambasts politicians and newscasters. For something more comprehensible, catch the ABC news (in English) at 7 AM, also on Channel Four. Channel Five is the intellectual channel and is the only channel to subtitle its films instead of dubbing them. Channel Six is a rather pathetic MTV substitute.

THE METRO & RER

Except for the fact that it closes soon after midnight, the métro is the epitome of convenient public transportation. Thirteen métro lines and five main RER lines crisscross Paris and the suburbs, and you will almost never be more than a 10-minute walk from the nearest métro stop. Any station or tourist office can give you a free map of the whole system, or you can use the handy map in Chapter 2. Métro **lines are marked in the station both by line number and by the names of the stops at the end of each line.** Find the number of the line you want to take and the name of the terminus toward which you will be traveling, and follow the signs.

To transfer to a different line, look for orange signs saying CORRESPONDENCE and for the new line number and terminus you need. The blue-and-white signs that say SORTIE (exit) will lead you back above ground. You can identify métro stations by the illuminated yellow M signs, by the round red-and-white METRO signs, or by the old, green, art nouveau arches bearing the full name, METROPOLITAIN. The métro trains (but not those heading to the suburbs, or *banlieus*) tend to be pretty safe at night, as nocturnal Parisians will often be accompanying you on whatever train you take. Of course, bringing a companion is always a good idea. Otherwise, just look mean and uncommunicative.

The first métro of the day heads out at 5:30 AM, the last at 12:30 AM. Often the directional signs on the quays indicate the times at which the first and last trains pass that station. Individual billets (tickets) cost 8F, but **it's much more economical to buy a carnet (book of 10) for 48F.** You can use one ticket each time you go underground for as many transfers as you like. For extended stays **consider getting a Carte Orange,** for which you need a photo of yourself. (Large métro stations usually have photo booths that cost 25F or you can try photo stores.) You can fill the card with a coupon semaine (weekly pass; 75F, valid Mon.–Sun.) or coupon mensuel (monthly pass; 255F, valid from the first day of the month). You can buy these in any station or at a tabac with "RATP" on the window. Whatever kind you use, **hang on to your ticket until you exit the métro** in case one of the mean, green-uniformed RATP employees wants to see it, a particular danger toward the end of the month. Not having a ticket or hopping the barriers could land you a fine of up to 250F.

Several **métro stations also act as RER stations.** The RER is a high-speed rail system that extends into the Parisian suburbs and is a fast way to travel between major points in the city. The five principal RER lines are marked on the métro maps. You can use normal métro tickets on them within Zones 1 and 2, which will get you pretty much anywhere in Paris. To venture farther into Zones 3–5, to Versailles, for example, or to the airports, you need to buy a separate, more expensive ticket.

PUBLIC TRANSPORT INFORMATION • Call **RATP** (tel. 08–36–68–77–14) between 6 AM and 9 PM, though you may find it difficult to get through.

MONEY

The units of currency in France are the franc and the centime (1 franc = 100 centimes). Bills come in denominations of 20, 50, 100, 200, and 500 francs. Coins are worth ½, 1, 2, 5, 10, and 20 francs and 5, 10, and 20 centimes. When you plan your budget, **allow for fluctuating exchange rates;** at press time, the exchange rate for the French franc was as follows:

START IN DOWNTOWN LONDON AND IN 3 HEURES, ARRIVEZ AU CENTRE DE PARIS.

Rail Europe Imagine traveling directly between London and Paris with no connections to run for, no busses to board, no taxis to hail. In fact, the only thing you have to change is the tongue you speak upon arrival.

That's exactly what you'll experience aboard the high-speed Eurostar passenger train.

Board the Eurostar at the center of one city, travel through the new Channel Tunnel, and arrive directly in the center of the other. Simple as that. And at speeds of up to 200 miles per hour, the entire trip lasts just three short hours. We can also get you between London and Brussels in three and a quarter.

For more information, contact your travel agent or Rail Europe at 1-800-EUROSTAR.

If a quick, comfortable trip between London and Paris is on your itinerary, you'll find we speak your language perfectly.

EUROSTAR. DIRECT.   **CALL 1-800-EUROSTAR**

Eurostar is a service provided together by the railways of Belgium, Britain and France

Pick up
the phone.

Pick up
the miles.

MCI   Calling Card

415 555 1234 2244
J.D. SMITH

WorldPhone

Use your MCI Card® to make an international call from virtually anywhere in the world and earn frequent flyer miles on one of eight major airlines.

Enroll in an MCI Airline Partner Program today. In the U.S., call **1-800-FLY-FREE.** Overseas, call MCI collect at **1-916-567-5151.**

1. To use your MCI Card, just dial the WorldPhone access number of the country you're calling from. (For a complete listing of codes, visit www.mci.com.)
2. Dial or give the operator your MCI Card number.
3. Dial or give the number you're calling.

# Austria (CC) ♦	022-903-012	# Netherlands (CC) ♦	0800-022-91-22
# Belarus (CC)		# Norway (CC) ♦	800-19912
From Brest, Vitebsk, Grodno, Minsk	8-800-103	# Poland (CC) ÷	00-800-111-21-22
From Gomel and Mogilev regions	8-10-800-103	# Portugal (CC) ÷	05-017-1234
# Belgium (CC) ♦	0800-10012	Romania (CC) ÷	01-800-1800
# Bulgaria	00800-0001	# Russia (CC) ÷ ♦	
# Croatia (CC) ★	99-385-0112	To call using ROSTELCOM ■	747-3322
# Czech Republic (CC) ♦	00-42-000112	For a Russian-speaking operator	747-3320
# Denmark (CC) ♦	8001-0022	To call using SOVINTEL ■	960-2222
# Finland (CC) ♦	08001-102-80	# San Marino (CC) ♦	172-1022
# France (CC) ♦	0-800-99-0019	# Slovak Republic (CC)	00-421-00112
# Germany (CC)	0130-0012	# Slovenia	080-8808
# Greece (CC) ♦	00-800-1211	# Spain (CC)	900-99-0014
# Hungary (CC) ♦	00▼800-01411	# Sweden (CC) ♦	020-795-922
# Iceland (CC) ♦	800-9002	# Switzerland (CC) ♦	0800-89-0222
# Ireland (CC)	1-800-55-1001	# Turkey (CC) ♦	00-8001-1177
# Italy (CC) ♦	172-1022	# Ukraine (CC) ÷	8▼10-013
# Kazakhstan (CC)	8-800-131-4321	# United Kingdom (CC)	
# Liechtenstein (CC) ♦	0800-89-0222	To call using BT ■	0800-89-0222
# Luxembourg	0800-0112	To call using MERCURY ■	0500-89-0222
# Monaco (CC) ♦	800-90-019	# Vatican City (CC)	172-1022

Is this a great time, or what? :-)

MCI

U.S.	Canada	Britain	Australia	New Zealand
$1=5F79	C$1=4F52	£1=9F34	AUS$1=4F55	NZ$1=4F45
1F=17¢	1F=22¢	1F=11p	1F=21¢	1F=22¢

The French use two methods of listing prices that include centimes. While 5 francs is always 5F, a price of 4 francs and 70 centimes may be rendered either 4F70 or 4,70F. In all our price listings we use the first method.

A major U.S. credit card (especially Visa, known in France as Carte Bleue) with accompanying personal identification number (PIN) is often the safest and most convenient way to pay for goods and services in Paris. Many **hotels, restaurants, and shops accept credit cards** (though there is often a 100F–150F minimum), and **you'll find numerous ATMs** that will give you cash advances at favorable rates (*see* ATMs, *below*). Traveler's checks also come in handy. Although few merchants accept them in foreign currencies, you can exchange them for cash at many banks and almost all bureaux de change. Keep in mind that you lose money every time you exchange currency, so try to avoid changing so much of your money to francs that you end up having to exchange it back when you leave the country. Whichever method of payment you use, **protect yourself by carrying cash in a money belt or "necklace" pouch** and by keeping records of your credit card numbers and traveler's check serial numbers in several, separate safe places.

ATMS

Using an ATM is often one of the best ways to get francs at the excellent commercial exchange rate. Before leaving home, to increase your chances of happy encounters with cash machines in Paris, **make sure that your card has been programmed for ATM use there.** ATMs in Paris accept PINs of four or fewer digits only; if your PIN is longer, ask about changing it. If you know your PIN as a word, learn the numerical equivalent, since most Paris ATM keypads show numbers only, no letters. You should also have your credit card programmed for ATM use (note that Discover is accepted mostly in the United States); a Visa or MasterCard can also be used to access cash through certain ATMs, although fees may be steep and the charge may begin to accrue interest immediately even if your monthly bills are paid up. The transaction fees for using your bank card may be lower than the interest charged by your credit card for cash withdrawals. However, local bank cards don't always work overseas or may access only your checking account; **ask your bank about a MasterCard/Cirrus or Visa debit card,** which works like a bank card but can be used at any ATM displaying a MasterCard/Cirrus or Visa logo. These cards, too, may tap only your checking account; check with your bank about their policy. In any case, make sure you have a back-up method of getting money.

Images from St-Exupéry's Little Prince grace 50F bills, and an intricate design of Paris's most famous monument and its illustrious creator, Gustav Eiffel, decorates the new rose-colored 200F bills.

In Paris, most ATMs are affiliated with the Cirrus and Plus systems only. In theory, the ubiquitous BNP (Banque National de Paris) machines will accept cards on both systems, but your card may only work sporadically. When it does, withdraw as much as you think safe to carry (especially because most banks charge you each time you withdraw). The most reliable Cirrus ATMs are housed at Crédit Mutuel banks. Plus-system cardholders should try Bred banks with Right Bank–only locations. Citibank Citicard users can go to Citibank on avenue des Champs-Elysées, where the ATM works around the clock, and the English-speaking staff can help you transfer funds from U.S. Citibank accounts. Other Citibank offices are for business use and do not have ATMs or staffs particularly sympathetic to the woes of the cashless traveler.

ATM LOCATIONS • For ATM locations in Paris, contact **Cirrus** (tel. 800/424–7787) or, for a list of **Plus** locations, your local bank. **BNP** (16 blvd. des Italiens, 9e, tel. 01–44–83–53–99, métro Opéra; 147 blvd. St-Germain, 6e, tel. 01–40–46–73–99, métro St-Germain-des-Prés). **Bred** (33 rue de Rivoli, métro Hôtel de Ville; 14 blvd. des Capucines, métro Opéra). **Citibank** (30 av. des Champs-Elysées, 8e, tel. 01–40–76–33–00, métro Franklin-D.-Roosevelt). **Crédit Mutuel** (8 rue St-Antoine, 4e, métro St-Paul; 2 rue de l'Arrivée, 15e, métro Montparnasse-Bienvenue; 13 rue des Abbesses, 18e, métro Abbesses).

CURRENCY EXCHANGE

You'll get a better deal buying francs in Paris than at home. Nonetheless, it's not a bad idea to exchange a bit of money into francs before you arrive in France in case the exchange booth at the train station or airport at which you arrive is closed or has a long line. At other times, **to get the most favorable rates, change money at banks or at ATMS.** Although fees charged for ATM transactions may be higher abroad than at home, Cirrus and Plus exchange rates are excellent, because they are based on wholesale rates offered only by major banks. You won't do as well at exchange booths in airports or rail and bus stations, in hotels, in restaurants, or in stores, although you may find their hours more convenient. The Orly and Charles de Gaulle airports both have cash machines that will accept credit cards with PIN numbers. If you do exchange at the airport, don't go overboard—the rates here feed off your lack of choice. But you do need at least 50F to get to the city center by public transport.

During business hours (from 9 or 10 AM to 5 or 6 PM) you can **get good currency-exchange rates around the Opéra Garnier, the Champs-Elysées, and the Palais Royal** (rue de Rivoli); just be sure you stop in at an official bank and not one of the bureaux de change, which keep longer hours but get away with worse rates. Banque de France is your best bet, with no commission and strong rates. The bureaux at the train stations stay open until at least 8 PM, sometimes as late as 10 PM, and have slightly worse rates than banks. There are other bureaux around the Champs-Elysées and the Quartier Latin around the intersection of boulevards St-Germain and St-Michel.

For late-night currency exchange, use one of the automatic cash-exchange machines that are popping up all over. To use exchange machines you need cash—and relatively crisp cash at that—and the exchange rate is not that great but, at 3 AM, who cares?

BANKS • Banque de France (31 rue Croix des Petits Champs, 1e, tel. 42–92–42–92; call for other locations).

EXCHANGE SERVICES • International Currency Express (tel. 888/842–0880 on the East Coast or 888/278–6628 on the West Coast for telephone orders). **Thomas Cook Currency Services** (tel. 800/287–7362 for telephone orders and retail locations).

24-HOUR EXCHANGE MACHINES • Crédit du Nord (29 blvd. Sébastopol, 1er, métro Châtelet–Les Halles). **CCF** (103 av. des Champs-Elysées, 8e, métro George-V).

TRAVELER'S CHECKS

Whether or not to buy traveler's checks depends on where you are headed. Traveler's checks work well in cities, but you should **take cash if your trip includes rural areas** and small towns. If a thief makes off with your checks, they can usually be replaced within 24 hours. Always pay for your checks yourself—don't delegate—or there may be problems if you need a refund later on.

COSTS

LODGING • Although hostels are probably the best deal if you're traveling solo, **you're better off splitting a hotel room if you're traveling with other people.** Expect to pay 500F or less for a nice double room (about 50F less for a single), and a minimum of 250F just for a basic, clean, and, perhaps, slightly threadbare double with toilet and shower. If you don't mind sharing bathroom facilities, you can land equally simple quarters with only a sink for about 175F–200F. If you're a woman traveling alone in Paris, you would be wise to pay more for a well-lit and safer location—at least while you get your bearings. *See* Chapter 3 for more details.

FOOD • Plan to sit down for a Parisian multicourse meal at least once during your trip. A three-course dinner will run you at least 70F, though the same meal will cost a lot less (maybe 50F) at lunchtime. Unless you're from New York, expect to pay twice what you would at home for the same quality food. Throw yourself at the mercy of the markets, where you can survive quite well (and inexpensively) on fresh produce, cheese, and bread. Snacks like *tarte aux pommes* (apple tart) and *chocolate croissants* run anywhere from 5F to 15F, and wine worth drinking starts at about 15F a bottle. *See* Chapter 4 for more details.

GETTING AROUND • Métro and bus tickets run 8F per trek, but you can save money with weekly or monthly passes (*see* Bus Travel *and* The Métro & RER, *above*) and you should use your feet whenever possible—Paris is a great city for walking. Expect to pay 40F–50F for a short taxi ride, though often at night there'll be 20F or more on the meter when you get in.

ENTERTAINMENT • This is where you can go broke fast. Cover charges for nightclubs range 70F–140F and usually include one drink. Drinks in clubs are outrageously expensive—about 80F each, and the price is no guarantee of quality. A beer in a bar costs 15F–50F and a glass of wine 15F–40F. Movies are pretty expensive (about 50F), but every theater has discount nights or matinées with tickets as low as 25F. Classical music and theater tickets are reasonable, and discounted rush, student, and youth tickets are often available. Museums can run 35F–45F, though some have one discount day a week or month.

MOTORBIKES & MOPEDS

Any two-wheeled vehicle that goes over 50 km (31 mi) per hour needs to be registered and licensed at the nearest préfecture (local police department). This means most mopeds don't have to be registered and most motorbikes do. Renting a moped is expensive but may be worth doing to really get off the beaten track for a day or two. It's also a good way to zip through Parisian traffic—most Parisian drivers are used to mopeds and won't try too hard to run you over. To buy a used moped or motorcycle, check the listings in *Argus,* a weekly publication available at most newsstands.

SCOOTER RENTALS • Dynamic Sport (149 rue Montmartre, 2e, tel. 01–42–33–61–82).

PACKING FOR PARIS

Paris is a fashionable city where locals don't just throw on sweats to run to the store. Though it's important to pack pragmatically (comfortable, easy-to-clean clothes), you may feel uncomfortable if you're always dressing down. It's better to have one decent shirt you can wear every other day (as the Parisians do) than a whole slew of T-shirts. Athletic clothes are rarely worn outside the gym, and berets on foreigners will provoke derision. Shorts or ski jackets will immediately mark you as a tourist. But you'll blend in nicely with snug Levi's and nice t-shirts or oxfords, or skirts and slacks for day wear; expect to get a little more dressed up at night. If you plan an extended stay, **pack for all possible climates,** and, whatever you do, don't forget your comfortable walking shoes or some sort of rain gear. And you've heard it before, and you'll hear it again: **Pack light.** The heaviness of your luggage is always directly proportional to how many days you've been carrying it around.

Bring all the paraphernalia you need to conduct chemical warfare on your contact lenses if you wear them. Also take an extra pair of contact lenses and eyeglasses in your carry-on luggage. Tampons, soap, shampoo, and toothpaste can all be bought in Paris, though they're generally more expensive. If you have a health problem, **pack enough medication** to last the entire trip or have your doctor write you a prescription using the drug's generic name, because brand names vary from country to country. To avoid problems with customs officials, carry medications in the original packaging. It's important that you **don't put prescription drugs, your passport, or other valuables in luggage to be checked**: it might go astray. Also, don't forget the addresses of offices that handle refunds of lost traveler's checks.

Note that many hostels require you to use a sleep sheet (two sheets sewn together so that you can easily make your bed), though some do rent sheets. If you plan to be staying in a lot of hostels, **you might want to bring a sleep sheet, or a sleeping bag,** just in case. Other stuff you might not think to take but will be glad to have: a miniature flashlight, good in dark places; a pocket knife for cutting fruit, spreading cheese, and opening wine bottles; a water bottle; sunglasses; several large zip-type plastic bags, useful for wet swimsuits, leaky bottles, and rancid socks; a travel alarm clock; a needle and a small spool of thread; extra batteries; a good book; and a day pack.

LUGGAGE

In general, you are entitled to check two bags on flights within the United States and on international flights leaving the United States. A third piece may be brought on board, but it must fit easily under the seat in front of you or in the overhead compartment. If you are flying between two foreign destinations, note that baggage allowances may be determined not by piece but by weight—generally 88 pounds (40 kilograms) in first class, 66 pounds (30 kilograms) in business class, and 44 pounds (20 kilograms) in economy. If your flight between two cities abroad *connects* with your transatlantic or transpacific flight, the piece method still applies.

At check-in, **make sure that each bag is correctly tagged** with the destination airport's three-letter code. If you're traveling with a backpack, tie all loose straps to each other or onto the pack itself, so that they don't get caught in luggage conveyer belts. If your bags arrive damaged or not at all, file a written report with the airline before leaving the airport.

Airline liability for baggage is limited to $1,250 per person on flights within the United States. On international flights it amounts to $9.07 per pound or $20 per kilogram for checked baggage (roughly $640 per 70-pound bag) and $400 per passenger for unchecked baggage. Insurance for losses exceeding these amounts can be bought from the airline at check-in for about $10 per $1,000 of coverage; note that this coverage excludes a rather extensive list of items, which is shown on your airline ticket.

PASSPORTS & VISAS

Once your travel plans are confirmed, **check the expiration date of your passport.** It takes a while to get a new passport, so be sure to check right away. It's a good idea to **make photocopies of the data page**; leave one copy with someone at home and keep another with you, separate from your passport. If you lose your passport, promptly call the nearest embassy or consulate and the local police. Having a copy of the data page can speed replacement.

AUSTRALIAN CITIZENS • Citizens of Australia need a valid passport and visa to enter France. **Passport Office** (tel. 008/131–232).

CANADIANS • You need only a valid passport to enter France for stays of up to 90 days. **Passport Office** (tel. 819/994–3500 or 800/567–6868).

NEW ZEALAND CITIZENS • Citizens of New Zealand need only a valid passport to enter France for stays of up to 90 days. **Passport Office** (tel. 04/494–0700 for information on how to apply, 0800/727–776 for information on applications already submitted).

U.K. CITIZENS • Citizens of the United Kingdom need only a valid passport to enter France for stays of up to 90 days. **London Passport Office** (tel. 0990/21010) for fees and documentation requirements and to request an emergency passport.

U.S. CITIZENS • All U.S. citizens, even infants, need only a valid passport to enter France for stays of up to 90 days. **Office of Passport Services** (tel. 202/647–0518).

ROLLERBLADING

Rollerblades are taking over the world, and Paris is no exception. Rollerbladers of all ages zip around unsuspecting pedestrians, especially along the Seine, the Arche de le Défense, the Trocadéro, and even on the métro. If you've arrived in Paris without wheels, you'll have to shell out some cash; you can't rent them (yet), and **the cheapest pairs are at Go Sport** (Forum des Halles, 1er, métro Châtelet–Les Halles) for around 500F.

SAFETY

Money belts may be dorky and bulky, but it's better to be embarrassed than broke. You'd be wise to **carry all cash, traveler's checks, credit cards, and your passport in your money belt** or in some other inaccessible place: front or inner pocket, or a bag that fits underneath your clothes. Keep a copy of your passport somewhere else. Waist packs are safe if you keep the pack part in front of your body. Keep your bag attached to you if you plan on napping on the train. And never leave your belongings unguarded, even if you're only planning to be gone for a minute.

PRECAUTIONS FOR WOMEN

Although times are changing, the idea still exists that women traveling alone are fair game for lewd comments, leering looks, and the like. The Left Bank tends to be less troublesome than the Right Bank, which, thanks to the sex trade that goes on around Les Halles, St-Denis, and on boulevard Clichy in Pigalle, deserves extra precaution, as do many off-the-beaten-path neighborhoods. Harassment is usually verbal—always annoying, but not often violent. *Dragueurs* (men who persistently profess their undying love to hapless female passersby) tend to be very vocal, but the threat they pose is usually very minimal.

There are precautions you can take to avoid some harassment. Dressing conservatively helps, depending on the area you are in. Walk with a deliberate step and don't be afraid to show your irritation. Avoiding eye contact and conversation with potential aggressors also helps. Finally, be aware of your surroundings and use your head; **don't do things abroad that you wouldn't do at home.** Hitchhiking alone, for example, is not the brightest idea, nor is walking back to your hotel at night along deserted streets. Stay off the suburban trains at night, which tend to be stomping grounds for amateur criminals. If you get into an uncomfortable situation, move into a public area and make your fear widely known. That said, Paris is one of the safest big cities for the lone female, especially in areas that stay up late. Stick to the boulevards, memorize the time of the last métro train to your station, and ride in the first car by the conductor.

RESOURCES • SOS Viol (tel. 0–800–05–95–95) is a rape crisis hot line; they'll answer calls weekdays 10–6.

STUDENTS

To save money, look into deals available through student-oriented travel agencies and the various other organizations involved in helping out student and budget travelers. Typically, you'll find discounted airfares, rail passes, tours, lodgings, or other travel arrangements, and you don't necessarily have to be a student to qualify.

The big names in the field are STA Travel, with some 100 offices worldwide and a useful Web site (www.sta-travel.com), and the Council on International Educational Exchange (CIEE or "Council" for short), a private, nonprofit organization that administers work, volunteer, academic, and professional programs worldwide and sells travel arrangements through its own specialist travel agency, Council Travel. Travel CUTS, strictly a travel agency, sells discounted airline tickets to Canadian students from offices on or near college campuses. The Educational Travel Center (ETC) books low-cost flights to destinations within the continental United States and around the world. And Student Flights, Inc., specializes in student and faculty airfares.

Most of these organizations also issue student identity cards, which entitle you to special fares on local transportation and discounts at museums, theaters, sports events, and other attractions, as well as a handful of other benefits, which are listed in the handbook that most provide to cardholders. Major cards include the International Student Identity Card (ISIC) and Go 25: International Youth Travel Card, available to non-students age 25 and under as well as students age 25 and under; the ISIC, when purchased in the United States, comes with $3,000 in emergency medical coverage and a few related benefits. Both the ISIC and Go 25 are issued by Council Travel or STA in the United States, Travel CUTS in Canada, at student unions and student-travel companies in the United Kingdom, and STA in Australia. The International Student Exchange Card (ISE), issued by Student Flights, Inc., is available to faculty members as well as students, and the International Teacher Identity Card (ITIC), issued by Travel CUTS, provides similar benefits to teachers in all grade levels, from kindergarten through graduate school. All student ID cards cost between $10 and $20.

STUDENT IDS AND SERVICES • Council on International Educational Exchange (CIEE, 205 E. 42nd St., 14th floor, New York, NY 10017, tel. 212/822–2600 or 888/268–6245, fax 212/822–2699), for mail orders only, in the United States. **Council Travel in the United States**: Arizona (Tempe, tel. 602/966–3544). California (Berkeley, tel. 510/848–8604; Davis, tel. 916/752–2285; La Jolla, tel. 619/452–0630; Long Beach, tel. 310/598–3338; Los Angeles, tel. 310/208–3551; Palo Alto, tel. 415/325–3888; San Diego, tel. 619/270–6401, San Francisco, tel. 415/421–3473 or 415/566–6222; Santa Barbara, tel. 805/562–8080). Colorado (Boulder, tel. 303/447–8101; Denver, tel. 303/571–0630). Connecticut (New Haven, tel. 203/562–5335). Florida (Miami, tel. 305/670–9261). Georgia (Atlanta, tel. 404/377–9997). Illinois (Chicago, tel. 312/951–0585; Evanston, tel. 847/475–5070). Indiana (Bloomington, tel. 812/330–1600). Louisiana (New Orleans, tel. 504/866–1767). Maryland (College Park, tel. 301/779–1172). Massachusetts (Amherst, tel. 413/256–1261; Boston, tel. 617/266–1926; Cambridge, tel. 617/497–1497 or 617/225–2555). Michigan (Ann Arbor, tel. 313/998–0200). Minnesota (Minneapolis, tel. 612/379–2323). New York (New York, tel. 212/822–2700, 212/666–4177, or 212/254–2525). North Carolina (Chapel Hill, tel. 919/942–2334). Ohio (Columbus, tel. 614/294–8696). Oregon (Portland, tel. 503/228–1900). Pennsylvania (Philadelphia, tel. 215/382–0343; Pittsburgh, tel. 412/683–1881). Rhode Island (Providence, tel. 401/331–5810). Tennessee (Knoxville, tel. 423/523–9900). Texas (Austin, tel. 512/472–4931; Dallas, tel. 214/363–9941). Utah (Salt Lake City, tel. 801/582–5840). Washington (Seattle, tel. 206/632–2448 or 206/329–4567). Washington, D.C. (tel. 202/337–6464). **Council Travel in Paris** (6 rue de Vaugirard, 6e, tel. 01–44–41–89–89, métro Odéon; open weekdays 9:30–6:30, Sat. 10–5. 22 rue des Pyramides, 1er, tel. 01–46–55–55–65). **Educational Travel Center** (438 N. Frances St., Madison, WI 53703, tel. 608/256–5551 or 800/747–5551). **STA in the U.S.**: California (Berkeley, tel. 510//642–3000; Los Angeles, tel. 213/934–8722; San Francisco, tel. 415/391–8407; Santa Monica, tel. 310/394–5126; Westwood, tel. 310/824–1574). Florida (Miami, tel. 305/461–3444; University of Florida, tel. 352/338–0068). Illinois (Chicago, tel. 312/786–9050). Massachusetts (Boston, tel. 617/266–6014; Cambridge, tel. 617/576–4623). New York (Columbia University, tel. 212/865–2700; West Village, tel. 212/627–3111). Pennsylvania (Philadelphia, tel. 215/382–2928). Washington (Seattle, tel. 206/633–5000). Washington, D.C. (tel. 202/887–0912). **STA in Paris** (tel. 01–43–43–46–10 for information or try CPS Voyages, 20 rue des

Carmes, 5e, tel. 01–43–25–00–76, métro Maubert-Mutualité). **STA elsewhere**: Australia (Adelaide, tel. 08/223–2434; Brisbane tel. 73/229–2499; Cairns, tel. 70/31–41-99; Canberra, tel. 06/247–8633; Darwin, tel. 89/41–29–55; Melbourne, tel. 39/349–2411; Perth, tel. 09/227–7569; Sydney, tel. 29/368–1111 or 29/212–1255). Belgium (Brussels, tel. 02/524–0178). Canada (Calgary, tel. 403/282–7687; Edmonton, tel. 403/492–2592; Montreal, tel. 514/284–1368; Toronto, tel. 416/977–5228; Vancouver, tel. 604/681–9136). Czech Republic (Prague, tel. 02/26–64–66). Denmark (Holstebro, tel. 97/42–67–33; Copenhagen, tel. 33/55–75–33). Germany (Berlin, tel. 30/285–9826 or 30/311–0950; Cologne, tel. 22/144–2011; Frankfort, tel. 69/70–30–35 or 69/43–01–91; Hamburg, tel. 40/450–3840; Heidelberg, tel. 62/212–3528). Greece (Athens, tel. 01/322–1267). Holland (Amsterdam, tel. 20/624–0989 or 20/626–2557). Hungary (Budapest, tel. 01/111–9898). **Student Flights** (5010 E. Shea Blvd., Suite A104, Scottsdale, AZ 85254, tel. 602/951–1177 or 800/255–8000). **Travel Cuts** (187 College St., Toronto, Ontario M5T 1P7, tel. 416/979–2406 or 800/667–2887) in Canada.

HOSTELS

If you want to save on accommodations, look into hostels. In some 5,000 locations in more than 70 countries around the world, Hostelling International (HI), the umbrella group for a number of national youth hostel associations, has single-sex, dorm-style beds and, at many hostels, "couples" rooms and family accommodations (3 in Paris, over 100 in France). You don't just have to be a student to stay at a hostel: **Membership in any HI national hostel association is open to travelers of all ages** and allows you to stay in HI-affiliated hostels at member rates (one-year membership about $25 for adults; hostels about $10–$25 per night). Members also have priority if the hostel is full; they're eligible for discounts around the world, even on rail and bus travel in some countries. There are also two international hostel directories, one on Europe and the Mediterranean, the other covering Africa, the Americas, Asia, and the Pacific ($13.95 each). The French division of Hostelling International is the Fédération Unie des Auberges de Jeunesse (FUAJ); your HI card is good at all FUAJ hostels. There are a number of nice, privately-run hostels in Paris, as well as other hostelling organizations. Maisons Internationales des Jeunes Etudiants (MIJE) hostels, for example, are more comfortable than many budget hotels, but you must be between the ages of 18 and 30 to stay at them. BVJ Foyers also has clean, centrally located rooms, but you must be between 16 and 35 to stay at them. *See* Chapter 3 for more information.

ORGANIZATIONS • Hostelling International—American Youth Hostels (HI–AYH; 733 15th St. NW, Suite 840, Washington, DC 20005, tel. 202/783–6161, fax 202/783–6171). **Hostelling International—Canada** (HI–C; 400-205 Catherine St., Ottawa, Ontario K2P 1C3, tel. 613/237–7884, fax 613/237–7868). **Youth Hostel Association of England and Wales** (YHA; Trevelyan House, 8 St. Stephen's Hill, St. Albans, Hertfordshire AL1 2DY, tel. 01727/855215 or 01727/845047, fax 01727/844126). **Australian Youth Hostels Association** (YHA; Level 3, 10 Mallett St., Camperdown, New South Wales 2050, tel. 02/565–1699). **Youth Hostels Association of New Zealand** (YHA; Box 436, Christchurch 1, tel. 3/379–9970).

STUDYING IN PARIS

Studying in Paris is the perfect way to shake up your perception of the world, make international friends, and improve your language skills. You may choose to study through a U.S.-sponsored program, usually through an American university, or to enroll in a program sponsored by a French organization. Do your homework: **programs vary greatly** in expense, academic quality, exposure to language, amount of contact with locals, and living conditions. Working through your local university is the easiest way to find out about study-abroad programs in Paris. Most universities have staff members who distribute information on programs at European universities, and they might be able to put you in touch with program participants.

RESOURCES • American Institute for Foreign Study (102 Greenwich Ave., Greenwich, CT 06830, tel. 203/869–9090 or 800/727–2437, fax 203/869–9615). **American Council of International Studies** (ACIS; 19 Bay St., Boston, MA 02215, tel. 617/236–2051 or 800/888–2247). **Council on International Educational Exchange** (*see* Students, *above*). **Institute of International Education** (IIE; 809 U.N. Plaza, New York, NY 10017, tel. 212/984–5413). **World Learning** (Kipling Rd., Box 676, Brattleboro, VT 05302, tel. 802/257–7751 or 800/451–4465, fax 802/258–3248).

TAXIS

Getting a taxi in Paris can be frustrating, especially in summer. During peak times (7–10 AM and 4–7 PM), allow yourself a couple of hours to secure one—only taxis with lit signs are available, and these are few and far between. Your chances of picking one up are best if you **go to major hotels.** In the better-traveled parts of the city, people **line up at makeshift taxi stations**; try to find one of these, or **call individual taxi companies.** Rates are approximately 8F per kilometer; they may go up a bit after dark, but not more than 50 centimes or so per kilometer. Your taxi driver may be able to speak an English word or two, but don't expect him or her to understand complicated directions; a map, finger, and half-coherent verb phrase ought to do the trick.

RADIO CABS • Taxis Radio 7000 (tel. 01–42–70–00–42). **Taxis Bleus** (tel. 01–49–36–10–10).

TELEPHONES

The country code for France is 33. Each region of France has a two-digit prefix: 01 for Paris and Ile-de-France; 02 for the northwest; 03 for the northeast; 04 for the southeast; and 05 for the southwest. When dialing a French number **from abroad, drop the initial 0 from the two-digit prefix.** But when calling **in France, dial the whole, ten-digit number,** even if you are calling another region of the country.

Public phones are never far away in Paris; you will find them at post offices and often in cafés. Local calls cost a minimum of 1F for six minutes. Almost all French phones only accept the Télécarte, a handy little phone card you can buy at tabacs, post offices, or métro stations; it costs 41F for 50 units or 96F for 120 units. The digital display on the phone counts down your units while you're talking and tells you how many you have left when you hang up. Dial 12 to reach directory inquiries from any phone (though operators rarely speak English).

Within France, you can call collect by dialing 12 for the operator and saying "en PCV" (pronounced "on pay say vay"). If you want international directory information, dial 00–33–12 and then the country code (listed in all phone booths).

CALLING LONG DISTANCE

To dial direct to another country, dial 00 + the country code (61 for Australia, 64 for New Zealand, 44 for the United Kingdom, and 1 for the United States and Canada) plus the area code and number. The cheapest time to call is between 10:30 PM and 6 AM (about 4F10 per minute to the States, 3F70 per minute to Britain). Middling rates apply 6–8 AM and 9:30–10:30 PM; rates are reduced all day Sunday and holidays.

AT&T, MCI, and Sprint long-distance services make calling home relatively convenient, but you may find the local access number blocked in many hotel rooms. First ask the hotel operator to connect you. If the hotel operator balks, ask for an international operator, or dial the international operator yourself. One way to improve your odds of getting connected to your long-distance carrier is to **travel with more than one company's calling card** (a hotel may block Sprint, for example, but not MCI). If all else fails, call your phone company in the United States collect, or make your call from a pay phone in the hotel lobby.

ACCESS CODES • AT&T USADirect (tel. 0–800–99–00–11). **MCI** Call USA (tel. 0–800–99–00–19). **Sprint** Express (tel. 0–800–99–00–87).

MINITEL

The Minitel is a monitor/modem system that can dole out addresses and telephone numbers for all of France, receive electronic mail, conduct data searches, and even tell you the weather. You can **use Minitel terminals for free in any post office,** where they have for the most part replaced telephone books. Here's how it works: Press the button with a phone-receiver symbol on it and dial "11." When you hear the high-pitched tone, press CONNEXION/FIN. Database fields will then appear on the screen. Type in the nom (name), activité (subject), localité (city), or address relating to the information you're seeking. To advance a line press SUITE, to go back a line press RETOUR, to backspace press CORRECTION, and to begin a new search press ANNIHILATION. Press ENVOI to send your query; responses will then appear on the screen. To end your session, press CONNEXION/FIN.

TIPPING

At restaurants, cafés, and brasseries, service is included, and it's 100% normal not to leave a centime. If you love the service or you're in a more swanky establishment, then leave anywhere from 2F to 10F extra. Tip taxi drivers and hairdressers 10%; ushers who help opera- and theater-goers to their seats should get about 5F; and sometimes ushers movie theaters expect 1F–2F for showing you to your seat.

TOUR OPERATORS

Buying a vacation package can sometimes make your trip to Paris less expensive. The tour operators who put them together may handle several hundred thousand travelers per year and can use their purchasing power to give you a good price. Their high volume may also indicate financial stability. But some small companies provide more personalized service; because they tend to specialize, they may also be more knowledgeable about a given area.

The more your package includes, the better you can predict the ultimate cost of your vacation. Make sure you know exactly what is covered, and **beware of hidden costs.** Are taxes, tips, and service charges included? Transfers and baggage handling? Entertainment and excursions? These add up. If the package you are considering is priced lower than in your wildest dreams, **be skeptical.** Ask about the hotel's location, room size, beds, and whether it has a pool, room service, or programs for children, if you need them.

Each year consumers are stranded or lose their money when tour operators—even large ones with excellent reputations—go out of business. So **check out the operator.** Find out how long the company has been in business, and ask for references that you can check. And don't book unless the firm has a consumer-protection program. Members of the National Tour Association and United States Tour Operators Association are required to set aside funds to cover your payments and travel arrangements in case the company defaults. Nonmembers may carry insurance instead. Look for the details, and for the name of an underwriter with a solid reputation, in the operator's brochure. And when it comes to tour operators, don't trust escrow accounts. Although there are laws governing charter-flight operators, no governmental body prevents tour operators from raiding the till. For more information, *see* Consumer Protection, *above.*

TOUR-OPERATOR RECOMMENDATIONS • **National Tour Association** (NTA; 546 E. Main St., Lexington, KY 40508, tel. 606/226–4444 or 800/755–8687). **United States Tour Operators Association** (USTOA; 342 Madison Ave., Suite 1522, New York, NY 10173, tel. 212/599–6599, fax 212/599–6744).

USING AN AGENT

A good travel agent is an excellent resource. When shopping for one, collect brochures from several sources and remember that some agents' suggestions may be skewed by promotional relationships with tour and package firms that reward them for volume sales. If you have a special interest, find an agent with expertise in that area (*see* Travel Agencies, *below*).

SINGLE TRAVELERS

Remember that prices for vacation packages are usually quoted per person, based on two sharing a room. If traveling solo, you may be required to pay the full double-occupancy rate.

PACKAGES

The companies listed below offer vacation packages in a broad price range.

AIR/HOTEL • **American Airlines Fly AAway Vacations** (tel. 800/321–2121). **Continental Vacations** (tel. 800/634–5555). **Delta Dream Vacations** (tel. 800/872–7786). **DER Tours** (11933 Wilshire Blvd., Los Angeles, CA 90025, tel. 310/479–4140 or 800/937–1235). **United Vacations** (tel. 800/328–6877).

TRAIN TRAVEL

The railway system in France is fast, extensive, and efficient. All French trains have a first and second class. First class is 30%–50% more expensive, though the difference in comfort between the two is minimal, except on the lightening-fast TGV (*Trains à Grande Vitesse,* or Very Fast Trains) on which first class is really deluxe. First-class sleeping cars are very expensive, but second-class couchettes, bunks that come six to a compartment, cost only 90F more (check in advance to make sure that's what you're getting). When you're **going long distances, it's best to take the TGV.** Be sure to **make a seat reservation** (20F–80F), which is usually required, though SNCF now runs some Train Verts, which don't require a reservation and are less expensive. For information on the various passes available, *see* Rail Passes, *below.*

Be aware that trains fill fast on weekends and holidays, so purchase tickets well in advance at these times. Don't forget to validate them (*composter le billet*) at the orange ticket punchers, usually at the entrance to the platforms (*quais*). If you board your train on the run and don't have time to punch it, look for a conductor (*contrôleur*) as soon as possible and get him to sign it. Otherwise, you're in for a nasty fine (*amende*). Train schedules for individual lines are available at all stations through which the line runs. Complete SNCF timetables are available at information counters in large stations. Bring food and drink with you on long trips, as the food sold on the train is very expensive and very bad.

TRAIN RESERVATIONS

For information or to make reservations on any train, call 08–36–35–35–35 (there's a 2F per minute charge); for the most part, you can't make reservations by calling individual train stations (their numbers are for station information hours, etc.), but you can buy tickets at any station.

STATIONS

Six major train stations serve Paris; all have cafés, newsstands, bureaux de change, and luggage storage. Unfortunately, most luggage lockers have been closed for security measures, though it's worth checking if there are any available. Most train stations have tourist offices, and each is connected to the rest of Paris by the métro system.

GARE D'AUSTERLITZ • Trains serve southwest France and Spain, including Toulouse (7 hrs, 510F), Barcelona (10–14 hrs, 495F), and Madrid (11 hrs, 598F).

GARE DE L'EST • Trains serve eastern France, Germany, Austria, and Eastern Europe, with trains leaving daily for Frankfurt (6 hrs, 568F), Prague (16 hrs, 1,039F), and Vienna (13 hrs, 1,058F). The station is smaller than nearby Gare du Nord and its services are more limited, but there's still a tourist office and a Thomas Cook bureau de change (open daily 7 AM–6:45 PM). The neighborhood is a bit scary at night.

GARE DE LYON • Trains serve the south of France, the Alps, Switzerland, and Italy. Plenty of trains run to Lyon (5 hrs, 372F), Lausanne (4 hrs, 506F), Milan (7½ hrs, 411F), and Rome (14 hrs, 550F). This is one of the bigger stations, with a full range of services, including a bureau de change (open 7 AM–11 PM).

GARE MONTPARNASSE • Trains serve Brittany and southwestern France. Daily trains run to Bordeaux (3 hrs, 371F), Rennes (2 hrs, 280F), and Biarritz (5 hrs, 493F).

GARE DU NORD • Trains serve northern France (Calais and Lille), and to Belgium, the Netherlands, and points in Scandinavia. Regular trains run to Amsterdam (6 hrs, 378F), Copenhagen (16 hrs, 1,091F), and London (*see* The Channel Tunnel, *above*). Showers cost 20F; soap and towels are extra. The neighborhood gets sketchy at night.

GARE ST-LAZARE • Trains serve Normandy and some destinations in northern France. International destinations include Amsterdam (6 hrs, 390F). This is the only major station without a tourist office.

RAIL PASSES

If you plan to do a lot of train traveling, **compare costs for rail passes and individual tickets.** If you plan to cover a lot of ground in a short period, rail passes may be worth your while; they also spare you the time waiting in lines to buy tickets. To price costs for individual tickets of the rail trips you plan—**ask a travel agent or call Rail Europe, Railpass Express, or DER Tours.** If you're under 26 on your first day of travel, you're eligible for a youth pass, valid for second-class travel only (like Europass Youth, Eurail Youth Flexipass, or Eurail Youthpass). If you're older, you must buy one of the more expensive regular passes, valid for first-class travel, and it might cost you less to buy individual tickets, especially if your tastes and budget call for second-class travel. Be sure to **buy your rail pass before leaving the United States**; those available elsewhere cost more. All Eurail- and Europass holders get a discount on Eurostar fares through the Channel Tunnel (*see* The Channel Tunnel, *above*).

A France Railpass is valid within France only for three days of travel within a one-month period. First-class passes go for $185, second-class for $145; added days (up to six allowed) cost $30 each for either class. The France Railpass isn't available once you arrive (in fact, it can't even be used by residents or citizens of France), so be sure to pick one up before leaving home. Another good deal is the France Rail 'n Drive Pass; for only a bit more than the plain old train pass, you get three days of train travel and two days of Avis car rental within one month. A second-class pass goes for $219, and you can add car days for $39 each and rail days for $30 each (per person). You get unlimited mileage and can pick up and drop off the car anywhere in France at no extra charge (Avis has 520 agencies in France), so this might not be a bad deal for seeing out-of-the-way châteaux. Car-rental reservations must be made directly with Avis at least seven days in advance (tel. 800/331–1084 in U.S.), and drivers must be age 24 or older. Neither the France Rail nor the France Rail 'n Drive pass is valid for travel in Corsica.

Finally, **don't assume that your rail pass guarantees you a seat** on every train—seat reservations are required on some trains (see above).

FRENCH RAIL DISCOUNTS

If you purchase an individual ticket from SNCF in France and you're under 26, you will automatically get a 25% reduction (a valid ID, such as an ISIC card or passport, is necessary). If you're under 26 and are going to be using the train quite a bit during your stay in France, **consider buying the Carte 12–25** (270F), which offers unlimited 50% reductions for one year (providing that there's space available at that price, otherwise you'll just get the standard 25% discount).

When traveling together, **two people can save money (and don't have to be a couple) with the Prix Découverte à Deux.** Just buy your tickets together or say you're traveling together when you reserve, and you'll get a 25% reduction during "périodes bleus" (blue periods; weekdays and not on or near any holidays).

The **Carte Vermeil is a good value if you're over age 60.** There are two options: The first, the Carte Vermeil Quatre Temps, costs 143F and gives you a reduction on four trips: 50% off in the blue periods and 20% off during the more crowded "périodes blanches" (white periods; weekends and on or around holidays). The second, the Carte Vermeil Plein Temps, is 279F and allows you an unlimited number of 30% reductions on trips within France and a 30% discount on trips outside of France for one year.

You can **get a discount for children with the Carte Kiwi.** With the card, up to four children under 16 accompanying an adult can get a 50% discount for a full year. It's 285F for four trips and 444F for an unlimited number of trips.

If you don't benefit from any of these reductions and you plan on traveling at least 1,000 km (620 mi) round trip (even with several stops), **look into Billets Séjours.** This ticket gives you a 25% reduction if you stay over a Sunday and if you travel only during the blue periods. It may be a major organizational feat, but you can save a lot of cash this way.

If you don't actually want a rail pass and are under 26, you might want to **consider a Billet International de Jeunesse (International Youth Ticket),** usually known as a BIJ or BIGE ticket. Here's how it works: You can purchase a second-class ticket between two far-flung European cities at a 20%–30% savings and then make unlimited stops along the way for up to two months. BIJ tickets are available throughout Europe at budget travel agencies; try the European offices of STA and Council Travel (see Students, above).

TRANSPORTATION

When you've had enough walking and you just want to get there, the city has an excellent public transportation system consisting of the métro and the RER (which make up the subway system) and the municipal bus system, all operated by RATP (see The Métro & RER, above). If you plan to stay in Paris for only a short time, stick to the métro; it's easier to use and faster than the buses. If you have time, take a bus; not only is it a way to get around Paris, but is also a cheap way to get a tour of the city (see Bus Travel, above). To avoid getting lost on a regular basis, **as soon as you arrive buy an indispensable *Plan de Paris par Arrondissement,*** a booklet of detailed maps showing all métro stops and sights. An index at the front alphabetically lists all streets and their arrondissement. It costs 35F–60F and is available at large bookstores such as the FNAC (see Bookstores in Chapter 6), smaller bookstores marked Presse, and some newsstands. You can also get less useful but free maps from the tourist offices (see Visitor Information, below). Other ways to get around the city are bicycling or rollerblading, by motorbike or moped, or with a taxi (see individual topics, above).

TRAVEL AGENCIES

PLANNING YOUR TRIP

Find a good travel agent who puts your needs first when you're planning your trip. Your best bet is to **look for an agency that specializes in your destination, has been in business at least five years, and emphasizes customer service.** If you're looking for an agency-organized package, choose an agency that's a member of the National Tour Association or the United States Tour Operators Association (see Tour Operators, above).

TRAVEL AGENT REFERRALS • American Society of Travel Agents (ASTA; 1101 King St., Suite 200, Alexandria, VA 22314, tel. 703/739–2782, fax 703/684–8319). **Alliance of Canadian Travel Associations** (Suite 201, 1729 Bank St., Ottawa, Ontario K1V 7Z5, tel. 613/521–0474, fax 613/521–0805). **Association of British Travel Agents** (55–57 Newman St., London W1P 4AH, tel. 0171/637–2444, fax 0171/637–0713).

DISCOUNT TRAVEL AGENCIES IN PARIS

Several places in Paris offer discount plane tickets and other travel services for the cash-strapped voyager. Though they are primarily aimed at students, a number of agencies in Paris are good for any traveler looking for cheaper rates. Council Travel has a couple offices in Paris, as does STA (*see* Students, *above*). Nouvelles Frontières is the best place for discounted plane tickets all over France. Wasteels is the best-represented youth travel organization in Paris, with branches near most train stations. If you're under 26, you can get 20% discounts on all train tickets beginning or terminating in France here. O.T.U. Voyages is also a haven if you're under 26; this agency will help you make hostel and hotel reservations, organize trips throughout France, and book discount plane tickets.

TRAVEL AGENCIES • Access Voyages (6 rue Pierre-Lescot, 1er, tel. 01–44–76–84–50, métro Rambuteau; open weekdays 9–7, Sat. 10–6). **Forum Voyages** (140 rue du Faubourg-St-Honoré, 8e, tel. 01–42–89–07–07, métro Champs-Elysées–Clemenceau; open weekdays 9:30–7, Sat. 10–1 and 2–5). **Nouvelles Frontières** (offices all over Paris; call tel. 08–03–33–33–33 for reservations and information). **O.T.U. Voyages** (39 ave. Georges Bernanos, 5e, tel. 01–44–41–38–50, métro Port-Royal; 2 rue Malus, 5e, tel. 01–43–36–80–27, métro Monge). **Usit Voyages** (6 rue de Vaugirard, 6e, tel. 01–42–34–56–90, métro Odéon; open weekdays 9:30–6:30, Sat. 1:30–5). **Wasteels** (113 blvd. St-Michel, 5e, tel. 01–43–26–25–25, RER Luxembourg; other location: 5 rue de la Banque, 2e, tel. 01–42–61–53–21, métro Bourse; both open weekdays 9–1 and 2–6:30).

TRAVEL GEAR

Travel catalogs specialize in nifty items that can save space when packing. They also sell dual-voltage appliances, currency converters, and foreign-language phrase books.

MAIL-ORDER CATALOGS • Magellan's (tel. 800/962–4943, fax 805/568–5406). **Orvis Travel** (tel. 800/541–3541, fax 540/343–7053). **TravelSmith** (tel. 800/950–1600, fax 800/950–1656).

VISITOR INFORMATION

Before you go on your trip, you can **get all kinds of information from the French Government Tourist Office or the Maison de la France.** In Paris, the main tourist office is an attraction in itself, with its gift shop, lodging desk, and multitude of glossy brochures—all a few seconds' walk from the Arc de Triomphe on the famed Champs-Elysées. The helpful multilingual staff can give you information on public transport and other practicalities, and they're happy to tell you about current cultural events. The office sells Télécartes (*see* Telephones, *above*), museum passes (*see* Museums *in* Chapter 2), and Paris Visite passes. Paris Visite passes are good for one, three, or five days of unlimited travel on métro, bus, and RER lines; if you plan to hop on the métro six or more times a day it might be worth it, otherwise buy a carnet or a pass (*see* The Métro & RER, *above*).

If you're in a bind, the tourist office can find lodging for you, but only if you come down to the office in person. They'll charge you 8F to find you a hostel, 20F to put you in a one-star hotel, and 25F to set you up in a two-star hotel—needless to say, this is not how you'll find the cheapest places to crash. They run out of brochures pretty regularly during peak tourist season, but try to secure "Les Marchés de Paris," which lists all the markets in Paris, and "Paris la Nuit," which highlights nightclubs and late-night restaurants. Both are free and in French. There are also six branch offices that also reserve rooms and dole out general information on the city.

BEFORE YOU GO • French Government Tourist Office: California (Beverly Hills, tel. 310/271–6665 or 900/990–0040 [50¢ per min]). Illinois (Chicago, tel. 312/751–7800 or 900/990–0040 [50¢ per min]). New York (New York, tel. 212/838–7800 or 900/990–0040 [50¢ per min]). **Maison de la France**: Canada (Montréal, tel. 514/288–4264; Toronto, tel. 416/593–4723).

PARIS TOURIST OFFICES • For 24-hour information in English on upcoming art exhibits and festivals, dial the **cultural hot line** (tel. 01–49–52–53–56). **Main tourist office** (127 av. des Champs-

TACKLING PARIS

If you don't get anything else straight, for God's sake learn the difference between the Rive Gauche (Left Bank) and the Rive Droite (Right Bank) before you step off that plane. The simplest directions will refer to these two sides of the Seine River, and if you have to ask which is which, you're likely to be scoffed at. In the most stereotypical terms, the Rive Gauche is the artistic area; the Sorbonne and the Quartier Latin are here, along with the former haunts of literary greats, budding artists, and intellectual dissidents. The Rive Droite, on the other hand, is traditionally more elegant and commercial, though its less central areas (the Marais, the Bastille, and Belleville, for example) are the hip places of the moment. The fancier parts of the Right Bank are home to ritzy shopping districts and most of the big-name sights like the Louvre and the Arc de Triomphe. Between the two banks you have the Ile de la Cité, where you'll find the Cathédrale de Notre-Dame, and the smaller Ile St-Louis.

Once you have the Left and Right Banks figured out, move on to the arrondissements, or districts, numbered 1 through 20. (For all addresses in this book, the arrondissement number is given, since it's the most common way to describe a location.) Arrondissements one through eight are the most central and contain most of the big tourist attractions, while the ninth through 20th gradually spiral outward toward the outskirts of the city.

More than 2 million people somehow manage to cram themselves into the apartments, cafés, restaurants, bars, and streets of Paris. The long-running joke is that the streets—narrow and labyrinthine (except for the grands boulevards, which urban planner Baron Haussman created in the late 19th century)— were paved according to the paths the cows wandered in more pastoral times. You will get lost—hell, most of the natives do, too (and many carry maps). But that's part of the fun.

Elysées, 8e, tel. 01–44–11–10–30, métro Charles de Gaulle–Etoile; open daily 9–8). **Branch offices**: Eiffel Tower (7e, tel. 01–45–51–22–15, métro Bir Hakeim, RER Champ de Mars; open May–Sept. only, 11–6). **Main train station branch offices:** Gare d'Austerlitz (13e, tel. 01–45–84–91–70); Gare de l'Est (10e, tel. 01–46–07–17–73); Gare de Lyon (12e, tel. 01–43–43–33–24); Gare Montparnasse (15e, tel. 01–43–22–19–19); and Gare du Nord (10e, tel. 01–45–26–94–82). They are open 8–8 most of the year and until 9 in summer (though Austerlitz closes at 3 PM); all of them are closed on Sunday. **Maison de la France** (8 av. de l'Opéra, tel. 01–42–96–10–23).

OTHER RESOURCES

The **American Church** is an indispensable resource for wayward expatriates. It hosts concerts, workshops and holiday meals; houses the Paris *Free Voice;* and updates postings for jobs and apartments daily. It's a great place to meet other Americans staying in the city. There are a number of very informative English-language publications (*see* English-Language Publications, *above*) where you can find information about events and opportunities in Paris.

AMERICAN CHURCH • 65 quai d'Orsay, 7e, tel. 01–40–62–05–00, métro Invalides. Open Mon.– Sat. 9 AM–10:30 PM and Sun. 2 PM–7:30 PM.

VOLUNTEERING

A variety of volunteer programs are available. CIEE (*see* Students, *above*) is a key player, running its own roster of projects and publishing a directory that lists other sponsor organizations, *Volunteer! The Comprehensive Guide to Voluntary Service in the U.S. and Abroad* ($12.95 plus $1.50 postage). Service Civil International (SCI), International Voluntary Service (IVS), and Volunteers for Peace (VFP) run two- and three-week workcamps; VFP also publishes the *International Workcamp Directory* ($12). WorldTeach programs, run by Harvard University, require that you commit a year to teaching on subjects ranging from English and science to carpentry, forestry, or sports.

RESOURCES • **SCI/IVS** (5474 Walnut Level Rd., Crozet, VA 22932, tel. 804/823–1826). **VFP** (43 Tiffany Rd., Belmont, VT 05730, tel. 802/259–2759, fax 802/259–2922). **WorldTeach** (1 Eliot St., Cambridge, MA 02138–5705, tel. 617/495–5527 or 800/483–2240, fax 617/495–1599).

WHEN TO GO

Paris's main tourist season is between Easter and early September, as you'll notice from the babble of every language but French near the major sights. The hotel owners know it, too, and they often jack up prices 10F–20F in the high season. April–June is great for crowdless touring if you can bear the occasionally wet weather. July brings an unsavory mix of crowds and heat. In August many Parisians skip town for vacation, leaving a trail of closed stores and restaurants behind them, as well as a refreshingly quiet town. Cultural life has its annual renaissance in September, when the weather is usually glorious and music festivals abound. From November to January—if you can stand the biting weather—you'll find a full schedule of ballet, theater, and opera performances.

CLIMATE

Telling your friends that you are going to Paris in the springtime may sound romantic, but **it can be distressingly damp if you show up before Easter.** The weather tends to be pleasantly warm (70°F, 20°C) by June but can be sultry and dusty in July and August (80°F, 30°C). **September and early October are almost ideal,** with lots of sun and moderate temperatures. Come November, expect a mixed bag of wet-and-cold and warmish-and-sunny days. From December to March, the temperature sporadically falls below freezing. Whenever you go, remember that you can usually count on some rain—check the weather pages of the newspaper for the current situation and be sure to bring an umbrella or raincoat.

FORECASTS • **Weather Channel Connection** (tel. 900/932–8437), 95¢ per minute from a Touch-Tone phone.

FESTIVALS

Paris loves to *fête* (party), and they do it in style all year round. Most of the following festivals are Paris-specific, but some are celebrated nationwide. Check the tourist offices (*see* Visitor Information, *above*) for details on dates and tickets.

SUMMER • The **Fête de la Musique** is not to be missed. Held annually on June 21, the festival celebrates the summer solstice with an explosion of live music performed throughout the streets, cafés, and public spaces of Paris (and all of France). The Palais Royal, Bastille, and other areas host music until the sun comes up. The **Fête du Pont Neuf** in mid-June is a festival with street performers, booths, and other fun activities on Pont Neuf and place Dauphine. On June 21, **Gay Pride Day** is celebrated with flamboyant floats and throngs of men and women partying down boulevard St-Germain. The **Festival du Marais,** celebrated between mid-June and mid-July, stages music, dance, and theater in the churches and historic hotels of the Marais. Also in the classical music mode, the **Musique en l'Ile** series of concerts is held in the 17th-century Eglise St-Louis on the Ile St-Louis every July and August.

The **Fête du Cinema** in June is a silver screen dream. One regular-price ticket is your passport to as many movies as your eyeballs can bear on this one special day. Ask a tourist office for this year's schedule. **Course des Garçons de Café** is a notorious race in which more than 500 professional waiters dash through the streets of Paris carrying trays of bottles and glasses. The fastest racer who spills the least wins. The race takes place at the end of June and starts and finishes at the Hôtel de Ville. The **Foire International d'Art au Grand Palais** happens in early July, when artists from around the world show off their work in the colossal Grand Palais. **Bastille Day (July 14),** which celebrates the storming of the state prison during the early days of the Revolution, is a mix of parades, fireworks, alcohol, street music, and debauchery. The "bals des pompiers" (firemen's balls) in almost every arrondissement are the prime places to vive la France. Depending on your penchant for partying, it's either one of the worst or best days to be in Paris.

The **Tour de France,** held annually at the end of July, is the world's most famous bicycle race. Anyone who is not along the route itself is glued to the TV set, and when the race winds up on the Champs-Elysées in Paris, the whole city pours into the streets to cheer.

AUTUMN & WINTER • Mid-September through mid-October is the time for **Musique Baroque au Château de Versailles,** a festival that takes place at Versailles and is well worth the trip. Hot on its heels is October's **Festival de Jazz de Paris,** the culmination of a summer full of jazz all over France. Subscription tickets are good for events in clubs and concert halls; for more information call 01–40–56–07–17. The **Festival d'Automne** (for information call 01–42–96–96–04), held from mid-September to the end of December, features music, theater, and dance throughout Paris. Cafés and restaurants all over France celebrate the official release of new wine during **Beaujolais Nouveau** on the third Thursday of November. **Chinese New Year** is celebrated in the 13th arrondissement, between avenue d'Ivry and avenue de Choisy, in late January or early February, depending on when the New Year falls.

SPRING • The **Festival du Livre** (for information call 04–47–63–60–65) takes place in March, where book publishers, authors, and aspiring intellectuals peruse what's on the market for the coming season. May 1 is **May Day,** honoring workers worldwide. Trade unions organize marches through the streets of Paris, museums and shops close, and newspapers stop their presses. Street vendors sell lilies of the valley, symbolic of the labor movement.

The **French Open** brings tennis greats and their fans to beautiful Roland-Garros Stadium every year at the end of May. For information call the **French Tennis Federation** (tel. 01–47–43–48–00). Or write them (2 av. Gordon-Bennett, 75016 Paris) in January and ask for a reservation form. Tickets run from 45F to 295F.

WORKING IN PARIS

Working in France isn't easy to finagle, and obtaining the right to do it legally requires a lot of tenacity, especially for the non-student. France won't grant you a work permit unless you already have a French employer who can convince immigration officials that a native couldn't do the same job. However, **there are a few programs geared toward work exchanges between the two countries** that will help you obtain a long-term visa for work of a professional nature. Many native English speakers find work teaching their mother tongue through one of the city's many private language schools. Each with its own guidelines and restrictions, some (but not all) requiring a Teaching of English as a Foreign Language (TOEFL) certificate, which is obtainable after an expensive four-week training course. Look in the Parisian Pages jaunes (Yellow Pages) for addresses and phone numbers.

The easiest way to arrange for work in France is through CIEE's (*see* Students, *above*) Work Abroad Department, which enables U.S. citizens or permanent residents, 18 years or older, to work in Europe at a variety of jobs, for three to six months; you must have been a full-time student for the semester preceding your stay overseas and have a good working knowledge of French. CIEE publishes two excellent resource books with complete details on work/travel opportunities, including the valuable *Work, Study, Travel Abroad: The Whole World Handbook* and *The High School Student's Guide to Study, Travel, and Adventure Abroad* ($13.95 each, plus $3 first-class postage). The U.K.-based Vacation Work Press publishes the *Directory of Overseas Summer Jobs* ($14.95) and Susan Griffith's *Work Your Way Around the World* ($17.95). The first lists more than 45,000 jobs worldwide; the latter, though with fewer listings, makes a more interesting read.

Travel CUTS (*see* Students, *above*) has similar programs for Canadian students. And the Association for International Practical Training sponsors professional internships of 12 to 18 months in many foreign countries; you must be under 35 and seek a professional internship with a foreign company. Au Pair Abroad arranges board and lodging for people between the ages of 18 and 26 who want to work as nannies for three to 18 months in France. Basic language skills are required, and all applicants must go through a somewhat lengthy interview process.

Once you arrive in Paris, **buy a copy of *Paris Anglophone*** (140F) published by Association Frank. It has a comprehensive listing of businesses, resources, and all things anglophone (including potential employers) in the city. **CIDJ** (Centre d'information et de documentation de la jeunesse), in Paris, can provide you with all the bulletin boards and binders you need to research both short- and long-term job openings.

RESOURCES • Association for International Practical Training (10400 Little Patuxent Parkway, Suite 250, Columbia, MD 21044-3510, tel. 410/997–2200, fax 410/992–3924). **Au Pair Abroad** (1015 15th St. NW, Suite 750, Washington, D.C. 20005, tel. 202/408–5380, fax 202/480–5397, 708439@mcimail.com). **CIDJ** (101 quai Branly, 15e, tel. 01–44–49–12–00, métro Bir-Hakeim; open Mon.–Sat. 9:30–6). **Vacation Work Press** (c/o Peterson's, 202 Carnegie Center, Princeton, NJ 05843, tel. 609/243–9111).

EXPLORING PARIS

2

UPDATED BY SIMON HEWITT

P roudly bearing the scars of an illustrious 2,000-year history and home to 2 million people, Paris could take you multiple lifetimes to explore from top to bottom—and that's not counting the Louvre. If you have only a few days or weeks in the city, strategy is key. The efficient métro system is the backbone of see-and-flee sightseeing, but moving around by bus—or, better yet, by foot—will give you a much better feel for Parisian street life—its action, its glamour, its pooper-scoopers.

To get a sense of Paris, consider taking one of the following walks through the center of the city: Follow the Seine between the Eiffel Tower and the Ile St-Louis, to see the Palais de Chaillot, the Grand Palais, the Musée d'Orsay, the Louvre, the Institut de France, the Ile de la Cité, and Notre-Dame. Go from the Louvre to the Arc de Triomphe: Majestic with a capital "M," this walk hits many vestiges of aristocratic Paris, including the Jardin des Tuileries, the place de la Concorde, and the Champs-Elysées. Head from the Louvre to the Panthéon: Cross the Pont Neuf, walk through place Dauphine toward Notre-Dame, cross the bridge at the west of place Parvis, and walk along rue St-Jacques to explore the crowded little streets of the Quartier Latin. Walk from the place de la Bastille to the Jardin des Tuileries, by heading west through the Marais via place des Vosges, toward Beaubourg and the vibrant Les Halles area. Head south to rejoin rue de Rivoli around the Louvre, and rest your aching feet in the Jardin des Tuileries. To explore Montmartre, walk from the Blanche métro stop, weave up rue Lepic to the place du Tertre and Sacré-Coeur, then wander around the cobblestoned streets of Montmartre.

Be sure to visit the obelisk at place de la Concorde, where you can see 360° around Paris. You might also consider a ride on one of the riverboats—equipped with enough wattage to illuminate a small nation—that churn their way down the Seine, riling pedestrians and riverside habitants with their incomprehensible loudspeakers. But they do take you past some awesome sights, especially at night. Try **Bateaux Mouches** (Pont de l'Alma, tel. 01–42–25–96–10, 8e, métro Alma-Marceau) on the Right Bank, which runs 40F boat tours every half hour, 10 AM–11 PM. With luck, you'll also have time for a little aimless wandering: the **Bastille** (11e), **Belleville** (20e), the **Champs-Elysées** (8e), the **Marais** (4e), **Montmartre** (18e), the **Quartier Latin** (5e), and **St-Germain-des-Prés** (6e) (*see* Neighborhoods, *below*) will all treat you well if you get lost in their little streets.

Paris's sights are not cheap, but you may qualify for a discount. Youths and students can get discounts, though these vary from place to place (often, even as a student, you have to be 25 and under). Other discounts are available to the elderly, children, and the unemployed (though you must be a citizen of a European Union nation to get this one); in national museums, visitors using wheelchairs and their attendants also receive reduced rates. In addition, some sights have reduced admission one day of the week or after 3 PM. All kinds of other special stipulations exist, but no matter what the rule is, a reduction may depend largely on the mood of the person in the ticket booth—bring many forms of ID and hope for the best. We have noted only the standard admission prices for sights, as well as weekly discounts. If you believe that you qualify for a discount, it is always worth inquiring. For information on museum passes, see Museums, below.

Paris's major sights are listed first in alphabetical order in the following pages. Other sights are arranged by category (Museums, Houses of Worship, Dead Folk, Parks and Gardens, and Neighborhoods). You'll find descriptions and maps of individual neighborhoods in the Neighborhoods section at the end of the chapter.

MAJOR ATTRACTIONS

ARC DE TRIOMPHE

Never one renowned for subtlety or modesty, Napoléon I, celebrating his successful battles of 1805–06, commissioned architect Jean-François Chalgrin to design a permanent monument to his military prowess. Plans weren't finalized till 1809, and when Marie-Louise of Austria arrived in 1810 to marry Napoléon, only the foundations had been completed. No problem—he simply had a full-size wooden mock arch set up, disguised by a trompe l'oeil canvas. In 1815, when Napoléon met his waterloo, the Arc de Triomphe was still only half finished; Louis-Philippe finally completed it in 1836. Although the plaque on the arch calls it simply a "tribute to the French military," the names of Napoléon's 128 victorious battles and 660 generals are inscribed on the inner faces.

Napoléon's coffin was rolled under the Arc de Triomphe in 1840, inaugurating the arch as a site for public ceremonies. Victor Hugo's remains rested underneath for a night before being moved to the Panthéon. In 1919 the triumphal parade marking the end of the war passed below, and in 1920 the Unknown Soldier was buried here; an eternal flame, relit each evening, has watched over him ever since. Hitler strode through the arch in 1940 to encounter a largely deserted Paris; four years later Charles de Gaulle victoriously followed the same route, met by thousands of jubilant Parisians.

The Arc de Triomphe remains the largest triumphal arch in the world. The sculpture surrounding it includes François Rude's famous La Marseillaise, depicting the uprising of 1792. Climb the 164-foot arch for one of the better views of Paris, highlighting the city's unmistakable design. The arch marks the intersection of the 8th, 16th, and 17th arrondissements, and radiating out from the arch are 12 avenues, hence its traditional name—place de l'Etoile (Star Plaza). Gaze along the vista west to La Défense, then east down the Champs-Elysées to place de la Concorde and on to the Louvre. Pl. Charles de Gaulle, 16e, tel. 01–43–80–31–31. Take the underground passage from the Champs-Elysées, on the even numbers side. Métro: Charles de Gaulle–Etoile. Admission 32F. Open Apr.–Sept., daily 9:30–6 (Fri. until 10); Oct.–Mar., daily 10–5:30.

BASILIQUE DU SACRE-COEUR

This white concoction overlooking the city was dreamt up by overzealous Catholics to "expiate the sins" of the Paris Commune of 1871 (see box, The Paris Commune, below). Built between 1875 and 1914 to the designs of Paul Abadie, who made his name by sticking similar scaly domes onto cathedrals in Angoulême and Périgueux in southwest France, the neo-Byzantine Sacré-Coeur snubs aesthetes from the city's most spectacular hilltop site, basking in the dubious aura of Most Popular Postcard Subject In Paris. Its nouveau-riche gleam is down to the local stone (quarried in Château-Landon, southeast of Paris) which secretes calcite when wet; the more it rains, the whiter the Sacré-Coeur glows. The interior is a letdown after the exterior bombast; the mighty gold mosaic above the altar looks as if it could be exciting, but it's too murky to tell. The 15F admission fee to the 367-foot dome offers a magnificent view of the city, but you can get almost the same view for free from the front of the basilica. 35 rue du Chevalier-de-la-Barre, 18e, tel. 01–42–51–17–02. Métro: Anvers. Basilica open daily 6:45 AM–11 PM. Dome open summer, daily 9–7; winter, daily 9–6; admission 15F.

LEVALLOIS-
PERRET

blvd.
Bessières

av. de Clichy

blvd. Berthier

av. de St. Ouen

BATIGNOLLES

Cimitière de
Montmartre

av. de Wagram

av. de Villiers

blvd. des Batignolles

blvd

NEUILLY-SUR-
SEINE

TO
LA
DEFENSE

Porte
Maillot

TERNES

av. de La Grande
Armée

Bois de
Boulogne

blvd. de
Courcelles

Parc de
Monceau

Arc de Triomphe to O

Gare
St-Lazare

blvd.

Haussmann

blvd. Friedland

**Arc de
Triomphe**

av. Foch

av. Marceau

av. George V

av. des Champs

av. F. D. Roosevelt

-Elysées

Eglise de
la Madeleine

Opéra

pl.
Vendôme

av. Kléber

av. Victor Hugo

Petit
Palais

Grand Palais

pl. de la
Concorde

r. de Rivoli

Jardin des
Tuileries

CHAILLOT

pl. du
Trocadéro

av. du Pres.

Wilson

pont de
l'Alma

quai d'Orsay

Palais
de Chaillot

pont
d'Iena

av. de la Bourdonnais

Musée
d'Orsay

Tour
Eiffel

PASSY

av. de Suffren

Hôtel des
Invalides

blvd

av. du Pres.
Kennedy

blvd. de Grenelle

Ecole
Militaire

av. de
Breteuil

r. de Sèvres

Palais c
Luxembour

av. Emile Zola

r. de la Convention

r. du Commerce

ARENELLE

r. Lecourbe

r. de Vaugirard

blvd. Raspail

L

blvd. du Montparnasse

av. F. Faure

r. de Vaugirard

Gare
Montparnasse

Tour
Montparnasse

av. du Maine

Cimitière du
Montparnasse

blvd. Victor

r. d'Alésia

Montparnasse, Qu

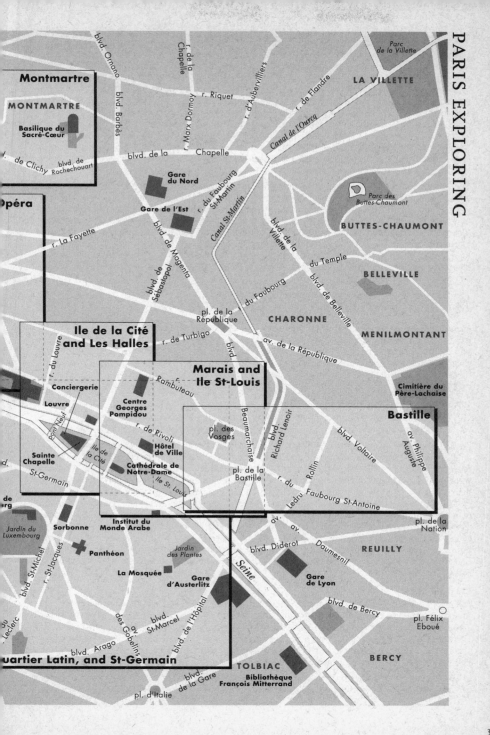

Montmartre

MONTMARTRE

Basilique du
Sacré-Cœur

blvd. Ornano

r. de
Chapelle

blvd. Barbès

r. Marx Dormoy

r. Riquet

r. d'Aubervilliers

r. de Flandre

Canal de l'Ourcq

Parc
de la Villette

LA VILLETTE

v. de Clichy

blvd. de
Rochechouart

blvd. de la   Chapelle

Gare
du Nord

r. La Fayette

Gare de l'Est

blvd. de Magenta

blvd. de Sebastopol

r. du Faubourg
St-Martin

Canal St-Martin

blvd. de la
Villette

du Temple

blvd. de Belleville

Parc des
Buttes-Chaumont

BUTTES-CHAUMONT

BELLEVILLE

MENILMONTANT

du Faubourg

pl. de la
République

r. de Turbigo

av. de la République

CHARONNE

Opéra

Ile de la Cité
and Les Halles

r. du Louvre

Conciergerie

Louvre

Pont Neuf

Sainte
Chapelle

St-Germain

Ile de
la Cité

Rambuteau

Centre
Georges
Pompidou

r. de Rivoli

Hôtel
de Ville

Cathédrale de
Notre-Dame

Ile St. Louis

Marais and
Ile St-Louis

pl. des
Vosges

Beaumarchaise

blvd. Richard Lenoir

pl. de la
Bastille

r. du

Ledru

Rollin

Faubourg St-Antoine

blvd. Voltaire

av. Philippe
Auguste

Cimitière du
Père-Lachaise

Bastille

pl. de la
Nation

Institut du
Monde Arabe

Jardin du
Luxembourg

Sorbonne

blvd. St-Michel

r. St-Jacques

Panthéon

La Mosquée

Jardin
des Plantes

Gare
d'Austerlitz

Seine

blvd. Diderot

Daumesnil

av.

av.

Gare
de Lyon

blvd. de Bercy

REUILLY

pl. Félix
Eboué

BERCY

du
Leclerc

blvd. Arago

des Gobelins

blvd.
St-Marcel

blvd. de l'Hôpital

uartier Latin, and St-Germain

pl. d'Italie

blvd.
de la Gare

TOLBIAC

Bibliothèque
François Mitterrand

CATHEDRALE DE NOTRE-DAME

For centuries, Notre-Dame (built between 1163 and 1361) has watched over Paris like a patient parent, emerging as one of the best-known houses of worship in the world. Fortunately, its current condition barely gives us an idea of its previous states: During the Gothic era, the fashion was to cover everything in bright paint, so the statuary on the facade was awash with color against a gilded background. The now-colorless portals depict (from left to right) the Virgin (to whom the cathedral is dedicated), the Last Judgment, and St. Anne, Mary's mother. Above is a row of statues depicting 28 kings of Judah and Israel. All lost their heads during the Revolution, when the cathedral became a Temple of Reason. Once all the fuss had died down, that crusading architect, Viollet-le-Duc, rolled up his sleeves and took on serious restoration, replacing the kings' heads. Turns out, some Royalist had stashed the originals away in his basement; they were discovered a couple of decades ago and are on display in the Musée National du Moyen-Age (*see* Museums, *below*).

The interior of Notre-Dame is vast and somber and usually crowded. Three spectacular rose windows shimmer with medieval stained glass. Notice the statues flanking the altar: One is Louis XIII, who, after years of unsuccessful trying, promised to repay the Virgin if she would grant him a son; and the other is Louis XIV, who carried out his father's vow by dressing up the choir area in fancy baroque stonework quite out of keeping with the rest of the building. Climb the cathedral's towers (around to the left as you face the building) for a gape at tons (literally) of gargoyles and the bells literally rung by Quasimodo. And for a terrific view of Paris. *Pl. du Parvis Notre-Dame, 4e, tel. 01–42–34–56–10. Métro: Cité. Admission to towers 30F. Cathedral open daily 8–7. Towers (tel. 01–43–29–50–40) open daily 9:30–6:30.*

CENTRE GEORGES-POMPIDOU AND MUSÉE NATIONAL D'ART MODERNE

Known to Parisians as Beaubourg, the Centre Georges-Pompidou brings a circuslike multitude of fire-eaters, tourists, and caricaturists to its plaza and fountains out front. Inside, a museum, library, theater, and cinema act as the "laboratory" envisioned when the center was conceived in the early 1970s. What wasn't envisioned was that the center would be so popular that it would need renovating a mere quarter-century after being built: The aim is to revamp the whole complex by December 31, 1999. In the meantime, various sections of the museum will be closed; call for information.

BASICS

The lobby is a huge tangle of signs, televised images, chairs, art, pipes, escalators, and people. In addition to the museum, public library, theater, and cinema, the center has countless conference rooms.

Two breeds of art exhibits exist here: Those that cost money and those that don't. The free ones are scattered throughout the temporary galleries on the ground floor and in the library halls; these are usually related to the blockbuster temporary exhibit housed in the fifth-floor Grande Galerie. For everything else you need to buy a ticket corresponding to the exhibits you want to see. The permanent collection is more than enough for one day, as is the Grande Galerie, though the ambitious will pace themselves and get an all-gallery pass. The cashier will issue you a ticket that you pop into a machine, métro-style, at the entrance to the galleries. The information desks have a bimonthly program of events printed in English, as well as a full listing of gallery events, prices, and the wheres and whens of guided tours in your mother tongue. *Pl. Georges Pompidou, 4e, tel. 01–44–78–12–33 or 01–42–77–11–12. Métro: Rambuteau. Admission to permanent collection 35F, Sun. free; Grande Galerie 45F; Forum and Galeries Nord and Sud 27F; all galleries and permanent collection 70F. Open weekdays noon–10 PM, weekends 10–10. Closed Tues.*

HISTORY

The decrepit Beaubourg district, in decline since the late 17th century, had an estimated five million rats when Georges Pompidou, the French president from 1969 to 1974, declared in December of 1969 that a new contemporary art museum and intellectual center would be placed in the decaying heart of Paris. The conservative, chain-smoking Pompidou seemed an unlikely cultural hero, but apparently the idea of creating a multimedia cultural center (with his name on it) seemed like a good urban renewal project. This new center, he promised, would be more than a building; it would be a statement.

In 1977, after six years of demolition and construction, the riot of steel crossbraces and snaky escalators designed by Italy's Renzo Piano and Gianfranco Franchini and Britain's Richard Rodger was inaugurated before an astonished city—the Pompidou looks like someone turned it inside out and then went to town with a box of crayons. The exposed pipes in bright primary colors (green for water, blue for air, yellow for electricity, red for communications) may be the most memorable part of the building, but it is with the interior structure that the architects were truly innovative. To eliminate the need for columns to hold the building up, steel beams were cross-strutted and hinged over its length and width, connecting to the exterior skeleton. Water fills the large steel tubes, stabilizing the outward push made on the structure from the pressure of the floors. This never-before-tried system was supposed to give the Center an unheard-of flexibility—walls could be taken down or put up anywhere at will, allowing the building to change shape to accommodate different exhibitions and displays.

While the building itself became the topic of architecture classes everywhere, its two major tenants, the museum and the **Centre des Créations Industriel** (CCI), soon defined the Pompidou's role in Parisian life. The CCI, the interactive part of the center, is composed of two parts: the **Bibliothèque Publique d'Information** (BPI; *see* Libraries *in* Chapter 1) and the **Institut de Recherche et Coordination de l'Acoustique et de la Musique** (IRCAM; Sound and Music Research Institute; *see* Opera, Classical Music, and Dance *in* Chapter 5). BPI, with its massive open stacks and technological resources (microfiche back then, CD-ROM today), was supposed to revolutionize the traditional library, while IRCAM offered a venue for contemporary dance, music, and theater performances, not to mention provocative colloquia and films.

THE COLLECTION

The Pompidou is justly proud of its permanent collection, which picks up around 1904, where the Musée d'Orsay leaves off: Encompassing more than 40,000 works, it is the largest single gathering of modern art in the world. Until recently, only 850 works could be displayed at any one time; transformation is under way to enlarge the galleries on the third and fourth floors. The fourth floor houses the historical part of the collection and the third has later pieces. The historical part starts off with Matisse, then takes off through the cubists, futurists, surrealists, Bauhaus, European abstractionists, abstract expressionists, pop artists, minimalists . . . don't worry, the museum has thoughtfully placed quartets of chairs throughout the galleries for you to collapse in.

For those in desperate need of some Internet contact, the café on the mezzanine of the Pompidou will grant you Web access (50F for an hour, 30F for half an hour) and strong coffee.

Because the museum got into the collecting business rather late in comparison to New York's Museum of Modern Art or Guggenheim Museum, there aren't as many postcard-famous works here as you'd expect. Of course, there are some stunners: **Alexander Calder**'s (1898–1976) *Josephine Baker* was one of the sculptor's earliest and most graceful versions of the mobile—a form he invented. Also here is **Marcel Duchamp**'s (1887–1968) *Valise,* a collection of miniature reproductions of his most famous dada sculptures and drawings conveniently displayed in their own ironic carrying case. One of the last works by the piously abstract **Piet Mondrian** (1872–1944), *New York,* marks one of the few breaks with the style of the Compositions he had been painting for the previous 25 years. The Russian **Kazimir Malevich** (1878–1935) declared that his *Black Square* was the point from which painting left behind the frivolity of illusionism in favor of abstraction. The museum displays his work where Malevich intended—hanging above eye level, as Eastern Orthodox Church icons were placed in pre-Revolution Russian homes. Also here is *Out of the Deep,* **Jackson Pollock**'s (1912–56) attempt a year before his death to return to the abstraction of his earlier drip paintings, though alcoholism and fame were suffocating his career.

Accessible only from an escalator within the fourth-floor galleries is the third floor, home to more recent works from the permanent collection. The fourth floor has the unspoken need to spell out a history of early modern art, but the third is far more playful. In general, though, the Musée National d'Art Moderne's best asset is the natural light, which shines through the building's large windows and gives the visitor the illusion of walking through an outdoor gallery.

SPECIAL EXHIBITIONS

Temporary shows play an important role in the life of the Pompidou; nine or so galleries are set up to serve that purpose, not to mention the countless partitions that pop up in the lobbies and other public spaces. The Grande Galerie on the fifth floor holds the big exhibitions, for which the Pompidou plasters the city with advertisements. Exhibition admission is separate (*see* Basics, *above*). Next door to the Grande Galerie is Studio 5, a cinema that screens films and videos related to the exhibition (screenings will be moved to a yet unannounced location during the renovation). Smaller displays relating to the main exhi-

JIM WHO?

If you're a Doors fan, check out the shrine to Jim Morrison at the Czech restaurant across the street from where Jimmy once lived (17 rue Beautreillis, 4e). To celebrate Jim's birthday on December 8, people start the festivities over his grave at Père-Lachaise and then bring the party back to Restaurant Le Beautreillis. You can sit in the same wicker chair where the Lizard King once slammed whiskey shots, and the restaurant owner will fill you in on all the "connections" he and Jim share. The catch is that Vieran never even heard of The Doors until he bought the restaurant . . . years after Jim died.

bition are scattered around the building; some are free, and the ones that charge admission are available in a package deal with the Grande Galerie. The Galerie Nord and Galerie Sud on the mezzanine level offer shows not connected to the big ones upstairs, and they usually focus on the work of a single artist.

CIMETIERE DU PERE-LACHAISE

The world's most celebrated necropolis, the 118-acre Père-Lachaise cemetery is the final stop for more illustrious people than you could ever meet in a lifetime. Plots on the former farm of Louis XIV's confessor, Father Lachaise, are prime real estate, and now only the outrageously wealthy can afford to be laid to rest with the famous. Jim Morrison fans rage on at the eternal party in Division 6, but otherwise a serene Gothic aura persists. Although the famous deserve a visit, it's just as fun to wander aimlessly amid the disorderly array of decaying tombstones.

The oldest residents at Père-Lachaise are the celebrated lovers **Abelard** (1079–1142) and **Héloïse** (1101–64). But let's face it, most young travelers are tromping out here to see lizard king **James Douglas Morrison** (1943–71). A gendarme is now posted to keep crowds from mussing up nearby graves; Jim's grave site is periodically cleaned of spray-painted messages left by well-intentioned devotees. There was once a bust of Jim here, but it was stolen. Die-hard Jim fans insist he must still be roaming the earth somewhere, because the grave is too small.

The precocious composer **Georges Bizet** (1838–75), best known for his blockbuster opera, *Carmen,* met a pitiful death in the bath (the water was too cold for his weak heart). Entombed with the negligent family he immortalized in over 3,000 pages of artful diatribes, **Marcel Proust** (1871–1922) now has the undivided attention of his mother. The dramatic death by strangulation (her long scarf got tangled up in a wheel of her sporty convertible) of dancer **Isadora Duncan** (1878–1927) wasn't the only freak accident in the family; 14 years earlier her children Deirdre and Patrick drowned after their limousine plunged into the Seine. The body of **Oscar Wilde** (1854–1900) was moved here nine years after his death—the quicklime that was supposed to decompose him actually preserved the corpse, shocking the poor guys who had to dig him up. Wilde's tombstone, by Sir Jacob Epstein, is famous for its fantastic penis; it was originally covered up by the order of the cemetery, only to be lopped off later by an adoring fan. In a similar vein, the family jewels of **Victor Noir** (1848–70) are in danger of being completely rubbed off. The journalist-gigolo, killed in a duel, is depicted in bronze at the moment of death; ever since the statue's, um, erection, young lovers have been petting his pride and joy for fortune and fertility. Irreverent fans pick at the face of the sculpted angel watching over the timid virtuoso **Frédéric Chopin** (1810–49), and have even gone so far as to tear off her fingers.

Even in death, there are those who are greater among equals. Here they include city planner **Baron Haussmann** (1809–91); writers **Colette** (1873–1954), **Honoré de Balzac** (1799–1850), **Gertrude Stein** (1874–1946) and (in the same grave) **Alice B. Toklas** (1877–1967), and 1967 Nobel Prize winner **Miguel Angel Asturias** (1899–1974); poet and critic **Guillaume Apollinaire** (1880–1918); playwrights **Jean-Baptiste Molière** (1622–73) and **Pierre-Augustin Beaumarchais** (1732–99); fabulist **Jean de La Fontaine** (1621–95); painters **Théodore Géricault** (1791–1824), **Jean-Auguste Ingres** (1780–1867),

Eugène Delacroix (1798–1863), Jacques-Louis David (1748–1825), Amedeo Modigliani (1884–1920), Camille Pissarro (1830–1903), Georges Seurat (1859–91), and Max Ernst (1891–1976); illustrator Honoré Daumier (1808–79); philosopher Auguste Comte (1798–1857); doctor and revolutionary François Raspail (1794–1878); actress Sarah Bernhardt (1845–1923); and singers Edith Piaf (1915–63) and Yves Montand (1921–92). Near the Mur des Fédérés in the southeast corner are equally humbling memorials to World War II concentration camp victims and Resistance workers. All of these graves (and oh-so-many more) are located on free photocopied maps occasionally available at the cemetery office. Or you can buy a detailed map (10F) from nearby florists. *Blvd. de Ménilmontant, 20e, tel. 01–43–70–70–33. Métro: Philippe-Auguste, Père-Lachaise, Gambetta. Open daily 8 AM–6 PM.*

GRANDE ARCHE DE LA DEFENSE

Paris's major monuments follow the longest urban axis in the world: A straight line starts at the Louvre, passes through the Jardin des Tuileries, the place de la Concorde, and the Arc de Triomphe, and terminates at the Grande Arche de La Défense, just outside Paris. Resembling a tremendous, mirrored Rubik's Cube floating in air with its center removed, the Grande Arche is a sort of monumental office building commissioned by the king of *grands projets* (great projects), François Mitterrand. Designed by Danish architect Otto von Spreckelsen and inaugurated on July 14, 1989, the futuristic structure is weirdly impressive: Uncomfortably perched on top of 12 narrow piers, the Grande Arche crosses the cold sleekness of its concrete beams and pure white marble with the optical brilliance of 2,800 panes of clear glass. Over the years, the French government has come to realize that stark concrete is a bit drab and has spruced up the plaza below with a monumental fountain and a few dozen sculptures. A 40F elevator ride will whisk you up through the belly of the building for a view of Paris. For tickets, head for the booth near the elevator; there's also a larger info booth just out front. *Tel. 01–49–07–27–57. Métro: Grande Arche de La Défense. Admission (arch) 40F. Open daily 10–7 (ticket booth closes at 6).*

". . . you have been trapped by this glass serpent that brings alive, with its flow of humanity, the facade of this big body. The joke is on you! You are a spectator on view!"—a reference to the Pompidou's glass-encased escalators, from its "Practical Guide."

HOTEL DES INVALIDES

The Hôtel des Invalides was commissioned by Louis XIV to house invalids, the soldiers wounded during his many military campaigns. The free digs must have come as a mixed blessing to the 4,000 veterans who lived here under Louis: Although they had what was essentially a small town within a stunning architectural complex, their lives were still dictated by the military, with captains supervising their daily work in artisanal studios. Napoléon Bonaparte, too, came to rest on his sickbed here, and the Musée de l'Armée, inside, not very logically displays his death mask as a souvenir (since he died on St-Helena). Along with all sorts of military paraphernalia, the museum has mildly interesting costumes, armor, weapons, maps, and models of soldiers in war garb, as well as some imposing cannons in the central courtyard. Admission to the museum also buys a visit to Napoléon's tomb, housed in the majestic Eglise du Dôme (Dome Church), where the great strategist enjoys the cover of five coffins within a bombastic case of reddish porphyry. Wounded soldiers are still housed in the Hôtel des Invalides, dutifully hobbling into mass in the airy, elegant Soldier's Church in the courtyard. *Esplanade des Invalides, 7e, tel. 01–44–42–37–67. Métro: La Tour–Maubourg or Varenne. RER: Invalides. Admission (valid for 2 days) 37F, 27F Sun. Open Apr.–Sept., daily 10–6; Oct.–Mar., daily 10–5.*

HOTEL DE VILLE

The first Hôtel de Ville (City Hall), built in 1532, was burned to the ground in the 1871 rebellion by the Communards (*see* box, The Paris Commune, *above*). Prompt construction spanned 14 years in an attempt to make the replica even better than the original (which, in 19th-century architectural terms, meant bigger). In 1944 German troops set up camp in the building, but not for long—General de Gaulle celebrated the liberation of the city from the place de l'Hôtel de Ville on August 25, 1944. Today, the building is the seat of local government, and hosts temporary exhibits in the east wing. *Pl. de l'Hôtel de Ville, 4e, tel. 01–42–76–43–43. Métro: Hôtel de Ville. Admission free. Official tour Mon. 10:30 AM.*

THE PARIS COMMUNE

While musicians and writers beeline toward the graves of cultural icons like Jim Morrison and Oscar Wilde, socialists, anarchists, and other freethinkers make a pilgrimage to the Mur des Fédérés (Communards' Wall) at the southeast corner of Père-Lachaise, where the last shots rang out during the Paris Commune of 1871, as 147 revolutionaries were executed.

The Commune was begun by left-wing Parisians determined to resist the Prussian invasion. On January 28, 1871, France capitulated to a dishonorable peace: the Treaty of Frankfurt granted the Prussians Alsace, part of Lorraine, five billion francs, and the right to parade victoriously through Paris and install their government at Versailles, a symbol of the old absolute order. Outraged Parisians resisted this treaty by electing a radical municipal government. Paris's National Guard soon joined the citizens, giving them the firepower they needed to form the independent Commune and resist the onslaught of troops faithful to the national government in Versailles. Statues were toppled, the Hôtel de Ville (City Hall) burned to the ground, and chaos ensued.

The Communards used their newly seized power to pass social legislation intended to shorten the workday, improve education, and empower the working classes. Parisians held outdoor concerts and parties during what Lenin later described as a "festival of the oppressed" and what Marx considered to be a precursor of the greater socialist revolution to come. The Communards' main goal was to organize the country into a system of politically autonomous, democratic enclaves. But their vision was short-lived. Government troops entered Paris only 72 days after the start of the Commune, brutally killing over 3,000 Parisians and summarily massacring over 25,000 others.

INSTITUT DU MONDE ARABE

More than a museum, the Institute of the Arab World is a monstrous multimedia cultural center. Built with funds from the French and most Arab governments, the institute is attempting to become a "cultural bridge" between Europe and Arab countries. In addition to its huge library and audiovisual center, the institute has two exhibition spaces, one for the permanent collection and the other for traveling exhibitions. The permanent collection (40F) is a combination of the institute's and some of the Louvre's Arab artifacts, with works dating from the pre-Islamic era to the present. The traveling exhibitions are usually blockbuster events, well-publicized by a large banner on the facade. Films are shown in the cinema on weekends, all in their original language with French subtitles (25F). A café and a restaurant reside on the ninth floor, though the former makes you pay dearly for the view (one of the best in Paris) and the latter serves surprisingly bland food.

The graceful glass institute, designed by Jean Nouvel (*see* box, Jean Nouvel, *below*), is famous for the way it manipulates light. Behind the glass south wall are 240 mechanized metal plates that act like the aperture on a camera—a contemporary interpretation of the *moucharabieh* (traditional Arab light-filtering latticework). Photo cells in the wall respond to the intensity of light outside, opening and closing the spiraling plates so that the interior of the institute is never too bright or too dim. The interior courtyard plays with light in a less flashy manner: Small squares of thinly cut white marble in the walls are carefully held in place by metal pins, allowing the sunlight to pass through the stone's patterns and illuminate the interior of the building with a soft glow. On top of this it's hard to get over the view—the spectacular panorama from the ninth-floor terrace encompasses Paris in all her glory. *1 rue des Fossés-St-Bernard, 5e, tel. 01–40–51–38–38. Métro: Jussieu or Cardinal Lemoine. Admission 40F (permanent collection); varied prices for special exhibits; 25F (films). Open Tues.–Sun. 10–6.*

MUSEE DU LOUVRE

One of the grandest and most spectacular museums in the world, and comfortably the biggest, the Louvre houses an overwhelming collection of art and artifacts from just about all cultures and regions, from ancient times up to the 19th century. Join the crowds of tourists flocking to the Mona Lisa for a photo or tarry amid the grandeur. For those under 26, the 100F *carte jeune* will give you unlimited access to the museum for the whole year. *Entrance off of pl. du Carrousel, 1er, tel. 01–40–20–53–17. Métro: Palais Royal–Musée du Louvre. Admission 45F, 26F daily after 3 PM and all day Sun., free 1st Sun. each month. Open Wed. 9 AM–10 PM, Thurs.–Mon. 9–6 (Richelieu open Mon. until 10 PM); galleries start emptying 30 mins before closing time. Cafés and stores in Carrousel du Louvre open daily 9 AM–10 PM.*

The Grande Pyramide is not the quickest way into the Louvre. Try the staircase alongside the Arc du Carrousel (called the Porte Jaujard), or enter through the métro stop Palais Royal–Musée du Louvre—both put you inside the underground mall.

BASICS

To get into the Louvre, you may have to wait in two long lines: one outside the Pyramide and another downstairs at the ticket booths. You can avoid the first by entering through the Carrousel du Louvre. You can't avoid the second. Your ticket will get you into any and all of the wings as many times as you like during one day.

The Louvre is enormous, so we've outlined a simple guide in the following pages that is broken up by location (wing, floor, collection, and room number). If you want more comprehensive stuff, the museum bookstore sells—in addition to the general maps at the information desk—books and leaflets outlining four different prepackaged strategies. The simplest is the **Guide for the Visitor in a Hurry** (20F), which directs you to the biggies with room numbers and illustrations. The **Visitor's Guide** (60F) ups the number of covered works but cuts the directions—it's an abridged catalog. The weighty **Louvre: The Collections** (130F) covers even more of the museum's works, but it's too cumbersome to be a good visitor's guide and too incomplete to be a true catalog. Finally, you've got the cellular-phone–style recorded tours (30F), which lead you through the galleries and explain the highlights. The Louvre is a great place to wander mapless in the hope of stumbling past fantastic bits of art, but don't get frustrated if you don't happen upon the Mona Lisa after hoofing it for five hours. Some pieces may also have been moved because of museum renovations.

HISTORY

The Louvre spent its first 600 years as a fortress and a palace. The original Louvre was a fortification built by Philippe-Auguste in the late 12th century. A young, nervous Charles V expanded the building in the mid-14th century to distance himself from the potential rebels on the Ile de la Cité, creating a Cinderella-like castle of moats and round towers. In the mid-16th century, François I demolished the old castle and started the Vieux Louvre, now encompassed within the Sully Wing, and initiated a cycle of major building projects that have continued more or less nonstop to this day. As construction lagged through the reign of Henri II, Catherine de' Medici started to build her Palais des Tuileries (named for the tileworks that stood close by) to the west of the Vieux Louvre. Catherine connected the two buildings with a hallway along the banks of the Seine, eventually to become the Galerie Medicis of the Denon Wing.

The construction of the stately Cour Carrée (Square Court), early in the reign of Louis XIV, marked the beginning of the Louvre as we see it today. When a competition for architects to design a suitably impos-

FRANÇOIS MITTERRAND

The death in 1996 of François Mitterrand, the Socialist president of France from 1981 to 1995, was met with mixed emotions. The driving force behind the construction of 11 grands projets, including the pyramids of the Louvre and the Grande Arche de La Défense, Mitterrand helped to infuse France with a new pride in its culture: His last project, the giant Bibliothèque de France (national library), was named for him in 1996. Recent revelations about Mitterrand's involvement with the Vichy government in WW II, however, not to mention indiscreet interludes with the likes of Coco Chanel models, have muddied his image.

ing east facade was held in 1668, a young draftsman named Claude Perrault teamed up with the seasoned illustrator and painter Charles Le Brun to produce the winning proposal. You'd have thought its muscular rhythms would have wowed the Sun King, but he left the city for Versailles in 1682.

The Louvre remained virtually untouched by royalty for the next century. The palace's apartments were rented out and very poorly kept; some even considered tearing it down in the mid-18th century. Then, in 1793, during the Revolution, the National Assembly voted to turn part of the Louvre into a public museum. The galleries were stocked with nationalized art taken from the churches, the king, and other members of the French nobility, but the greatest boon to the collection came when a Corsican corporal measured his power by how much Great Art he could ransack from the rest of the world. Napoléon Bonaparte moved into the Louvre in 1800 as his armies were marching across Europe. They bravely captured the world's most famous treasures, including entire fresco-covered walls, and brought them all back to the Louvre. With Napoléon's fall from grace, the new museum was forced in 1815 to return many of its works to the original owners. Not that everything found its way back home—certainly not a welter of Spanish and Italian paintings.

During the reign of Napoléon III (1852–71), the Louvre saw another feverish bout of building activity: The Denon and Richelieu Wings were finished, the Jardin du Carrousel was landscaped, and the facades overlooking the Cour Napoléon and the rue de Rivoli were completed in the baroque/Renaissance/neoclassical mishmash that came to be known as Second Empire. During the Commune, the royal apartments were stormed and the Tuileries Palace was burned to the ground, leaving the Cour Napoléon in its present, unfronted state. During World War II, the invading Germans looted the Louvre and used it as office space; a classical-art buff, Hitler had the *Victory of Samothrace* installed near his desk. Most of the stolen pieces were recovered after the Liberation, but no large-scale changes or innovations were made until Mitterrand was elected. In his first year in office, 1981, the president announced a plan to commence a 20-year, three-phase, 7-billion-franc ($1.3 billion) program of renovation and expansion.

THE LOUVRE TODAY

Mitterrand declared that the remaking of the Louvre was to be the central element of his *Grands Travaux* (Great Works), which makes it, according to the French, the most important building project in the world. I. M. Pei, a New York–based Chinese-American architect who made his reputation designing modernist megastructures, was commissioned. The French were nonplussed by both Pei's nomination and his proposal—for the relocation of all central services to an excavated Cour Napoléon, which would then be topped by a glass pyramid. Pei said that moving the ticket windows and stores underground would give the Louvre a single entrance capable of handling massive crowds of visitors (an estimated eight million in 1995). At the same time, he argued that the stark style of his design for the Pyramide, lobby, and gallery space would contrast with the older parts of the Louvre rather than mimic their frilly columns and statuary. In 1988 the Pyramide was inaugurated to a chorus of mixed reviews. Soon, however, in true Eiffel Tower tradition, pride replaced outrage and, when it came time to choosing an architect for the 2.7-billion-franc ($500 million) phase-two renovations, Pei topped the list.

In fact, the most controversial addition has proved to be the underground Carrousel du Louvre: a mall with upscale shops selling clothing, records, and other decidedly non-Louvre-related merchandise. There is even a massive fast-food court—now you can get a 30F Quick Burger and check out David's *Le Sacre de Napoléon 1er* (Coronation of Napoléon I) all in the same building. Lending the Carrousel du Louvre a semblance of aesthetic credibility is the inverted glass pyramid that plunges into the central hallway.

The most important part of the second phase has been the renovation of the old galleries, including 39 new rooms in the Sully Wing dedicated to French paintings. By annexing the Richelieu Wing, the Louvre also acquired three courtyards, transformed into stunning sculpture galleries. Just as the Pyramide became the symbol of the first phase of construction, these courtyards have become the postcard image of phase two. Pei was honored with a higher position in the Légion d'Honneur when the newest Louvre was inaugurated on November 18, 1993, exactly 200 years after the first Musée du Louvre opened to the public. Renovation is still marching on; painters, builders, and architects are furiously redoing, rearranging, and spiffing up the Louvre. For more info on changes or for up-to-date info on renovations, inquire at the knowledgeable, English-speaking information desk, or call 01-40-20-53-17.

RICHELIEU WING

BELOW GROUND AND GROUND FLOOR • As you enter the Richelieu Wing from the Pyramid, on the left and up a flight of stairs is a gallery that displays temporary exhibits that comprise the Louvre's most recent acquisitions in **French sculpture.** Straight ahead is **Salle 20,** filled with more French sculpture, including frilly busts of members of the court of Louis XIV, but most people pass through this room to get to the dramatic Cour Marly to the west or Cour Puget to the east. The

Every art thief's dream is to rip off the Mona Lisa (La Joconde). This daring feat was last accomplished in 1911 by a burglar disguised as a workman. It wasn't until two years later that Mona was found in Florence and safely returned to the Louvre.

Cour Marly is filled with sculptures taken from a garden commissioned to ultrapompous Versailles; you can just imagine all these Greco-Roman gods set into the bushes of the Sun King's garden, their clothes falling away from their perfect bodies for all eternity. The **Cour Puget** is named for the artist who created the sculpture at the place des Victoires, now mostly reassembled in the lower court. Sculptures that once dotted the estates of nobility fill the rest of the courtyard, and the upper level has busts of characters from the Revolution and the 1830 uprising.

Back to the southeast corner of Cour Marly: Here you will find **Salle 1** of French sculpture. The first truly French sculpture—that is, not Gallo-Roman—dates from the 11th century, when the carved column heads produced by regional artisans began to display figures or beasts instead of Corinthian capitals. In **Salle 2** are fragments of Romanesque chapels from Cluny, the powerful abbey in Burgundy that dominated French Catholicism in the 11th century. In **Salles 4–6** you can see the refinement of sculpture encouraged by the wealthy communities in the Ile de France. The funerary art of **Salles 7–10** ranges from spooky to risible. The late 15th-century tomb of Philippe Pot in **Salle 10** is especially eerie: You see Philippe stretched out in eternal prayer, held aloft by eight black-robed pallbearers.

Walking through **Salles 11–19,** you can see how the piety and stiffness of medieval French sculpture began to give way to the more natural style of the Italian Renaissance. Many local artists were traveling to Italy during the 16th and 17th centuries, and the French nobility were importing noted Italian sculptors. Bronze, out of favor since Roman times, was being cast again, and the subject matter, which had rarely strayed from Madonnas or saints, could now be mythological, allegorical, or classical.

To the north of the Cour Puget are **Salles 25–33,** filled with the products of the Académie Royale, *the* art school of 18th-century France. The smaller works in **Salle 25** are all qualification pieces for the Académie—once admitted into the school based on previous works, the student was asked to produce a sculpture as proof of continuing worth. Mythology was a popular subject, as in Jean Thierry's 1717 *Leda and the Swan,* which depicts the unorthodox seduction scene between the Queen of Sparta and Zeus in the form of a large bird. While beautiful art did emerge during the 18th century, the individual artists are of questionable creative merit: The Académie became a sort of aesthetics factory, churning out thousands of decorative marble statues depicting yet another stock Apollo figure.

To the east of the Cour Puget is the start of the Louvre's **Oriental Antiquities** collection. Within the glass case of **Salle 1** are many ancient Mesopotamian carvings, including a 5-centimeter (2-inch) neolithic figure dating from the 6th millennium BC. Facing the case are the pieced-together fragments of the 3rd millennium BC *Stela of the Vultures,* containing the oldest written history known to humankind: On one side, King Eannatum catches his enemies in a net and thanks the disembodied head of his patron goddess; on the other side, vultures eat the corpses of the enemy, while the king leads chariots and infantry over more bodies and a sacrifice is offered for the victory.

Farther along, **Salle 1b** has countless examples of the wide-eyed alabaster statues produced by the Sumerians during the 3rd millennium BC. **Salle 2** is filled with statues and fragments of Gudea, a prince who supported a neo-Sumerian artistic culture in his 23rd-century BC kingdom of Lagash. Gudea commemorated his achievements through countless portraits of himself he had carved from diorite, the hardest stone on earth; notice the one headless statue depicting Gudea presiding over the architectural plans for a temple.

The centerpiece of **Salle 3** is the "Codex of Hammurabi," an 18th-century BC diorite stela that contains the oldest written laws known to humanity. Near the top of the text you can see Hammurabi, king of the first Babylonian dynasty, meeting a seated Shamash, the god of justice. On the east side of **Salle 3** is a lion glazed onto a piece of a terra-cotta–tile wall—just one of hundreds of similar beasts that decorated the multistory 6th-century BC Gates of Babylon. (The rest of the Gates have been reerected in the Pergamon Museum in Berlin.)

Salle 4 is the Cour Khorsabad, a re-creation of the temple erected by the Assyrian king Sargon II in the 8th century BC at the palace of Dur-Sharrukin. Walking among the temple's five massive, winged bulls known as *lamassu,* or benign demigods, is one of the most spectacular experiences in the Louvre, even though only three of the bulls and almost none of the reerected reliefs are authentic. The originals were lost on a sunken frigate.

FIRST FLOOR • The restored rooms from the **royal apartments** of Napoléon III fill the southwestern portion of the first floor of the Richelieu Wing. **Salle 79** is the most spectacular; the corner reception room, decorated for Napoléon III's secretary of state, gives you a good idea of the crass luxury of the Second Empire. The **gallery** running between the Cour Marly and the Cour Puget is filled with **French medieval artifacts** saved from the Revolution's zeal to destroy all things Christian and Roman. It also contains **Byzantine objects** taken as booty from non–Roman Catholic churches in Constantinople during the Crusades.

SECOND FLOOR • Just to the east of the escalators is **Salle 1,** which begins the section devoted to **French and Northern School paintings.** At the entrance to this room is a single 14th-century gold-backed painting of John the Good—the oldest known individual portrait from north of Italy. In **Salle 4** is the *Madonna* and *Chancellor Rolin,* by the 15th-century Dutch master Jan van Eyck. The first artist to extensively use oil paints, van Eyck defined what became known as the "northern style," characterized by a light source illuminating one area on an otherwise dark background. One of the first self-portraits ever painted—a bizarre and disheveled offering by Albrecht Dürer (1471–1528)—hangs in **Salle 8.** Walking through **Salles 9–17,** you can see how the Dutch developed a fluid and comfortable representation of the body while playing with the shiny, dark palette of oil paints. **Salle 12** houses the 1514 *Banker and His Wife,* where Quentin Metsys (1456–1530) deftly depicts the effect of light on glass, gold, and mirrors.

The most dramatic gallery in this section is **Salle 18,** where a cycle of giant matching canvases by Peter Paul Rubens (1577–1640) recounts the journey Maria de' Medici made from Florence to Paris—an overbearing immortalization of a relatively cushy trip. The swirling baroque paintings were commissioned by Maria herself and originally hung in the Palais du Luxembourg. The riveting *Disembarkation of Maria de' Medici at the Port of Marseille* depicts an artificially slimmed-down Maria about to skip over the roly-poly daughters of Poseidon as a personified France beckons her to shore.

Though the still-life genre may seem dull today, it was loaded with meaning for the Dutch. Ambriosius Bosschaert's (1573–1621) *Bouquet of Flowers in an Arch* (1620) in **Salle 27** is meant to represent the power of the colonially minded Dutch merchants: The flowers brought together in the vase in this painting couldn't have been gathered at any one moment in real life because of their diverse and exotic origins. In **Salle 31** are several paintings by Rembrandt van Rijn (1606–69), including a late self-portrait in which he goes nuts with the chiaroscuro. In his 1648 *Supper at Emmaüs,* he challenges many painting conventions, such as centering the subject and delineating objects with bold brush strokes. The masterpiece of the Dutch collection is the *Lacemaker,* by Jan Vermeer (1632–75), in **Salle 38.**

Obsessed with optical accuracy, Vermeer painted the red thread in the foreground as a slightly blurred jumble, just as one would actually see it if focusing on the girl.

SULLY WING

The entrance into the **Sully Wing** is more impressive than the entrances to the other wings—you get to walk around and through the foundations and moat of the castle built by Philippe Auguste in the 12th century and expanded by Charles V in the 14th.

BELOW GROUND • The foundations of Philippe Auguste's castle were accidentally discovered during renovations of the building in 1988. Notice that many of the stones have squares, circles, or hearts cut roughly into them: These were used by the illiterate masons to identify the parts. Take a look at the model in the side room to get an idea of what the place used to look like.

GROUND FLOOR • The northern galleries of the Sully are a continuation of the ancient **Iranian collection** started on the ground floor of the Richelieu Wing. Conflicting styles emerged as the Greco-Roman art exported by the Roman and Byzantine empires influenced the work of indigenous artisans.

Adjacent to the Egyptian galleries—renovated in 1997—is **Salle 13,** housing the Greek, Etruscan, and Roman collections and the famous 2nd-century BC *Venus de Milo.* The armless statue, one of the most reproduced and recognizable works of art in the world, is actually as beautiful as they say—it is worth your trouble to push past the lecturing curators and tourist groups to get a closer look at the incredible skill with which the Greeks turned cold marble into something vibrant and graceful. **Salles 13–17** are filled with all kinds of statuary: funerary stelae, body fragments, architectural detailings. One important form for Greek figurative statues was the *kouros,* which depicts an idealized youth standing staring straight ahead, an "archaic smile" (the lips are pulled back to resemble a grin, but the mouth isn't actually smiling) on his face, his shoulders squared with his hands at his sides, and one foot slightly in front of the other. You can see in these galleries how sculptors relaxed and naturalized the stance over the centuries. The statues in **Salle 17,** known as the Caryatid Room (named for the 16th-century female figures standing as columns at either end of the hall), are Roman copies of original Greek works.

The French philosopher-writer Roland Barthes noted that only the Dutch painters allowed patricians and cows to look out and make eye contact with the viewer—glance around Salle 34 of the second floor of the Louvre's Richelieu Wing and see if you agree.

FIRST FLOOR • The northern galleries of the first floor continue with **the objets d'art collection** started in the Richelieu Wing, picking up at the 17th century and continuing through the Revolution to the Restoration. Running alongside the Egyptian galleries to the south are works from the early period of the **Greek collection**—a smattering of coins, pottery, and other everyday objects from the 7th to 3rd centuries BC.

SECOND FLOOR • Sully picks up French painting where the Richelieu Wing leaves off, somewhere around the 16th century. At this point, a conscious battle was under way in French art between the northern style—epitomized by Georges de La Tour and the Le Nain brothers, and centered on the work of the Dutch—and the southern one—headed by Poussin, and coming from Florence, Venice, and Rome. The result was a blending of northern style and technology (darkly painted interiors and oil paints) with southern subjects and technique (ruined landscapes and one-point perspective). Charles Le Brun (1619–90), Louis XIV's principal adviser on the arts, painted massive "History Paintings," jampacked with excruciating details depicting biblical, historical, or mythological stories. Displayed in **Salle 32** are the four colossal canvases of his late 17th-century *Story of Alexander,* with a powerful view of the trials of the emperor (and no small reference to Louis XIV).

An academic painter of a different genre was Jean-Antoine Watteau (1684–1721). In scenes such as his 1717 *Pilgrimage to the Island of Cythera* in **Salle 36,** he depicted in wispy pastel brush strokes the bucolic and often frivolous lifestyle of the baroque-age court set. In the same room is Watteau's enigmatic 1718 *Pierrot* (also called *Gilles*), a portrait of a boyish-looking actor whose costume and surroundings reflect the popularity of Italian commedia dell'arte at the time. Maurice Quentin de La Tour (1704–88) was another favorite court painter; his 1755 *Marquise de Pompadour* in **Salle 45** captures the frivolous pomp of Louis XV's court. Madame de Pompadour, mistress to the king, is shown with everything a good courtesan should have: books, music manuscripts, engravings, fine clothing, and, of course, pale skin.

One revolution and two republics after the court painters of the 17th and 18th centuries, the Académie continued to define Good Taste. In **Salle 55** you can see the paintings of Jean-Auguste Ingres (1780–1867), which depict the exotic themes popular in the Age of Empires. His 1862 *Turkish Bath* portrays an orgy of steamy women who look anything but Turkish. You can see more of his work in **Salle 77** of the Denon Wing and across the Seine at the Musée d'Orsay (*see below*).

DENON WING

BELOW GROUND • To the south and east from the Pyramide entrance are galleries displaying **Italian sculpture** from the early Renaissance, including a 15th-century *Madonna and Child* by the Florentine Donatello (1386–1466).

GROUND LEVEL • In **Salle 9** you can see the 1513–15 *Slaves of Michelangelo* (1475–1564). Carefully selecting his slab of marble, Michelangelo would then spend days envisioning the form of the sculpture within the uncut stone. The sculptures that finally emerged openly eroticized the male body. The fact that many were left "unfinished" (i.e., parts of the marble were left rough, making it look as if the sculptures were trying to free themselves from the stone blocks) was controversial at first, but the style was to inspire Rodin and other modern artists. In **Salle 10** is the 1793 *Eros and Psyche* by the great Italian neoclassicist Antonio Canova (1757–1822), whose delicate and precise touch made him the darling of European royalty.

To the east of the Italian sculpture collection are the galleries containing the sculptures of the **Greek, Etruscan,** and **Roman** periods. In **Salle 18** is the 6th-century BC Etruscan *Sarcophagus from Cerveteri,* pieced together from thousands of clay fragments.

FIRST FLOOR • Stretching out from a tiny entry next to the Sully Wing is the **Galerie d'Apollon,** a 17th-century hall decorated by the painter Charles Le Brun (who immortalized himself in one of the portraits on the wall) that now holds what remains of France's **Crown Jewels.** Around the corner from the jewels, the *Victory of Samothrace* stands regally, if headless, at the top landing of the staircase leading down to the ground floor. The spectacular 2nd-century BC statue, found on a tiny Greek island in the northern Aegean, was probably a monument to a victorious battle at sea.

The **Italian painting** collection begins at the western end of the Denon Wing. The paintings in **Salle 6** are large-scale canvases from the 16th-century Venetian School. Dominating the room is the massive 1562 *Feast at Cana* by Veronese (1528–88), a sumptuous scene centered on Jesus turning water into wine. Spread across the canvas are hundreds of still lifes and portraits, all little masterpieces within this huge painting; it is said that the great painters of the Venetian School—Titian, Bassano, Tintoretto, and even Veronese—are depicted as the musicians. In the same room is the 1525 *Entombment* by the quintessential Venetian painter, Titian (1488–1576), who used the translucent shine of the oil paints characteristic of Venetian art while contrasting dark colors against extreme whites to create a sense of light. The last great artist from the Venetian School was Tintoretto (1518–94), whose latter works look almost impressionistic, since he rejected a brush in favor of smearing the paint onto the canvas with his fingers.

And now for **Salle 7,** home to the Most Famous Painting in the World, the **Mona Lisa** (officially known as *La Gioconda,* or *La Joconde* to the French). Somewhere behind the legion of videotaping tourists (think about it: videotaping paintings!) and layers of bulletproof glass is the painting that has inspired so much awe, emulation, and disbelief—you, too, may find yourself asking "Is this it?" when you are faced with this 2½-by-1¾-foot painting of an eyebrow-less woman with yellowing skin and an annoyingly smug smile. But if you can somehow move to the front of the crowd to squint through the glare of the protective coating, you'll have a close look at a truly beautiful painting.

The 1458 *Calvary* in **Salle 8,** painted by Andrea Mantegna (1431–1506), a follower of the Florentine architect Brunelleschi's treatises on perspective, is one of the first paintings ever with a vanishing point. The angling of the roads and people may seem severe, but Mantegna opened the door for exploration of the concepts of background and foreground. Although more accomplished during his lifetime as an anatomist and inventor, Leonardo da Vinci (1452–1519) was originally trained as a painter. His 1483 *Virgin of the Rocks* has a pretty nifty sense of spatial relationships—the four figures create the four corners of a pyramid, while their glances and gestures keep all activity contained within this form. On the way from Salle 8 to the landing where the *Victory of Samothrace* is standing, you'll pass by Sandro Botticelli's (1445–1510) *Venus and the Graces,* a fresco chipped out of its villa in Tuscany. The painting is full of the sidelong glances and lengthy fingers associated with the Mannerist movement.

Behind the *Feast at Cana* are two passages leading to **Salles 75–77,** home of the great epic-scale canvases produced in Paris during the 19th century. When official court painter Jacques-Louis David

(1748–1825) produced the 1806 *Coronation of Napoléon, 2 December 1804,* now hanging in **Salle 75,** he wisely decided not to capture the moment when Napoléon snatched the crown from the hands of Pope Pius VII to place it upon his own head—choosing instead to paint the new emperor turning to crown Josephine. In the same room is the 1805 painting *Empress Josephine* by Pierre-Paul Prud'hon (1758–1823), depicting the wife of Napoléon one year after her crowning.

Also in **Salle 75** hang two of the most famous works in the history of French painting: the 1819 *Raft of the Medusa* by Théodore Géricault (1791–1824) and the 1830 *Liberty Leading the People* by Eugène Delacroix (1798–1863). The *Medusa,* painted when Géricault was only 27 years old, was inspired by the real-life story of the wreck of a French merchant ship: The captain lost control, the ship was without lifeboats or supplies, and ultimately the survivors resorted to cannibalism. The painting caused a stir with the government, which took offense at the stab made at the inefficiency of authority. The Académie was aghast for formal reasons: The painting had no central subject, no hero, no *resolution.* The survivors are a mess of living and dead bodies jumbled in and out of ominous, sickly green shadows.

Even though Delacroix wasn't directly involved in the "Trois Glorieuses"—a three-day revolution in 1830 that ousted Charles X's autocracy and brought in a parliamentary monarchy with Louis-Philippe as king—he was compelled to paint *Liberty* to commemorate the Parisians who attempted to restore the Republic. Once again, it is an unorthodox subject for a painting: Poorly armed bourgeoisie and pugnacious street urchins step over the dead bodies of comrades and kill other French folk in the name of an ultimately short-lived government. The allegorical figure of Liberty is quite a character: She is shown walking barefoot over barricades, her peasant dress falling away from two nippleless breasts, the Tricolore (French flag) held aloft with one well-muscled limb while the other grips a rifle. The painting was immediately bought by an appreciative Louis-Philippe, who hid it to keep from inciting his enemies.

If you're lucky enough to have a 100F note in your possession, you'll notice Delacroix's famous "Liberty Leading the People" gracing its design. Might make you think twice about spending the cash on postcards in the museum shop.

SPECIAL EXHIBITIONS AND EVENTS

Temporary photography shows, exhibits of new acquisitions and donations, and events honoring individual painters or subjects usually take place in either the Salle Napoléon, the basement galleries of the Richelieu and Sully Wing, the second-floor galleries of the Denon Wing, or the showrooms of the Carrousel du Louvre. Your Louvre ticket may give you free access, or you may have to shell out another 28F, depending on the exhibit. Lectures and films take place in the Louvre Auditorium on topics such as archaeology, architecture, and art criticism (25F–50F); the films showcase everything from silent works to the history of art in Paris (25F–100F). Chamber music concerts happen infrequently in the auditorium as well (100F–130F). A smattering of films, lectures, concerts, and exhibits are included in what's called **Les Midis du Louvre;** these noontime events cost 25F–50F. For a recorded message announcing the week's agenda, call 01–40–20–52–99; if you'd rather talk to a human being, call 01–40–20–51–86 between 9 AM and 7 PM. You can also pick up the free three-month schedule of events called *Louvre* at the information desk under the Pyramid, or look at the TV monitors behind the desk.

MUSÉE D'ORSAY

If you've just visited the Louvre and are oozing antiquity from every orifice, the Musée d'Orsay presents a refreshingly modern collection, encompassing art produced between 1848 (where the Louvre drops off) and about 1908 (where the Pompidou picks up). Since the most talented artists at this time, at least according to the French, were French, the Musée d'Orsay has a peculiar bias for French works. Not unfair comment: Renoir, Monet, and Cézanne spell genius in any language. Less familiar are the meticulous paintings and sculptures of highly trained "academic" artists that haunt the plentiful nooks and crannies not occupied by van Gogh and co. *62 rue de Lille, 7e, tel. 01–40–49–48–14. Métro: Solferino. RER: Musée d'Orsay. Admission 39F; separate admission for temporary exhibits. Open Tues.–Sat. 10–6 (Thurs. until 9:45), Sun. 9–6; in summer (mid-June–mid-Sept.), from 9 AM.*

BASICS

Although not as chaotic as the Louvre, the interior of this former train station may overwhelm you with its weighty postmodern architecture, sculptures, and hordes of people furiously milling around. The museum shop sells the **Guide for Visitors in a Hurry** (20F), an abbreviated outline of the most important works of the collection, and the **Guide to the Orsay** (110F), a more comprehensive look at the collection with better pictures.

General English-language tours are given Tuesday through Saturday at 11 AM (also 7 PM Thursday); tours at 11:30 are in French. Tours related to the special exhibitions vary—ask for the monthly calendar **Au Jour le Jour** when you buy your ticket to learn what's being offered that day.

HISTORY

Orsay only became a "musée" (that rhymes in French) in 1986. Built in 1898, the original Gare d'Orsay was meant to handle the onslaught of trains expected for the 1900 World's Fair. Architect Victor Laloux, a professor at the nearby Ecole des Beaux-Arts, designed all kinds of ornamental frippery appropriate to the dawning of the modern age. The platforms of the station were soon too short, however, and main-line trains had skedaddled downriver to Austerlitz by 1939. Suburban trains kept chugging in till the sixties, when the station hit the buffers. A few tenuous tenants moved in—Orson Welles shot *The Trial* here, and the city auction house moved in briefly—but it was slated for demolition as a part of the urban renewal schemes of the 1970s. Parisians couldn't stand the thought of this beloved, neo-rococo dinosaur being torn down, so they successfully petitioned President Pompidou to designate it a national monument in 1973. Four years later, a competition was announced for a design to turn the old station into a museum.

Yet when François Mitterrand became president in 1981, the renovation of the Orsay had completely stalled. The culture-conscious Mitterrand promptly tripled the reconstruction budget. Five years later the Musée d'Orsay was inaugurated, displaying the combined collections of the Jeu de Paume (*see* Museums, *below*) and the 19th-century galleries of the Louvre (*see above*). The crowds love architect Gae Aulenti's renovation design: While preserving a single grand, statue-lined promenade along the length of the building, Aulenti broke up the spacious shell of the old train station by dividing and subdividing the galleries into smaller rooms.

THE COLLECTION

Earlier paintings and sculptures are displayed on the ground level, later sculpture and architectural design on the middle level, and the heart of the impressionist collection on the upper level. If impressionism is this museum's draw for you, take an elevator directly to the third floor—otherwise, all the walking will have you beat by the time you hit your favorites.

GROUND FLOOR • As you walk up the Grande Promenade, the first gallery on the right contains the works of sensualist **Jean-Auguste Ingres** (1780–1867), whose erotic style was called "classic" by the other sensualists at the Académie des Beaux-Arts. The next gallery along the promenade has the works of **Eugène Delacroix** (1798–1863) who, despite his image as a fiery Romantic, maintained enough high-placed clout to land prestigious commissions to paint frescoes in several churches across the city. His vivid colors and flowing brushwork were a deliberate challenge to the staid precision of Ingres and his ilk.

Back across the promenade, the first gallery has figurines by the satirical illustrator **Honoré Daumier** (1808–79). Working at the beginning of the popular-press age, Daumier spent his energies mocking various members of the government and intelligentsia with biting little etchings. The caricatures included wicked likenesses of members of the National Assembly; you can see some of his paintings on the upper level. In the next gallery are works by **Camille Corot** (1796–1875). His deft, softly lit landscapes are associated with the Barbizon School, an approach to painting inspired by the writings of Rousseau and the invention of the camera.

In the first room on the left in the next bank of galleries on the promenade is the notorious *Olympia* (1863) by **Edouard Manet** (1832–83). When it was unveiled at the Salon des Refusés, it drew scathing remarks: The image of a nude, youngish courtesan with unfinished hands (they were described as monkey paws), stretched out next to a black cat (a symbol of female sexuality), was too hot to handle for the outwardly prudish denizens of the decadently prurient Second Empire.

Between the banks of galleries running along the Seine side of the Orsay is a large, open room containing the works of **Gustave Courbet** (1819–77), arguably the first modernist. Courbet's subjects—muddy country roads, poor farmers, rural dogs—embodied everything the sophisticated Parisian art scene was not, making the artist a hero to future generations of realists. His controversial *Origine du Monde*, a portrait of female genitals, was one of a stream of works commissioned by Turkish patrons. For more Courbet, check out the Petit Palais (*see* Museums, *below*).

In case you want to see the world.

At American Express, we're here to make your journey a smooth one. So we have over 1,700 travel service locations in over 120 countries ready to help. What else would you expect from the world's largest travel agency?

do more ®

AMERICAN
EXPRESS

Travel

In case you want to be welcomed there.

We're here to see that you're always welcomed at establish-ments everywhere. That's why millions of people carry the American Express® Card – for peace of mind, confidence, and security, around the world or just around the corner.

do more ®

AMERICAN EXPRESS

Cards

In case you're running low.

We're here to help with more than 118,000 Express Cash locations around the world. In order to enroll, just call American Express before you start your vacation.

do more

Express Cash

And just in case.

We're here with American Express® Travelers Cheques and Cheques *for Two.*® They're the safest way to carry money on your vacation and the surest way to get a refund, practically anywhere, anytime.
Another way we help you...

do more ®

AMERICAN
EXPRESS

Travelers
Cheques

Standing under the twin battlements at the end of the promenade is the **Salle Garnier,** a spiffy cluster of rooms devoted to the architect **Charles Garnier** (1825–98) and his crowning achievement, the Opéra Garnier (*see* Opera, Classical Music, and Dance *in* Chapter 5). Here you can look at models and sketches examining the Opéra's structure, but the best part is the scale model of the Opéra and its surrounding neighborhood set into the floor under see-through tiles. Trailing up along the staircase in the northeast corner of the museum is a montage of Parisian facades, starting from the Restoration and moving chronologically through the July Monarchy, Second Republic, Second Empire, and Third Republic.

MIDDLE FLOOR • On the terrace overlooking the promenade are early 20th-century sculptures, including works by **Auguste Rodin** (1840–1917) and **Camille Claudel** (1864–1903). Rodin, arguably the greatest sculptor of his era, spent the last 37 years of his career working on figures for his never-finished bronze *La Porte de l'Enfer* (*Gate of Hell*), a plaster version of which stands between the two battlements. (For more on the *Gate* and on Rodin and Claudel, *see* Museums, Musée Rodin, *below.*)

The galleries on either sides of the battlements are filled with architecture and furniture design from the turn of the century. To the north are several rooms filled with art nouveau, including a completely reconstructed dining room by **Alexandre Charpentier** (1856–1909). Across the terrace are rooms dedicated to non-French designers of the same period, including the American "Prairie School" architect **Frank Lloyd Wright** (1867–1959) and Scot **Charles Rennie Mackintosh** (1868–1928), whose straight-lined furniture echoes Viennese Jugendstil.

UPPER FLOOR • Entering the first gallery from the northeastern stairs or elevator, you'll find the impressionists, who challenged the status quo with their theories about the effects of light, movement, and color. In 1863 Manet painted his controversial *Déjeuner sur l'Herbe* (*Picnic on the Grass*). The subject, naked ladies and clothed men in a bucolic setting, wasn't new to the French public; many were familiar with a similar scene from the Italian Renaissance hanging in the Louvre. But there was something about the modern dress of the men, the discarded clothes of the women, and the way two of the figures look out at the viewer with a slightly confrontational glance that upset the critics.

In the next gallery is the famous portrait of the mother of **James McNeill Whistler** (1834–1903), embodying all the spartan puritanism associated with the rural United States and the late 19th-century American aesthetic. In the next gallery, the work of **Claude Monet** shows how the painter replaced hard delineation with soft brush strokes and colors from a muted palette. His *Fête du 30 juin 1878* tries to capture the shimmering vitality of a Paris street celebration. In the same gallery is the work of **Pierre-Auguste Renoir** (1841–1919), who used to spend long hours in Parisian parks catching the newly idle petite bourgeoisie at play.

The last gallery in this series is devoted to **Paul Cézanne** (1839–95), who challenged the salons of Paris by entirely ignoring them. Though he had contact with other painters like Degas and Manet, and a few young artists who came to study with him in his Aix-en-Provence studio, Cézanne painted almost entirely for himself. And he painted and painted, continually playing with color and spatial relationships while selling only a few works to a wealthy doctor.

Around the corner, beyond the café behind one of the giant clocks, is a room filled with the work of **Vincent van Gogh** (1835–90), the firebrand Dutchman who spent most of his career in France. Van Gogh was doomed to a bizarre life from the outset—he was named for a dead brother who'd had the same birthday. Sure, there's the ear story, and the problems he had with prostitutes and his brother Theo, but the contribution he made to painting cannot be overestimated. Van Gogh painted a stone bridge yellow and a wheat field red because that's the way he painted them—a simple idea for later generations of artists to figure out.

Turn the corner and you can figure out **Le Douanier Rousseau** (1844–1910), doyen of naive artists, whose cool and flattened touch delineated fairy-tale-like jungle scenes complete with exotic animals hidden in the dense underbrush. This jungle motif was popular with the style-conscious French, who were eager to get images of what they imagined to be Edenic colonies in Africa, East Asia, and the Caribbean. The penniless Rousseau dreamt up his world overview during visits to city hothouses. **Paul Gauguin** (1848–1903) also used flat expanses of color, but his titillating Tahiti maidens are overladen with fatalistic imagery.

Farther along are works by **Georges Seurat** (1859–91), whose use of dots of color became known as pointillism (though he found the term "divisionism" much more appropriate). At the end of the hallway are early works by **Henri Matisse** (1869–1954), whose 1904 *Luxe, Calme, et Volupté* helped him earn the label *fauvist,* an uncomplimentary term coined by the critics, who thought his bright colors were

JEAN NOUVEL

Jean Nouvel, an emerging visionary of Parisian architecture, designed the Institut du Monde Arabe and the Fondation Cartier. His philosophical obsession with "transparency" inspired the light-manipulating wall at the Institute and the mobile 26-by-10-foot glass panels at Cartier. Critics have dubbed his style "façadism," but Nouvel is quick to differentiate his innovative use of glass—panes that fog, LCD-tinted panels—from run-of-the-mill corporate architecture. His latest project is to build the 1,300-foot Tour Sans Fin (Endless Tower) at La Défense, to be enclosed entirely by, of course, glass.

comme un fauve (like a beast). The Fauves—Vlaminck and Derain were other exponents—mark the official end (at least according to French museums) of postimpressionism and the beginning of modern art—for more Matisse, go to the Pompidou (*see above*). For another big batch of impressionists and postimpressionists in a smaller setting, make time for the Musée de l'Orangerie; and Monet fans won't want to miss the Musée Marmottan Claude Monet (for both, *see* Museums, *below*).

PLACE DE LA CONCORDE

In no other spot in Paris can you turn 360° and see so many monuments. Place de la Concorde is a Kodak dream come true, provided you aren't flattened by the hundreds of cars that tear through it. Architect Jacques-Ange Gabriel designed the square for Louis XV; in 1763 a statue of Louis XV was erected in the center of the square, named after his egotistical majesty. In 1792 the statue was replaced by a big symbol of Liberty (and complemented, ironically enough, by a guillotine that same year). It was at this spot that Louis XVI lost his head (literally), as did Marie-Antoinette and hundreds of others. In 1795 it was hopefully dubbed place de la Concorde.

The square is flanked on the northern side by Gabriel's 1763 mansions, the **Hôtel de la Marine** and the **Hôtel Crillon** (now a super luxurious hotel), with the **Madeleine** (*see* Houses of Worship, *below*) rising up in the middle-distance. To the west you can stare up the Champs-Elysées to the **Arc de Triomphe** and, on unusually clear days, to **La Défense.** On the eastern side is the **Jardin des Tuileries,** leading to the **Louvre.** To the south is the fancy **Pont de la Concorde,** built in 1788, with the colonnaded **Assemblée Nationale** (parliament) at the far side. Smack-dab in the middle of the square, and looking decidedly un-French, is the **Obelisque de Luxor,** given to King Louis-Philippe in 1831 by Egypt's Mohammed Ali. The obelisk originally stood before the gates of Thebes; the hieroglyphics, running 75 feet high, tell the story of Ramses II. The more modern tale of how the 230-ton monument was shipped from Egypt to Paris is engraved on the bottom (it took a vessel specially equipped with cranes and pulleys). The eight matronly statues encircling place de la Concorde, added in 1871, represent the biggest cities in France. *8e, Métro: Concorde.*

SAINTE-CHAPELLE

Sainte-Chapelle is a Gothic chapel made sublime by its fantastic room of stained glass. Ascending to the upper chapel, especially on sunny days, is like climbing into a jewel box: Brilliantly colored windows flood the interior with light—you get the exhilarating feeling that the building has walls of glass. The less-grand lower chapel, once reserved for the king's servants, is paved with the faceless, worn tombstones of clerics and forgotten knights.

This chapel remains a fine example of the extremes to which people will go when they get hold of a holy relic or two. In the mid-13th century, Louis IX bought the alleged crown of thorns and a part of the Cross from Constantinople. In order to house these treasures, as well as a portion of John the Baptist's skull and Mary's milk and blood, he commissioned the Sainte-Chapelle. The elegant result was completely unlike its massive contemporary nearby, Notre-Dame (*see above*). Louis's influence is everywhere; he even had his own private entry to the chapel so he wouldn't have to mix and mingle with the rabble. His fleur-de-lis (lily) emblem is painted all over the place, as is the symbol of his mother, a golden church. Glorious instrumental and vocal concerts are held here (130F–200F); check the *Officiel des Spectacles* for dates. *Inside Palais de Justice, 4 blvd. du Palais, 1er, tel. 01–53–73–78–50. Métro: Cité. Admission 32F. Open Apr.–Sept., daily 9:30–6:30; Oct.–Mar., daily 10–5.*

TOUR EIFFEL

Strange to think that the Eiffel Tower, a construction so abhorred by Parisians when it was built, should become the symbol of France. Soaring to an obscene height yet graciously straddling all of Paris, this old hulk o' steel is instantly recognizable the world over. Chances are you'll be cursed with some vague sense of emotional unfulfillment until you've actually been to pay it your respects.

It all started in 1885, when the city held a contest to design a 300-meter (984-foot) tower for the 1889 World Exposition. Competing with proposals for a monster sprinkler and a giant commemorative guillotine, Gustave Eiffel, already well-known for his iron works, won the contest with his seemingly functionless tower, slated as scrap even as it was being built. Somewhere along the way, however, people realized it might actually have a practical use or two; it went on to help decipher German radio codes during World War I, capture Mata Hari, measure atmospheric pressure, and act as the ideal launch pad for 350 airborne suicides.

The Eiffel Tower was the world's tallest building until New York's Chrysler Building went up in 1930. When you visit, get your postcards stamped with the famous Eiffel Tower postmark; the post office here is open daily 10–7:30.

The close-up view of the tower—10,000 tons of brown metal—is overpowering. It remains a source of awe to legions of visitors, especially at night when every girder is illuminated. The hour-long lines to ascend the tower in summer are decidedly less wonderful; to avoid them, try visiting early in the morning or late at night. The best view, though, is on a clear day an hour before sunset, when visibility from the top extends 90 km (56 mi). You can walk up to the second level to save money and work off some crepes and take the elevator from there to the top. *Champ de Mars, 7e, tel. 01–44–11–23–23. Métro: Bir-Hakeim. RER: Champ de Mars. Admission (elevator) 20F to 1st level, 42F to 2nd level, 57F to top. Admission (stairs) 17F to 2nd level. Open daily 9 AM–11 PM.*

Just across the Pont d'Iéna bridge from the Eiffel Tower is the **Trocadéro** plaza, home to gardens, spectacular fountains, and the Palais de Chaillot museum complex. The view of the Eiffel Tower from here is unsurpassed, especially when the fountains are shooting up and framing it.

MUSEUMS

Paris's museums range from the ostentatiously grand to the delightfully obscure—the French seem hellbent on documenting everything any of its citizens have ever done. In addition to the three biggies covered above in Major Attractions—the Louvre, the Musée d'Orsay, and the Pompidou—we've listed all sorts of smaller spaces that may fit your various moods, including science and history museums, photography galleries, and world culture centers. The city also has many galleries that have no permanent collections but host traveling shows; check *Pariscope* (*see* English-Language Publications *in* Chapter 1) and posted flyers to find out what's in town.

The association InterMusée spends a large sum of money advertising its **Carte Musées et Monuments** (Museums and Monuments Card), valid for entry to most of Paris's museums. The pass—valid for either one day (70F), three days (140F), or five days (200F) and sold at participating museums and most major métro stations—is only a deal if you both (a) don't qualify for any discount admissions (*see* introduction to Exploring Paris, *above*); and (b) have the stamina of a marathon runner. But if you plan to start at the Musée d'Orsay (39F) and then pay your respects to the Parisian dead at the Catacombs (27F) all in the same day, this pass might be for you. Keep in mind that after 3 PM at the Louvre you only have to pay 26F for 6,000 years of art.

ART MUSEUMS

ESPACE MONTMARTRE—DALI

This museum has more than 300 works by the self-proclaimed master of surrealism, Salvador Dalí (1904–89), but it isn't quite as exciting as the Dalí museum in Spain. Nonetheless, the dark, sunken chambers of Espace Montmartre contain an impressive display of the artist's dream landscapes, psychedelic sculptures, and illustrations of *Alice in Wonderland*. But be warned: Most of the works in the collection are lithographs and castings produced in the winter of the artist's life, when a sick and senile Dalí was signing his name to prints and sculptures that were mainly reproductions of his earlier works, and the museum uses somewhat tacky New Age music and light effects to display them. *11 rue Poulbot, 18e, tel. 01–42–64–40–10. Métro: Anvers or Abbesses. Admission 35F. Open July–Aug., daily 10–7; Sept.–June, daily 10–6.*

FONDATION CARTIER

The Fondation Cartier has a reputation as one of the corporate world's greatest patrons of contemporary art. Designed by Jean Nouvel (*see* box, *above*), the building is one of Paris's most stunning—a mélange of vast glass panes, complicated steel structures, and exposed mechanical work, all done so elegantly that you can't accuse the building of being some cheesy, high-tech cliché. The watch-and-jewelry empire executives work upstairs in the Cartier headquarters, and the basement and ground floor of this ultra-modernist building hold galleries and museum staff who act like they genuinely want to help you enjoy yourself. Exhibitions are always changing and manage to be extremely sophisticated in such a relatively small space—it *is* Cartier, after all. The best way to experience both the art and Nouvel's building is to come on Thursday nights for the series "**Les Soirées Nomades**" (Nomadic Evenings), when there is dance, performance art, or live music around and about the art (except in July and August). *261 blvd. Raspail, 14e, tel. 01–42–18–56–50 or 01–42–18–56–51. Métro: Denfert-Rochereau. Admission 30F; "Les Soirées Nomades" included in admission. Open Tues.–Sun. noon–8 (Thurs. until 10).*

GRAND PALAIS AND PETIT PALAIS

Intended as temporary additions to the Parisian landscape for the 1900 Exposition Universelle, these self-styled palaces dodged the wrecking ball to become full-time tourist attractions. Behind its pompous facade with sugary mosaics and trite neoclassical details, the Grand Palais hides a cathedral-size concourse with a glass roof and art nouveau metalwork. After several years of repairs, it may or may not be open again for exhibitions come 1998. In the meantime, exhibitions are confined to the more modest halls in the wings. *3 av. du Général Eisenhower, 8e, tel. 01–44–13–17–17. Métro: Champs-Elysées–Clemenceau. Admission 25F–50F, depending on exhibit. Open Thurs.–Mon. 10–8, Wed. 10–10.*

The Petit Palais, across the road, has a majestic entrance hall splattered with outsize belle epoque frescoes. In addition to temporary exhibits, there's a permanent museum that focuses on 19th-century French painters, including large and plentiful works by Courbet—his risqué 1866 *Le Sommeil*, of two naked women napping together, is especially popular—and a healthy handful of impressionist-era pieces, such as Cézanne's *Les Baigneuses* (1880). There is also turn-of-the-century jewelry, including many art nouveau items. *Av. Winston-Churchill, 8e, tel. 01–42–65–12–73. Métro: Champs-Elysées–Clemenceau. Admission 27F; temporary exhibits 30F–40F extra. Open Tues.–Sun. 10–5:40.*

JEU DE PAUME

Named for the indoor tennis court that once stood in the royal Jardin des Tuileries, the Jeu de Paume housed much of the national impressionist collection until the Musée d'Orsay opened in 1986. The trim, rectangular 19th-century building stood neglected for five years before reopening as one of Paris's most exciting exhibition spaces, with large, gleaming white halls hosting some of the city's best shows of contemporary art. There's a small, loungeable café and a bookstore with a strong collection of French- and English-language art books. Admission prices and hours vary with exhibits. *Pl. de la Concorde, 1er, tel. 01–47–60–69–69. Métro: Concorde. Admission 35F. Open Tues. noon–9:30, Wed.–Fri. noon–7, weekends 10–7.*

MUSEE D'ART MODERNE DE LA VILLE DE PARIS

Even though the City of Paris's Museum of Modern Art occupies one of the city's most striking art deco buildings in a prime site by the Seine across from the Eiffel Tower, this museum has had a difficult time convincing the world that there is another major venue for modern art in Paris besides the Pompidou (*see* Major Attractions, *above*). Many of the 30,000 works forming the permanent collection were donated by artists such as Henri Matisse and Robert Motherwell, but there is a dearth of high-profile pieces. Wisely deciding not to compete with the Goliath across town, the Museum of Modern Art focuses on the contemporary works of more controversial artists, although not ignoring those of historical importance. The museum also hosts great temporary exhibits, as well as occasional concerts.

The museum has been housed in the east wing of the Palais de Tokyo since 1967. Originally constructed for the Exposition Universelle in 1937, this building stands where Louis XII's royal rug factory once operated. The columned modern terrace offers a great view of the Eiffel Tower and is popular with skate rats, whose racket echoes off the building's walls. On the way to the top floor it is impossible not to notice **Raoul Dufy**'s (1877–1953) *Fée Electricité,* in which 720 square yards of bright colors fervently depict the harnessing of electricity by humanity. At its creation, this was the largest displayed painting known in the world. Down the steps as you enter is another giant canvas, Delaunay's essay in psychedelic circles, and a roomful of fauves. Off the terrace on the ground floor are a café and a bookstore that stocks a diverse selection of art books and journals in English and French. *11 av. du Président-Wilson, 16e, tel. 01–47–23–61–27. Métro: Iéna. Admission permanent collection 27F, joint ticket with temporary exhibitions 45F. Open Tues.–Fri. 10–5:30, weekends 10–6:45.*

MUSEE DES ARTS DECORATIFS

You'll realize just how big the Louvre is when you consider that this major collection of decorative arts occupies only a modest part of its north wing. Spread confusingly over the museum's four floors are chairs, vases, sword cases, and other necessities of life from the Middle Ages to the present. There are also many rooms that have been meticulously redecorated with furniture and other period items: The game room has a backgammon board, the bathroom a soap dish, the salon an ostentatious number of chairs. The art-nouveau era is best represented in a fine collection of furniture and objets d'art. *107 rue de Rivoli, 1er, tel. 01–44–55–57–50. Métro: Palais Royal. Admission 35F. Open Wed.–Sat. 12:30–6, Sun. noon–6.*

If you want to pop into a museum just before closing, keep in mind that ticket offices close 15–45 minutes before the posted closing time of the galleries.

MUSEE GUSTAVE MOREAU

Symbolist painter Gustave Moreau (1826–98), the mentor of an entire generation of young artists and teacher of Matisse and Rouault, spent the final years of his life forming a little collection in his apartment. At his death, the collection became a public museum. Other than a few small works by Rembrandt and Poussin, the museum is devoted to the works of Moreau himself. On cloudy days it can seem a bit drab, as most of the lighting comes from the glass roof. It takes sunshine to come to terms with Moreau's unfettered imagination, obsession with intricate detail, and love of obscure, scantily clad mythological heroines. *14 rue de La Rochefoucauld, 9e, tel. 01–48–74–38–50. Métro: Trinité. Admission 17F, 11F Sun. Open Thurs.–Sun. 10–12:45 and 2–5:15, Mon. and Wed. 11–5:15.*

MUSEE JACQUEMART ANDRE

Showcased in this elegant town house is one of the most beautiful private art collections in Paris, amassed in the 19th century by Edouard André and Nélie Jacquemart, a wealthy, bourgeois couple. Italian Renaissance art, including works by Botticelli, Donatello, Tintoretto, and Canaletto, and Uccello's *St. George Killing the Dragon,* compete for attention with lavish 18th-century furnishings. The entrance fee includes an audio guide (in English or French) that explains the entire collection in detail. *158 blvd. Haussmann, 8e, tel. 01–42–89–04–91. Métro: St-Philippe du Roule or Miromesnil. Admission 45F. Open daily 10–6.*

MUSEE MARMOTTAN CLAUDE MONET

A couple of years ago, this museum, in an elegant 19th-century mansion, tacked "Claude Monet" onto its official name—and justly so, as this may be the best collection of the artist's works anywhere. Monet shares the ground floor with Boilly and priceless illuminated medieval manuscripts. You'll find such spectacular works as the *Cathédrale à Rouen* (1892–96), *Parlement à Londres* (1899–1904) series, and *Impression: Soleil Levant* (1872), the work that helped give the impressionist movement its name. Other exhibits include letters exchanged by impressionist painters Berthe Morisot and Mary Cassatt. Some of the rooms, graced with Empire furniture from Napoléon's time, make you feel as if you're at an actual salon, with comfortable couches and grand windows overlooking the Jardin de Ranelagh on one side and the hotel's private yard on the other. *2 rue Louis-Boilly, 16e, tel. 01–42–24–07–02. Métro: La Muette. Admission 40F. Open Tues.–Sun. 10–5:30.*

MUSEUMS STRANGE AND OBSCURE...

MUSÉE GRÉVIN. Since 1882, this wax museum has been covering all the big names from French history and American pop culture. Your overpriced ticket also grants you a magic show and entrance into the 1900 Palace of Illusion. 10 blvd. Montmartre, 9e, tel. 01–42–46–13–26. Métro: Rue Montmartre. Admission 55F. Open daily 1–7.

MUSÉE DE LA CONTREFAÇON. The Paris Manufacturers' Union, egged on by companies like Cartier, opened this tiny museum to document the problem of product counterfeiting. 15 rue de la Faisanderie, 16e, tel. 01–45–01–51–11. Métro: Porte Dauphine. Admission 10F. Open Mon. and Wed. 2–4:30, Fri. 9:30–noon.

MUSÉE DE LA CURIOSITÉ. Built in the underground caves (basements) of the former residence of the Marquis de Sade, this museum has rotating exhibits on magic and all the trademark funhouse mirrors and optical illusions, as well as magic shows. 11 rue St-Paul, 4e, tel. 01–42–72–13–26. Métro: St-Paul. Admission 45F. Open Wed. and weekends 2–7.

MUSÉE DU VIN. This museum explains all you need to know about winemaking, in a musty 14th-century cellar. 5 square Dickens, rue des Eaux, 16e, tel. 01–45–25–63–26. Métro: Passy. Admission 35F, glass of wine included. Open daily 10–6.

MUSEE NATIONAL DU MOYEN-AGE

The National Museum of the Middle Ages, formerly known as the Musée de Cluny, began in 1832 as the private—most people thought quirky—medieval art collection of Alexandre du Sommerand in an *hôtel particulier* (mansion) built over and around the ruins of some Roman baths. The state purchased the mansion and collection soon after and turned the place into a full-time museum. Today the collection features medieval stained glass, furniture, jewelry, carvings, music manuscripts, and some exquisite tapestries. One of the finest tapestry series—found half-eaten by rats before being brought here—is *The Lady and the Unicorn,* comprising six panels in which a refined lady demonstrates the five senses to a unicorn. The museum recently acquired a set of sculpted heads of the kings of Judea that once looked out from the facade of the Cathédrale de Notre-Dame (*see* Major Attractions, *above*); thought to have been lost during the Revolution, they were rediscovered in a bank vault in 1977. *6 pl. du Paul-Painlevé, 5e, tel. 01–43–25–62–00. Métro: Cluny–La Sorbonne. Admission 28F, 18F Sun. Open Wed.–Mon. 9:15–5:45.*

MUSEE DE L'ORANGERIE

This small but rewarding collection of impressionist and postimpressionist paintings sits peacefully across from the Jeu de Paume and overlooks place de la Concorde. Like the Musée Marmottan (*see above*), this is a place to visit if you're in the mood for turn-of-the-century art but can't deal with the enormity of the Musée d'Orsay. Below walls lined with Renoirs, Cézannes, Manets, and Modiglianis is the museum's most popular room: a magical, watery oval space with Monet's huge water-lily paintings. Inspired by Monet's home at Giverny (*see* Chapter 7), the *Nymphéas* (1914–26) are perhaps the best-known of his "series" works—repeated studies of the effects of different lighting upon the same subject. After the 1918 armistice, Monet donated the *Nymphéas* to the state, though he requested they not be displayed until after his death. *Pl. de la Concorde, 1er, tel. 01-42-97-48-16. Métro: Concorde. Admission 27F, 18F Sun. Open Wed.-Mon. 9:45-5:45.*

MUSEE NATIONAL EUGENE-DELACROIX

This modest museum is housed in the last apartment Delacroix occupied before his death in 1863. Bits of Delacroix paraphernalia and furniture—a paint box here, a divan there—decorate the tiny complex of rooms, and prints and paintings cover the walls. Knowing that he painted in this space is, however, more exciting than the artwork itself. Through the back is his high-ceilinged, generously windowed studio, overlooking a quiet courtyard. *6 rue de Furstenberg, 6e, tel. 01-43-54-04-87. Métro: St-Germain-des-Prés. Admission 15F. Open Wed.-Mon. 10-5.*

MUSEE PICASSO

When Pablo Picasso's family couldn't come up with enough cash to settle the taxes on his estate, they decided to donate a large number of his works to the French government. These are now displayed in a stately mansion, the 17th-century Hôtel Salé, in the heart of the Marais. Rooms in the museum are arranged chronologically, and information in each (in English) tells about major events in the artist's life. Although he was known as the greatest artist of his generation, Picasso was also an arrogant, misogynistic cad who enjoyed seducing other artists' wives; when his contemporaries (including Georges Braque and Guillaume Apollinaire) were shipped off to World War I, Picasso used his Spanish passport to stay safely in Paris. Taking their cues from the field of physics, Picasso, Braque, and Juan Gris reformulated the way three-dimensional space was represented on canvas. Though best known as a painter, Picasso was also an innovative sculptor, constructing cubist guitars and using a toy Renault for the snout of a bronze baboon. This collection represents a sampling of every stage of Picasso's work, but there are no blue-chip pieces to be found here—those are all in New York. Still, this is one of the most popular museums in Paris. The covered garden out back makes a pleasant setting for a summertime café and shades many of his sculptures. *5 rue Thorigny, 3e, tel. 01-42-71-25-21. Métro: Chemin Vert. Admission 30F, 20F Wed. Open Wed.-Mon. 9:30-6.*

MUSEE RODIN

The Musée Rodin is one of the most pleasant museums in Paris. The masterful French sculptor Auguste Rodin (1840-1917) left his house, the early 18th-century Hôtel Biron, and all the works in it to the state when he died. The mansion, with the second-largest garden in the neighborhood (after the prime minister's), is as much a part of the museum as the art. In addition to the beautiful garden (5F), there is also a pavilion exhibiting temporary shows. The main building houses numerous Rodin bronze and marble sculptures, as powerful and uncompromising as the man himself: His funeral, at the height of World War I, drew the largest nonmilitary crowd of the time (26,000); while alive, however, Rodin was stalked by controversy. His career took off in 1876 with *L'Age d'Airain* (The Age of Bronze), inspired by a pilgrimage to Italy and the sculptures of Michelangelo. Because the work was so realistic, some critics accused Rodin of having stuck a live boy in plaster, while others blasted him for what was seen as a sloppy sculpting and casting technique. His seeming messiness, though, was intentional; Rodin sought to capture the sculpting process through the imprints of fingers, rags used to keep the clay moist, and tools he left on his works.

Four years later, Rodin was commissioned to create the doors for the newly proposed Musée des Arts Décoratifs. He set out to sculpt a pair of monumental bronze doors in the tradition of Italian Renaissance churches, calling his proposal *La Porte de l'Enfer* (*Gate of Hell*). The *Gate,* a visual representation of stories from Dante's *Divine Comedy,* became his obsession: He spent the last 37 years of his life working on it. The *Gate* was never completed, and no metal casts of the masterpiece were made during Rodin's life—the museum's bronze out in the garden is posthumous.

Possibly Rodin's most celebrated work is his *Le Penseur* (*The Thinker,* ca. 1880), the muscular man caught in a moment of deep thought and flex. The version here in the garden is the original—the city of Paris, its intended owner, refused to accept it. Before installing the permanent bronze statue on the steps of the Panthéon, Rodin set up a full-scale plaster cast. Its physicality horrified the public; crowds gathered around the statue, debates ensued, and Rodin was ridiculed in the press. A man who was later tried and found criminally insane hacked away at some of the plaster cast with a hatchet, giving the city a convenient excuse to refuse the statue.

Rodin may have hogged the limelight, but his museum allows some space to works by his mistress **Camille Claudel** (1864-1943), a remarkable sculptor in her own right. Admire her dynamic 1900 work

FREE ART

To get a feel for Paris's current art scene, cruise through the multitude of galleries in the city. Most galleries are open Tuesday–Saturday 2–7. Anyone can enter for free, although looking rich and artsy helps deter snobby looks from gallery owners.

In the Bastille area, check out the huge, funky sculptures at Durand Desert (28 rue du Lappe, 11e, tel. 01–48–06–92–93), or the fantastic photography at Galerie Carlihan (37 rue de Charonne, 11e, tel. 01–47–00–79–28). In the Marais, Farideh Cadot (77 rue des Archives, 4e, tel. 01–42–78–08–36) has avant-garde work, and Galerie Laage-Salomon (54 rue du Temple, 4e, tel. 01–42–78–11–71) shows well-known, international contemporary artists. Rue Quincampoix is a good place to look for abstract art. On the Left Bank, rue de Seine, rue Daguerre, and rue du Bac all have lots of small galleries. Near the Montmartre cemetery, the Hôpital Ephémère (2 rue Carpeaux, 18e, tel. 01–46–27–82–82) is a collection of artist studios, a theater, and an auditorium. Another collection of artist work spaces, the Quai de la Gare (91 quai de la Gare, 13e, tel. 01–45–85–91–91), hosts frequent "portes ouvertes" (open doors) where you can wander freely among the 250 studios.

L'Age Mûr (Maturity): The young girl is Claudel, the man Rodin, and the old woman his wife. Shunning the monumental, except for her Persée et Méduse (Perseus and the Medusa), in which Medusa's face was a self-portrait, Claudel experimented with smaller figures in well-defined, almost architectural settings. Her torturous relationship with Rodin drove her out of his studio—and out of her mind. In 1913 she was packed off to an asylum on the Ile St-Louis (see Neighborhoods, below), where she remained, barred from any artistic activities, until her death in 1943. Had Claudel's talent not been straitjacketed, her work might have its own space today instead of being squished in among Rodin's. 77 rue de Varenne, 7e, tel. 01–47–05–01–34. Métro: Varenne. Admission 28F, 18F Sun., 5F gardens only. Open Tues.–Sun. 9:30–5:45.

MUSEE ZADKINE

The former studio of Ukrainian-born Ossip Zadkine (1890–1967) is one of the most appealing museums in the city—regardless of what you think of Zadkine's work. Dozens of sculptures from his Parisian career (he moved here in 1909) pack the small, bright rooms; feeling the sculptures is particularly tempting, since Zadkine worked with natural and treated woods, brass, and stone, giving the materials varying levels of shine. No great innovator, Zadkine was instead a skilled imitator of the styles that passed through Paris during the early to mid-20th century—cubism, futurism, primitivism, you name it. Check out the free sculpture garden in front. 100 bis rue d'Assas, 6e, tel. 01–43–26–91–90. Métro: Vavin. Admission 17F. Open Tues.–Sun. 10–5:30.

PHOTOGRAPHY

CENTRE NATIONAL DE LA PHOTOGRAPHIE

Photographs previously found in the Palais de Tokyo have been relocated to the ground floor of the expansive Hôtel Salomon de Rothschild, home of the National Photography Center. Big-name shows focusing on a single genre or artist dominate the main gallery, though peripheral rooms may display works from the permanent collection. Institutes related to photography are on the upper floors. The sizable grounds are well tended but off-limits, affording a strictly visual appreciation of nature. Balzac died in 1850 in a house that once stood in the west garden. *11 rue Berryer, 8e, tel. 01–53–76–12–31. Métro: George V. Admission 30F. Open Wed.–Mon. noon–7. Closed Aug.*

ESPACE PHOTO DE PARIS

Despite its location in the Forum des Halles mall, this tiny gallery stages consistently great photography exhibits, thanks to an association with the cultural muscle of the Mairie de Paris (Paris Mayor's Office). *4–8 Grande Galerie des Halles, 1er, tel. 01–40–26–87–12. Métro: Les Halles. Admission 10F. Open Tues.–Fri. 1–6, weekends 1–7.*

FNAC GALERIE PHOTO

FNAC Forum Les Halles hosts some wonderful free photography shows, as do the lesser branches in Montparnasse and in the 17th arrondissement on avenue Wagram, close to the Arc de Triomphe. Monthly brochures provide details on the exhibits. *1 rue Pierre-Lescot, 1er, tel. 01–40–41–40–00. Métro: Châtelet–Les Halles. Open Mon.–Sat. 10–7:30.*

MAISON EUROPEENNE DE LA PHOTOGRAPHIE

This beautiful museum in two, old, converted hôtels particuliers comes complete with creaky floorboards, a basement housing experimental projects, and a café. Despite its name, the museum also has an impressive selection of American works, with a focus on recent fashion photography and photojournalism. Check out the rare documentaries shown in the *videotheque* (video library) or attend one of the lectures on historical and contemporary issues in photography. *5 rue de Fourcy, 4e, tel. 01–44–78–75–00. Métro: St-Paul. Admission 30F, free Wed. after 5 PM. Open Wed.–Sun. 11–8.*

The Ecole Vétérinaire d'Alfort, in Maisons-Alfort just south of the Bois de Vincennes, contains the gruesome yet fascinating works of anatomist Honoré Fragonard (1732–99), including flayed bodies and preserved peculiarities like a 10-legged sheep.

MISSION DU PATRIMOINE PHOTOGRAPHIQUE

Set up by the Ministry of Culture, this small photography gallery, with continually changing exhibits, frequently focuses on avant-garde and contemporary work. Housed in a corner of the Hôtel Sully, the gallery overlooks a beautiful courtyard leading into place des Vosges. *62 rue St-Antoine, 4e, tel. 01–42–74–30–60. Métro: St-Paul. Admission 25F. Open Wed.–Mon. 1–6.*

FRENCH HISTORY AND CULTURE

LA CONCIERGERIE

This complex of towers and halls served as the royal palace until 1358, when a young Charles V sought to place a safe distance between himself and his potentially revolutionary masses by building the Louvre across the Seine. Since the 14th century, the Conciergerie (the name for the official who administered the castle) has served as a tribunal hall and prison, but its most macabre period came in the 18th century when the Revolutionary court mercilessly issued death proclamations—2,780 to be exact—from its halls. Although much of the nobility passed through these cells, the most famous resident was Marie-Antoinette, who spent her final days here before being hauled off on a garbage cart to be guillotined. The court disbanded after the execution of Robespierre, who became the victim of the Terror he had himself initiated. Now the Conciergerie is merely the basement of the Palais de Justice (Law Courts), though the Salle des Gens d'Armes (Hall of the Men-at-Arms), an impressive vaulted hall, and a motley collection of dusty cells, are still worth visiting. *1 quai de l'Horloge, 1er, tel. 01–43–54–30–06. Métro: Cité. Admission 32F. Open Apr.–Sept., daily 9:30–6:30; Oct.–Mar., daily 10–5.*

MAISON DE VICTOR HUGO

The former home of France's literary hero has become a two-story museum in his honor. His unsuspected gifts as a draughtsman emerge on the first floor via a number of gloomily atmospheric gothic-horror watercolors; illustrations for his writings by other painters, including Bayard's rendition of Cosette from *Les Misérables* (now a famous T-shirt), can also be found here. The rooms upstairs represent Hugo's living style in several of his many homes; the central room of the floor, for instance, is decorated with Chinese-theme panels and woodworks he created for his mistress's home outside town. *6 pl. des Vosges, 4e, tel. 01–42–72–10–16. Métro: St-Paul. Admission 27F. Open Tues.–Sun. 10–5:40.*

MUSEE CARNAVALET

It takes two hôtels particuliers in the Marais—the Carnavalet and Le Peletier de St-Fargeau—to house this worthy homage to Parisian history. Basically, the Carnavalet (through which you enter) covers ancient Paris through the reign of Louis XVI, the Peletier the Revolution through the 20th century—though you could go crazy trying to move through the poorly marked rooms chronologically. In the courtyard off rue de Sévigné stands the last remaining bronze statue of a Louis: Louis XIV, whose representation by Antoine Coysevox was saved from Revolutionary meltdown only by oversight—the people simply didn't notice it in the too-obvious Hôtel de Ville. Back inside, other treasures include Jean-Jacques Rousseau's inkwell and blackened blotting sponge, keys to the Bastille, and Napoléon I's death mask. Most entertaining, however, are the re-created rooms, particularly Marcel Proust's bedroom, the turn-of-the-century Fouquet jewelry shop, and a room from the art nouveau Café de Paris. *23 rue de Sévigné, 3e, tel. 01–42–72–21–13. Métro: St-Paul. Admission 27F. Open Tues.–Sun. 10–5:40.*

MUSEE DE LA MODE ET DU COSTUME

In the 1920s, Paris decided it needed a fashion museum, and after a couple of trial runs at World Expos, this is where it wound up. The strictly temporary exhibits, usually centering on fashionable aspects of Paris's past, feature hundreds of items of clothing and accessories. *10 av. Pierre-1er-de-Serbie, 16e, tel. 01–47–20–85–23. Métro: Iéna. Admission 35F–40F. Open Tues.–Sun. 10–5:40.*

MUSEE DE MONTMARTRE

This space houses a fascinating but small collection of photos and changing exhibits on life in Montmartre, including displays about famous former inhabitants, drawings by Toulouse-Lautrec, and minor works by Modigliani, Vlaminck, Utrillo, and others. *12 rue Cortot, 18e, tel. 01–46–06–61–11. Métro: Lamarck-Caulaincourt. Admission 25F. Open Tues.–Sun. 11–6.*

MUSEE DES MONUMENTS FRANCAIS

Architects will appreciate this collection, which displays models of all of Paris's great monuments in one small space. Hundreds of reproductions of portals, statues, and other pieces—many of them full size—represent all the blockbuster structures in France from Chartres to Mont-St-Michel. *1 pl. du Trocadéro, 16e, tel. 01–44–05–39–10. Métro: Trocadéro. Admission 22F. Open Wed.–Mon. 10–6.*

MUSEE DE LA POSTE

This museum is dedicated to stamps and the history of written communication, including the balloon used to get mail out of Paris during the 1870 Prussian siege. *34 blvd. de Vaugirard, 15e, tel. 01–42–79–23–45. Métro: Montparnasse. Admission 25F. Open Mon.–Sat. 10–6.*

MUSEE DE LA VIE ROMANTIQUE

See the memorabilia of woman writer, bohemian, and cross-dresser George Sand (1804–76) in the onetime studio of painter Ary Scheffer, where Chopin, Delacroix, Liszt, and other greats would gather in the evenings to swap artistic views and perform for one another. The museum occasionally hosts temporary exhibits, such as "The life and work of Ary Scheffer." On sunny days, take advantage of the opportunity to picnic on the patio. *16 rue Chaptal, 9e, tel. 01–48–74–95–38. Métro: Pigalle or St-Georges. Admission 27F. Open Tues.–Sun. 10–5:40.*

PAVILLON DE L'ARSENAL

In a spacious late 19th-century iron-and-glass hall, the Centre d'Urbanisme et d'Architecture de la Ville de Paris is devoted to documenting and exploring the buildings of Paris. Dominating the ground floor is the Grande Modèle, a 432-square-foot model of Paris, complete with interactive computer screens—you can direct a CD-ROM to display any of 30,000 images of the city and its buildings. Temporary exhibits take up the ground floor and upper loft, and a library (*see* Libraries *in* Chapter 1) provides art and architecture periodicals and books, plus 70,000 photographs of Paris. *21 blvd. Morland, 4e, tel. 01–42–76–33–97. Métro: Sully-Morland. Admission free. Open Tues.–Sat. 10:30–6:30, Sun. 11–7.*

WORLD HISTORY AND CULTURE

MUSEE DES ARTS AFRICAINS ET OCEANIENS

This art deco palace, with a monumental frieze on the facade detailing scenes from former colonies, was designed for the 1931 Colonial Exposition. The museum, first named the Musée des Colonies (Museum of the Colonies), was updated and renamed the Musée de l'Outre-Mer (Museum of France Overseas) after World War II—the "Virtues of French Colonization" display, however, still held a prominent position. In 1960 the museum settled upon its current name under the advice of France's Ministry of Cultural Affairs.

Today, the slightly run-down museum—its glorious Expo days are definitely over—is unjustly ignored by most visitors to Paris. The displays are divided by region and explained in French. The ground floor showcases South Pacific culture, notably from New Guinea, plus temporary exhibits often featuring contemporary African artists. The first floor turns to central African cultures, looking at great kingdoms in the Congo and Benin. The importance of funerary rites in this region, particularly among the Ashanti, is evidenced in death masks and other funerary objects. The top floor is dedicated to the Maghreb (Algeria, Tunisia, and Morocco), with some impressive Algerian jewelry that will instill new respect in you for your mostly intact earlobes and neck. In the basement, in a ditch that curators have tried hard to transform into a natural habitat, lurk crocodiles of the Nile. The calm aquarium surrounding the crocs is home to a second ditch filled with turtles. Psychedelic fish float around in the tanks that line the walls. A small library, open weekdays 10–6, is on the east side of the building. *293 av. Daumesnil, 12e, tel. 01–44–74–84–80. Métro: Porte Dorée. Admission 28F. Open Mon. and Wed.–Fri. 10–5:30, weekends 10–6.*

MUSEE NATIONAL DES ARTS ASIATIQUES—GUIMET

This enormous collection of religious and secular artwork from China, Japan, India, Indochina, Indonesia, and central Asia spans more than 3,000 years of history. Highlights include statues of Hindu gods and stunning finds from the Chinese Silk Route. Unfortunately, it's all under wraps until 1999 as part of a giant renovation program overseen by President Jacques Chirac, keen to foster his image as an Asian art buff. In the meantime, you can still visit the annex at 19 avenue d'Iéna, to see Buddhist images from China and Japan. *6 pl. d'Iéna/19 av. d'Iéna, 16e, tel. 01–47–23–61–65. Métro: Iéna. Admission 15F. Open Wed.–Mon. 9:45–6.*

The Musée de l'Homme's prize piece is Descartes's skull, the solution to the mind-body problem preserved forever in a little glass case.

NATURAL HISTORY

GRANDE GALERIE DE L'EVOLUTION

This natural history museum, popular with children, has a grand interior hall filled with stuffed bears, tigers, elephants, and whales. TV screens in front of comfortable leather chairs document the fascinating art of taxidermy. On Thursday nights, the museum hosts a debate, lecture, or film on some aspect of natural history, included in the admission price. *Jardin des Plantes, 36 rue Geoffroy St-Hilaire, 5e, tel. 01–40–79–39–39. Métro: Gare d'Austerlitz or Censier-Daubenton. Admission 40F. Open Wed.–Mon. 10–6 (Thurs. until 10).*

MUSEE DE L'HOMME

Visiting this anthropology museum in the Palais de Chaillot is like taking a trip around the world and through about three million years of history. Permanent exhibits show clothing, musical instruments, and other artifacts of the major cultures of the world (African, Asian, Middle Eastern, European, Native North and South American, indigenous Australian, South Pacific, Arctic) and fossil displays from prehistory to the present. Excellent temporary exhibits highlight topics like prehistoric funeral rites and traditions of Turkish households. The museum is slated for renovation, extension, and a new title (Musée des Arts Primaires) by 1999. *Pl. du Trocadéro, 16e, tel. 01–44–05–72–72. Métro: Trocadéro. Admission 30F. Open Wed.–Mon. 9:45–5:15.*

SCIENCE AND TECHNOLOGY

CITE DES SCIENCES ET DE L'INDUSTRIE

This museum at the Parc de la Villette (*see* Parks and Gardens, *below*) is a sleek glass-and-steel temple to everything industrial and scientific. Many of the exhibits are interactive. Give yourself at least half a day to see everything: It's three times the size of the Pompidou. The permanent exhibit is dedicated to scientific exploration, with multilingual explanations. Hands-on experiments include futuristic musical instruments, environmental manipulation, a simulated space voyage, and cutting-edge photography.

The second-floor planetarium is well worth a stop. The magnificent steel sphere in front of the exhibit building is the Géode cinema (tel. 01–40–05–80–00), which has the largest projection screen in existence that completely surrounds the spectators; tickets for films (usually nature flicks) are sold separately for 57F. *Parc de la Villette, 30 av. Corentin-Cariou, 19e, tel. 01–40–05–70–00. Métro: Porte de la Villette. Admission 50F. Open Tues.–Sun. 10–6.*

PALAIS DE LA DECOUVERTE

The worst thing about the Palace of Discovery, a museum in a back wing of the Grand Palais (*see above*), is the preponderance of grammar-school student groups. The best thing is its quality displays on all branches of science, from the solar system to the human brain. The exhibits are rarely hands-on, but they are informative and eye-catching. Planetarium shows cost an extra 13F. *Av. Franklin D. Roosevelt, 8e, tel. 01–40–74–80–00. Admission 27F. Open Tues.–Sat. 9:30–6, Sun. 10–7.*

HOUSES OF WORSHIP

Unfortunately, many of the important houses of worship in Paris tend to be dwarfed by the existence of big timers like the Cathédrale de Notre-Dame and the Basilique du Sacré-Coeur (*see* Major Attractions, *above*). Their isolation from the Kodak crowd and their own historical importance, however, make them more pleasant places to reflect, admire the architecture, or even lounge around naked sipping tea (although only in the Mosquée, and only in their Turkish baths, at that). Many of them offer free concerts; check *Pariscope* for listings.

CATHEDRALE DE ST-DENIS

The first major Gothic building in the world, the Cathédrale (also known as the Basilique) de St-Denis sits in the square of the eponymous suburb, north of Paris. Legend has it that at the foot of the Montmartre hill Paris's first bishop, St-Denis, had his head lopped off by angry Romans in AD 250. Not one to give up without a few dramatics, St-Denis picked up his head and made his way to the top of the hill before calling it quits at the site where the Cathédrale de St-Denis now looms. In the 12th century, Abbot Suger decided to build a church on the site according to his notion that God equaled light, and that daring expanses of glass allowing light into a cathedral would bring worshipers closer to the divine. The resulting cathedral—with loads of stained glass, high-pointed arches, and a rose window with the signs of the zodiac—would set the style for French cathedrals over the next four centuries.

Admission to the choir, ambulatory, and crypt allows access to 15 centuries of French royalty, including peeks at their mismatched bones and a delightful cabinet of embalmed hearts—one is even encased in a glass bulb. All of the favorites are here—Catherine de' Medici (depicted in one statue conspicuously young, dead, and naked), Marie-Antoinette (gently grazing her right nipple for all eternity), and Louis XIV (buried under a modest black stone). While checking out the corpses, note the foundations of previous crypts; the site has been used as a necropolis since Roman times. *Tel. 01–48–20–02–47. Métro: St-Denis–Basilique. Admission to choir, ambulatory, and crypt 28F. Crypt open summer, Mon.–Sat. 10–6:30, Sun. noon–6:30; winter, Mon.–Sat. 10–5:30, Sun. noon–5:30;. Sun. Mass at 7:30, 8:30, and 10 AM.*

EGLISE DE LA MADELEINE

Under sporadic construction for 80 years, the Eglise de la Madeleine (known as La Madeleine) finally opened its huge bronze doors in 1842, becoming one of the largest French neoclassical buildings. The church stands alone in the center of a busy thoroughfare as a proudly inflated, though unfaithful, version of the classic Greek temple. The loose interpretation was intentional: The overproportioned porticoes, the interior barrel vaults-cum-domes, and the opulent versions of the Ionic and Corinthian orders were meant to be Parisian one-uppings of anything Athens had to offer. Changing political moods continued to alter the building's purpose—a Greek basilica one day, a temple to Napoléon's glory another, a National Assembly hall the next. The building suffered from all these vacillations, as designers razed foundations and eliminated details; much of the church's gloominess results from one architect filling in the stained-glass windows of another. Nowadays the opulent interior witnesses lots of expensive concerts, as well as daily masses. And if sitting in the cool interior of a Catholic church is not enough to make you reflect upon your sins, try viewing the huge fresco of the Last Judgment above you.

A world away from the scale and politics of the church proper is the **crypt** (admission free), in whose intimate chapel weekday masses (7:30 and 8 AM) are held. The crypt is accessible from either the nave of the church or the northwest side of place de la Madeleine. *Pl. de la Madeleine, 8e, tel. 01–42–65–52–17. Métro: Madeleine. Open daily 8–7. Sun. mass at 8, 9, 10 (choral mass), and 11 AM, 12:30 and 6 PM.*

EGLISE ST-ETIENNE-DU-MONT

The ornate Gothic, Renaissance, *and* baroque facade of St-Etienne-du-Mont peeps out from behind the grandiose Panthéon. Inside you'll find subtle interpretations of various forms of the Gothic style: Arches blend into the nave's columns without capitals, and a double-spiral staircase ascends the only remaining rood screen in Paris. A stroll behind the altar reveals plaques marking the remains of Pascal, Racine, Marat, and St-Geneviève, who became the patron saint of Paris when her prayers rebuffed Attila the Hun in 451. A faded red engraving at the portal end of the nave indicates where Monseigneur Sibour, a 19th-century archbishop of Paris, was stabbed to death by a mad priest. Come here to look and to rest your weary feet in its cool interior. *1 rue St-Etienne-du-Mont, 5e, tel. 01–43–54–11–79. Métro: Cardinal-Lemoine. Sun. mass at 9 AM, 11 AM, and 6:45 PM.*

EGLISE ST-EUSTACHE

Right next door to the ultramodern Forum des Halles, St-Eustache presents a ponderous reminder that this area wasn't always all glitz and neon: The site was once the city's main marketplace and happening spot, which Emile Zola called "the belly of Paris." Over the years St-Eustache has seen lots of famous people: The composer Rameau was buried here; little Louis XIV took his first communion here; and both Richelieu and Molière were baptized here. Lesser notables have also left their mark: Much of the chapel and artwork were donated by the food guilds and merchants of the old Les Halles.

> *Few people realize that the huge head and hand in front of St-Eustache are modeled after those of Henry Miller.*

The structure was built over nearly a hundred years (1537–1632), at the tail end of the Gothic era, but it was during the 19th century, when Liszt directed his *Messe de Gran* here and Les Halles was still a real market, that the cathedral was at its height. The bland reconstructed facade is a letdown, but the gloomy interior will intrigue architecture buffs with its uncertain lurch from late Gothic toward Renaissance. The presence of a Rubens painting in one of the side chapels also potentially salvages the church's appeal, except that no one is quite able to prove which Rubens did it. Do look for the painting *The Departure of the Fruits and Vegetables from the Heart of Paris* (1968), Raymond Mason's animated and very unchurchlike interpretation of the closing of Les Halles marketplace. *Pl. René-Cassin, 1er, tel. 01–42–36–31–05. Métro: Les Halles. Open daily 8:30–7 in winter, 8:30–8 in summer. Sun. mass at 8:30, 9:30, and 11 AM and 6 PM.*

EGLISE ST-GERMAIN-DES-PRES

The oldest church in Paris, St-Germain-des-Prés traces its roots to the 6th century, when then-archbishop Germanus (now known as St-Germain) built an altar to St-Symphorien on land left to the Benedictine monks by Childebert I. Though most of the present church dates from the 12th and 13th centuries, the purported remains of the original altar still stand near the south side of the entrance. The abbey became one of the great centers of learning in France, with its complex of buildings stretching from the Seine well into the present-day Quartier Latin. Here the Benedictines busied themselves completing the first French translation of the Bible in 1530 and amassing a library that would be appropriated during the Revolution to found the Bibliothèque Nationale (*see* Libraries *in* Chapter 1). Almost all of the abbey buildings were torn down in the years after the Revolution, and a renovation in the 1950s removed the paint on the ceiling ribbing. Some of the remains of René Descartes (his heart, to be precise) have found peace in the seventh chapel. The church now holds a series of usually choral concerts, alas, rarely free (80F–200F). *Pl. St-Germain-des-Prés, 6e, tel. 01–43–25–41–71, 01–44–62–70–90 for concert info. Métro: St-Germain-des-Prés. Sun. mass at 9, 10, and 11:15 AM and 5 (in Spanish) and 7 PM.*

TURKISH DELIGHTS

For a decadent experience, spend an afternoon at the hammam (39 rue Geoffroy-St-Hilaire, 5e, tel. 01-43-31-38-20), the Turkish baths in la Mosquée. Lie around naked in one of the steam rooms or in the bathing area, listening to Arabic music and drinking mint tea (10F). To maximize your pleasure, bring something to slather all over your body, a sponge, and some water so you don't get dehydrated. Women are admitted Monday and Wednesday through Saturday; men on Tuesday and Sunday. Admission is 85F and towel rental is 12F. The baths are open Wednesday through Monday 10-9 and Tuesday 2-9.

EGLISE ST-SEVERIN

This ivy-covered Gothic isle of calm dates from the 11th century, though much of what you see comes from 16th-century construction efforts and 18th- and 19th-century renovations. The double aisle of the ambulatory has a subterranean feel, with the ribbing of the vaults looking more as if it were holding up the earth than soaring toward the heavens. The column behind the altar is twisted like a contorted tree trunk. The church is at its best at night, when the only lighting comes from the base of the columns and from behind the altar. Daylight, however, has the advantage of showing off the stained-glass windows (1966–70) depicting the Seven Facets of the Sacrament. Occasional free concerts are performed on Sundays. *3 rue des Prêtres-St-Séverin, 5e, tel. 01–43–25–96–63. Métro: St-Michel. Sun. mass at 10 AM, noon, and 6 PM.*

EGLISE ST-SULPICE

Facing a tranquil square not far from bustling boulevard St-Germain, St-Sulpice is an unusual departure from most Parisian churches: The double-story loggia with freestanding columns was the first example of French neoclassicism on a monumental scale. The facade was designed in 1736 (after most of the church had already been built) by painter Jean-Nicolas Servandoni, who conceived the scheme with little regard for stodgy architectural tradition. His right tower was never finished, lending the facade quirky asymmetry. Although not the most attractive church in Paris, there are some impressive Delacroix murals in the first chapel on the right, as well as a regular stream of free concerts of the recently restored 18th-century organ. The fountain in front matches the church in hulking scale, but both are softened by nighttime lighting. Star-watcher alert: Catherine Deneuve lives on the square. *Pl. St-Sulpice, 6e, tel. 01–46–33–21–78. Métro: St-Sulpice. Sun. mass at 7, 9, 10:15 AM, noon, and 6:45 PM. ½-hr organ concerts Sun. 11:30–noon; call for other scheduled concerts.*

LA MOSQUEE

Behind the Jardin des Plantes, the city's main mosque is the religious and intellectual center of the Parisian Muslim community. Built in the 1920s as a memorial to North African Muslims who died fighting for France in World War I, its modest white walls enclose colorful, intricately tiled courtyards, which surround the prayer room, *hammam* (baths), and an equally opulent tearoom (*see* Salons de Thé *in* Chapter 4), all designed in the tradition of North African secular architecture. Upstairs from the peaceful public gardens are institutes devoted to the study of Islam and Arab cultures.

Since the prayer room is used continually throughout the day (daily prayer times are posted inside), you should be aware of some basic customs before entering. Cover all skin above the elbow and above the calf and remove your shoes; the more traditional insist that you also cleanse your face, neck, ears, arms, and hands with water. The carved wooden altar indicates the direction of Mecca; if you sit, point your feet away. Non-Muslims are never allowed in during daily calls to prayer, and at other times, depending on the orthodoxy of the person nearest the door, women, non-Muslims, or both may be asked to view the prayer room only from the courtyard. *Pl. du Puits-de-l'Ermite, 5e, tel. 01–36–68–70–05. Métro: Monge. Admission to entire complex 15F; garden free. Open for tours Sat.–Thurs. 10–noon and 2– 6:30; in winter, until 5:30.*

DEAD FOLK

From carefully tended plots of crumbling tombstones to eerie, skull-filled channels leading deep into the bowels of the city, Paris has been perfecting its postmortem practices since the Revolution. More than just eternal hangouts for famous dead folk, Paris's cemeteries also have tree-lined cobblestone paths, well-tended flowers, and ample benches where mortals can sit and contemplate the erosive quality of time. Seeking the ultimate mortal experience? Venture through the Catacombes—miles and miles of bones and grinning skulls ensconced in dark, dank passages.

Père-Lachaise (*see* Major Attractions, *above*), Montmartre, and Montparnasse hog the limelight, but there are plenty of enchantingly haunting burial grounds where the famed can remain a little more incognito. The intimate, high-walled **Cimetière de Passy** (2 rue du Commandant-Schlœsing, 16e, métro Trocadéro) is particularly inviting; it's also the everlasting home of French impressionist **Edouard Manet** (1832–83), and modern music pioneers **Gabriel Fauré** (1845–1924) and **Claude Debussy** (1862– 1918).

For a more offbeat funerary excursion, head to the **Cimetière des Chiens** (Dog Cemetery, along the Seine, Asnières-sur-Seine, métro Gabriel-Péri). The privately owned pet cemetery has hundreds of lap-dogs, cats, and even a wolf and bear. On the second-highest point in all of Paris you'll find the **Cimetière de Belleville** (40 rue du Télégraphe, 20e, métro Télégraphe), with no famous folks, but a fabulous view. *All city cemeteries open Mar. 16–Nov. 5, weekdays 8–6, Sat. 8:30–6, Sun. 9–6; Nov. 6–Mar. 15, weekdays 8–5:30, Sat. 8:30–5:30, Sun. 9–5:30.*

LES CATACOMBES

"Arrête! C'est ici l'Empire de la Mort" ("Stop! This is the Empire of Death"). This message scrawled at the entrance was enough to convince German troops in World War II to leave promptly before they guessed that Resistance fighters used the tunnels in the catacombs as a base. This dire warning now welcomes you after a winding descent through dark, clammy passages to Paris's principal ossuary and most disturbing collection of human remains. Bones from the notorious Cimetière des Innocents, a stinky, overcrowded plot of common graves under what is now place des Innocents, were the first to be transplanted here in 1786, when decomposing bodies started seeping into neighboring cellars, bringing swarms of ravenous rats with them. Other churchyard cemeteries, also facing unhealthy conditions, were happy to dispose of the decomposed in the catacombs. The legions of bones dumped here are arranged not by owner but by type—witness the rows of skulls, stacks of tibias, and piles of spinal disks. There are also some bizarre attempts at bone art, like skulls arranged in the shape of hearts. It's macabre and makes you feel quite . . . mortal. Among the bones in here are those of **Mirabeau** (1749– 91), the Revolution leader who found an early resting place in the Panthéon (*see below*) but was trans-ferred when his ideas became unfashionable; keeping him company are the remains of fellow rebels, many of them brought fresh from the guillotine. Sixteenth-century satirist and writer **Rabelais** (1490– 1553) was transplanted from the former cemetery at the Eglise St-Paul–St-Louis, and famous courtesan **Madame de Pompadour** (1721–64) is mixed in with the rabble after a lifetime spent as the mistress to Louis XV. Be prepared to walk long distances when you come here—the tunnels stretch for kilometers, and the only light comes from the flashlight that you bring yourself. *1 pl. Denfert-Rochereau, 14e, tel. 01–43–22–47–63. Métro: Denfert-Rochereau. Admission 27F. Open Tues.–Fri. 2–4, weekends 9–11 and 2–4.*

CIMETIERE DE MONTMARTRE

Though it's crammed underneath a busy traffic bridge, the Montmartre cemetery still manages to be a beautiful resting place, with trees hanging over crumbling stones and the occasional prowling cat. A

THAT WHICH LURKS BELOW

Since the Middle Ages, Paris has been abused, prostituted, and exploited for her earthy treasures—mostly limestone, clay, and sand quarried with the use of a 300-km (186-mi) labyrinth of passageways and immense caverns beneath the streets of Paris. Mining didn't stop until the early 1800s, despite ominous warnings that the weight of the city was too great for the caverns to support. And it wasn't until whole streets began collapsing (taking with them buildings, trees, and poodles) that Parisians wised up, mining was stopped, and most passages were closed off. Today, the greatest danger is not a cave-in but getting lost: All the tunnels look virtually the same.

The subterranean "égouts" (sewers) of Paris were immortalized in "Les Misérables," in which Jean Valjean used them to escape, and in "The Phantom of the Opera," which places the phantom's lair in the depths below the Paris Opéra. The Communards used the quarries in 1871 to flee from approaching government troops; and in 1944 occupying Germans set up offices here with lights, pumped-in air, and communication lines. Legally, the passageways are off-limits, but that doesn't mean they aren't still used for late-night carousing.

smaller and more peaceful version of the Cimetière du Père-Lachaise (*see above*), it has the advantage of not being mobbed by Jim Morrison fans. The neighborhood was once home to a lively art scene, but today the dead artists draw more attention than the breathing ones. Among the former is **François Truffaut** (1932–84), who turned from critic to filmmaker with *Les 400 Coups* (1959), the flick that kicked off the French New Wave. (Ironically, Truffaut was once booted out of the cemetery, while still living, for trying to film here without permission.) You can also seek out composer **Jacques Offenbach** (1819–80)—the Montmartre soirée scene is forever indebted to his legendary cancan.

Other colorful residents include painters **Edgar Degas** (1834–1917) and **Jean-Honoré Fragonard** (1732–1806), writers **Stendhal** (1783–1842) and **Alexandre Dumas** *fils* (1824–95), composer **Hector Berlioz** (1803–69), Russian ballet dancer **Vaslav Nijinski** (1890–1950), physicist **Jean-Bernard Foucault** (1819–68), and German poet **Heinrich Heine** (1797–1856). **Emile Zola** (1840–1902) had a brief stint here—until he was moved to the Panthéon (*see below*), where he has remained. If you don't want to get lost among the tombstones, pay close attention to the map next to the front gate. *20 av. Rachel, 18e. Métro: Blanche or Place de Clichy.*

CIMETIERE DU MONTPARNASSE

A leafy canopy hides the modern buildings looming above this peaceful cemetery of flat, orderly rows of tombstones. Residents include angst-ridden existentialist **Jean-Paul Sartre** (1905–80), who is buried with longtime companion and early feminist **Simone de Beauvoir** (1908–86). **Charles Baudelaire** (1821–67) is memorialized here with a striking sculpture; the poet reclines nearby in a tomb with other members of his family. Avant-garde playwright, novelist, and poet, **Samuel Beckett** (1906–89) also has a place among the intellectuals here. American actress **Jean Seberg** (1938–79) became France's sweetheart when she relocated to Paris and started adding her girlish accent to French films like Jean-Luc Godard's *Breathless*. Admirers of sculptor **Constantin Brancusi** (1876–1957) can pay their respects twice: once at his grave, and again at his famous sculpture *The Kiss,* which portrays the close bodies of two lovers. You'll find the couple hovering over **Tanosa Gassevskaia** (1888–1910), who killed herself over unrequited love.

The eternal party also includes author **Guy de Maupassant** (1850–93), theater-of-the-absurd guru **Eugène Ionesco** (1912–94), composer **Camille Saint-Saëns** (1835–1921), American artist **Man Ray** (1890–1976), musician **Serge Gainsbourg** (1928–1991), Russian sculptor **Ossip Zadkine** (1890–1967), anarchist **Pierre-Joseph Proudhon** (1809–65), carmaker **André Citroën** (1879–1935), and **Alfred Dreyfus** (1859–1935), the Jewish army captain falsely convicted of spying for the Germans. *3 blvd. Edgar-Quinet, 14e. Métro: Raspail or Edgar Quinet.*

PANTHEON

Official home to the country's late and great, the Panthéon was originally intended to replace nearby St-Etienne-du-Mont (*see* Houses of Worship, *above*) as home to the relics of St-Geneviève. Construction began in 1755, topped by Germain Soufflot's dome on a scale never before seen—a soaring master-piece of technical achievement. Soufflot had the vision thing all right, but he was a terrible engineer, and the building has been falling apart ever since. The original windows had to be filled in, interior columns braced, the dome restructured; in 1985 falling stones prompted its temporary closure. The structure was finished in 1790, 10 years after the death of the architect, and just in time for . . . the Revolution. Thereafter, the building alternated as a church and a nondenominational burial ground—until the funeral procession of Victor Hugo came rolling up from the Arc de Triomphe into the crypt, cementing its status as the tomb for French VIPs.

The remains of Nobel Prize–winning scientist Marie Curie were moved to the Panthéon on April 19, 1995, making her the first woman to earn a berth among France's great dead citizens solely on merit (Berthelot's wife is here with her husband).

Victor Hugo (1802–85), the prolific author and social chroni-cler, wasn't the first resident of the Panthéon; he was joining philosophers **Jean-Jacques Rousseau** (1712–78) and **Voltaire** (1694–1778). The heart—yep, we mean heart—of **Léon Gambetta** (1838–82), a leader of the Paris Commune (*see* box, *above*) and eponym for countless French streets, sits quietly in its little vase. Novelist **Emile Zola** (1840–1902) was a populist intellectual and a supporter of the working class. His courageous exposure of an army cover-up during the Dreyfus Affair, and outspoken condemnation of its attendant anti-Semitism, brought out as many supporters as blinkered protesters to his funeral. **Louis Braille** (1809–52) was considered worthy of a spot in the Panthéon, too—100 years after his death—except for his all-important hands, which remain in his parish churchyard. Blind, Braille taught himself to read by feeling embossed Roman letters, eventually devising the system of raised dots we know today. Resis-tance leader and Nazi victim **Jean Moulin** (1899–1943) has also found an eternal place in the base-ment of the Panthéon. Climb to the top of the dome for an ethereal view of Paris, or just rest a moment on the main floor to watch Foucault's pendulum swing back and forth across the nave. *Pl. du Panthéon, 5e, tel. 01–43–54–34–51. RER: Luxembourg. Admission 32F. Open daily 9:30–6:30.*

PARKS AND GARDENS

If you need a rest from Paris's bustling streets and just want a place to sit down without having to order a cup of coffee, over 350 green spots come to the rescue. Watch for kids floating boats in fountains, gos-siping old ladies, poodle-walkers, and randy French men preying on tourists. Two large *bois* (woods) on the western and eastern edges of the city make you feel like you've escaped Paris altogether. Parks are either *à l'anglaise,* which means they're artfully landscaped like English gardens, or *style français,* which means everything's even more artfully planted in neat, symmetrical rows. In most parks, you can stroll along paths and read on benches, but stay the hell off the grass—the *gendarmes* (police) will not hesi-tate to lecture (and pursue) trespassers. Exceptions to the rule include the user-friendly grass in the Bois de Boulogne, the Bois de Vincennes, the Parc des Buttes-Chaumont, and the Parc de la Villette. Most parks open at dawn and are locked at dusk.

PICK A PARK

BASSIN DE L'ARSENAL. This small canal-side park, complete with a café-restaurant, is a peaceful spot to eat lunch and watch the boats. Napoléon created the canal to increase water movement through the city, and Jacques Chirac commissioned the park in the '80s. 12e. Métro: Bastille.

PARC ANDRÉ-CITROËN. Named for the automobile magnate, this park has greenhouses, shallow waterways, carpetlike lawns you can play on, and trees arranged like an army regiment. 15e. Métro: Balard.

PARC GEORGES-BRASSENS. Once an abattoir (slaughterhouse), this park has secluded paths, rocks to climb, Ping-Pong, and a theater. There's also a huge used-book market on weekends. 15e. Métro: Porte de Vanves.

PARC MONCEAU. In the posh 8th arrondissement, this garden was the setting for love scenes in Zola's "La Curée." Besides au pairs pushing strollers, you'll find fake grottoes, made-to-look-ancient Greek sculptures, a waterfall, and the Musée Cernuschi—a small museum of Chinese art. 8e. Métro: Monceau.

SQUARE DU VERT-GALANT. Created in 1884, this square on the tip of the Ile de la Cité is the place to go to smooch, catch a sunset, and watch the Seine flow by. 1er. Métro: Pont-Neuf.

BOIS DE BOULOGNE

Stretched along the western side of the 16e arrondissement, the Bois de Boulogne—"Le Bois"—is the largest park in Paris and has played an important role in Parisian life for the past 100 years. It owes its existence to Louis XI, who protected the park's game with his personal guards; Napoléon III shaped it into its present form, modeling the previously unlandscaped grounds after London's Hyde Park. The late 19th-century Bois became one of Paris's great social hot spots, a place to ride disdainfully on horseback or in carriages watching everybody watching everybody else. It was the playground of the wealthy, with polo fields, a racetrack, tennis lawns, and the court that eventually became the **Stade Roland-Garros** of French Open fame (*see* When to Go, Festivals *in* Chapter 1).

The Bois is such a convenient and pleasant place to get away from the crowds of Paris that only the Eiffel Tower has more annual visitors. You are allowed to sit on (most of) the lawns, climb the trees, and do all those other park-type things you never thought you'd miss until you visited the Jardin du Luxembourg (*see below*). Boating on **Lac Inférieur** is an integral part of many a Parisian Sunday; you can rent a boat here for 45F per hour (200F deposit). Or take the ferry to the lake's islands, well worth the 7F round-trip ticket. The café out there serves expensive snacks and 17F cafés; you may want to bring a picnic and sit under the cherry trees with the strutting peacocks. Other attractions include the **Jardin d'Acclimatation,** a hands-on kiddie park-zoo-playground at the north end of the park, and the incredible flower collection of the **Parc de Bagatelle.**

Families and nice folks frequent the Bois during the day, but at night sleaze creeps down the access roads and into the park. The Bois has always been the city's prostitution center; it is estimated that over five million francs—about $1 million—change hands here every night. Unless you yearn for the attentions of a transvestite, her/his pimp, and a police officer dogging you all, avoid the park at night.

The park is huge and can be difficult to navigate, so look at the métro station map carefully to orient yourself. The métro stops at the perimeter, and buses (like the 52 and 241 from Porte d'Auteuil or 244 from Porte Maillot) cross the Bois. You can also rent bikes (25F per half hour, 40F per hour) from the stand at the entrance to the Jardin d'Acclimatation and close to the Pavillion Royal, on the northwest of Lac Inférieur. *16e. Métro: Porte Maillot, Porte Dauphine, or Porte d'Auteuil. RER: Avenue Foch.*

BOIS DE VINCENNES

Southeast of the city is another huge, relatively unmanicured, wooded area. You can rent a rowboat on either of two major lakes (30F per half hour, 55F per hour), **Lac des Minimes** or **Lac Daumesnil**, at which you can also rent bikes (25F per half hour, 40F per hour). Also near Lac Daumesnil are the **Musée des Arts Africains et Océaniens** (*see* Museums, *above*), a zoo, and a Buddhist center, including a Tibetan Buddhist temple where you can meditate on Saturday and Sunday at 5 PM (métro Porte-Dorée). The **Château de Vincennes** (métro Château-de-Vincennes) was a long time coming: Started by Philippe VI in 1337, it wasn't completed until his grandson, Charles V, rolled around. The château served as, among other things, a country home for François I, and, later, a fortified bastion under Emperor Napoléon I—his failing empire's last stronghold against the invading western European powers. The proud general on guard, Daumesnil, refused to capitulate to the Russians, British, Austrians, and Prussians, waiting until he could surrender to a Frenchman. The château now houses a museum. The **Parc Floral,** near the château, features diverse displays of aquatic and land-bound flowers. The **Zoo de Vincennes** (métro Porte-Dorée), open daily 9–5 (35F), attracts hordes of schoolchildren who want to gape at wild animals. A look at the exotic birds in "virtual" freedom is well worth the trip. *12e. Métro: Château-de-Vincennes, Porte-Dorée, or Liberté. RER: Nogent-sur-Marne.*

Paris has not one but TWO tiny models of the Statue of Liberty (a likeness of sculptor Frédéric Bartholdi's mom): one in the west gardens of the Jardin du Luxembourg, the other on the Allée des Cygnes (15e, métro Charles-Michels).

JARDIN DU LUXEMBOURG

The Jardin du Luxembourg possesses all that is unique and befuddling about Parisian parks: swarms of pigeons, cookie-cutter trees, ironed-and-pressed dirt walkways, and immaculate lawns meant for admiring, not touching. The tree- and bench-lined paths offer a reprieve from the incessant bustle of the Quartier Latin, as well an opportunity to discover the dotty old women and smooching university students who once found their way into Doisneau photographs. Somewhat austere during the colder months, the garden becomes intoxicating as spring fills the flowerbeds with daffodils, tulips, and hyacinths; the pools teeming with boats nudged along by children (17F per hour to rent), and the paths with Parisians thrusting their noses toward the sun. The park's northern boundary is dominated by the **Palais du Luxembourg,** surrounded by a handful of well-armed guards; they are protecting the senators who have been deliberating in the palace since 1958. Feel free to move the green chairs around to create your own picnic area or people-watching site.

Although the garden may seem purely French, the original 17th-century planning took its inspiration from Italy. When Maria de' Medici acquired the estate of the deceased Duke of Luxembourg in 1612, she decided to turn his mansion into a version of the Florentine Medici home, the Palazzo Pitti. She ended up with something more Franco-Italian than strictly Florentine. The land behind the palace was loosely modeled on the Boboli Gardens. The landscapers, like the architects, didn't design a true version of the Florentine garden, opting for the emerging style of heavy-handed human manipulation of nature—linear vistas, box-trimmed trees, and color-coordinated flowerbeds—thereby further defining the "French" garden. A tiny corner of the park still possesses that nature-on-the-brink-of-overwhelming-civilization look that was the trademark of the Renaissance Italian garden—namely, the intentionally overgrown cluster of trees and bushes lining the 1624 **Fontaine de Medicis.** The park captured the hearts of Parisians when it became public after the Revolution; thousands turned out in the mid-1800s to prevent a Haussmann-directed boulevard from being built through its middle.

One of the great attractions of the park is the **Théâtre des Marionnettes,** where on Wednesday, Saturday, and Sunday at 3 and 4 PM you can catch one of the classic *guignols* (marionette shows) for 22F. The wide-mouthed kiddies, though, are the real attraction; their expressions of utter surprise, despair, or glee have fascinated the likes of Henri Cartier-Bresson and François Truffaut.

And finally, for those eager to burn off those pastry breakfasts: The Jardin de Luxembourg has a well-maintained trail around the perimeter, and it is one of the few public places the French will be seen in athletic clothes. It takes an average jogger 20 minutes to get all the way around, and water fountains are strategically placed along the way. Men of all ages are also strategically placed; their comments to female runners are irritating, but otherwise this is a great escape. *Bordered by rues de Vaugirard, de Medicis, Guynemer, and Auguste Comte and blvd. St-Michel, 6e. RER: Luxembourg.*

JARDIN DU PALAIS ROYAL

It's odd that the "Royal Palace" is the only palace in the city that never sheltered a monarch. Cardinal Richelieu laid claim to the land, buying up property until he found himself with a palace. When he died in 1642 he left the digs to the crown. Anne of Austria promptly took advantage of the gift, moving here in 1643 to escape the stuffy Louvre. Five years later, La Fronde, a period of unrest between nobility and royalty, broke out; Anne fled Paris, and the Orléans family took her place, sticking around until the Revolution. The last Orléans, Philippe Egalité, expanded the complex in a clever attempt to make some francs by selling lots and building town houses. It quickly became a fashionable place to live, and the ground level filled with cafés and bordellos. The garden became a public forum for voicing complaints against the government, ultimately witnessing many of the key meetings leading up to the Revolution. People gathered here on July 14, 1789, before stomping off to the Bastille.

The Jardin du Palais Royal as we know it today is devoid of bordellos, and little old men talking to sparrows have replaced the dissenters. You can still order a cup of coffee from one of the cafés overlooking the grounds, and it's a good place to take a break. The park itself is the picture of Parisian romance, with lines of trees, a dramatic central fountain, and benches for snuggling couples. The southern end of the park, however, receives the most attention—and controversy. In truly Parisian style, in 1986 artist Daniel Buren decided to juxtapose the traditional with the ultramodern. His black and white columns rise up from water flowing beneath the courtyard, accompanied by fountains of rotating silver balls. At night, airport runway lights glow green and red, and blue lights illuminate the columns. Although conservative Parisians shudder at the sight of all this modernity in royal surroundings, skateboarders and roller skaters give the smooth concrete the thumbs-up. *1er. Métro: Palais Royal–Musée du Louvre. Open Apr.–May, daily 7 AM–10 PM; June–Aug., daily 7 AM–11 PM; Sept., daily 7 AM–9:30 PM; Oct.–Mar., daily 7 AM–8:30 PM.*

JARDIN DES PLANTES

In 1626 Louis XIII intended for this park to become "The King's Garden of Medicinal Herbs." Today, the Jardin des Plantes is the city's official botanical garden and houses over 10,000 varieties of plants (all tidily arranged in little rows and labeled, of course), a zoo (the animals also tidily arranged—in 19th-century cages), a vivarium (reptiles), huge collections of rocks and insects, the **Musée National d'Histoire Naturelle,** and lots of traffic from students attending the nearby Ecole Normale Supérieure and Jussieu. With the Gare d'Austerlitz along its southeastern edge, the park is a great discovery if you have a long wait for your train, as is the **Open-Air Sculpture Garden** between the Jardin des Plantes and the Seine. *57 rue Cuvier, 5e. Métro: Jussieu, Monge, or Gare d'Austerlitz. Admission to museums, zoo, and vivarium 15F–40F.*

JARDIN DES TUILERIES

A stroll around this stately (albeit dusty) onetime royal garden is like an abbreviated monument tour: You'll see the Louvre, place de la Concorde, the Musée d'Orsay, the Eiffel Tower, and the Seine. Look in one direction down the Champs-Elysées all the way to the Arc de Triomphe, and in the other down a long, orderly expanse of garden to the Louvre. A palace by the same name had been around for centuries when Catherine de' Medici arrived in the mid-16th century, bringing Renaissance influences from Tuscany and coercing architect Philibert de l'Orme to design a private park; the result was the first classical French garden in the structured, manicured style we know today. A century later, André "Versailles" Le Nôtre gave the place a face-lift before it was opened to the public; it instantly became the fashionable center for strolling and showing off. The palace was burned down during the Commune of 1871, but the gardens stuck it out.

Besides small lawns you can't sit on and a huge pick-up scene for gay men along the Seine, the Tuileries has a series of women sculpted by **Aristide Maillol** (1861–1944) as well as a place to rest your weary feet after the trek down the Champs-Elysées. Hanging by the big fountain near place de la Concorde is about as relaxing as it gets in the heart of Paris. If the summer heat makes you delirious, take refuge in one of the two art museums at the west end, the Orangerie and the Jeu de Paume (for both, *see* Museums, *above*). *1er. Métro: Tuileries or Concorde. Open summer, daily 8–9; winter, 8–7.*

PARC DES BUTTES-CHAUMONT

The Parc des Buttes-Chaumont wins the prize for most dramatic transformation: It's been a quarry for plaster of paris, a garbage dump, a slaughterhouse, and refuse pile for dead horses. A treatise on the merits of simulated nature, this park near Belleville now has steep lawns, a mountain made of cement and rock, and a waterway and grotto. One of the most comfortable places in the city to collapse, the hill and the small lake are a welcome relief after you've seen one too many stodgy French gardens. The park has gorgeous views of the city below, ducks to feed, and a small neoclassical temple at the top of the hill. This little oasis is brought to you by Napoléon III and Baron Haussmann, who wanted to give the working folk a green spot where they could take their families. Kids (big and small) will enjoy a stop at the **Théâtre de Guignols** (puppet theater) on the northern side of the park. Shows start daily (weather permitting) at 3 PM and cost 10F. *Bordered by rues de Crimée, Manin, and Botzaris, 19e. Métro: Buttes-Chaumont.*

> *Running across the waterway at the Parc des Buttes-Chaumont you'll find the Pont des Suicidés (Suicide Bridge). So many distraught young lovers leapt from here to a watery death that a barricade was put up.*

PARC MONTSOURIS AND CITE UNIVERSITAIRE

Another Haussmann project, Parc Montsouris almost succeeds in convincing you that you have found an arcadian paradise. The hilly park (its name means mouse mountain) is filled with sloping fields, clusters of stately trees, and a pond. Unfortunately, abandoned railway tracks and active RER lines cross the park, and traffic speeds around its perimeter. Across boulevard Jourdan from the park is the Cité Universitaire, a collection of residences built by foreign countries to house their nationals while they study at Parisian universities. Funded by John D. Rockefeller in the 1920s, each of the 35 buildings was designed with a world's fair–like attitude toward national identity and architectural design. Le Corbusier designed two houses, the Fondation Suisse and Fondation Franco-Brasil, and both continue to attract architectural pilgrims. The cité is a nice complement to the Parc Montsouris across the street, and you can run around, throw a Frisbee, or climb a tree without being pestered by park police. *14e. RER: Cité Universitaire.*

PARC DE LA VILLETTE

What was Paris's largest complex of slaughterhouses and stockyards is now a giant park with tons of high-tech buildings and toys to run around in and play with. The sheep that were once driven through this neighborhood on their way to becoming mutton left in the mid-1970s; you can check out photos documenting these days at the **Maison de la Villette** (tel. 01–40–03–75–10; closed Mon.). Most people come here to enjoy the lawns, nifty mega-playgrounds, and bike paths. The largest park this side of the Bois de Boulogne, it's also the city's most fun. There are things like Claes Oldenberg's oversize *Buried Bicycle* to ogle, a monstrous dragon slide, catwalks, and no fewer than 11 special theme gardens, including the meditative **Jardin des Bambous** (Bamboo Garden), the steamy **Jardin des Brouillards** (Fog Garden), the **Jardin des Miroirs** (Mirror Garden), the **Jardin des Vents** (Wind Garden), and the **Jardin des Frayeurs Enfantines** (Garden of Childhood Frights). Park architect Bernard Tschumi divided the area into a 5- by 9-unit grid and put a big red steel contraption called a *folie* (whimsical building) at each grid point. Each has some sort of artistic or other purpose—like the *folie vidéo*, the *folie arts plastique*, or the *Quick folly*, which sells nasty fast food.

The park is bordered by the canal St-Denis to the west and is split by the canal de l'Ourcq through the middle; the information folie (211 av. Jean Jaurès, tel. 01–40–03–75–03, métro Porte de Pantin), near the confluence of the canals, dispenses maps and general park info. To the north of the canal de l'Ourcq is the **Cité des Sciences et de l'Industrie** museum and the **Géode** cinema (*see* Museums, *above*), as

THE REVOLUTION

In the late 18th century, the aristocracy was frantically trying to hold on to its privileges; the middle class was frustrated by its lack of power; and the peasants were furious about being taxed into oblivion. It all exploded with the French Revolution. The bourgeois members of the government kicked things off on June 17, 1789, by proclaiming themselves a new legislative body called the National Assembly. On July 14, Parisians of every political stripe joined the fray, storming the Bastille in search of arms for the citizen militia. During the next two years, aristocrats fled the country in droves—their property was being taken away, and they figured their heads would be next. (Some were right.) Louis XVI was forced to leave his palace in Versailles and slum it at the Tuileries, where he could be watched. He and his wife, Marie "Let them eat cake" Antoinette, later tried to flee France but were caught.

In September 1791, the National Assembly adopted a constitution, all but shutting Louis out. Unfortunately for him, that wasn't enough for the radical antimonarchists, the Jacobins, who eventually gained control. They tried and executed the king in January 1793 at place de la Révolution (place de la Concorde). Throughout the year, the newly appointed Committee of Public Safety manned the guillotines, beheading thousands of "enemies of the Revolution" during a period known as "The Terror." Revolutionary ideals seemed to fall by the wayside as more and more heroes of the Revolution were tried on unlikely treason charges. In 1794 the frenzy reached such a pitch that Jacobin leader Maximilien Robespierre lost his own head. With Robespierre out of the way, the quasi-tyrannical Directory of Five took over until Napoléon Bonaparte worked his way up from General of the Interior to First Consul and ultimately "Emperor of the French."

well as the semiburied Argonaute, a 1950s nuclear submarine. To the south of the canal de l'Ourcq is the slaughterhouse-turned-concert-venue **Grande Halle,** which hosts jazz festivals and other big events, and the **Théâtre Paris-Villette** (tel. 01–42–02–02–68). Nearby is the **Cité de la Musique,** an assortment of theaters and recital rooms, including a museum of musical instruments and the campus of the Conservatoire National Supérieur de Musique et de Danse (*see* Opera, Classical Music, and Dance *in* Chapter 5). On the western corner is the **Zénith** (*see* Live Music *in* Chapter 5), a major concert hall hosting big-name international acts. *19e. Métro: Porte de la Villette or Porte de Pantin.*

NEIGHBORHOODS

One of the many names for Paris is *la cité aux cent villages*—the city of a hundred villages. The modernization of the 19th century meant grand boulevards and imposing government buildings cut wide swaths into these villages, sometimes obliterating them entirely. With the waves of immigration from former colonial territories in this century, new "villages" have formed within Paris. To really experience the hidden Paris, explore the winding side streets; they frequently squirm through tiny communities that huddle in the shelter of modern high-rises.

The following neighborhoods are ordered alphabetically. If you'd rather tackle things geographically, the neighborhoods on the Right Bank are the Bastille, Belleville, Bercy, the Champs-Elysées, La Défense, the Gares de l'Est and du Nord, Les Halles and Beaubourg, Louvre to Opéra, the Marais, and Montmartre. On the Left Bank you'll find Montparnasse, the Quartier Latin, St-Germain-des-Prés, and Tolbiac. In the heart of the city are the Seine's two islands: Ile de la Cité and the smaller Ile St-Louis.

BASTILLE

You probably won't feel compelled to visit place de la Bastille, at the intersection of the 4e, 11e, and 12e arrondissements, just to see the monument erected here—it's just a column, after all. But as you'll almost certainly end up in the neighborhood surrounding it, either going to bars or shopping, you may at least want to have a vague idea of what once happened here.

The original Bastille was a fortress built during the reign of Charles V with the works: a moat, drawbridges, and towers. It was designed to defend the eastern entrance to Paris, but was gradually transformed into a prison for political offenders. On July 14, 1789, thousands of French citizens, frustrated by Louis XVI's hapless rule, tore apart the Bastille prison to liberate the contents of the meager arsenal (rather than its seven prisoners, as you might expect). Nowadays, all you see around the place de la Bastille are swarms of Parisian drivers circling a pole with an angel on top of it—the **Colonne de Juillet** (July Column), erected in memory of the 504 victims who died during the "Trois Glorieuses" revolution of 1830. These victims are supposedly buried in a vault underneath the column. The victims of the 1848 revolution were also buried here and added to the inscription on the column.

The only folks likely to storm the Bastille these days are Opéra-goers lining up for seats at the **Opéra Bastille** (see Opera, Classical Music, and Dance in Chapter 5) and Parisians out on the town. Today the area around the former prison is gentrified: Galleries, shops, theaters, cafés, restaurants, and bars replaced the formerly decrepit buildings and alleys, bringing an artsy crowd to mingle with blue-collar locals—and jacking up prices. Already the artists and penniless students are defecting to cheaper places like Belleville. Don't expect too much activity and excitement during daylight hours—what's left of the hip Bastille spirit wakes up (and keeps going) after dark.

To get away from the crowds, try exploring **rue de la Roquette** and **rue de Charonne,** which lead you into areas largely inhabited by African and Arab Parisians. A myriad of small streets between the two, such as **rue Keller** and **rue des Taillandiers,** hide cool art galleries and nifty clothing and music stores. On **avenue Daumesnil,** check out the **Viaduc des Arts,** a redbrick viaduct—originally, the last mile of the suburban railroad that led to place de la Bastille (the site of the Bastille Opéra was once a station)— now a stylish walkway with shrubs, flowers, and benches, and arts and crafts shops. Nocturnal activities are the Bastille's specialty. **Rue de Lappe, rue de la Roquette,** and **rue de Charonne** are packed with bars, restaurants, and gaggles of hipsters.

BELLEVILLE

Belleville is one of Paris's most atmospheric and, unhappily, quickly changing neighborhoods. Victim to the city's urban renewal frenzy, the area's pleasant old buildings are being replaced with ugly modern structures. When the powers that be suggested virtually demolishing Belleville's oldest, most characteristic, western corner (crossed by rue de Belleville and boulevard de Belleville), neighbors united to fight the plan, forming a group known as the "Bellevilleuse"; they've had mixed success in gaining promises to restore rather than raze some areas. But the stretch between the original Belleville and Père-Lachaise cemetery still warrants rambling. Take **rue de Ménilmontant,** which goes up, up, up, from boulevard de Belleville and is still lined with many old buildings. Other good places to experience the area's slightly run-down charm are the **Parc de Belleville, rue Dénoyez,** and **rue de Belleville** up to **rue des Pyrénées.**

A more refreshing change taking place in Belleville is the recent influx of artists, musicians, and young people who can afford to live in this part of town. Part of the area's appeal stems from the fact that it never charmed the bourgeoisie. Originally a country village with farmland and vineyards, it had less than 1,000 inhabitants right up to the Revolution. The late 18th century saw the beginning of a long, slow migration into Belleville, and in the mid-19th century the village was incorporated into Paris. Pushed out

BASTILLE

of central Paris by Haussmann's huge boulevards, the laboring class came here to live. The arrival of waves of immigrants in the 20th century, most fleeing persecution in their homelands, has contributed to Belleville's international esprit: Polish, Russian, German, and Sephardic Jews; Armenians; Greeks; Africans; Eastern Europeans; Chinese . . . all have brought their specialties to shops, markets, and restaurants throughout the district. Groups of men chat amicably on corners and doorsteps in this approachable, friendly quartier—although women traveling alone might find it a little too friendly. If you need a respite from the picture-book Paris of grand boulevards and Chanel boutiques, this is the neighborhood for you.

BERCY-TOLBIAC

The Bercy-Tolbiac neighborhood in east Paris, currently the focus of massive redevelopment, is testimony to the French genius for urban renewal. Tucked away on the far Right Bank, the Bercy district was for decades filled with crumbling wine warehouses. Now sports and money set the tone, with the mighty glass walls of the **Ministère des Finances** (Finance Ministry) facing off against the odd, grass-covered slopes of the **Palais Omnisports** stadium. Leading east is the ultimate designer garden, with trim lawns, rose-strewn arbors, glass follies, and artfully arrayed grapevines nostalgically evoking the vanished vintners' village that once stood here. Across the garden is American architect Frank Gehry's witty, postmodern **American Center,** opened in 1994 but closed two years later for lack of funds. Gehry described it as a "dancing figure in the park," though, now empty and forlorn, it has about as much spring as a rag doll.

Towering directly across the Seine are the four, glass, L-shaped towers of Dominique Perrault's **Bibliothèque François-Mitterrand,** the new national library opened in 1996 and named for the late bookworm president who masterminded the project. With 11 million volumes, it surpasses the Library of Congress as the largest library in the world. The library, with its lavish, airy interior that is open to visitors, anchors the Tolbiac district. The area's most salient feature is still the myriad train tracks heading into Gare d'Austerlitz. But these are being covered as new housing sprouts up all around. The neighborhood will be linked to the rest of Paris by the new Météor métro line.

CHAMPS-ELYSEES

What was once an aristocratic pleasure park is now a commercialized tourist trap living off its former glory. Although there's a certain thrill to strutting down the world's most famous street, in the shadow of the **Arc de Triomphe,** the abundance of bland shops and restaurant chains (and the lack of actual Parisians) makes the experience feel suspiciously like a trip to the mall. The city's attempt at bringing back splendor has included widening the white-granite sidewalks and planting lots of trees, but it still feels like the world's grandest outdoor shopping mall: lots of French kids and tourists cruising around, scoping each other out. The only exclusive things left in the area are the power-lunch bistros, the private nightclubs, and the haute-couture shops on the surrounding streets, particularly **avenue Montaigne.**

Originally an expanse of green frequented by cattle, the Champs was built for Louis XIV by the landscape designer Le Nôtre to extend the line of the Tuileries. Though **place de la Concorde,** at the eastern end, saw plenty of activity—including a few hundred heads rolling around during the Revolution—the extending stretch stayed rural, except for a few wealthy folks' homes. In the mid-1800s, the Champs became a popular Sunday strolling ground, encouraging more ice-cream stands, pavilions, and parties as the century went on. The decline of World Expos in the mid-20th century saw a parallel decline in the Champs-Elysées, which had been the stomping grounds of many a fair-goer. A few designer names and fancy shops still hang around the avenue, but it has lost its novelty. For a map of the Champs, *see* map Arc de Triomphe to Opéra, *below.*

LA DEFENSE

With sleek modern buildings and funky urban art, La Défense is Paris's version of Disney's Futureland. About 2 km (1¼ mi) outside Paris proper, La Défense does not exactly fit the traditional idea of a "neighborhood." The 35,000 residents who live in the high-rise housing projects are easily eclipsed by the 110,000 people who work in the complex of business towers and shops. Development of this huge commercial conglomeration of hypermodern architecture and sculpture began in 1958 on what had been

17e

blvd. de Courcelles

Parc de Monceau

blvd. Malesherbes

av. Niel

Wagram

pl. des Ternes

r. P. le Grand

r. Daru

av. de

pl. de Rio de Janeiro

r. de Courcelles

Monceau

av. de Messine

r. de Miromesnil

r. de

av. MacMahon

av. Beaujon

av. Hoche

r. de l'Arc de Triomphe

Arc de Triomphe

pl. G. Guillaumin

av. Myron T. Herrick

blvd. Haussmann

r. du Faubourg

r. La Boétie

r. de Penthièvre

pl. Charles

av. d'Iéna

de Gaulle

av. Marceau

r. Balzac

av. de Friedland

r. Washington

r. d'Artois

St-Honoré

8e

pl. Beauvau

r. du P

av. des Champs-Elysées

r. de Berri

r. de Ponthieu

av. George-V

r. Galilée

r. Pierre Charron

r. Marbeuf

r. Robert-Estienne

r. François-Ier

Cl. Marot

r. de Boccador

av. Montaigne

av. Franklin D. Roosevelt

av. Matignon

av. Gabriel

Rond-Point des Champs-Elysées

av. de Marigny

16e

av. Pierre-Ier-de-Serbie

av. du Président Wilson

av. W. Churchill

Palais de Tokyo

New York

av. de

pl. de l'Alma

cours Albert Ier

cours la Reine

Seine

l'Alma

Pl. de

quai d'Orsay

Pl. des Invalides

Pl. Alexandre III

quai d'Orsay

Palais Bourbon

r. Jean-Goujon

7e

KEY

AE American Express Office

The American Church, 9
Bibliothèque Nationale Richelieu, 18
Centre National de la Photographie, 2
Comédie Française, 21
Eglise de la Madeleine, 23
Grand Palais, 11

Jardin du Palais Royal, 19
Jeu de Paume, 24
Musée des Arts Decoratifs, 22
Musée Cernuschi, 3
Musée Gustave Moreau, 15
Musée Jacquemart André, 4
Musée Marmott au Claude Monet, 7

Musée de la Mode et du Costume, 6
Musée National des Arts Asiatiques - Guimet, 5
Musée de l'Orangerie, 25
Musée de la Vie Romantique, 14
Opéra Comique, 17
Opéra Garnier, 16
Palais de la Dècouverte, 10

Palais de l'Elysée, 13
Palais Royal, 20
Petit Palais, 12
Salle Pleyel, 1
Théâtre des Champs-Elysées, 8

r. Chaptal ⑭

0 _____ 440 yards
0 _____ 400 meters

r. des Londres

r. d. Rome Ⓜ

r. du Rocher

Foy

Bienfaisance

Gare St-Lazare

r. d'Amsterdam

r. de Clichy

Ⓜ

r. Pigalle

r. de la Rochefoucauld

Ⓜ d'Aumale

⑮

Notre-Dame-de-Lorette

r. Clauzel

r. des Martyrs

r. St-Lazare

Ⓜ r. de Châteaudun

9e

r. de la Chaussée-d'Antin

r. Taitbout

r. de Provence

r. La Fayette

Ⓜ

r. Laffitte

r. Geoffroy-Marie

Ⓜ

r. St-Lazare Ⓜ

pl. St-Augustin

r. de la Pépinière Ⓜ

blvd. Haussmann

r. Auber Ⓜ

r. Tronchet

r. de Caumartin

r. Pasquier

r. Scribe

Ⓜ AE

⑯

pl. de l'Opéra

Ⓜ

blvd. des Italiens

Ⓜ

⑰ r. Favart

r. St-Marc

blvd. de la Madeleine

blvd. des Capucines

r. du Quatre-Septembre

2e

blvd. de la Madeleine

r. des Capucines

r. de la Paix

r. Daunou

r. St-Augustin

r. Ste-Anne

r. Chabanais

r. Vivienne

⑱

blvd. Malesherbes

d'Aguesseau

bourg St-Honoré

r. de Boissy-d'Anglas

Duras

⑳③ ②③

pl. de la Madeleine Ⓜ

r. Royale

pl. Vendôme

r. de Castiglione

r. St-Honoré

r. St-Roch

av. de l'Opéra

r. des Petits-Champs

pl. des Victoires

r. de Richelieu

⑲

1er

Ⓜ

pl. de la Concorde

②④

②⑤

Pl. de la Concorde

quai des Tuileries

r. de Rivoli Ⓜ

Jardin des Tuileries

r. des Pyramides

②②

②①⑳

Jardin du Carrousel

Ⓜ pl. du Palais Royal

Louvre

the site of the ultimately ill-fated Parisian defense (hence the name) against the invading Prussians. By the time the developers came to the area, La Défense was just a large traffic circle with a statue in the middle commemorating the battle—the statue still stands today, oddly isolated on an elevated island of grass. The developers sought to create an American-style business park, and they succeeded in building one of Europe's largest and most prestigious commercial neighborhoods with typical French flair.

La Défense is designed to continue the longest urban axis in the world, from the Louvre westward to the **Grande Arche de La Défense** (*see* Major Attractions, *above*), an enormous arch that hides an office building within its walls. The Grande Arche, along with La Défense's first building, the concrete, curvaceous **CNIT** (Centre National des Industries et des Techniques), draws thousands of tourists daily. The **esplanade,** the wide concrete promenade extending along the axis, is lined with big-name art, including a sculpture by Joan Miró that sparked furious controversy over its bizarre shape; Yaacov Agam's *Waterfall,* a fountain powered by 50 computer-controlled jets; and Takis's funky fountain filled with traffic signal–like lights. The Grande Arche de La Défense and the area surrounding it is especially worth a trip at night, when the bright lights and harsh geometrical shapes create a surreal atmosphere.

And the axis isn't stopping yet. Development contracts have been added past the original 1988 time line, and construction crews are extending métro lines and unearthing cemeteries to the west of the Grande Arche to make room for new buildings. New proposals include the Tour Sans Fin (Endless Tower) designed by Jean Nouvel (*see* box, *above*), which would be the tallest building in Europe and the fifth-tallest in the world. The Jardin de l'Arche, a huge park over an underground freeway, will probably be completed in 1998. Though it may not jibe with your sense of aesthetics, La Défense is too enormous, popular, and spectacular to ignore. Visit the information center by the Grande Arche to pick up a map outlining all the sculptures and architectural details, including information about the history of La Défense. *Métro: Grande Arche de La Défense or Esplanade de La Défense.*

GARE DE L'EST AND GARE DU NORD

You may breeze through this quarter on your way from the center up to Montmartre, but if you stop you can get a more satisfying taste of Paris than you could soak up from 38 portrait sittings on place du Tertre. This is a neighborhood filled with working-class people who shop at functional stores and eat at reasonably priced restaurants. Many of Paris's old *passages* (shopping arcades) are here, but unlike the spruced-up ones in the center, these passages are old and crumbling, housing Indian restaurants or used-book vendors. If you're attracted to crumbly Old World charm, check out some passages (such as **passage Brady** and **passage Reilhac**) that branch off from **boulevard de Strasbourg.** The area right around the train stations can get a little sleazy, but if you head south toward **rue du Château-d'Eau** or east toward **quai de Valmy,** you'll be rewarded with a down-to-earth look at Paris. A few of the grand old cafés still call the area home, but their facades practically disappear amid the worn streets and stores around them.

A large Jewish population sustains kosher restaurants and bakeries, especially in the area above métro Rue Montmartre, and Indian and Eastern European joints crowd the 10th. Head to **rue d'Enghien** for a great marketplace. Unfortunately, it isn't a good idea to come to this area alone at night, particularly if you're a woman or if you don't know exactly where you're going; it's one of Paris's worst areas for theft.

LES HALLES AND BEAUBOURG

Many Parisians believe that the day Les Halles marketplace left Beaubourg in 1969 was the day Paris irrevocably shuffled its priorities; tourism and consumerism were allowed to oust centuries of local tradition in a move that some call "McDonaldization." The Paris market had been here for nearly 800 years—ever since Philippe-Auguste divided up the space, with central buildings for shops and surrounding open spaces for the fresh food market. The market became the central Paris meeting, drinking, and entertainment spot. In the mid-19th century, when Napoléon III complained that the market was disorganized, Victor Baltard created a covered market with glass-roofed pavilions supported by an iron frame, a design that became the model for markets all over Europe.

When the demolition of the market was decided upon in 1962, Parisians showed surprisingly little resistance; in 1969 the food merchants were chased out to a concrete modern complex at Rungis near Orly Airport, and the 19th-century market hall was torn down and replaced with a gaping hole. As politicians haggled over the fate of the site, the wasteland came to be known as the "Largest Urban Hole in Europe." After 10 years of wrangling, developers had a brilliant idea: Build a shopping mall. The multi-

Cathédrale
Notre-Dame, **10**

Conciergerie, **12**

Crypte
Archéologique, **11**

Eglise
St-Eustache, **2**

Eglise St-Merri, **4**

Forum des Halles, **3**

Hôtel de Ville, **8**

Louvre, **1**

Mémorial de la
Déportation, **9**

Palais de
Justice, **13**

Sainte-Chapelle, **14**

Square du
Vert-Galant, **15**

Théâtre du
Chatelet, **6**

Théâtre de
la Ville, **7**

Tour St-Jacques, **5**

level, soulless structure you see today, the **Forum des Halles,** is the best they could come up with. Though the mall below ground is an indisputable mess, at least the streets of Les Halles have been spared from the property boom and hawkish developers. Sitting on top of the underground shopping monstrosity is a ghastly collection of fast-food stalls and tourist shops, but many old-time bistros have held on in the narrow surrounding streets. The area gets going at about 5 AM, when butchers and fish merchants arrive to set up shop, and the cafés fill up soon after with folks getting a coffee before work. Throughout the rest of the day, the streets fill up with students and street musicians, beer-drinking punk rockers and their dogs, wide-eyed tourists, and patrons of the porno video parlors. **Rue St-Denis** is both one of the sleaziest and one of the most inviting streets around; its bustling restaurants share centuries-old building space with equally busy sex shops. Northern Les Halles has evolved into a hot spot; a city project to redo the streets has proved successful, and hip cafés surround **rue Montorgueil,** lined with food markets and restaurants.

The **Eglise St-Eustache** (*see* Houses of Worship, *above*), at the northern edge of the **Jardin des Halles,** is a 16th-century Gothic wonder. In the other direction, to the south of the Forum, is the **Fontaine des Innocents,** for ages the site of a common-trench cemetery, which was emptied into the **Catacombes** (*see* Dead Folk, *above*) after the overabundance of bodies pushed themselves above street level and the smell became unbearable. Now the public square here is filled day and night with Rasta bongo players, hair weavers, and tourists.

Farther south are small streets filled with jazz clubs and trendy shops. Then hit **place du Châtelet** and its facing theaters. The square takes its name from a notoriously harsh prison that sat on the present site of Théâtre du Châtelet until its destruction in the 19th century. That random tower just off the place is the **Tour St-Jacques,** built as an addition to a church that was torn down during the Revolution. The tower has since served as Pasteur's lab for experiments on gravity, as a quarry, and currently as a meteorological observatory.

A couple blocks northeast of Châtelet is the best-known landmark of the neighborhood: the **Centre Georges-Pompidou** (*see* Major Attractions, *above*). Street musicians and performers gather on the sloping desert of a plaza in front of the Centre. Around the corner at **place Igor-Stravinsky** is Jean Tinguely's wild and fanciful fountain. A pair of big red lips, a rotund woman, a treble clef, and other wacked sculptures turn and gurgle in the spitting streams of water, a stark contrast to the venerable Gothic **Eglise St-Merri** nearby.

ILE DE LA CITE

The strategic location of this island in the Seine first drew a Gallic tribe, the Parisii, to the place they dubbed Lutetia in about 300 BC. Settling mainly on the island itself, they built wood bridges to the mainland. Caesar's rapid expansion plan hit Paris around 50 BC, and the Romans moved the hub to the Left Bank (though as late as the 4th century AD, Roman governors still slept in a palace on the island). Frankish kings took over that palace—now known as the Conciergerie—a couple centuries later, and it remained a royal residence until the 1300s; the Capetians alone lived here for 800 years.

Today, the tough Gauls have been replaced by tourists flocking to **Sainte-Chapelle** and **Notre-Dame** (*see* Major Attractions, *above*) and milling around the expensive tourist shops that surround them. The desire to showcase Notre-Dame altered the soul of the island in the late 19th century: The tiny winding streets, churches, stalls, and houses crouching below it, along with an orphanage and invalids' hospital, were bulldozed to make way for the Haussmann aesthetic. The **Crypte Archéologique** (tel. 01–43–29–83–51), under the place du Parvis in front of the cathedral, became a museum after ruins were discovered in 1965 while building an underground parking structure here. Among the excavated details are parts of the 3rd-century wall of Lutetia; a Merovingian cathedral (Notre-Dame's predecessor) from AD 600; and bits of Roman and medieval houses. Plenty of diagrams, pictures, and photographs go along with the ruins, detailing the history of the isle. Admission to the crypt is 28F. It's open daily 10–6 (shorter hours off-season).

For the most tranquil moment you are likely to have on the Ile de la Cité, head to the **square du Vert-Galant** (*see* box, Pick a Park, *above*) at the island's western tip for a view out over the Seine, or picnic in shady **place Dauphine** opposite. The small garden behind Notre-Dame is another peaceful spot, where you can gaze at flying buttresses all day long. From the back of Notre-Dame head across the street and down the steep granite stairs to the **Mémorial de la Déportation,** a striking tribute to the 200,000 French sent to death camps by the Vichy government during World War II. Inside, 200,000 crystals memorialize the victims, and the walls are lined with moving quotations by famous French writers, poets, and philosophers, etched in angular, blood-red letters. It's worth bringing a dictionary to translate the passionate sentiments.

ILE ST-LOUIS

If it weren't sitting directly behind Notre-Dame, attached by a bridge, you probably would never think of going to Ile St-Louis. But it is, and you should: There is an entire street of restaurants and shops waiting to greet you. Actually, the narrow **rue St-Louis-en-l'Ile** may be one of the most charming streets in Paris, and as a result plenty of locals join visitors here on warm days and clear evenings. You'll find most of them standing in line outside **Berthillon** (31 rue St-Louis-en-l'Ile, 4e, tel. 01–43–54–31–61), Paris's best ice creamery. The relatively ignored Seine-side streets of the Ile St-Louis are some of the most enjoyable, with shady spots perfect to sit and savor your purchase.

Once a canal divided the current Ile St-Louis in two; the halves were dubbed the Ile Notre-Dame and Ile aux Vaches, the latter given over to dairy cows and their attendants. And so it remained until the 17th century, when some land speculators joined the two islands, connecting them by bridges to the Ile de la Cité and the Left and Right Banks, and sold plots to town house developers. After a time in the spotlight, the posh residences lost their appeal among the bourgeoisie, and artists, writers, and intellectuals like Cézanne and Baudelaire moved in. The **Hôtel de Lauzun** (17 quai d'Anjou, 4e) was one of Baudelaire's haunts. As you wander around, keep an eye out for the building plaques describing who lived where when, and why it's important. The **quai d'Anjou** and **quai de Bourbon** have some beautiful hôtels particuliers. A somber plaque adorns 19 quai de Bourbon: "Here lived Camille Claudel, sculptor, from 1899 to 1913. Then ended her brave career as an artist and began her long night of internment." Claudel's family committed her to an insane asylum where she was forbidden to practice her art for the rest of her life. Some of her works are displayed in the Musée Rodin (*see* Museums, *above*).

LOUVRE TO OPERA

Yes, it's terribly expensive, snobbish, and packed with tourists. But any neighborhood that has the centers of the Western art, theater, and music worlds all within a 15-minute walk can't be all bad. The **Louvre** (*see* Major Attractions, *above*) is the biggie here, displaying thousands of works in what was originally a royal palace. Just a block above it is the **Comédie Française** (*see* Theater *in* Chapter 5), tacked onto another royal residence, the **Jardin du Palais Royal** (*see* Parks and Gardens, *above*), and pointing the way up one of Haussmann's favorite boulevards, avenue de l'Opéra. On the avenue, notice the monotony of the structures and how closely the teeny balconies cling to the buildings; Haussmann wanted to ensure that you'd be struck by the grandeur of the street as a whole, with no one well-designed building stealing the show and no protruding terraces breaking the line straight down the street. At the end of this promenade is, of course, the **Opéra Garnier** (*see* Opera, Classical Music, and Dance *in* Chapter 5).

If you aren't coming to this district to follow the museum trail, pose with the pretentious, or shop in the nearby *grands magasins* (department stores), you're probably coming for practical reasons—it's home to all of the major airlines, travel agencies, and tourist bureaus. Off **avenue de l'Opéra,** however, you'll find the famous restaurants, age-old bistros, and upscale shops that form the opulent heart of the quarter. Lately, a sizable Japanese population has moved in, bringing restaurants, bookstores, and specialty shops with them. North of the Jardin du Palais Royal is **rue des Petits-Champs,** whose bounty of iron-and-glass passages makes it one of the neighborhood's best spots for roaming. The street ends in the intimate **place des Victoires;** its matching facades were designed in 1685 by Versailles architect Hardouin-Mansart. Louis XIV was so pleased with the results that he had Hardouin-Mansart do another, the **place Vendôme,** on the other side of avenue de l'Opéra. Snobbish and self-important, place Vendôme is also gorgeous; property laws have kept away cafés and other such banal establishments, leaving the plaza stately and refined, the perfect home for the Ritz and Cartier (Chopin lived and died at No. 12). The column in the center of the place Vendôme has had numerous face-lifts, depicting everything from Louis XIV's curls blowing in the breeze to Napoléon's mug, depending on who needed a little self-glorification. The most noteworthy change was the toppling of Napoléon's statue in 1871, when enraged Communards followed the lead of artist Gustave Courbet, heave-hoing and bringing the whole thing down into a pile of manure (which they'd heaped at the base). Courbet made a quick escape to Switzerland to avoid imprisonment and hefty fines, and eventually Napoléon was cleaned up and put back in the saddle, so to speak.

N

1er

r. B-de-Clairvaux

r. Michel Le Comte

r. Rambuteau

r. Brantôme

r. Beaubourg

r. du Temple

r. des Haudriettes

r. des

Archives r. Pa

r. de Braque

r. des 4 Fils

r. Quincampoix

r. St-Martin

(2)

r. Simm Le Franc

pl. Igor Stravinsky

r. des

r. du Temple

r. des Blancs Manteaux

Archives

r. Vieille du Ten

r. Bo

blvd. de Sébastopol

r. des Lombards

(1)

r. de la Verrerie

r. St-Merri

r. du Renard

r. du Plâtre

r. des

r. Ste-Croix de la Bretonnerie

r. des Francs

M

M

M

pl. de l'Hôtel de Ville

(3)

r. de Rivoli

r. de Moussy

r. du Bourg Tibourg

Vieille du Temple

r. des Hospitalières St-Gervais

r. des Rosiers

r. Vier. du Trésor

r. des Écouffes

r. F. Duval

r. du Roi de Sicile

Pont Notre Dame

r. de Lobau

pl. St-Gervais

quai de l'Hôtel de Ville

r. François Miron

r. Pavée

M

Pont d'Arcole

M

Ile de la Cité

r. Geoffroy l'Asnier

r. de Jouy

(5)

(8)

r. de Foucy

4e

r. Cha

r. du Cloître Notre Dame

r. du Pont Louis Philippe

r. de l'Hôtel de Ville

r. du Fauconnier

r. de l'Ave Mai.

(7)

des

M

Notre Dame

Pont Louis Philippe

Pont St-Louis

quai de Bourbon

Pont Marie

quai des Célestins

quai de Montebello

r. le Regrattier

r. St-Louis en l'Île

(6)

r. des Deux Ponts

quai d'Anjou

(11)

r. des

quai d'Orléans

Ile St-Louis

M

pl. Maubert

5e

Pont de la Tournelle

quai de Béthune

de Sully

quai de la Tournelle

Pont

blvd. St-Germain

82

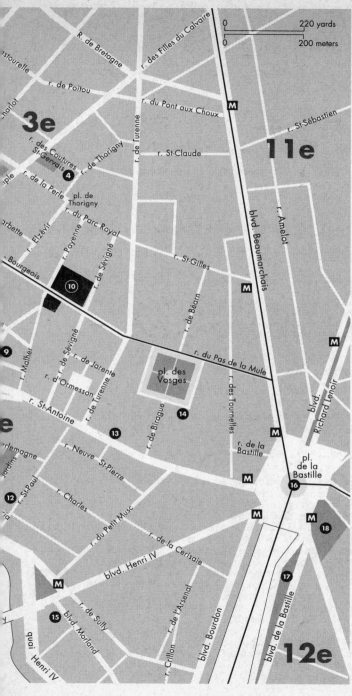

1913 Synagogue, **9**

Bassin de l'Arsenal, **17**

Camille Claudel's home, **6**

Centre Georges Pompidou, **2**

Colonne de Juillet, **16**

Eglise St-Merri, **1**

Hôtel de Lauzun, **11**

Hôtel de Sens/ Bibliothèque Forney, **7**

Hôtel de Ville, **3**

Maison de Victor Hugo, **14**

Maison Européenne de la Photographie, **8**

Mémorial du Martyr Juif Inconnu/Centre de Documentation Juive Contemporaine, **5**

Mission du Patrimoine Photographique/ Hôtel de Sully, **13**

Musée Carnavalet, **10**

Musée de la Curiosité, **12**

Musée Picasso, **4**

Opéra Bastille, **18**

Pavillon de l'Arsenal, **15**

ARTIST ADDRESS BOOK

Do the bogus artists on Monmartre's place du Tertre seem so tacky that you can't believe anyone cool ever lived around here? Well they did, and here's where you could have found them:

CÉZANNE: *15 rue Hégésippe-Moreau*

MANET: *77 rue d'Amsterdam and 39 rue de Léningrad*

TOULOUSE-LAUTREC: *21 rue Caulaincourt, 19 rue Fontaine and 30 rue Fontaine*

VAN GOGH: *54 rue Lepic*

RENOIR: *12 rue Cortot, 13 rue Ravignan, 8 allée des Brouillards, 22 rue Tourlaque, 73 rue Caulaincourt, 57 boulevard de Clichy, and 64 rue de La Rochefoucauld*

West of the Louvre and the Opéra is the decadent **Eglise de la Madeleine** (*see* Houses of Worship, *above*); the surrounding area is where rich French do their shopping. **Place de la Madeleine** is home to a great flower market Tuesday–Sunday. To stroll among the well-heeled of Paris, head to its version of Rodeo Drive, **rue du Faubourg-St-Honoré,** where ridiculously expensive clothes grace the windows of ridiculously expensive boutiques. While you're in the area, stop in and tell the president what you think of his country—the **Palais de l'Elysée** on place Beauvau (look for all the humorless cops hanging around) has been the official residence of the head of state since 1873.

LE MARAIS

Le marais translates as "the swamp." Although this title indicates the formerly overwhelming presence of the Seine in this area, the lively neighborhood of today is anything but stuck in the mud. The Marais covers the 3e and 4e arrondissements, and though its narrow streets become a bit too crowded in the summer, its eternally lively atmosphere makes it one of Paris's best areas for eating, drinking, singing, walking, and simply living.

Between its original existence as a swamp and its current one as a fashionable district inhabited by stylish Parisians and a thriving gay community, the Marais has seen royalty move in and out. When Henri IV installed his court here in the 17th century and built the place Royale (now the place des Vosges), the Marais was *the* place to live. Nobles flaunted money and prestige, building big, beautiful hôtels particuliers in the area. However, as soon as Versailles became the hot ticket, all those fickle French aristocrats followed Louis out there to kiss his feet, leaving the Marais virtually abandoned. Taking advantage of what had become basically worthless property, waves of Jewish immigrants put down stakes. The Revolution granted Jews religious freedom, and 100 years later Jews fleeing persecution in Poland and Russia came to Paris, living in squalid conditions in the Marais ghetto working mainly as peddlers and merchants. During World War II, the French police arrested thousands of Jews living in the Marais; the Vél d'Hiv roundup of July 16, 1942, when over 12,000 Jews were arrested in one day, marks the low point of the French collaboration. After the decimation of World War II, the Marais remained an old, decaying quarter until a 1962 law, the Loi Malraux, established a restoration program and saved the buildings from ruin. Developers started buying up property, fixing the facades of historic buildings, installing shops and galleries, and jacking up property values. The last 20 years have seen the transformation of the Marais into the trendy, artsy neighborhood that it is today, with a good mix of artists' studios and working-class folk.

The **Jewish quarter,** centered on **rue des Rosiers** and **rue des Ecouffes,** adds to the Marais's bustling, sometimes bizarre, character: Hasidic Jews with beards and yarmulkes emerge from the kosher stores, passing young men in tight shirts heading to gay bars. Jewish immigrants from North Africa have brought new life to the quarter, and you'll discover a hodgepodge of falafel stands, kosher butchers, and bookstores with tomes in Hebrew, Arabic, and French. Though interior visits are discouraged (most effectively by the locked gate), at least walk past the **1913 synagogue** (10 rue Pavée, 4e), designed by art nouveau whiz Hector Guimard. The **Mémorial du Martyr Juif Inconnu** (Memorial of the Unknown Jewish Martyr) and the **Centre de Documentation Juive Contemporaine** (17 rue Geoffroy-l'Asnier, 4e, tel. 01-42-77-44-72) share the same building. The memorial houses temporary art and history expositions, as well as the ashes of concentration camp victims; the center is a great resource for Jewish studies (*see* Libraries *in* Chapter 1).

At the end of rue des Francs-Bourgeois is the elegant **place des Vosges:** One look at the stylish red- and white-brick residences, flowing fountains, and manicured garden, and you'll understand why back in the old days this square was all the rage. In 1605 Henri IV initiated work to transform the square into the place Royale, though the poor guy died before he could move in. The king's and queen's residences, with the largest facades, face each other from across the plaza. Between them lay what belligerent Parisians used as jousting grounds, and so they remained until finally becoming an English-style park later in the century. The stately arcades under the mansions harbor the open gardens of the Hôtel de Sully and the **Maison de Victor Hugo** (*see* Museums, *above*). Try to come on a weekend afternoon, when sporadic free classical music concerts add to the already royal atmosphere.

Between the Seine and the rue de Rivoli lies the calmer part of the Marais, packed with beautiful old mansions and green patches. Look for the tiny garden behind the **Hôtel de Sens,** a mansion transformed into the **Bibliothèque Forney,** an art-history library (*see* Academic and Cultural Resources *in* Chapter 1). **Rue St-Paul** and **rue de l'Hôtel-de-Ville** overflow with dusty, insignificant-looking antiques shops that sometimes hide treasures. There are also plenty of cool-looking overpriced shops that offer everything but bargains.

MONTMARTRE

Rising above the city on the highest hill in Paris is Montmartre, site of the **Basilique du Sacré-Coeur** (*see* Major Attractions, *above*) and once home to a hefty artist community. Even now, after many of the artists have headed for cheaper quarters and tour buses deliver hordes to its minuscule streets, Montmartre remains first and foremost a village where a special breed of Parisian lives and drinks. A trip through the streets of this neighborhood will reward you with glimpses of gardens, small cafés filled with locals, and perhaps the sound of a practicing violinist. An essential part of the Montmartre experience is to sweat your way up the steep stairways that have graced many a Robert Doisneau photograph and afford incredible views of Paris. In the 19th century, vineyards and over 40 windmills covered Montmartre, then a country village. The only surviving windmill is the **moulin de la Galette,** on the corner of rue Lepic and rue Girardon. It is immortalized in Auguste Renoir's *Le Bal du Moulin de la Galette* (*Ball at the Windmill of the Galette*).

After Haussmann razed most of the working-class homes in the city center, this area saw a population boom. Among the newcomers were artists, drawn by cheap rents and the bohemian atmosphere. Picasso, Renoir, Dalí, Braque, and writer-poets like Apollinaire and Baudelaire all lived and worked here. The **Bateau-Lavoir** (13 pl. Emile-Goudeau, 18e, métro Abbesses) was an artists' colony where Picasso, Braque, Gris, and others had studios. Picasso painted the Cubist classic *Les Demoiselles d'Avignon* here; supposedly a pack of prostitutes from Barcelona posed for the painting. Head south one block to the **place des Abbesses,** a tranquil old square with one of the two remaining art nouveau métro entrances designed by Guimard. For more on the history and illustrious personalities of Montmartre, visit the **Musée de Montmartre** (*see* Museums, *above*), in the building where Renoir once had his studio.

Where artists go, rich folk soon follow, and the area gradually filled with galleries, boutiques, and tourists. Today, the aggressive third-rate painters clustered around **place du Tertre,** one of the most tourist-attacked spots in the entire city, are the unfortunate reminders of Montmartre's artistic heritage. Real artists live behind the hill, often in million-dollar homes on **avenue Junot** or the picturesque **villa Léandre** just off it. To the east, on **rue des Saules,** is the last remaining vineyard in Paris, producing 125 gallons of wine per year. Nearby, off **place des Quatre-Frères-Casadesus,** is a small park where old men

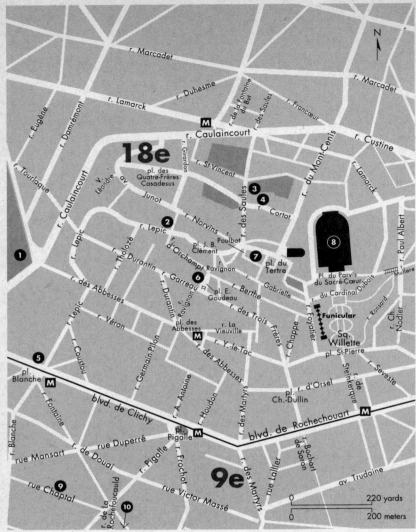

N

r. Marcadet

r. Duhesme

r. Lamarck

r. Marcadet

r. Custine

M r. Caulaincourt

r. Eugène

r. Dammémont

r. Caulaincourt

r. Tourlaque

r. de la Fontaine du But

r. des Saules

r. Francœur

r. du Mont-Cenis

r. Lamarck

18e

pl. des Quatre-Frères Casadesus

r. Girardon

av. Léandre

V.

r. St-Vincent

Junot

3

4

Cortot

r. des Saules

r. Paul Albert

r. Lepic

2

r. Norvins

r. Tholozé

r. Durantin

d'Orchamps

Poulbot

pl. J. B. Clément

Ravignon

7

pl. du Tertre

8

1

r. Lepic

r. des Abbesses

r. Garreau

6

Berthe

Gabrielle

Muliere

r. Durantin

r. Ravignon

pl. E. Goudeau

r. des Trois Frères

Pl. du Parvis du Sacré-Cœur

du Cardinal Dubois

r. Ronsard

r. Véron

pl. des Abbesses

r. La Vieuville

Chappe

r. Foyatier

Funicular

Sq. Willette

r. Ch. Nodier

M

r. Y.-le-Tac

pl. St-Pierre

r. des Abbesses

5

pl. Blanche

M

r. Coustou

r. Lepic

Germain-Pilon

r. A. Antoine

Houdon

r. d'Orsel

pl. r. d'Orsel

Ch.-Dullin

r. de Steinkerque

Séveste

r. de Bochart

r. Fontaine

blvd. de Clichy

r. des Martyrs

blvd. de Rochechouart

M

r. Blanche

rue Mansart

r. de Douai

rue Duperré

pl. Pigalle

M

r. Pigalle

Frochot

de Saron

rue Tellier

av. Trudaine

rue Chaptal

9

r. de la Rochefoucauld

10

rue Victor Massé

9e

r. des Martyrs

0   220 yards

0   200 meters

Basilique du Sacré-Cœur, **8**

Bateau-Lavoir, **6**

Cimetière de Montmartre, **1**

Espace Montmartre–Dali, **7**

Moulin de la Galette, **2**

Moulin Rouge, **5**

Musée de la Vie Romantique, **9**

Musée de Montmartre, **4**

Musée Gustave Moreau, **10**

Vineyard, **3**

gather every day to play pétanque. The guy holding his head in his hands in the statue here is St-Denis, Paris's first bishop (*see* Cathédrale de St-Denis, *above*).

Rue Ste-Croix-de-la-Bretonnerie and **rue Vieille-du-Temple** are the center of gay life in Paris. Here you'll find bars, bookstores, cultural info, and all the accessories needed for a night out at Le Queen (*see* Dance Clubs *in* Chapter 5). **Rue des Francs-Bourgeois** is another great street, full of sleek cafés and homey restaurants, and just north of it are a couple of the city's best museums: the **Musée Picasso** and **Musée Carnavalet** (*see* Museums, *above*).

Montmartre became famous between 1880 and 1914, from the time when the first cabarets opened to the start of World War I. The cabarets, at the bottom of the hill near **place Pigalle** and **place de Clichy,** provided new excitement for the area's bohemians, as well as for students and bourgeois couples who came to the neighborhood for a show. The **Moulin Rouge** (*see* Cabaret *in* Chapter 5), immortalized in Toulouse-Lautrec's posters and paintings, still cashes in on Paris's reputation as a city of sex and sin. The cabaret culture and the artistic community fed off each other: The artists provided the cabarets with patronage and publicity, and the cabarets provided the artists with the intrigue, alcohol, and occasional glimpse of dancers', uh, ankles they needed to stay "inspired."

In eastern Montmartre, demarcated by **rue Doudeauville** to the north and **boulevard de la Chapelle** to the south, is the **Goutte d'Or** (Drop of Gold), named after the white wine the vineyards here used to produce. A bastion of the Algerian independence party (the FLN) during the Franco-Algerian war, the area has absorbed constant waves of immigrants, most recently from the Antilles and Africa. Today, Muslim markets sit next to African textile manufacturers, wholesale grocers, and old horse butchers in this multiethnic working-class quarter. Huge crowds of people move through the streets and groups of men debate on corners; lone women may feel uncomfortable with the unwanted attention from men and the lack of other women. The neighborhood gets most festive on Sunday; streets are often blocked off for daylong street markets, and shops stay open later. Like Belleville, however, this center for immigrant communities is struggling against the modern "renovations" being inflicted upon many of its charming (albeit decrepit) buildings. Rents will soon shoot up, forcing many immigrants out of Paris and into cheaper, utilitarian, concrete housing in the suburbs.

In the wall of the arcade-lined building across from the Senate (26–36 rue Vaugirard, 6e) is the last original marble "Mètre," one of 16 plaques put up in Paris in 1796 by the National Convention to familiarize the public with the new "enlightened" metric system.

MONTPARNASSE

The name Montparnasse is burdened with images of all kinds of brilliant expatriates doing silly drunken things in the years surrounding World War I. A quartet of cafés on the corner of **boulevard du Montparnasse** and **boulevard Raspail**—La Coupole, Le Dôme, Le Sélect, and La Rotonde—became the center for American writers who lived, lolled, loved, and left if the service displeased them. When the owner of Le Dôme fired his manager, threatened his waiters, and insulted his customers, they all regrouped a few weeks later at La Coupole, newly opened by the ex-manager. Americans liked to think that they held court on these corners, pointing to the presence of Ernest Hemingway, Gertrude Stein, Alice B. Toklas, Paul Bowles, Zelda and F. Scott Fitzgerald, Henry Miller, and Peggy Guggenheim. But they weren't the only people around—Pablo Picasso, Georges Braque, Juan Gris, Piet Mondrian, Leon Trotsky, Jean-Paul Sartre, Simone de Beauvoir, Albert Camus, Lawrence Durrell, Anaïs Nin, Jean Arp, Meret Oppenheim, Yves Tanguy, and Marcel Duchamp completed the picture, while an exiled Lenin spent most of his time here shunning chitchat and honing his chess game.

The four cafés are still here, though only Le Sélect still has a stylish crowd. The rest of the neighborhood, on the surface anyway, looks like the same mixture of old buildings, manicured parks, and out-of-place new buildings that you see in the rest of Paris. The huge **Tour Montparnasse,** finished in 1973 and the tallest office building in the city (at 690 feet), detracts substantially from the neighborhood. You can take an elevator to its rooftop bar where an overpriced drink will get you a spectacular view (but why subsidize an enterprise that ruins the skyline from every other vantage point?). Stretching out from the tower and the Gare Montparnasse train station are several uninspired commercial and residential developments, as well as a few more adventurous buildings. Ricardo Bofil's semicircular **Amphithéâtre** housing complex, with its whimsical postmodernist quotations of classical detail, is the most famous. The glass-

7e

6e

14e

1e

Louvre

Seine

Musée
d'Orsay

Palais du
Luxembourg

Jardin
du
Luxembourg

Gare
Montparnasse

Cimetière
du
Montparnasse

pl.
Dauphine

pl.
St-Germain-
des-Prés

pl.
St-Sulpice

pl. de
l'Odéon

pl. de la
Sorbonne

pl. du
18 juin 1940

pl.
Denfert
Rochereau

carrefour
de Buci

r. de l'Ancienne
Comedie

St-André des
Arts

St-Mich

blvd. St-Germain
quai Anatole France
quai du Louvre
quai Malaquais
quai de Conti
quai des Grands Augustins

Pont Royal
Pont du Carrousel
Pont des Arts
Pont Neuf
Pont St-Mi

r. de Solférino
r. St-Dominique
r. de Bellechasse
r. de Grenelle
r. de Varenne
r. de Babylone
r. Vaneau
r. du Bac
r. de l'Université
r. de Lille
r. Perronet
r. Sts-Pères
r. Jacob
r. Visconti
r. de Seine
r. Mazarine
r. Dauphine
r. Grégoire-de-Tours
r. de Buci
blvd. St-Germain
r. du Dragon
r. du Four
r. des Canettes
r. Princesse
r. Guisarde
r. Mabillon
r. de Tournon
r. de l'Odéon
r. Monsieur-le-Prince
r. de l'Ecole de Medecine
blvd. St-Germain
r. de Bac
sq. Boucicaut
r. de Sèvres
r. du Vieux-Colombier
r. Madame
r. de Vaugirard
r. Bonaparte
blvd. Raspail
blvd. St-Germain
r. de Sèvres
r. du Cherche-Midi
r. St-Placide
r. de Rennes
r. de Fleurus
r. Auguste Comte
r. Moyet
r. de Vaugirard
r. du Montparnasse
r. de Stanislas
r. d'Assas
r. Notre Dame des Champs
r. Vavin
blvd. du Montparnasse
r. Toullier
r. Soufflot
r. Gay Lussac
blvd. St-Michel
r. de l'Arrivée
r. du Départ
r. d'Odessa
r. Delambre
blvd. Edgar Quinet
r. de la Gaîté
av. du Maine
av. Froidevaux
r. Daguerre
r. Gassendi
r. Balard
Général Leclerc
blvd. Raspail
av. Georges-Bernanos
av. de l'Observatoire
r. du Faubourg St-Jacques
r. St-Jacques
r. D. Rochereau
blvd. de Port Roy
blvd. Arago
r. de Santé
blvd. St-Jacques

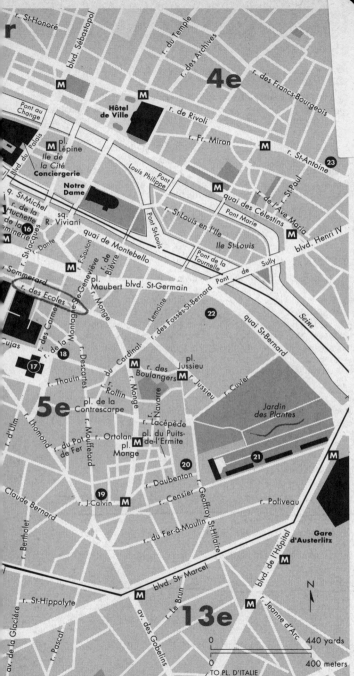

cubed **Fondation Carti**
with its giant glass fa
more historical p
Charles de G
student po
the late
tuck

Cartier, **11**

Grand Galerie de l'Evolution/Musée National d'Histoire Naturelle, **21**

Institut de France, **4**

Institut du Monde Arabe, **22**

Mission du Patrimoine Photographique, **23**

La Mosquée, **20**

Musée National Eugene-Delacroix, **3**

Musée National du Moyen-Age, **14**

Musée de la Poste, **10**

Musée Rodin, **1**

Musée Zadkine, **8**

Panthéon, **17**

Parc Montsouris/Cité Universitaire, **12**

Sorbonne, **15**

Théâtre de l'Odéon, **7**

Tour Montparnasse, **9**

440 yards

400 meters

N

TO PL. D'ITALIE

r (*see above*), a center for contemporary art, and the Montparnasse train station cade and designer garden above the tracks, are other outstanding examples. On a ote, just north of the tower, the **place du 18 juin 1940** commemorates the speech ulle gave in exile in London urging the French to resist the German invaders. The huge pulation in Montparnasse, having fled the expensive 5e and 6e arrondissements, ushers in t (but not necessarily greatest) developments in nightlife along boulevard du Montparnasse and d into offshoots of **avenue du Maine.**

few sights are worth visiting. The **Parc Montsouris** and **Cité Universitaire** area (*see* Parks and Gardens, *above*) is a great place to meet other foreigners in Paris. The **Cimetière du Montparnasse** has been packing them in for years, and the entrance to the network of **catacombs** is at place Denfert-Rochereau (*see* Dead Folk, *above*).

Montparnasse is probably best explored during the day, as you turn off the tree-lined boulevards onto scores of tiny streets and culs-de-sac lined with ivy-covered houses that look more like they belong in a country village than in Paris. **Villa Adrienne,** off avenue du Général-Leclerc, and **villa Hallé,** off avenue René-Coty, are both especially picturesque. Each house on villa Adrienne bears the name of a famous artist or philosopher instead of a numerical address. **Villa Seurat,** off rue de la Tombe-Issoire, saw the many comings and goings of Anaïs Nin, Henry Miller, and Lawrence Durrell. Several little streets leading away from Parc Montsouris off rue Nansouty, especially **square de Montsouris,** are likely to make you want to become a fabulously wealthy homeowner.

QUARTIER LATIN

The center of French intellectual life for over 700 years, the Quartier Latin has drawn the metaphysically restless, the politically discontent, the artistically inspired, and their hopeful wanna-bes to the neighborhood's universities, cafés, garrets, and alleys. In 1099 Peter Abelard came to the area to study with a local monk. He became a master of dialectics (the discovery of truth through debate), and students from all over Europe came to study with him, including the young Héloïse, whose uncle had Abelard castrated when he learned of the couple's love. In 1215 the Parisian crown and the Roman papacy officially recognized the teachings going on in the area, though the growing school wasn't baptized until 1257, when it took on the name of Robert de Sorbon's (chaplain to Louis IX) neighboring boarding house. Latin became the fashionable language in and out of the classroom, hence the neighborhood's name.

The conservative **Sorbonne** had strong ties to the church; because of this, Rabelais was particularly fond of taking jabs at the university. In 1530 some disgruntled students and professors set up camp next door, establishing the Collège de France, where the classics were taught in—gasp!—Greek instead of Latin. Intellectual life plodded along for the next 250 years, until the Revolution turned all the abbeys and cloisters of the universities into quarries. The curriculum fell under the direction of the government until 1808, when the University of Paris took over the Sorbonne. It took the 1968 student uprisings against conservative faculty and obsolete teaching methods to bring the Sorbonne into the 20th century and to "encourage" the formation of the 13 specialized schools of the University of Paris.

The presence of several institutions of higher learning, including the **Ecole Normale Supérieure** on rue d'Ulm, keeps the neighborhood youthful, creative, and relatively liberal. Cafés, bookstores, bars, and cheap restaurants proliferate, and even the presence of millions of tourists doesn't break the mood (though it can seriously dampen it in summer). Down toward the Seine, the maze of streets surrounding **rue de la Huchette** are the ultimate experience in crowd tolerance, though you might find some good crepes or street music there. Napoléon Bonaparte settled at 10 rue de la Huchette. Just to the west, **place St-Michel** and its fountain act as a good meeting spot.

An excellent place to get "lost" is in the labyrinthine streets between **place Maubert** and the Seine; these streets manage to retain their medieval feel despite the presence of fast-food joints and expensive residences (Mitterrand's private home was at 22 rue de Bièvre). The **square René-Viviani,** just east of the Huchette madness, is a pleasant little park with the oldest tree in Paris, sprouted in 1601. **Shakespeare & Company,** a handy refuge for Anglophones, is next door (*see* English-Language Bookstores *in* Chapter 6). Don't forget to check out the bibliophilic *bouquinistes* (booksellers) along the Seine, where you can rummage through rare books, posters, and postcards.

The area around the Sorbonne and behind the **Panthéon** (*see* Dead Folk, *above*) merits serious exploration as well. Pretty **place de la Contrescarpe,** and tumbling **rue Mouffetard** leading off it, are lively day and night when students from the nearby Grandes Ecoles congregate here. After walking the length of rue Mouffetard, take a peek at the **Eglise St-Médard** (141 rue Mouffetard). Between 1728 and 1732, there was a series of miracles, séances, and visions in one of the chapels, causing the government great consternation; an anonymous pundit scrawled on a side door, "The King has decreed that God is prohibited from making miracles in this place." **Rue de la Montagne-Ste-Geneviève,** winding between the Panthéon and **place Maubert,** is one of the oldest streets in Paris, with a number of buildings dating from the Middle Ages.

If you're in search of a less perfectly packaged part of the Quartier Latin, keep to the fringes and note the Eastern influence in the 13e arrondissement, where many Asian communities thrive. **Avenue des Gobelins** goes by the famous tapestry factory, the Manufacture des Gobelins (a turn down the side street brings you to the leafy **Square René-Le Gall**) and directly to the **place d'Italie.** Continue south on rue Bobillot to the charming **rue de la Butte-aux-Cailles,** a perfectly preserved example of old Paris. The little streets in this area have inexpensive bars and restaurants, but the locals will not take kindly to a passel of loud Americans plunking down at a table—go exploring quietly by yourself or with one unobtrusive friend.

ST-GERMAIN-DES-PRES

The time-honored tradition of barricading streets in the Quartier Latin with pried-up cobblestones was brought to a close during the student rebellions of 1968: The government poured tar over every last tempting stone.

The venerable tower of St-Germain-des-Prés, the oldest church in Paris, anchors a neighborhood of bookstores, art galleries, designer boutiques, and cafés where Picasso, Camus, Sartre, and de Beauvoir spent their days and nights. The cynical and the nostalgic bemoan that the area has relinquished its spirit to the hands of the mainstream, the upscale, and the comfortable—and it's true that in summer you'll encounter many tourists in the shops and cafés. But wander off the traffic-clogged boulevard St-Germain, and you'll find winding streets, ancient facades, and hidden courtyards that defy the onrush of modernity.

A short walking tour: Start at **Eglise St-Germain-des-Prés,** where monks once set up camp and blessed the area with an intellectual reputation, bringing international art and culture to the city. Rousseau and Voltaire, unable to get support elsewhere, were published in the St-Germain abbey. Literati continue to haunt the tables of **Les Deux Magots** and **Café Flore,** two overpriced cafés on boulevard St-Germain. Les Deux Magots was the favorite of Verlaine and Mallarmé, the Flore of Jean-Paul and Simone, Camus, and Picasso, although only the Flore is still populated by French intellectuals. From the Eglise St-Germain, take rue Bonaparte toward the river and you'll soon reach the once-great **Ecole Nationale Supérieure des Beaux-Arts** (the art school). Take a detour to your right down **rue Visconti**: At No. 17 a young Balzac founded an unsuccessful press. On the other side of the Beaux-Arts school, Serge Gainsbourg had his Parisian digs at 5 bis rue Verneuil (today covered with spray paint) until his death in 1991. Similar in style and impact to American Bob Dylan in his songwriting and general presence, Gainsbourg became a folk hero and national idol for his poetic but risqué songs. He's buried in the Cimetière du Montparnasse (*see* Dead Folk, *above*). Turn right at the river and walk past the **Institut de France** (at the corner of quai de Conti and Pont des Arts), the seat of the Académie Française, which Richelieu created in 1635 in an attempt to supervise the activities of Parisian intellectuals. The Académie is still around, defending the French language from foreign invaders—its latest stroke of brilliance was to *outlaw* the commercial use of non-French (read: English) words in France, though this was soon declared unconstitutional.

Walking along the Seine toward the Louvre, you pass **rue des Grands-Augustins,** where at No. 5–7 Picasso enjoyed his last—and most luxurious—Parisian home from 1936 to 1955. Turn away from the river again on rue Dauphine, veering left at the fork a few blocks up, and you'll hit the **cour de Rohan,** where Dr. Joseph-Ignace Guillotin invented an execution device he described as a "puff of air on the neck" of the victim. Farther ahead, near place de l'Odéon, a statue of Danton marks where this great revolutionary once lived (Haussmann had his way with the actual building). Great streets branch south off place Henri-Mondor, including the tiny **rue de l'Ecole-de-Médecine,** where Sarah Bernhardt was born at No. 5. To the west lies **rue Monsieur-le-Prince;** No. 14 was home to American writer Richard Wright (from 1948 to 1959) and composer Camille Saint-Saëns (from 1877 to 1889). Head west a few

RODIN AND BALZAC

It made perfect sense that the greatest French writer of his time should be sculpted by the greatest French artist of his time: so Société des Gens de Lettres president Emile Zola commissioned Auguste Rodin to immortalize Honoré de Balzac. Despite the objections of society members, who saw the artist as out-of-touch and incompetent, Rodin accepted the proposal to erect a sculpture at the small place Guillaumin. Though his health was failing, Rodin traveled to the town where Balzac was born and sketched local peasants as models for the long-dead writer.

The final version of the sculpture, unveiled in 1898, was a towering image of the writer with a backward-arching body, shoulders draped by a formless gown, and hands clutched at the waist. Rodin insisted that the work be mounted on a tall pedestal, forcing viewers to gaze up. The similarity between the work and a phallus is hardly accidental—both Rodin and Balzac were notorious for their high opinions of their own virility. The society refused the work and gave the commission to A. Jolguière who obediently produced a larger-than-life image of Balzac sitting fully clothed in an armchair. This work was installed in the square in 1900 and has been largely neglected ever since. The original Rodin Balzac is on a traffic island on boulevard du Montparnasse at boulevard Raspail.

blocks to **rue de Tournon,** whose 18th-century hôtels particuliers have housed too many celebrities to mention (read the plaques), among them Casanova (No. 27) and Balzac (No. 2). If you roam St-Germain with your eyes tilted upward, you'll find plenty of commemorative plaques to keep you busy.

Don't miss **rue St-André-des-Arts,** a pedestrian street roughly between place St-Michel and carrefour de Buci, lined with crêperies, postcard shops, and a good experimental cinema. The nearby **cour du Commerce St-André** (an alley between rue St-André-des-Arts and boulevard St-Germain) was opened in 1776 and saw all sorts of revolutionary activity, including the printing of Marat's *L'Ami du Peuple* at No. 8, the beheading of subversives at No. 9, and the daily life of Danton in his seven-room apartment at No. 20.

WHERE TO SLEEP

UPDATED BY SUZANNE ROWAN KELLEHER

nless you have well-placed friends, Paris isn't the cheapest place to spend a night. Nonetheless, soaking up the City of Light doesn't have to break the bank. It's possible to get a nice double room for 500F or less. The bottom line is that you should expect to pay a minimum of 250F just for a basic, clean, and, perhaps, slightly threadbare double with toilet and shower. If you don't mind sharing bathroom facilities, you can land equally simple quarters with only a sink for about 200F. Anything much cheaper than that and you're likely to be in a dark, dingy room with a cigarette-burned bedspread. But, frankly, at that price you're better off in one of Paris's nicer hostels, which are a bargain and in some of the city's choicest locations.

HOTELS

Even with Paris's huge choice of hotels, you should always reserve well in advance, especially if you're determined to stay in a specific hotel. You can do this by telephoning ahead, then writing or faxing for confirmation. If you're asked to send a deposit, be sure to discuss refund policies before releasing your credit card number or mailing your check or money order. During peak seasons, some hotels require total prepayment. Always demand written confirmation of your reservation, detailing the duration of your stay, the price, the location (overlooking street or courtyard) and the type of your room (single, twin, or double), and bathroom specifics (private bathroom, etc.). If you're in Paris from July to August or December to March—considered the city's low seasons—it's worth asking if lower rates are available.

Be prepared for a room that is considerably smaller than you're used to back home. Think of it as an authentic experience: rooms were built on a smaller scale two and three centuries ago. Although air-conditioning has become de rigueur in middle- to higher-priced hotels, it is generally not a prerequisite for comfort (thankfully it's not hot in Paris for long).

Keep in mind, too, that the less you pay, the more likely it is that you will have to share bathroom facilities. If you're willing to pay 300F or more, you'll probably get a private bathroom. When booking a room in a rock-bottom budget hotel, don't assume that what is billed as a bathroom will necessarily contain a tub. Some rooms have toilets (what the French call *wc* or *cabinet de toilet*) or bidets only—with shower or bath facilities down the hall (and often at an extra charge). When you book, you need to specify if you

AN AMERICAN IN PARIS

Disillusioned by America's Prohibition laws and the aftermath of World War I, and lured by favorable exchange rates and a booming artistic scene, many American writers, composers, and painters moved to Paris in the 1920s and 1930s. Here's where some of those early expats lived:

AARON COPLAND: 30 rue de Vaugirard, 15e.

E. E. CUMMINGS: 46 rue St-André-des-Arts, 6e.

JAMES BALDWIN: 170 boulevard St-Germain, 6e.

NATALIE BARNEY: 20 rue Jacob, 6e.

ZELDA and F. SCOTT FITZGERALD: 14 rue de Tilsitt, 8e.

JANET FLANNER: 36 rue Bonaparte, 6e.

FORD MADOX FORD: 32 rue Vaugirard, 15e.

ERNEST HEMINGWAY: 44 rue Jacob, 6e; 74 rue du Cardinal-Lemoine, 5e; 113 rue Notre-Dame-des-Champs, 6e; and others.

WILLIAM FAULKNER: 26 rue Servandoni (entrance at 42 rue de Vaugirard), 15e.

HENRY MILLER: most notably at 100 rue de la Tombe-Issoire, 14e.

JOHN DOS PASSOS: 45 quai de la Tournelle, 5e.

COLE PORTER: 269 rue St-Jacques, 5e.

GERTRUDE STEIN and ALICE B. TOKLAS: 27 rue de Fleurus, 6e; and 5 rue Christine, 6e.

require a private bathroom (*salle de bain privée*) with a tub (*baignoire*) or shower (*douche*). Hall showers (typically 5F–25F) are usually decent, but bring thongs just in case.

Almost all hotels in Paris charge extra for breakfast, starting at around 25F. For anything more than the standard Continental breakfast of café au lait (coffee with hot milk) and baguette or croissants, the price will be higher. Be sure to inform the desk staff if you don't plan to have breakfast at the hotel, so that they don't charge you for it. You're usually better off finding the nearest café or *boulangerie* (bakery).

You'll notice that stars appear on a shield on the facade of most hotels. The French government grades hotels on a scale of one to four stars based on a complex evaluation system. At the bottom end are one-star hotels, where you might have to share a bathroom and do without an elevator. Two- and three-star hotels generally have private bathrooms, elevators, and in-room televisions. The ratings are sometimes misleading, however, since many hotels prefer to be understarred for tax reasons.

Price categories in this book refer to the cost of a double room plus tax. If a hotel has doubles in a wide range of prices, our price category generally refers to the less expensive doubles. It's worth asking whether a hotel has singles, which are generally around 50F less than doubles. Rates must be posted in all rooms (usually on the backs of doors), with all extra charges clearly shown. There is a small *séjour* tax of 7 francs per person, per night. Unless otherwise stated, the hotels reviewed below accept most major credit cards.

ARC DE TRIOMPHE AND MONCEAU

The 16th and 17th arrondissements, sprawling out from the Arc de Triomphe and the Parc Monceau, are Paris's most hoity-toity residential neighborhoods. Walk out the door and you'll be steps away from true Parisian elegance. Not surprisingly, the area isn't a bastion of budget finds, but you can find a few good, affordable options.

UNDER 400F • Hôtel des Deux Acacias. This fin-de-siècle hotel was modernized in the early nineties (in unimaginative but inoffensive pastels), though some of the belle epoque details remain. Doubles with shower are 350F, tubs are a little more; singles with shower are 310F. In summer, breakfast is served in the garden under the two acacias for which the hotel is named. *28 rue de l'Arc de Triomphe, 75017, tel. 01–43–80–01–85, fax 01–40–53–94–62. Métro: Charles-de-Gaulle–Etoile. 50 rooms with toilet and shower or bath.*

L'Ouest. Montmartre, the Parc Monceau, and the *grands magasins* (department stores) are all within easy reach of this unpretentious hotel. Although it overlooks the railroad tracks near Pont-Cardinet station, you'll get a restful sleep—rooms are soundproof. They are also clean and simple, and some are sunnier or more spacious, so make your preference known. Doubles run 375F, whether the room has a tub or shower; singles are 325F. *165 rue de Rome, 75017, tel. 01–42–27–50–29, fax 01–42–27–27–40. Métro: Rome, Villiers. 16 rooms with toilet and bath, 32 with toilet and shower. Bar.*

Palma. The friendly and efficient Couderc family runs this small, old-fashioned hotel between the Arc de Triomphe and Porte Maillot. Rooms are decorated with bright floral wallpaper, which gives the place a cheery, if generic, feel; ask for one of the top-floor rooms so you can have a view of the arch. Doubles with shower cost 380F; those with tub are 400F. Five rooms have air-conditioning. *46 rue Brunel, 75017, tel. 01–45–74–74–51, fax 01–45–74–40–90. Métro: Argentine. 13 rooms with toilet and bath, 24 with toilet and shower.*

UNDER 450F • Keppler. Near the Champs-Elysées, on the edge of the 8th and 16th arrondissements, this small hotel in a 19th century building is a cut above other budget options in the neighborhood. The spacious and airy rooms are simply decorated with wood furnishings and bright fabrics, and have satellite TV. Singles and doubles with toilet and shower cost 400F. *12 rue Keppler, 75016, tel. 01–47–20–65–05, fax 01–47–23–02–29. Métro: George V. 31 rooms with toilet and bath, 18 with toilet and shower. Bar.*

BASTILLE

Spreading over the 11th and 12th arrondissements on the Right Bank, the Bastille is all about cool cafés, cheap restaurants, and lively bars full of young people. If you're a night owl, the Bastille is right up your alley—it's the only area in Paris still humming at 4 AM. For you quieter types, there are some nice side streets that evoke Paris of yore.

DIRT CHEAP • Hôtel de l'Europe. This small but impersonal hotel has roomy, clean, basic doubles, and is popular with mostly German tourists. The cheapest rooms, without showers, go for 185F. A shower (with a shared toilet) will cost you 220F, a private bathroom 240F. Ask for a room with a balcony for no extra charge. *74 rue Sedaine, 75011, tel. 01–47–00–54–38, fax 01–47–00–75–31. Métro: Voltaire. 6 rooms with toilet and shower, 10 rooms with shower only, 6 rooms with sink only.*

Hôtel de la Herse d'Or. The Golden Gateway, right off the place de la Bastille, is popular with young travelers and backpackers. Rooms are basic and spotless. Doubles with toilet and no shower are 200F; a room with a shower will run you 260F, and a tub more. Singles are 160F. The rooms off the street are infinitely quieter, but darker—so you'll have to decide what you need more, sunlight or sleep. *20 rue St-Antoine, 4e, tel. 01–48–87–84–09, fax 01–42–78–12–68. Métro: Bastille. 23 rooms with toilet and shower, 12 with sink only.*

UNDER 300F • Pax Hôtel. The Pax is no palace, which the 1970s-style lobby will clue you into right away. But a young, very trendy crowd makes it their own. If you want to be in the thick of Bastille action, you can't beat the location near all the galleries and clubs. Rooms are spartan but meticulously maintained and have TVs. Doubles with shower go for 290F; singles with sink only are 210F. *12 rue de*

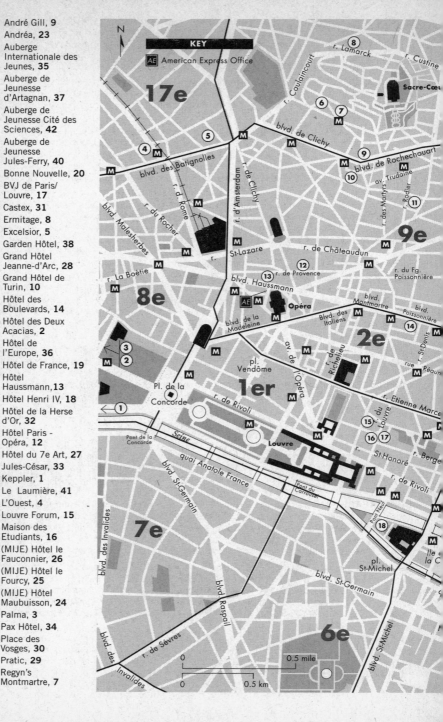

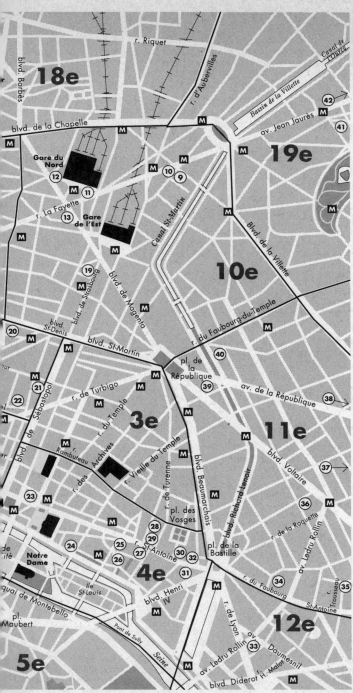

Résidence
Alhambra, **39**
Roubaix, **21**
Tiquetonne, **22**
Utrillo, **6**
Woodstock, **11**

18e

r. Riquet

blvd. Barbès

r. d'Aubervilles

Canal de l'Ourcq

Bassin de la Villette

av. Jean Jaurès

42

41

blvd. de la Chapelle

M

19e

Gare du Nord

12

10 9

M

11

r. La Fayette

13

Gare de l'Est

M

Canal St-Martin

Blvd. de la Villette

19

M

blvd. de Strasbourg

blvd. de Magenta

10e

blvd. St-Denis

20

blvd. St-Martin

r. du Faubourg-du-Temple

M

40

pl. de la République

39

av. de la République

38

M

21

r. de Turbigo

de Sébastopol

22

3e

r. du Temple

11e

M

blvd. Voltaire

37

r. Rambuteau

r. des Archives

r. Vieille du Temple

r. de Turenne

blvd. Beaumarchais

blvd. Richard Lenoir

36

M

r. de la Roquette

23

M

pl. des Vosges

28

24

25

29

r. St-Antoine

30

32

av. Ledru Rollin

Notre Dame

27

26

pl. de la Bastille

4e

31

r. du Faubourg

34

St-Antoine

35

r. Trousseau

île St-Louis

blvd. Henri IV

r. de Lyon

12e

quai de Montebello

Pont de Sully

Seine

r. de Ledru Rollin

33

av. Daumesnil

pl. Maubert

av. Ledru Rollin

M

blvd. Diderot

H. Malot

5e

Charonne, 11e, tel. 01–47–00–40–98, fax 01–43–38–57–81. Métro: Bastille. 37 rooms with toilet and shower, 10 with sink only.

UNDER 350F • Jules-César. This hotel, open since 1930, has a rather glitzy marble lobby. Thankfully, rooms are more subdued, with plain wood furnishings and beige fabrics to match. Ask for one of the rooms facing the street; they are larger and sunnier than the ones in the back, but go for the same price: 345F for a double (with bath or shower). Best of all, the hotel is only a short walk from the Gare de Lyon and the Opéra Bastille. *52 av. Ledru-Rollin, 75012, tel. 01–43–43–15–88, fax 01–43–43–53–60. Métro: Gare de Lyon, Ledru-Rollin. 4 rooms with toilet and bath, 44 with toilet and shower.*

Résidence Alhambra. You won't be right in the midst of the Bastille nightlife—a blessing or a burden depending on your perspective—if you stay at this hotel in a 19th-century building. But you will be within walking distance of the Marais and the place de la République, where five métro lines converge. Rooms are smallish, spartan, and innocuously decorated in pastels, and have satellite TV. The quietest overlook the pretty back garden. The least expensive doubles (with shower) run 320F. *13 rue de Malte, 75011, tel. 01–47–00–35–52, fax 01–43–57–98–75. Métro: Oberkampf. 10 rooms with bath, 48 with shower.*

BELLEVILLE AND PERE-LACHAISE

As the Bastille becomes too trendy for its own good, young people, attracted to the cheaper prices around Belleville, in the northern part of the 20th arrondissement, have started to move to this immigrant-dominant neighborhood. A stay here can mean respite from the swarm of August tourists—and it's a must for Jim Morrison devotees who plan on spending days elbowing crowds at nearby Père-Lachaise.

UNDER 300F • Le Laumière. At this family-run hotel near the rambling Buttes-Chaumont park, request one of the rooms overlooking the pretty garden. Though all the rooms share the same stiff, contemporary style, the warm, enthusiastic welcome more than makes up for it. Doubles range from 280F (with shower) to 360F (with tub). *4 rue Petit, 75019, tel. 01–42–06–10–77, fax 01–42–06–72–50. Métro: Laumière. 18 rooms with toilet and bath, 36 with toilet and shower.*

UNDER 350F • Garden Hôtel. This family-run hotel is on a pretty garden square 10 minutes from Père-Lachaise. Be prepared to try out your French, as the staff speaks little English. Rooms have private bathrooms and are spotless, if functionally decorated. Ask for one overlooking the square; the view costs nothing extra. Those with shower only are 300F. It's not worth springing the additional 50F for one of the four rooms with half-size tubs. *1 rue du Général-Blaise, 75011, tel. 01–47–00–57–93, fax 01–47–00–45–29. Métro: St-Ambroise. 4 rooms with toilet and bath, 38 with toilet and shower.*

GARE DE L'EST

This part of Paris, surrounding the train station, isn't one of the city's most beautiful (or quietest) spots. But it's a convenient place to stay if you're on your way in or out of the city.

UNDER 300F • Hôtel de France. This modest, turn-of-the-century hotel is the biggest bargain near the Gare de l'Est. Don't expect frills: just a clean room with inoffensive pastel decor for 250F. *3 rue Jarry, 75010, tel. 01–45–23–50–00, fax 01–45–23–30–65. Métro: Gare de l'Est. 35 rooms with toilet and shower. In-room safes.*

LES HALLES

Lively and a bit more downscale than the rest of central Paris, Les Halles makes for a cheap but not necessarily quiet place to get some sleep. Also known as Beaubourg, the quarter has some good inexpensive shopping and nightlife. It's also steps away from the Centre Pompidou and the Louvre. But steer clear of rue St-Denis, a sleazy (though fairly safe) pocket of prostitution and sex shops.

DIRT CHEAP • Andréa. You can get a relatively spacious double at this modest hotel, but insist on a room away from noisy rue de Rivoli. For the five smallish, bargain 200F doubles (with sink only) be sure to book months in advance; the others are more expensive. *3 rue St-Bon, 75004, tel. 01–42–78–43–93. Métro: Hôtel de Ville or Châtelet. 21 rooms with toilet and shower, 5 with sink only.*

Hôtel des Boulevards. A short walk from Les Halles, this hotel has immaculate, basic rooms with bright chenille bedspreads and beige walls. The bargain option is the doubles for as little as 185F with a shower but no toilet. A toilet and shower will run you 255F, and a tub 290F. Breakfast is included in the deal. *10 rue de la Ville-Neuve, 75002, tel. 01-42-36-02-29, fax 01-42-36-15-39. Métro: Bonne Nouvelle. 6 rooms with toilet and tub, 8 with toilet and shower, 4 with shower but no toilet.*

Tiquetonne. If all you need is a simple, clean room on a quiet street near Les Halles, then this place is for you. If you're traveling solo, ask for one of the dozen singles that share facilities and cost under 140F. Doubles (with private bathrooms) are 225F. *6 rue Tiquetonne, 75002, tel. 01-42-36-94-58, fax 01-42-36-02-94. Métro: Etienne Marcel. 35 rooms with toilet and shower, 12 with sink only.*

UNDER 350F • Bonne Nouvelle. Reproductions of famous paintings and photos from bygone eras give this clean, comfortable hotel near Les Halles a warm, slightly retro feel. Rooms range in size from very small (310F for a double) to spacious rooms with two twin beds overlooking the street (410F). *17 rue Beauregard, 75002, tel. 01-45-08-42-42, fax 01-40-26-05-81. Métro: Bonne Nouvelle. 20 rooms with toilet and shower.*

Roubaix. There's a friendly, slightly kitschy atmosphere at this hotel just north of Les Halles. The cheapest rooms are 330F, the most expensive are 370F (it depends on the size). Singles go for 185F. For this, you'll get an impeccably maintained, comfortable room with double-glazed windows, satellite TV, and floral wallpaper. *6 rue Grénéta, 75003, tel. 01-42-72-89-91, fax 01-42-72-58-78. Métro: Réaumur-Sébastopol. 53 rooms with toilet and shower.*

LOUVRE AND OPERA

You can't get any more central than this—smack in the historic heart of Paris amid the city's grandest monuments. As a bonus, the area is one of the most beautiful in Paris. Although you'd never call it a bargain-hunter's playground, the neighborhood does have some inexpensive hotels.

DIRT CHEAP • Hôtel Henri IV. Backpackers and young travelers consider this hotel a well-situated haven, but older folks might not see the romance. Actually, it's amazing to find such good prices for the location—on the northernmost tip of the Ile de la Cité, blessedly near Notre-Dame and far away from Parisian traffic. Sure, the lobby is bleak and the creaky halls extremely narrow, but it all adds to the place's rustic charm. The rooms with just a sink go for under 200F, and the two with toilet and shower are 250F. The place is almost consistently full, so book well ahead. *25 pl. Dauphine, 75001, tel. 01-43-54-44-53. Métro: Pont Neuf. 2 rooms with toilet and shower, 20 with sink only. Cash only.*

UNDER 300F • Hôtel Haussmann. Near the grands magasins and right behind the Opéra, you'll find this clean, small, professionally run place. Mostly French people stay here, hence the slightly smoky rooms and ubiquitous mirrors. Book ahead: At this price (285F for a double), rooms go fast. *89 rue de Provence, 75009, tel. 01-48-74-24-57, fax 01-44-91-97-25. Métro: Havre-Caumartin. 34 rooms with toilet and bath.*

Hôtel Paris-Opéra. This place is right around the corner from the Opéra and the grands magasins. Request a room that's not facing the street and you'll get a quieter night's sleep. Doubles go for 265F, singles (with sink only) for 185F. *76 rue de Provence, 75009, tel. 01-48-74-12-15, fax 01-40-16-43-34. Métro: Chaussée d'Antin. 29 rooms with toilet and shower, 3 with sink only.*

UNDER 400F • Louvre Forum. The central location and the eager-to-please staff make this hotel a good place to stay, not to mention the clean, comfortable, well-equipped rooms (featuring satellite TV) starting at 350F. Breakfast is served in the vaulted cellar. *25 rue du Bouloi, 75001, tel. 01-42-36-54-19, fax 01-42-33-66-31. Métro: Louvre. 11 rooms with toilet and bath, 16 with toilet and shower. Bar.*

LE MARAIS

The Marais, a Seine-side neighborhood sandwiched between Les Halles and the Bastille, is one of the best places to stay in Paris. Brimming with Revolution-era architecture, funky shops, a clutch of kosher delis, an active gay community, and myriad wine bars and cafés, the quarter is Paris's answer to New York's Greenwich Village.

UNDER 300F • Pratic. The best thing about this hotel is its location, just a block from the place des Vosges. Rooms are done in a casual, mix-and-match style; ask for one facing the little place du Marché-Ste-Catherine. Count on paying 290F for a double with a shower only, and 340F for one with toilet and shower. A caveat: If you go for one of the showerless rooms (245F), you may have to descend as many as four flights to bathe. *9 rue d'Ormesson, 75004, tel. 01-48-87-80-47, fax 01-48-87-40-04. Métro: St-Paul. 5 with toilet and shower, 10 with shower only, 7 with neither toilet nor shower.*

UNDER 350F • Castex. This hotel in a Revolution-era building has rooms that are low on frills but squeaky clean. Doubles with shower and shared toilet are 300F; a private bathroom with shower or tub will run you 320F–340F; the one triple goes for 440F. A big plus is the extremely friendly owners. Many Americans stay here, which means that the place is often booked months ahead—so make reservations early. There's no elevator, and the only TV is in the ground-floor salon. *5 rue Castex, 75004, tel. 01–42–72–31–52, fax 01–42–72–57–91. Métro: St-Paul. 4 rooms with toilet and bath, 15 with toilet and shower, 8 with shower only.*

Grand Hôtel Jeanne-d'Arc. At this standard hotel you'll get a good-size, spotless, modern double with a bathroom, TV, telephone, and maybe even a couch for 310F and up. It's a good place for families, as there are rooms with extra single beds (an additional 70F) and the friendly, English-speaking manager will help you set up cribs or cots as needed. *3 rue de Jarente, 75004, tel. 01–48–87–62–11. Métro: St-Paul. 36 rooms with toilet and shower.*

UNDER 450F • Hôtel du 7e Art. Many a hipster has inked this hotel into his or her journal. The name fits the theme ("Seventh Art" is what the French call filmmaking): Hollywood from the '40s to the '60s, and posters of Cagney, Marilyn, Chaplin, and others cover the walls. Rates start at 410F (but go as high as 650F), so ask for one of the cheaper rooms. They're small and spartan, but they're also clean and quiet—and have cable TV. Be prepared to walk up: There's no elevator, but there is a pleasant bar to help you prepare your way. *20 rue St-Paul, 75004, tel. 01–42–77–04–03, fax 01–42–77–69–10. Métro: St-Paul. 9 rooms with toilet and bath, 14 with toilet and shower. Bar, in-room safes.*

UNDER 500F • Place des Vosges. A loyal and eclectic clientele swears by this small, historic hotel on a pretty little street off place des Vosges. The Louis XIII-style furniture in the lobby, and oak-beamed ceilings and rough-hewn stone in the rooms evoke that old Marais feeling. Ask for the top-floor room, the hotel's largest, for the view over the rooftops. Be aware that the least expensive rooms (400F with shower) are the size of walk-in closets; springing for one of the decent-size doubles will only set you back 460F. *12 rue de Birague, 4e, tel. 01–42–72–60–46, fax 01–42–72–02–64. 11 rooms with toilet and bath, 5 with toilet and shower. Métro: St-Paul.*

MONTMARTRE

Perched on the northern edge of the city, Montmartre epitomizes Paris's bohemian alter ego (it was the haunt of Picasso, Baudelaire, and Renoir, among others). Most major attractions are just 10 minutes away by métro, so it's a good bet if you're budget-minded and into experiencing more than just the main sights. At the bottom of Montmartre is Pigalle, where you'll find all the hokey cabarets, sex shops, and cross-dressing prostitutes—you may want to avoid it, or just pass through it for a look (it's fairly safe). It's better to stick to the streets near place des Abbesses and rue Lepic (where there's a market on weekends) for inexpensive and infinitely more respectable options.

DIRT CHEAP • Grand Hôtel de Turin. Although it's on the seedy side of Montmartre near the Moulin Rouge, this hotel has clean, surprisingly spacious rooms with comfortable beds. Doubles go for 245F. *6 rue Victor-Massé, 75009, tel. 01–48–78–45–26, fax 01–42–80–61–50. Métro: Pigalle. 14 rooms with toilet and bath, 37 with toilet and shower.*

UNDER 300F • André Gill. Not only does this hotel have a friendly staff, but the rooms are also some of the nicest in Montmartre—the plush carpeting does wonders for tired feet and some even have stained-glass windows. Don't fret that it's only two blocks from Pigalle's sex shops; it's only one block away from pretty rue des Abbesses. Doubles (with private bathrooms) go for 285F; singles with sink-only can be had for 190F. Rates include breakfast. *4 rue André-Gill, 75018, tel. 01–42–62–48–48, fax 01–42–62–77–92. Métro: Abbesses. 22 rooms with toilet and shower, 10 with sink only.*

UNDER 400F • Excelsior. Five minutes from place des Abbesses, this hotel has a rustic and homey atmosphere. For 385F you'll get a small, spotless room furnished with country-style antiques and big armoires; request one overlooking the little garden. *16 rue Caroline, 75017, tel. 01–45–22–50–95, fax 01–45–22–59–88. Métro: Place de Clichy. 19 rooms with toilet and bath, 3 with toilet and shower. Laundry.*

UNDER 450F • Ermitage. This elfin, family-run hotel dates from Napoléon III's time. Rooms are filled with antiques and evoke the feel of the old Montmartrois village days. The building is only two stories high, but the *butte* (hill) of Montmartre ensures that some rooms have a good view of Paris. Doubles (with shower) start at 425F; a tub will cost you 50F extra. *24 rue Lamarck, 75018, tel. 01–42–64–79–22, fax 01–42–64–10–33. Métro: Lamarck-Caulaincourt. 3 rooms with toilet and bath, 9 with toilet and shower. Cash only.*

Regyn's Montmartre. Rooms start at 430F at this owner-run hotel right on place des Abbesses. Many are on the small side, but they are clean and have firm beds. Each floor is dedicated to a Montmartre artist, and poetry by local writers is framed and hung in the hallways. Request a room on the top two floors for a great view of the Eiffel Tower or the Sacré-Coeur at no extra charge. The courteous service and the relaxed atmosphere make this place just the ticket. *18 pl. des Abbesses, 75018, tel. 01–42–54–45–21, fax 01–42–23–76–69. Métro: Abbesses. 14 rooms with toilet and bath, 8 with toilet and shower. In-room safes.*

Utrillo. Check it out: For 440F you get fabulous views of the city *and* the use of the sauna. This hotel is on a quiet side street at the foot of Montmartre, near rue Lepic. The impressionist prints and the marble-top breakfast tables in every room make the place feel old-fashioned, and the white-and-pastel color scheme gives them a bright and spacious feel. Ask for Room 61 or 63; both have views of the Eiffel Tower. *7 rue Aristide-Bruant, 75018, tel. 01–42–58–13–44, fax 01–42–23–93–88. Métro: Abbesses. 5 rooms with toilet and bath, 25 with toilet and shower.*

MONTPARNASSE

Montparnasse expands across the sprawling 14th arrondissement and nudges its way into neighboring Left Bank districts, including the Quartier Latin and St-Germain. In Montparnasse's famous cafés, once the intellectual playground for the likes of Hemingway, Fitzgerald, and Miller, you'll find students, professors, and business people conversing over a coffee or an aperitif. Along the busy streets, be prepared to dodge shoppers and high-heeled speedwalkers.

The métro station Abbesses, near the Sacré-Coeur, has one of the few remaining art nouveau métropolitain archways. It also has a seven-flight, spiral staircase: Climb it, and you'll wonder why the place isn't called the Abyss.

DIRT CHEAP • Hôtel de l'Espérance. The "Hotel of Hope" is on a small street in the southern, less tourist-infested part of Montparnasse. Book well in advance for a 190F double with toilet; those with a sink only can be had for 140F. Rooms (with lace curtains and TV) either look worn and shabby or hopelessly romantic, depending on your disposition. But the proprietress is energetic and eager to please. It's also near a great market on rue Daguerre, so you can stock up on all your picnic needs. *1 rue de Grancey, 75014, tel. 01–43–21–41–04, fax 01–43–22–06–02. Métro: Denfert-Rochereau. 6 rooms with toilet, 4 with toilet and shower, 4 with sink only.*

UNDER 300F • Beaunier. A friendly welcome, a flower-filled patio, satellite TV, and well-kept, if basic, rooms make this hotel a good choice. Doubles go for 260F. *31 rue Beaunier, 75014, tel. 01–45–39–36–45, fax 01–45–39–33–55. Métro: Porte d'Orléans. 23 rooms with toilet and bath.*

Broussais Bon Secours. This little hotel is ideal if you require little more than a clean room and a good bed (doubles are 280F). A communal refrigerator in the salon is available so that you can keep your picnic supplies fresh and your beer or white wine cold. *3 rue Ledion, 75014, tel. 01–40–44–48–90, fax 01–40–44–96–76. Métro: Plaisance. 26 rooms with toilet and shower.*

Paris-Didot. The decor in this quiet hotel is a tad dated (stuck in the '70s/early '80s), but rooms are spotless and beds are firm. A double will run you 280F. *20 rue Ledion, 75014, tel. 01–45–42–33–29, fax 01–45–42–02–58. Métro: Plaisance. 30 rooms with toilet and shower.*

UNDER 350F • Parc Montsouris. This modest hotel in a 1930s villa (really more of a small house) is on a quiet residential street next to the Parc Montsouris. You can expect your room to be small but tastefully done in pastels and basic wood furnishings. There's even satellite TV. Rooms with shower are 320F; tubs cost an extra 60F. *4 rue du Parc-Montsouris, 75014, tel. 01–45–89–09–72, fax 01–45–80–92–72. Métro: Montparnasse-Bienvenue. 28 rooms with toilet and bath, 7 with toilet and shower.*

UNDER 400F • Midi. The facade and the reception area call to mind a chain hotel, but rooms are comfortably furnished in French provincial style and have large floor-to-ceiling windows. Those facing the street are quite spacious and no more expensive. Doubles with shower cost 360F; you'll pay about 70F more for a tub. *4 av. Réné-Coty, 75014, tel. 01–43–27–23–25, fax 01–43–21–24–58. Métro and RER: Denfert-Rochereau. 25 rooms with toilet and bath, 19 with toilet and shower. Refrigerators.*

Map labels

Seine

Pont de l'Alma
Pont des Invalides
Pont Alexandre III
Pont de la Concorde
Seine
Pont Solférino

pl. de la Résistance

quai d'Orsay
quai d'Orsay
quai Anatole France

r. de l'Université

av. Rapp
av. Bosquet
r. St-Dominique
av. de la Bourdonnais
r. de Grenelle
av. G-Eiffel

blvd. St-Germain
r. de Lille
r. de l'Université

Musée d'Orsay

av. de Suffren

Parc du Champ de Mars

av. de la Motte Picquet
av. de la Tour-Maubourg

Hôtel des Invalides

r. de Bourgogne
r. de Bellechasse
r. de Grenelle
r. du Bac

Ecole Militaire

av. de Tourville
av. de Villars
blvd. des Invalides

Vaneau
r. de Varenne
av. de Varenne

r. de Babylone

7e

av. de Lowendal
av. de Ségur
av. de Breteuil

blvd. de Commerce
blvd. de Grenelle
r. du Commerce

r. Frémicourt
blvd. Garibaldi
r. Cambronne
r. de la Croix-Nivert

r. de Sèvres
r. de Sèvres

blvd. Raspail
blvd. de Rennes

pl. du 18 Juin 1940

r. Lecourbe
r. Boromée
r. de Vaugirard
blvd. Pasteur
blvd. des Invalides

15e

r. d'Odessa
r. Delambre
blvd. Edgar Quinet

Cimetière du Montparnasse

0   1/2 mile
0   500 meters

Lodging index

3e

N

Louvre

1er

r. de Rivoli

blvd. Sébastopol

r. Beaubourg

4e

r. de Rivoli

Pont Royal

Pont du Carrousel

Pont des Arts

Pont Neuf

r. Jacob

r. de Seine

r. Mazarine

r. Dauphine

20

Pont au Change

Ile de la Cité

Pont d'Arcade

quai des Célestins

Notre Dame

Ile St-Louis

r. des Sts-Pères

blvd. St-Germain

19

r. St-André des Arts

pl. St-Michel

quai de Montebello

Pont de la Tournelle

Pont de Sully

r. du Four

r. de Rennes

r. de l'Odéon

Monsieur le Prince

r. St-Jacques

pl. Maubert

r. des Ecoles

24

25

r. Monge

27

quai St-Bernard

18

pl. St-Sulpice

21

26

r. Descartes

r. de Vaugirard

17

r. Guynemer

6e

Jardin du Luxembourg

r. Gay Lussac

22

23

r. Cujas

pl. du Panthéon

5e

Jardin des Plantes

r. d'Assas

blvd. St-Michel

r. d'Ulm

r. Lhomond

pl. de la Contrescarpe

r. Mouffetard

pl. Monge

r. Monge

blvd. du Montparnasse

r. de la Grande Chaumière

28

r. Claude Bernard

r. Berthollet

r. Censier

4 15 16

blvd. Raspail

14e

29 30

blvd. St-Marcel

NEAR THE EIFFEL TOWER

This is the Left Bank at its poshest. Fancy apartment buildings line the wide, tree-lined avenues of the 7th arrondissement, often invisible to the hordes of tourists rushing to the Eiffel Tower and Les Invalides. Although bargains are more illusive here than elsewhere, following are some good options.

UNDER 300F • Family. This well-run hotel has clean rooms and an efficient staff. For 290F you'll get a spic-and-span, if basic, double equipped with a kitchenette—a great way to save a few francs by doing a little home cooking. *23 rue Fondary, 75015, tel. 01–45–75–20–49, fax 01–45–77–70–73. Métro: Dupleix. 1 room with toilet and bath, 20 with toilet and shower. Kitchenettes.*

UNDER 400F • Champ de Mars. This little hotel is only a stone's throw from the rue Cler market, the Eiffel Tower, and Les Invalides. The look is blue-and-yellow French country-house style and the rooms are comfortable. They're also equipped with satellite TV. The ones on the ground floor open onto a leafy courtyard and are 390F, as are all the doubles with tub. Those with shower are only 360F. *7 rue du Champ de Mars, 75007, tel. 01–45–51–52–30, fax 01–45–51–64–36. Métro: Ecole Militaire. 19 rooms with toilet and bath, 6 with toilet and shower.*

Grand Hôtel Lévêque. It's hard to resist the location on one of Paris's most loved market streets, or the eager-to-please staff and comfortable, old-style rooms with satellite TV. There's no elevator, so try to avoid the top floors unless you're ready for a hike. Doubles are 380F, but the five singles without private bathrooms go for 225F, and the hall showers are free. *29 rue Cler, 75007, tel. 01–47–05–49–15, fax 01–45–50–49–36. Métro: Ecole Militaire. 45 rooms with toilet and shower, 5 with sink only. In-room safes.*

Turenne. The 19th-century facade is as elegant looking as the tony neighborhood surrounding it. Rooms have a more modern, neutral look. Doubles with shower go for 390F; tubs are 50F more. *20 av. de Tourville, 75007, tel. 01–47–05–99–92, fax 01–01–45–56–06–04. Métro: Ecole-Militaire. 18 rooms with toilet and bath, 16 with toilet and shower.*

UNDER 450F • Nevers. Despite its name, there's nothing negative about this place. In a cozy, 18th-century town house—on one of the city's ritziest streets—this hotel epitomizes unpretentious charm. Rooms are tiny, but they get lots of light and individual touches give them a homey atmosphere. Ask for No. 60, which has the best view over the streets. Doubles are 420F. *83 rue du Bac, 75007, tel. 01–45–44–61–30, fax 01–42–22–29–47. Métro: Sèvres-Babylone. 11 rooms with toilet and bath.*

UNDER 500F • Tour Eiffel Duplexix. Since you're this close, ask for one of the rooms with a great view of the Eiffel Tower. All are impeccably kept and done in basic neutral shades. They also have new, modern bathrooms, cable TV with CNN, and double-glazed windows. Doubles with shower are 460F, but during low season (July–August), they go for 390F; a tub will cost you another 70F. The buffet breakfast is a bargain at 35F. *11 rue Juge, 75015, tel. 01–45–78–29–29, fax 01–45–78–60–00. Métro: Dupleix. 30 rooms with toilet and bath, 10 with toilet and shower. Laundry.*

PLACE D'ITALIE

The often overlooked 13th arrondissement has traditionally been a working-class district. Here you'll find Paris's Chinatown and the appealing Butte aux Cailles neighborhood, with its hilly cobblestone streets and old houses. The hub of this area is busy place d'Italie.

DIRT CHEAP • COYPEL. Rooms at the Coypel are immaculate and basic in style, and have sound-proof windows to block out the noise from the street below. Doubles with private bathrooms run 210F; those with sink only can be had for under 160F. *2 rue Coypel, 75013, tel. 01–43–31–18–08, fax 01–47–07–27–45. Métro: Place d'Italie. 15 rooms with toilet and shower, 28 with sink only.*

UNDER 300F • Hôtel de la Place des Alpes. For 280F you can expect a clean, but spartan double with toilet and shower, and a friendly welcome. If you're willing to settle for just a shower, the rate drops to 220F. *2 pl. des Alpes, 75013, tel. 01–42–16–92–93, fax 01–45–86–30–06. Métro: Place d'Italie. 27 rooms with toilet and shower, 15 with shower only.*

QUARTIER LATIN

The Quartier Latin remains one of the most heavily visited districts in all of Paris. Its web of narrow streets and passages has been the stomping ground of students and intellectuals since the Middle Ages, though the cobblestone lanes now attract a more mixed crowd. Today you'll find as many natives as tourists hanging out here, especially in summer. Nonetheless, the area still delivers a very real, if laid-back, Paris experience, as well as a number of affordable hotels.

DIRT CHEAP • Marignan. A friendly French-American couple owns this modest hotel. Everything is very simple, from the look of the place to the functionally decorated rooms. A double with shared facilities is 220F; a private bathroom costs 270F. An added bonus is that you can do your laundry free. *13 rue du Sommerard, 75005, tel. 01–43–54–63–81. Métro: Maubert-Mutualité. 10 rooms with toilet and shower, 20 with sink only. Laundry.*

UNDER 400F • Cluny-Sorbonne. Overlooking the Sorbonne, this hotel has neo-classic furnishings and old-fashioned glass lampshades. The staff is friendly and the feel of the place is relaxed. Doubles start at 380F. *8 rue Victor-Cousin, 75005, tel. 01–43–54–66–66, fax 01–43–29–68–07. Métro: Luxembourg. 12 rooms with toilet and bath, 12 with toilet and shower.*

UNDER 500F • Familia. With owner Eric Gaucheron and his family bending over backward for you, it's hard not to feel like you're almost home. Rooms start at 380F, then climb to above 450F for one on the second or fifth floor with a walk-out balcony overlooking a typical Latin Quarter street (well worth the price). Or ask for one with a fresco depicting a Paris monument (painted by a Beaux-Arts graduate); others are furnished with fine Louis XV–style furnishings. *11 rue des Ecoles, 75005, tel. 01–43–54–55–27, fax 01–43–29–61–77. Métro: Cardinal Lemoine. 14 rooms with toilet and bath, 16 with toilet and shower.*

Grandes Ecoles. Okay, so we're cheating: Rooms here actually cost 510F, but this place is so nice you'll want to plunk down those extra francs. The hotel, off the main drag on a beautiful, leafy garden, looks and feels like a country cottage in the middle of Paris. Parquet floors, fancy Louis-Philippe-style furnishings, lace bedspreads, and the absence of TV all add to the rustic ambience. *75 rue du Cardinal Lemoine, 75005, tel. 01–43–26–79–23, fax 01–43–25–28–15. Métro: Cardinal Lemoine. 45 rooms with toilet and bath, 6 with toilet and shower.*

Grand Hôtel St-Michel. Between the boulevard St-Michel and the Panthéon, you'll find this hotel in a large, 19th-century town house. Rooms are clean and have modern bathrooms. Ask for one with a balcony; the best views are from the sixth floor. Doubles start at 490F and go all the way up to 700F. *19 rue de Cujas, 75005, tel. 01–46–33–33–02, fax 01–40–46–96–33. Métro: Cluny–La Sorbonne. 56 rooms with toilet and shower.*

Sorbonne. As you might expect from the name, this early 18th-century hotel has a slightly scruffy, academic ambience. Rooms are small but comfortably furnished with good beds and brightened with fresh flowers. Try to get one overlooking the little garden. Doubles are all 470F. *6 rue Victor-Cousin, 75005, tel. 01–43–54–58–08, fax 01–40–51–05–18. Métro: Cluny–La Sorbonne. 11 rooms with toilet and bath, 26 with toilet and shower.*

ST-GERMAIN-DES-PRES

This Left Bank district bordering the Seine cradles the oldest church in Paris (Eglise St-Germain) and has some of the most captivating, romantic streets in the city. It is also one of Paris's safest neighborhoods and it is near good shopping, a big park, and plenty of well-dressed French people. All this charm comes at a price, however. Following are some more affordable options.

UNDER 300F • Jean Bart. You can't beat this hotel's location right near the Jardin du Luxembourg. Rooms are clean and decorated in *style ancienne* (old-fashioned French style), with sturdy armoires and comfy beds. Doubles with shower are 280F; tubs are 30F extra. *9 rue Jean-Bart, 6e, tel. 01–45–48–29–13, no fax. Métro: St-Placide. 17 rooms with toilet and bath, 17 with toilet and shower.*

UNDER 350F • Hôtel du Globe. Find a little bit of the country at this tiny hotel in the heart of the 6th arrondissement. Very French, dark floral fabrics, wood beams, and, if you're lucky, a canopy bed add to the rustic ambience. Though the cheapest rooms (340F) are very small, they make you feel like you're in your own little garret. Reserve at least two weeks ahead to get one of them—their romantic appeal makes them very popular. *15 rue des Quatre-Vents, 75006, tel. 01–46–33–62–69. Métro: Mabillon. 6 rooms with toilet and bath, 9 with toilet and shower. Closed Aug.*

Nesle. This laid-back, no frills hotel is especially loved by backpackers. For 300F you'll get a clean, simple double with sink only; you'll pay 50F more for a private bathroom. Reservations are not accepted. *7 rue de Nesle, 75007, tel. 01–43–54–62–41, fax 01–45–23–30–65. Métro: Odéon. 10 rooms with toilet and shower, 10 with sink only. Cash only.*

Petit Trianon. Overlooking the lively rue de Buci market, this little hotel has sunny rooms with old-style upholsteries and a better quality of furnishings than you normally get for this price. The least expensive doubles (with toilet and shower) are 300F, but they go up to 700F. Singles are 170F–300F. But be forewarned: Prices vacillate according to season, so always get confirmation in writing. *2 rue de l'Ancienne-Comédie, 75006, tel. 01–43–54–94–64, no fax. Métro: Odéon. 12 rooms with toilet and shower, 1 with sink only.*

UNDER 450F • Acacias St-Germain. If you book early enough, you can snag one of the least expensive rooms in the hotel (doubles start at 400F but go up as high as 700F). The whole place is done up in the *style anglais*, which means it sort of looks like an English country inn with sturdy pine furniture and summery, floral fabrics. The staff is friendly. Ask about weekend discounts. *151 bis rue de Rennes, 75006, tel. 01–45–48–97–38, fax 01–45–44–63–57. Métro: St-Placide. 33 rooms and 4 apartments with bath, 8 rooms with shower. In-room safes, laundry.*

UNDER 500F • Aramis-St-Germain. The six cheapest rooms at this hotel barely make it into this category at 490F (the others climb to 590F). But for your money you'll get understated elegance, damask bedspreads, and cherry-wood armoires, as well as cable TV. Harvey's Piano Bar, on the ground floor, is popular with business types. *124 rue de Rennes, 75006, tel. 01–45–48–03–75, 800/528–1234 in the U.S., fax 01–45–44–99–29. Métro: St-Placide. 36 rooms with bath, 6 with shower. Bar, air-conditioning, laundry.*

HOSTELS AND FOYERS

Most of Paris's hostels and foyers are clean, reliable, and safe. Not only are they a bargain at 100F–170F a night for a bed with free showers and a baguette and coffee wake-up call, but they're also in some of the city's prime locales. Furthermore, they're great places to meet people, get tips, and hear about other travelers' adventures (or misadventures). And if you're traveling solo—and sick of being stiffed for a double rate by hotels—this is definitely the cheapest way to go, regardless of your age. Travelers of all ages stay in the hostels, though for the most part they are students or recent graduates, particularly in summer. The only drawback might be the early lockout hours at some of the hostels.

In summer, you should reserve *in writing* a month in advance, particularly for hostels in the **Latin Quarter** (5e), **St-Germain-des-Prés** (6e), the **Marais** (4e), and near the **Louvre** (1er). You'll probably have to provide a credit card number or fork over a deposit for the first night, so don't forget to get written confirmation in case of a mix-up. Because hostels book up quickly in summer, it's a good idea to check in as early as 7 AM. Accueil des Jeunes en France, or AJF (*see* Visitor Information *in* Chapter 1), can find you a last-minute cheap bed for a 10F fee, but don't expect miracles in high season. Unless otherwise noted, assume that hostels take MasterCard and Visa.

Auberges de jeunesse (youth hostels) are operated by Hostelling International (HI) or by private parties. Although *foyers* (student hostels) tend to house young workers and students, they often offer dormlike accommodation for travelers of all ages. Rates run 100F–130F for a bed. To get a room in high season, arrive between 8 AM and 10 AM or try reserving a room at HI hostels. Hostels and foyers often have fairly strict rules regarding curfews, late-night carousing, and alcohol intake, but be prepared for the occasional rowdy group making your night a sleepless hell.

HI HOSTELS

All three HI hostels are run by the Fédération Unie des Auberges de Jeunesse (FUAJ), the French branch of Hostelling International. For 130F, you'll get a bed, sheets, shower, and breakfast. Best of all, there's no curfew, which is a rare thing among Paris's youth hostels. Most rooms are single-sex, although if it's really crowded they'll put you wherever they can. To reserve a space ahead of time at the Cité des Sciences or d'Artagnan hostels, call the HI-AYH office in Washington, D.C. (tel. 202/783–6161) and give them your credit card number; they'll charge you for the price of a night's stay plus a $6 booking fee. The third HI hostel is at 84 boulevard Jules Ferry and doesn't take reservations. Show up before 10 AM to secure a spot. Be sure to note the afternoon lockout hours (noon–3 PM). But first you'll need a hostel card, which you can buy for 100F at any of the four FUAJ offices in Paris. **FUAJ Beaubourg:** 9 rue Brantôme, 3e, tel. 01–48–04–70–40, métro Châtelet. **FUAJ Ile de France:** 9 rue Notre-Dame-de-Lorette, 9e, tel. 01–42–85–55–40, métro Notre-Dame de Lorette. **FUAJ République:** 4 blvd. Jules-Ferry, 11e, tel. 01–43–57–02–60, fax 01–40–21–79–92, métro République. **FUAJ Centre National:** 27 rue Pajol, 18e, tel. 01–44–89–87–27, métro La Chapelle.

Auberge de Jeunesse d'Artagnan. This clean, enormous hostel is only steps away from Père-Lachaise. It gets packed and loud in summer. A bed in a three- or four-bed dorm costs 110F (including sheets and breakfast); beds in double rooms go for 121F (130F with private shower). Three meals are served daily (menus for 28F–50F) at the very social bar and cafeteria. *80 rue Vitruve, 20e, tel. 01–43–61–08–75, fax 01–40–32–34–55. Métro: Porte de Bagnolet. 411 beds. Reception open 8 AM–midnight, lockout noon–3. Laundry.*

Auberge de Jeunesse Cité des Sciences. Although technically in the suburbs, this hostel is well served by the ever-efficient métro, so you can be in the center of Paris in less than 20 minutes. A mellow staff welcomes you to standard four- to six-bed dorm rooms. Though the rooms close every day noon–3 PM, the reception desk and a small common room stay open 24 hours. Beds cost 110F per night. *24 rue des Sept-Arpents, 93000, tel. 01–48–43–24–11, fax 01–48–43–26–82. Métro: Hoche. 128 beds. Reception open 24 hrs. Laundry.*

Auberge de Jeunesse Jules-Ferry. Come early and be ready to socialize. This one is extremely popular with friendly and rowdy backpackers. It's also centrally located, overlooking a canal of the Seine and close to place de la République and the Bastille. Bed and breakfast in a dorm runs 110F (115F per person for the few doubles). Cheap food and groceries are close by, as are clubs and cafés. *8 blvd. Jules-Ferry, 75011, tel. 01–43–57–55–60, fax 01–40–21–79–92. Métro: République. 100 beds. Reception open 24 hrs, lockout noon–2. Luggage storage 5F.*

PRIVATE HOSTELS

Aloha Hostel. This welcoming place has rooms that sleep two to six. Supermarkets, laundromats, and La Tour Eiffel are all nearby—you'll feel particularly safe in the midst of the hubbub if you're traveling alone. The friendly, English-speaking staff will usually let the one-week maximum stay (550F) slide during the school year. You'll pay 87F per person for a double, 97F for a dorm bed, plus 10F extra during the summer. You can use the kitchen, but access is limited. *1 rue Borromée, 75015, tel. 01–42–73–03–03, fax 01–42–73–14–14. Métro: Volontaires. 130 beds. Curfew 2 AM, lockout 11–5. Reception open 8 AM–2 PM. Kitchen.*

Three Ducks Hostel. This American-infested hostel-bar is rambunctious and fun, what with all the cheap beers being consumed (9F). Try to land a room with a shower; if not, you'll be queuing up in the communal courtyard for a shower booth. Beds rent for 77F (97F in a double), plus 20F extra during the summer; sheet rental is 12F, and towels cost 5F. There's laundry next door and a safe-deposit box. Book ahead May–October by sending payment for the first night. Otherwise, call or arrive before 11 AM or after 5 PM to nab one of the remaining beds. *6 pl. Etienne-Pernet, 75015, tel. 01–48–42–04–05, fax 01–48–42–04–05. Métro: Commerce. 95 beds. Curfew 2 AM, lockout 11–5. Kitchen.*

Woodstock. Sounds retro, eh? But this recently opened hostel was created in the same vein as the others. In rooms with three to six beds, you'll pay 97F, including showers. Sheets rent for 15F, towels 5F. *48 rue Rodier, 75009, tel. 01–48–78–87–76. Métro: Anvers. 75 beds. Curfew 2 AM, lockout 11–5. Kitchen.*

Young and Happy Youth Hostel. Among the cafés, shops, and restaurants of rue Mouffetard in the Latin Quarter, this hostel is no stranger to young American and Japanese travelers. The two- to six-bed rooms are basic but spotless and cost 97F per person, including breakfast. Sheets rent for 15F, towels 5F. Arrive before 11 AM or reserve with a deposit for the first night. *80 rue Mouffetard, 75005, tel. 01–45–35–09–53. Métro: Monge. 75 beds. Curfew 2 AM, lockout 11–5.*

BVJ FOYERS

Both of these two foyers for travelers aged 16–35 are in great locations and have immaculate rooms that hold up to 10 people. You'll get a bed, breakfast, sheets, and a shower for 120F, plus access to kitchen facilities, 10F lockers, and a 24-hour reception desk. Unfortunately you can't make reservations, so show up early in the morning. If one branch is booked, the staff will call the other for you. Singles cost 10F more in the Latin Quarter. The Louvre location has a restaurant where guests at any of the four other foyers can eat for 55F. There's also a shuttle service to Orly (59F) and Charles de Gaulle (69F), which you can reserve at the desk. **BVJ de Paris/Louvre:** 20 rue J.-J. Rousseau, 75001, tel. 01–42–36–88–18, fax 01–42–33–82–10, métro Palais Royal. **BVJ de Paris Quartier Latin:** 44 rue des Bernardins, 75005, tel. 01–43–29–34–80, fax 01–42–33–40–53, métro Maubert-Mutualité.

MIJE FOYERS

In a trio of medieval palaces and 18th-century Marais town houses, **Maisons Internationales des Jeunes Etudiants (MIJE)** foyers are more comfortable than many budget hotels. The catch is that you must be between the ages of 18 and 30. The 125F rate includes a bed, sheets, breakfast, showers, and free luggage storage. Doubles with private bath cost 150F. MIJE foyers don't accept reservations, so show up between 7 and 8:30 AM for one of the 450 beds. There's a seven-night maximum and a 1 AM curfew. A restaurant in the Fourcy location serves meals (menus 32F–52F). The lockout is between noon and 4 PM. **Hôtel le Fauconnier:** 11 rue de Fauconnier, 75004, tel. 01–42–74–23–45, fax 01–42–74–08–93, métro St-Paul. **Hôtel le Fourcy:** 6 rue de Fourcy, 75004, tel. 01–42–74–23–45, fax 01–42–74–08–93, métro St-Paul. **Hôtel Maubuisson:** 12 rue des Barres, 75004, tel. 01–42–72–72–09, fax 01–42–74–08–93, métro St-Paul or Hôtel de Ville.

Auberge Internationale des Jeunes. This impeccable, modern hostel, right next to place de la Bastille and 10 minutes from the Gare de Lyon, is popular with young, international backpackers. If you're into going out at night, this is the place for you. The friendly (albeit harried) management accepts reservations. Rooms for two to six people rent for 81F–91F per person, breakfast included. *10 rue Trousseau, 75011, tel. 01–47–00–62–00, fax 01–47–00–33–16. Métro: Bastille or Ledru Rollin. 240 beds. Reception open 24 hrs, lockout 10–3. Laundry.*

Maison des Etudiants. In a fabulous house with a flower-filled courtyard, 140F will get you a double and 160F a single (150F if you stay three weeks or more). There's a four-night minimum stay and breakfast is included. The maison accepts students year-round and tourists of all ages in summer. *18 rue J.-J. Rousseau, 75001, tel. 01–45–08–02–10. Métro: Palais Royal. 52 beds.*

RESIDENCE HOTELS

If you will be staying longer than a week, want to do your own cooking, or need a base large enough for a family, consider a residence hotel. The cost is about 3000F–4000F a week for four. Policies differ from company to company, but you can generally expect a minimum required stay of one week; a refundable deposit (expect 1000F–2500F), payable on arrival; and weekly or biweekly maid service. Four good-value residence hotels, each with multiple properties in Paris, are **Orion** (30 pl. d'Italie, 75013, tel. 01–40–78–54–54, 800/546–4777 or 212/688–9538 in the U.S.; fax 01–40–78–54–55, 212/688–9467 in the U.S.); **Citadines Résidences Hôtelières** (18 rue Favart, 75002, tel. 01–44–50–23–23, fax 01–44–50–32–50); **Adagio** (20 esplanade Charles-de-Gaulle, 92000, Nanterre, tel. 01–46–69–79–00, fax 01–47–25–46–48); and **Paris Appartements Services** (69 rue d'Argout, 75002, tel. 01–40–28–01–28, fax 01–40–28–92–01).

FOOD

UPDATED BY ALEXANDER LOBRANO

Experiencing the French appreciation for fine food is much more than selecting a restaurant with "Chez" in the title, forking out a minimum of a three-digit sum in francs, and knowing the best vintages of *vin rouge* (red wine) and *vin blanc* (white wine). The best introduction to French food is the marketplace, where you'll see butchers nonchalantly toting pig carcasses over their shoulders, barrows of vegetables and fruits being transferred into neat pyramids, and whole fish artfully arranged on beds of crushed ice at the *poissonerie* (fish market). Whether you buy the baguettes lined up soldier-style at the *boulangerie* (bakery), pastries displaying themselves wantonly at the patisserie, or one of the exotic cheeses emitting a stiff but enticing odor at the *fromagerie* (cheese shop), you'll soon discover that your francs will go much further at the markets than at those vulturous restaurants that advertise "cuisine traditionelle" and print their menus in English.

That said, it is imperative that you indulge in at least one drawn-out meal and treat the event with as much nonchalant reverence as the French do. There are several places where you can accomplish this. One option is a **bistro,** which is primarily a wine bar that offers plates of cheese and *charcuterie* (cold cuts) or even full meals as accompaniments. Bistros that fit this description are listed near the end of this chapter (*see* Bistros and Wine Bars, *below*). A **brasserie** is a French pub that offers standard, single-course dishes traditionally (but not necessarily) served with beer. Although not quite an eating institution, the most Parisian of all creatures is the **café** (*see* Cafés, *below*)—a mélange of sidewalk tables, saucy waiters, and Parisians enjoying many an espresso and a Gaulois cigarette.

In addition to the many **crêperies** (crepe stands) and sandwich joints springing up on Paris's side streets, you'll no doubt get the chance to sample the international culinary scene as you wander from one ethnic restaurant to another. The **Marais** (3e, 4e) has some of the best falafel stands in Paris, and **Belleville** (20e) and the 13th arrondissement are chock-full of Vietnamese, Chinese, and Thai restaurants. The large West African and Algerian immigrant population in **Montmartre** (18e) and near the **Bastille** (11e) has brought couscous to the forefront of Parisian food, although you might want to avoid the ghastly Tex-Mex eateries currently invading Montparnasse and the Quartier Latin. You can always trust the **Quartier Latin** (5e) to have anything from Greek to Lyonnais food at prices low enough to keep its student population sated.

The best deals for a full meal in restaurants are usually the prix-fixe (fixed-price) menus, which include an *entrée* (appetizer), a *plat* (main course), and *dessert,* for 60F and up. The lunch and dinner menus are usually the same, although lunch often costs a third less than dinner. It might sound elegant, but

ALL-NIGHT EATERIES

After-party hunger pangs at 3 AM may make you slink into one of Paris's "24/24" (open 24 hours) restaurant chains. Batifol Opéra (36 blvd. des Italiens, 9e, tel. 01–45–23–09–34, métro Richelieu Drouot) has hot and filling meals 24 hours daily. Pizza Pino (38 rue St-Séverin, 5e, tel. 01–43–54–70–53, métro St-Michel–Notre-Dame; 43 rue St-Denis, 7e, tel. 01–40–26–39–07, métro Châtelet–Les Halles) serves a variety of pizzas until 5 AM. Also try the Mustang Café (see Montparnasse, below), open until 5 AM, or the late-night bakery Le Terminus (10 rue St-Denis, 1er, tel. 01–45–08–87–97, métro Châtelet–Les Halles), which closes at 3 AM.

LE DÉPANNEUR. This diner-bar near Pigalle has artsy chrome touches and comfy chairs. Big salads, hamburgers, and sandwiches run 40F–70F, a small carafe of wine 25F (15F during the day). It's open 24 hours. 27 rue Fontaine, 9e, tel. 01–40–16–40–20. Métro: Blanche.

LE GRAND CAFÉ. Finally—an all-night café. Too bad it's in a neighborhood that goes to bed early. 40 blvd. des Capucines, 9e, tel. 01–47–42–19–00. Métro: Madeleine.

LE PIGALLE. Though not necessarily in the greatest neighborhood, it's open Monday–Saturday until 5 AM. Chill out with some Vietnamese specialties after grooving all night at one of the nearby clubs. 22 blvd. de Clichy, 18e, tel. 01–46–06–72–90. Métro: Pigalle.

PUB ST-GERMAIN. Off boulevard St-Germain, this pub is always packed with foreigners. Over 450 international beers—26 on tap and more in bottles—accompany French pub food. Steak or lobster menus are 50F–78F. 17 rue de l'Ancienne-Comédie, 6e, tel. 01–43–29–38–70. Métro: Odéon.

ordering à la carte (separately) is a surefire way to dine yourself into poverty. Some restaurants offer a filling plat du jour (daily special), which includes meat, veggies, and pasta or potatoes for as little as 50F. The commonly seen words service compris mean that tip is included in the prices. You can leave an extra 2F–5F pourboire (tip) for an extra-friendly server, but it's not an insult to leave nothing.

The French start their day with a petit déjeuner (breakfast), which usually consists of coffee and bread or croissants. Déjeuner (lunch) is normally served from noon until 2 or 2:30 and dîner (dinner) from 7 to 10 or 11. We list hours when a restaurant is closed, otherwise you can assume it is open for lunch and dinner. In addition, we list when a restaurant takes cash only, otherwise you can assume Visa and MasterCard are accepted (and, less often, American Express).

RESTAURANTS

The following restaurants are arranged by neighborhood and price. If you're looking for a specific type of cuisine, flip to the Reference Listings at the end of this chapter. The price categories listed generally refer to the price of a three-course dinner and a drink—which means you can spend a bit less if you order carefully and forgo appetizers and wine.

BASTILLE

It's only fitting that a great nighttime area would have a great selection of restaurants. Take-out joints of all stripes serve cheap falafel and sandwiches along **rue de la Roquette;** on the rue's first block off place de la Bastille, you might want to take comfort in thick pizza from **Slice.** Otherwise, you'll find plenty of cafés open late and many opportunities for quality meals, often served in converted art galleries. Keep in mind that the artsy crowd is often willing to pay a higher price. Edge northwestward out of the Bastille toward **place de la République** and along **boulevard Voltaire;** prices drop and ethnic eateries pop up more often.

UNDER 60F • Le Bistrot du Peintre. This popular café and bar serves food until midnight and closes at 2 AM. The standard French cuisine includes a great *soupe à l'oignon* (onion soup; 30F) and the best *salade au chèvre chaud* (warm goat-cheese salad; 35F) in the city. The waiters are friendly and loyal regulars dominate the crowd, gobbling up hearty plats du jour like the *poulet moutarde* (mustard chicken; 62F). *116 av. Ledru-Rollin, at rue de Charonne, 11e, tel. 01–47–00–34–39. Métro: Ledru-Rollin.*

Crêpes-Show. A cadaverous-looking mannequin beckons you into the Crêpes-Show, but luckily teen horror-flick gore is not what they serve here. Instead, you'll find fast, cheap, and filling fare dished out to everyone from students to heels and suits. The 39F lunch menu gets you a salad, a main course crepe (like cheese and mushroom), and a dessert crepe, while the 59F dinner menu includes all of the above with wine thrown in. *51 rue de Lappe, 11e, tel. 01–47–00–36–46. Métro: Bastille. Cash only.*

UNDER 80F • Café Moderne. Despite its name, this restaurant is a classic old Paris bistro, with wooden tables, a mirrored bar, and *sympathique* atmosphere. Cherif, the congenial man behind the bar, won't take too many reservations (he likes to leave a bunch of tables free for friends and regulars). Some nights you'll hear as much Arabic as French, as local North Africans congregate for the house specialty: mounds of couscous with raisins and pimento garnish (50F–60F). The three-course lunch or dinner menu is 70F. If you want similar food and style, but with a high-powered fashion crowd, check out Chez Omar, run by Cherif's brother Omar in the Marais (*see* Le Marais, *below*). *19 rue Keller, 11e, tel. 01– 47–00–53–62. Métro: Bastille. Closed Sun.*

Le Petit Keller. Many of Paris's good budget places dish up foreign cooking, but this unprepossessing spot near the Bastille serves food that's resolutely French—and surprisingly good for the money. What pulls a discerning but penny-wise crowd of young trendies, including many resident Anglophones, is the 70F menu—three courses (that may include braised veal, roast duck, and crème caramel) and a quarter liter of wine. *13 rue Keller, 11e, tel. 01–47–00–12–97. Métro: Ledru-Rollin. Closed Sun., Aug.*

Restaurant Sarah. Ask locals where to get a great cheap meal, and they'll steer you toward the green doors of this Persian delight. The 35F plat du jour is always a good deal, or, for the total experience, get the 55F lunch menu with specialties like *tchelo kebab koubidee* (beef, onion, grilled tomatoes, and saffron rice). The four-course dinner menu is a deal at 65F. Add a quarter-bottle of wine (15F) and you'll be so happy you'll probably come back the next day. *10 rue Oberkampf, 11e, tel. 01–43–57–83–48. Métro: Oberkampf. Cash only.*

Le Temps des Cerises. This tiny lunch-only restaurant has been around since 1900; from the convivial atmosphere and the photos of old Paris, you might think you've jumped back in time. It's named after a revolutionary song, "The Time of Cherries"—if you didn't bring the sheet music, the words are written on the walls. Get here by noon to rub elbows with locals over a hearty 65F menu of traditional French home cooking, or one of the many meat and salad specials. Come later and you'll be in for a long, long wait. *31 rue de la Cerisaie, 4e, tel. 01–42–72–08–63. Métro: Sully-Morland or Bastille. Closed weekends and Aug.*

Tokaj. Duck past hand-painted murals and seat yourself before heaps of steaming goulash (62F) to the sounds of soft Gypsy music. Originally from Budapest, the Brandt family relocated to Paris, where they are happily filling the stomachs of Parisians and tourists alike. The atmosphere is warm and the food fantastic. Treat yourself to the *hortubagy* (chicken-filled crepe in paprika sauce; 58F) and a carafe of the house rosé (18F). *57 rue du Chemin-Vert, at blvd. Voltaire, 11e, tel. 01–47–00–64–56. Métro: Voltaire. Closed Sun., Mon.*

UNDER 100F • Naz Restaurant. A laid-back crowd lingers over meals at this Indian-Pakistani place, which is best known for its curry and tandoori specials. *Poulet palak* (chicken curry with creamed

I ORDERED WHAT?!

If you're an adventurous gourmet who has ordered one of the following dishes, here are some definitions to chew on:

ANDOUILLETTES: sausages stuffed with pork tripe.

BOUDIN: a blood sausage made with onions and wheat grains.

CERVELLE: pork or sheep brain cooked with butter and herbs.

FOIE GRAS: a rich paté of pure duck or goose liver.

PÂTÉ de foie gras is a less expensive version of it.

TÊTE DE VEAU: Boiled calf's head served with a pickle and caper sauce.

spinach) runs 65F; a three-course menu is 59F–69F for lunch, dinner is 100F. Vegetarians should try the amazing *raita d'aubergine* appetizer (25F), made with grilled eggplant and spicy yogurt sauce. *19 rue de la Roquette, 11e, tel. 01–48–05–69–19. Métro: Bastille. No lunch Fri.*

SPLURGE • Au Camelot. Book a table at this minuscule bistro, a 10-minute walk from the Bastille, the moment you get to town—it only seats 20 and it's one of the most popular places in the neighborhood. What draws the diverse but stylish crowd of Parisians is the outstanding and delicious 130F prix-fixe menu that includes soup, fish and meat courses, cheese, and dessert. Wines are nicely priced, too (75F for a fine Bordeaux). *50 rue Amelot, 11e, tel. 01–43–55–54–04. Métro: Chemin-Vert. Cash only. Closed Sun. No lunch Mon. or Sat.*

Chez Paul. A modest sign welcomes you to a reliably good splurge in the Bastille. The grilled salmon (80F), rabbit with goat-cheese sauce (75F), and escargots (40F) are delectable; spring for a bottle of wine (100F) and whip out that credit card. The place is crowded with locals and clued-in visitors, so make reservations. If you didn't plan ahead, get a drink at the bar or head over to Les Portes (*see* Bars *in* Chapter 5) across the street and work up an appetite during your long wait. *13 rue de Charonne, at rue de Lappe, 11e, tel. 01–47–00–34–57. Métro: Bastille.*

BELLEVILLE

Belleville's African, Asian, and Eastern European restaurants are a refreshing alternative to standard Parisian cuisine—and most of them offer pretty good food for fair prices, unlike the tourist traps around Les Halles and in the Quartier Latin. On **rue de Belleville, rue des Pyrénées,** and the streets stretching south from them, you can find some of the most varied and affordable dining in town. Boulevard de Belleville has cheap produce and scads of good Chinese and Laotian restaurants. Chinese residents prefer the well-stocked **Wing An** (7 rue de Belleville, 19e, tel. 01–42–38–05–24) for cooking ingredients, plus snacks to go. The Sephardic Jews in the area have opened up a kosher shop here and there; try the **Maison du Zabayon** (122 blvd. de Belleville, 20e, tel. 01–47–97–16–70), a kosher bakery with good pastries (8F–10F).

UNDER 60F • Da Lat. This flashy restaurant is full of folks downing Da Lat's excellent Chinese-Thai cuisine. Almond chicken (40F), Thai chicken curry (31F), and crab salad (27F) are some of the favorites here. The 65F three-course menu is served piping hot all day. *19 rue Louis-Bonnet, 11e, tel. 01–43–38–22–72. Métro: Belleville.*

Lao Siam. Laotian and Thai specialties fill the vast menu of this humble Belleville institution, which focuses on basics like chicken with bamboo shoots (38F). The egg foo yong (an omelette made with onions and served with rice; 23F) is a tasty option if you want to get filled up cheaply. *49 rue de Belleville, 19e, tel. 01–40–40–09–68. Métro: Belleville. Cash only.*

Modas. This small, artsy crêperie high up on the rue de Ménilmontant has as much personality as Gabriel, its owner—which means it's colorful, chaotic, and extremely eccentric. Come and enjoy the rotating art exhibits along with Belleville regulars munching on a broad selection of crepes (under 30F) and grilled meats (50F–60F). *110 rue de Ménilmontant, 20e, tel. 01–40–33–69–58. Metro: Ménilmontant. Cash only. Closed Mon.*

UNDER 80F • Au Rendez-vous des Chauffeurs. The name of this little bistro refers to its popularity with the cab drivers who once rendez-voused here. They still come today, but so do many students and artists—to order the 65F menu, served only before 8:30 PM. Start with pâté, followed, perhaps, by sautéed lamb and a fruit tart. The menu changes regularly, but the 30F-a-liter house wine remains a blessedly eternal fixture. The food is better than decent—if never remarkable—and you're not rushed through your meal. *11 rue des Portes-Blanches, 18e, tel. 01–42–64–04–71. Closed Tues., Wed., Aug.*

Restaurant Tai-Yien. The dining room may be a little dull, but mostly Asian customers stream in here for some of the best Chinese food in town. The simple stuff—like roast chicken with rice (42F)—is best. The adventurous should try the curried frogs' legs (48F) or lamb with ginger and onions (60F). The three-course dinner menu is 63F. *5 rue de Belleville, 19e, tel. 01–42–41–44–16. Métro: Belleville.*

Le Vieux Byzantin. On a street jam-packed with sorry-looking stands of greasy Greek food, this cheery restaurant stands above the rest with its Greek and Turkish delicacies. Daily specials such as chicken *tagine* (braised with vegetables) go for 35F. The 50F lunch menu is a deal. Fancier dinner menus run 70F to 95F. *128 rue Oberkampf, 11e, tel. 01–43–57–35–84. Métro: Ménilmontant. Cash only. No lunch Sun.*

UNDER 100F • Chez Justine. Chez Justine serves up heaps of traditional southern French cooking, complete with rustic log-cabin decor. The 74F lunch menu (56F without dessert and wine) and 87F dinner menu come with an all-you-can-eat appetizer buffet, a meat dish, such as *rôti de veau* (veal roast), dessert, and wine. *96 rue Oberkampf, 11e, tel. 01–43–57–44–03. Métro: St-Maur. Closed Sun. and Aug. No lunch Sat.*

SPLURGE • A la Courtille. Relax on the terrace of this sleek bistro with a breathtaking view over the city and the Parc de Belleville. Though decidedly off the beaten track, businesspeople fill it up at lunch and locals pack the place on evenings and weekends. Appetizers are 40F; courses like steak tartare are 75F–85F. Lunch is 70F–100F, dinner 150F–200F, but the wines are good value for money. *1 rue des Envierges, 20e, tel. 01–46–36–51–59. Métro: Pyrénées.*

A meal in Paris isn't complete without a glass of wine and a good toast. A few to try out on your friends: "Tchin tchin!" (a formal version of cheers!), "A votre santé!" (To your health!), "A la tienne!" (Here's to you!), "On bascule!" (Bottoms up!).

CHAMPS-ELYSEES

Though it's one of Paris's best-known boulevards, with loads of theaters and clubs, the area around it is a very tough neighborhood in which to find a decent meal for under 200F. Hunt around **rue La Boétie** and **rue de Ponthieu** for your most reasonable options. Restaurants here serve mostly traditional French fare for the ultrachic and ultrasleek. The rest of us just might have to grab a sandwich or duck into the closest MacDo (MacDonald's, to the French—you can't get away from them).

UNDER 60F • Barry's. This small, mirrored restaurant-deli is a popular lunch spot among the people who work in the area, which means it's chic but still affordable. Snag a seat indoors and try the 36F–49F roasted veal or curried chicken. Or get a 24F–29F *panini* (hot grilled sandwich) to go and picnic along the Champs-Elysées. *9 rue de Duras, 8e, tel. 01–40–06–02–27. Métro: Champs-Elysées–Clemenceau. Cash only. Closed weekends. No dinner.*

Chicago Pizza Pie Factory. Happy-hour drinks (Monday–Saturday 6–8 PM) are 50% off at this deep-dish pizza/sports bar institution. In addition to pizzas—84F for a two-person cheese pizza, 200F for the four-person everything-on-it—you can order all sorts of big salads (20F–55F), garlic bread (21F), and good ole California wine. *5 rue de Berri, 8e, tel. 01–45–62–50–23. Métro: George V.*

UNDER 100F • Chez Clement. This chain is sort of the French equivalent of Denny's or Howard Johnson's, which is to say, politely, that it serves decent and reasonably priced food to the middle-class hordes hailing from Toulouse, Toledo, and Tokyo. Two of their varying good-buys are all-you-can-eat offers of rotisseried meats or oysters. If you love kitsch, then the twee copper-sauce-pans and peasant-kitchen decor—the Gallic equivalent of American "colonial" style—is for you. *123 av. des Champs-Elysées, 8e, tel. 01–40–73–87–00. Métro: Franklin D. Roosevelt.*

VEGETARIAN GRAZING GROUNDS

There's no way around it: The French are major carnivores, and the honest displays in their butcher shops have sent more than one vegetarian running for cover. Still, it's not impossible to find a good, meatless meal. Here are some shops/restaurants that do their best to accommodate vegetarians:

AQUARIUS. 40 rue de Gergovie, 14e, tel. 01–45–41–36–88. Métro: Pernety.

LE BOL EN BOIS. 35 rue Pascal, 13e, tel. 01–47–07–27–24. Métro: Gobelins.

COUNTRY LIFE. 6 rue Daunou, 2e, tel. 01–42–97–48–51. Métro: Opéra.

ENTRE CIEL ET TERRE. 5 rue Hérold, 1er, tel. 01–45–08–49–84. Métro: Les Halles or Louvre-Rivoli.

GRANT APPÉTIT. 9 rue de la Ceuseiaie, 4e, tel. 01–40–27–04–95. Métro: Bastille.

LA PETITE LÉGUME. 36 rue des Boulangers, 5e, tel. 01–40–46–06–85. Métro: Cardinal-Lemoine.

LES QUATRE ET UNE SAVEURS. 72 rue du Cardinal-Lemoine, 5e, tel. 01–43–26–88–80. Métro: Cardinal-Lemoine.

SURMA. 5 rue Daubenton, 5e, tel. 01–45–35–68–60. Métro: Censier-Daubenton.

LA VILLE DE JAGANNATH. 101 rue St-Maur, 11e, tel. 01–43–55–80–81. Métro: St-Maur.

GARE DE L'EST AND GARE DU NORD

A jazzy, post–World War II expatriate crowd ushered in new life to this inconspicuously cool neighborhood that spreads southwest of the Gares de l'Est and du Nord. Rather than the intellectual types who had schmoozed in the cafés of Montparnasse 10 years earlier, these expats were serious swingers. Happily, the spirit of the 1940s has been quietly maintained in a few restaurants near **place St-Georges,** as well as in the hidden jazz joints sprinkled around the area. With a large Jewish population, this area is also a good place for cheap kosher meals, as well as for falafel around **rue de Montyon.**

UNDER 60F • Restaurant Chartier. Since the mid-1800s Chartier has served cheap, copious meals to workers, bankers, students, and (now) tourists. The old revolving door whirls you into a big space with touches of brass and stained glass. Erratic, near-frantic service demands that you assert yourself at times. The menu of basic, but by no means gourmet, French cooking changes daily; main dishes include grilled steak with fries (46F) and grilled mackerel (36F). Desserts are 8F–20F (though you're better off having one elsewhere), and half a carafe of passable red wine is 16F. You could also opt for the menus. 7 rue du Faubourg-Montmartre, 9e, tel. 01–47–70–86–29. Métro: Rue Montmartre.

Van Gölu. The food is excellent, with a wide range of lamb dishes and tasty baklava, but the entertainment is the main reason to come to this Kurdish institution. There's music every night, though the weekend show is best—when the belly dancer shimmies to the accompaniment of a saz (Turkish lute). You might even learn a few Turkish tunes from the crowd of regulars singing along. The 55F menu, complete

If you're stuck for cash on your travels, don't panic. Western Union can transfer money in minutes. We've 37,000 outlets in over 140 countries. And our record of safety and reliability is second to none. Call Western Union: wherever you are, you're never far from home.

WESTERN UNION | MONEY TRANSFER®

The fastest way to send money worldwide.

Austria 0660 8066 Canada 1 800 235 0000* Czech 2422 9524 France (01) 43 54 46 12 or (01) 45 35 60 60 Germany 0130 7890 or (0180) 522 5822 Greece (01) 927 1010 Ireland 1 800 395 395* Italy 167 22 00 55* or 167 464 464* Netherlands 0800 0566* Poland (022) 636 5688 Russia 095 119 82 50 Spain 900 633 633* or (91) 559 0253 Sweden 020 741 742 Switzerland 0512 22 33 58 UK 0800 833 833* USA 1 800 325 6000*.

*Toll free telephone No.

We'll give you a
$20 tip for driving.

See the real Europe with Hertz.

(I)t's time to see Europe from a new perspective. From behind the wheel of a Hertz car. And we'd like to save you $20 on your prepaid Affordable Europe Weekly Rental. Our low rates are guaranteed in U.S. dollars and English is spoken at all of our European locations. Computerized driving directions are available at many locations, and Free Unlimited Mileage and 24-Hour Emergency Roadside Assistance are standard in our European packages. For complete details call 1-800-654-3001. Mention PC #95384 So, discover Europe with Hertz.

Offer is valid at participating airport locations in Europe from Jan.1 – Dec.15,1998, on Economy through Full size cars. Reservations must be made at least 8 hours prior to departure. $20 will be deducted at time of booking. Standard rental qualifications, significant restrictions and blackout periods apply.

Hertz rents Fords and other fine cars.
® REG. U.S. PAT. OFF. © HERTZ SYSTEM INC., 1997/061-97.

Hertz europe

with dessert and wine, is a small price to pay for the great floor show. *3 rue d'Enghien, 10e, tel. 01–47–70–41–01. Métro: Strasbourg–St-Denis. Cash only. No lunch Sun.*

UNDER 80F • Bhai Bhai Sweets. South of the Gare de l'Est on boulevard de Strasbourg is a crumbling old *passage* (an iron- and glass-covered passageway created during the 19th century). It houses about a dozen cramped Indian eateries, but Bhai Bhai is the best. The 70F lunch or dinner menu includes three courses, among them *bharta* (eggplant puree with onions, tomatoes, and spices) and *dal* (lentils). Vegetable beignets cost 16F, or try the tandoori chicken (18F). *77 passage Brady, 10e, tel. 01–42–46–77–29. Métro: Château d'Eau.*

Chez Papa–Espace Sud Ouest. A friendly, young crowd packs this place for the lavish portions of very decent southwestern and Auvergant (central France) food. The salads are particularly good, including the trademark *garbure* (a veal chop, fried potatoes, cheese, and mushrooms on greens). The duck dishes—cassoulet (a casserole of preserved duck and bacon stewed with white beans and tomatoes under a crust of bread crumbs) and *confit de canard* (duck cooked in its own fat)—are hearty and authentic, and the house red at 44F a liter has never made anyone blind. *206 rue Lafayette, 10e, tel. 01–42–09–53–87. Métro: Louis-Blanc.*

Haynes. In 1947, former G. I. Leroy "Roughhouse" Haynes opened the first American restaurant in Paris, serving up a taste of his native Kentucky in the form of black-eyed peas, chicken hash, and whiskey sours. Haynes's kitchen not only gave Parisian cuisine a kick in the pants, it also became a favorite of expatriate hepcats looking for a piece of home. You can still feast on fried chicken, T-bone steaks, and barbecued ribs (60F–90F) in this dimly lit, smoky club. When there isn't live piano music, Leroy gets out his great collection of jazz and blues. *3 rue Clauzel, 9e, tel. 01–48–78–40–63. Métro: St-Georges. Closed Sun., Mon.*

For cheap and delicious crepes, head to the stand on the corner of rue de Rivoli and rue de Malher. Daniel, the ever-smiling cook, puts loads of Nutella in his 12F dessert crepes—a sure sign of a good chef.

Paparazzi. This boisterous Italian bistro just north of the 9th arrondissement's best nightspots sees a young, good-natured crowd diving into varied plates of pasta (50F–60F) and megapizzas. At lunch people crowd in for the 60F menu and the *scampi fritti* (fried scampi; 55F). *7 bis rue Geoffroy-Marie, 9e, tel. 01–48–24–59–39. Métro: Rue Montmartre. Closed Sun. and 2 wks in Aug. No dinner Mon.*

UNDER 100F • Chalet Maya. Get this straight: This is not a chalet, and there's nothing Maya about it. Gay actor Jean Marais, heartthrob of teenage girls in the '40s, is the godfather of the restaurant's proprietor—check him out in the arty photos on the walls. But the real reason to come is the food, with entrées like penne with smoked salmon and main courses like duck baked with peaches, or curried lamb with plantains (60F). The place fills up after 10:30 PM, when people file in for the 90F two-course menu. *5 rue des Petits-Hôtels, 10e, tel. 01–47–70–52–78. Métro: Gare de l'Est. Closed Sun. No lunch Mon.*

SPLURGE • Julien. This classy 1879 brasserie stands stylishly apart from its surroundings on a chaotic market street. High ceilings, mirrors, and tuxedoed waiters take you back to a golden era—on theater nights you'll still see decked-out dandies, playbills in hand, coming for the fantastic desserts (from 35F). The 51F profiteroles (ice cream inside a puff pastry smothered in chocolate) are Julien's specialty. Real food is good but expensive; try coming for lunch or after 10 PM, when the menu is 110F for two courses and a drink. *16 rue du Faubourg-St-Denis, 10e, tel. 01–47–70–12–06. Métro: Strasbourg–St-Denis.*

LES HALLES AND BEAUBOURG

Les Halles has the unique distinction of having the worst crepe stands in town, a trait indicative of the eating scene here as a whole. It's not that you can't eat well here—a few spots are actually quite good. However, plenty of places (particularly those south of the Forum des Halles) will happily take your francs for a plate of muck. The solution: On sunny days stroll down **rue Montorgueil**'s daily market and picnic in the park next to the Eglise St-Eustache. Or, grab a hot panini (18F–25F) from one of the stands lining **rue St-Denis** or **rue Rambuteau.** The best thing we can say about eating in Les Halles is that many restaurants stay open until the wee hours, including the **Pizza Pino** (open daily 11 AM–5 AM) on place des Innocents.

UNDER 60F • Dame Tartine. Squeeze in with the yuppies at this restaurant–cum–art gallery next to the Centre Georges Pompidou on place Igor-Stravinsky. The specialty is the *tartines* (hot or cold open-faced sandwiches); try the *poulet aux amandes* (chicken with almonds; 30F). Add an inspiring glass of Bordeaux (15F), ponder the works by local artists, and watch the afternoon go by. They also have an off-shoot called **Café Véry**, in the Jardin des Tuileries. *2 rue Brisemiche, 3e, tel. 01–42–77–32–22. Métro: Rambuteau or Châtelet–Les Halles. Cash only.*

Jip's. This boisterous Afro-Cuban café-restaurant blares continuous reggae and salsa from a corner of Les Halles. The friendly (sometimes a bit too friendly), dreadlocked clientele comes for dishes such as *pescado en salsa* (fish with fresh salsa; 45F) or *manioc en frites* (fried manioc; 28F). Drop in anytime for some strong punch (36F) and a vibrant atmosphere. *41 rue St-Denis, 1er, tel. 01–42–33–00–11. Métro: Châtelet–Les Halles. Cash only.*

La Tavola Calda. This tiny hole-in-the-wall is not only one of the best budget addresses in another otherwise barren area, but it also serves some of the best pizza in Paris. Assuming you prefer the real thing to global-chain-fodder, come let the friendly young Portuguese pizza-thrower toss one for you (45F). They also serve good pasta (60F) and chicken or veal dishes (70F). *39 rue des Bourdonnais, 1er, tel. 01–45–08–94–66. Métro: Les Halles.*

UNDER 80F • Au Petit Ramoneur. This family-run place has been dishing out solid meals in Les Halles since way before the sex shops moved in. The 68F menu includes goodies like fried potatoes and sausage, tripe cooked in Calvados brandy, andouillettes, and salads, not to mention a half liter of wine or beer. At lunch the place is packed with regulars who'll chat with anyone sitting nearby. *74 rue St-Denis, 1er, tel. 01–42–36–39–24. Métro: Les Halles or Etienne Marcel. Cash only. Closed weekends and end of Aug.*

Café de la Cité. Only a block from the Centre Georges Pompidou, this tiny brasserie is crowded with lunchtime regulars and offers good, hearty meals. At lunch all appetizers (including escargots or a meal-size avocado salad) are 15F, main dishes 40F, and desserts only 15F. At dinner try the two-course menu (65F), with appetizers like tabbouleh, and main dishes such as lasagna or grilled salmon. *22 rue Rambuteau, 3e, tel. 01–42–78–56–36. Métro: Rambuteau. Cash only.*

UNDER 100F • Chez Max. Even people who can afford much pricier fare are regulars here, since the 65F lunch menu and the 85F dinner menu are such good deals for the food (the beef bourguignon is heavenly). Max himself is the cook, and as soon as you meet him and experience his solicitous and cajoling ways—he can't stand it if you don't clean your plate and won't hear of your not having dessert—you'll understand why the food is so good: Max really cares. *47 rue St-Honoré, 1er, tel. 01–40–13–06–82. Métro: Châtelet. Closed Sun.*

Entre Ciel et Terre. This happy, crunchy place with wood-and-stone walls focuses on healthy gourmet meals of fruits and vegetables. They like to remind you of the great vegetarians of the world—Gandhi, Charles Darwin, Leonardo da Vinci, and Lenny Kravitz. The three-course vegetarian menu runs 90F, or try a tasty meal-size special like the *galette de céréales* (56F), a mix of different cereals and vegetables with a 15F glass of organic grape juice. The apple crumble (29F) is delicious. *5 rue Hérold, 1er, tel. 01–45–08–49–84. Métro: Les Halles or Louvre-Rivoli. Closed weekends.*

LOUVRE TO OPERA

Most of this neighborhood is going to be out of your range. On the upside, when you do sit yourself down for a bite here, it usually means you'll be served in true Parisian style. Employees of ritzy neighborhood shops find refuge on **rue du Faubourg-St-Honoré,** which has some good lunch deals. For Japanese restaurants and stores, check out **rue Ste-Anne** and, across avenue de l'Opéra, **rue St-Roch.** Some of the best sushi in town is served at **Foujita** (41 rue St-Roch, 1er, tel. 01–42–61–42–93), where a sushi sampler costs 100F.

UNDER 80F • Country Life. For health nuts, this may be the best deal in town: 65F gets you unlimited access to the quality pickings of both a hot and a cold vegetarian buffet (dessert and drinks are extra). The hot dishes vary daily, from tofu curry to veggie lasagna. You can also ask for a take-out tray (29F for a small one, 49F for a large), and eat it in the great outdoors. The health-food store in front will tempt even the pickiest of herbivores with its wide selection of dried fruits, nuts, organic vegetables, and soy products. *6 rue Daunou, 2e, tel. 01–42–97–48–51. Métro: Opéra. Closed weekends. No dinner Fri.*

Le Gavroche. *"Tout le monde bascule!"* is shouted as everyone pounds a glass of the house Beaujolais at this lively neighborhood bistro. A loyal group of middle-age locals has been coming for years for the 70F menu of provincial specialties such as hearty *pot-au-feu* (beef and vegetable broth). Plan to stay awhile, as evenings here often end with rowdy sing-alongs. *19 rue St-Marc, 2e, tel. 01-42-96-89-70. Métro: Richelieu-Drouot. Closed Sun. and Aug.*

Higuma. Japanese and French businesspeople gather at lunch for Higuma's 63F menu (also offered at dinner), which includes a minisalad, soup, and *gyoza* (Japanese ravioli)—nothing fancy, but surprisingly hearty. *Oyakadon,* a bowl of rice covered with chicken, eggs, and onions, will fill up even the emptiest stomach. Grab a spot at the counter and watch the chefs' knives flailing around. *32 bis rue Ste-Anne, 1er, tel. 01-47-03-38-59. Métro: Pyramides. Cash only.*

L'Incroyable. The name refers to the self-proclaimed "Incredibles," a corrupt, egotistical group of nouveaux riches who sprang up after the Revolution—before Napoléon took over and put them in their place. Pick between the rustic, wood-paneled interior and the brightly colored tables in the front patio. The 75F (lunch 67F) traditional French menu includes *blanquette de veau* (veal cooked in butter and stock) and dessert: Do as an Incredible and indulge in the handmade pastries. *26 rue de Richelieu, 1er, tel. 01-42-96-24-64. Métro: Palais Royal–Musée du Louvre. Cash only. Closed Sun. No dinner Mon. or Sat.*

Le Palet. Just above the Jardin du Palais Royal, Le Palet is so romantic and homey that you might find yourself falling for the suit-and-ties who come here for lunch. The filling 65F menu often includes tomato-and-mozzarella salad and steak; a slightly more elaborate 95F dinner menu has dishes like goat-cheese salad and *St-Pierre gratinée* (whitefish baked with cheese on top). *8 rue de Beaujolais, 1er, tel. 01-42-60-99-59. Métro: Palais Royal–Musée du Louvre. Closed Sun. No lunch Sat.*

UNDER 100F • Yamamoto. This crowded place serves excellent food to passing Japanese tourists—a sure sign that the food is good. Start off with a miso soup (20F), then try filling sushi rolls like *futo maki* (55F) or a sampler of six different kinds of sushi (95F). Wash it all down with a cold can of Sapporo (35F) or a warm sake (35F). *6 rue Chabanais, at rue des Petits-Champs, 2e, tel. 01-49-27-96-26. Métro: Quatre-Septembre or Pyramides. Cash only under 100F. Closed Sun.*

Have you noticed those signs on brasserie windows boasting that they serve Poilâne bread? It all comes from a sublime St-Germain bakery at 8 rue du Cherche-Midi, where specials include a wheat loaf with nuts (25F) and apple tarts (12F).

LE MARAIS

A variety of kosher restaurants, delis, and bakeries with Middle Eastern specialties indicate the strong presence of the Marais's Jewish community. Look no farther than the fantastic falafel stands on **rue des Rosiers** for the cheapest and tastiest meals in all of Paris. The Marais's other main contingent, its well-established gay crowd, means you'll also find more expensive, artsy, trendy joints; try instead the gay-owned restaurants, cafés, and bars on **rue Ste-Croix-de-la-Bretonnerie** and **rue Vieille-du-Temple.** The Marais café scene is swinging, so you won't have any trouble finding convivial spots to get your daily dose of espresso.

UNDER 40F • L'As du Fallafel. The long line of hungry folks waiting for their falafel fix shows that the "masters of falafels" are doing something right. Lenny Kravitz paid homage to this standing-room-only restaurant-grocery-deli in a Rolling Stone interview; now, it pays homage to him—the wall is adorned with pictures of Lenny and his girlfriend, the sexy French sugar-pop singer Vanessa Paradis. A falafel costs 20F, but shell out an extra 5F for the deluxe with grilled eggplant, cabbage, hummus, tahini, and hot sauce. Get a tiny 10F wine bottle to go with it, and you're set. *34 rue des Rosiers, 4e, tel. 01-48-87-63-60. Métro: St-Paul. Cash only. Closed Sat.*

Sacha et Florence Finkelsztajn. Walk through the brightly colored mosaic doorway and enter a world of Eastern European and Russian snacks and specialties. These store-delis are Paris institutions; the rue des Rosiers location has been open since 1946. Small *pirojki* (pastries filled with fish, meat, or vegetables) cost 10F (20F for a large, almost meal-size version). Heftier sandwiches are 30F–40F. You can also get blinis, gefilte fish, and blueberry muffins. *Sacha: 27 rue des Rosiers, 4e, tel. 01-42-72-78-91. Métro: St-Paul. Closed Mon., Tues., and July. Florence: 24 rue des Ecouffes, 4e, tel. 01-48-87-92-85. Métro: St-Paul. Cash only. Closed Tues., Sat., and Aug.*

UNDER 60F • Chez Rami & Hanna. This place serves hearty, filling meals and a mean falafel almost rivaling that of L'As du Fallafel (*see above*) down the street. You can get your falafel to go (21F–24F), or sit down to dishes like the Israeli Platter (hummus, tahini, and falafel balls; 35F), spicy Moroccan salad

(40F), or stuffed eggplant (60F) in the small, friendly dining room. *54 rue des Rosiers, 4e, tel. 01–42–78–23–09. Métro: Hôtel de Ville. Cash only.*

Le Petit Gavroche. You'll probably share a table and some smoke at this cramped bistro, which intimates what the quarter was like before the chic set moved in. All kinds install themselves at the bar for a nightly glass of Bordeaux, while diners head upstairs for a filling 48F meal served until midnight. Don't expect fancy cuisine or reverent service, just good, substantial food and a casual atmosphere. *15 rue Ste-Croix-de-la-Bretonnerie, 4e, tel. 01–48–87–74–26. Métro: St-Paul. Closed Sun.*

La Theière dans les Nuages. The setting of this creole restaurant is small, cozy, and somewhat nondescript, but the great food and friendly service more than make up for the lack of atmosphere. Tasty specialities such as *accras de morue* (salt-cod fritters) and *marmite créole* (pork and bean stew) are served up. The speciality dishes change daily, and you can get a two-course 52F or 55F lunch menu. *4 rue Cloche-Perce, off rue de Rivoli, between rue Vieille-du-Temple and rue des Ecouffes, 4e, tel. 01–42–71–96–11. Métro: St-Paul. Cash only. Closed Sun.*

UNDER 80F • Chez Marianne. You'll know you've found Marianne's place when you see the line of people reading the bits of wisdom and poetry painted across her windows. The restaurant-deli serves excellent Middle Eastern specialties like hummus and *babaganoush* (eggplant dish) and couscous weekdays for 55F. The sampler platter lets you try four items for 55F, five for 65F, or six for 75F. If you don't want to wait, make reservations, grab something to go from the deli (featuring piles of dried fruits and nuts in bulk), or get a fabulous 25F Israeli-style falafel (with beets and cabbage) from the window outside. *2 rue des Hospitalières-St-Gervais, 4e, tel. 01–42–72–18–86. Métro: St-Paul.*

UNDER 100F • Baracane. When you're traveling on a budget it can be really nice to step into a restaurant that doesn't immediately remind you of your own penurious circumstances—like this pleasant, easygoing place serving first-rate southwestern food. If you watch the price of wine, you'll be able to eat for less than 100F a head, especially if you order the 49F lunch menu or 78F dinner menu. Try the duck terrine or the cassoulet, a state-of-the-art version of this classic casserole. *38 rue des Tournelles, 4e, tel. 01–42–71–43–33. Métro: Bastille. Closed Sun.*

Chez Omar. This pretty, old-fashioned bistro is always packed with a good-looking and stylish international crowd eating some of the best couscous in Paris. Looking after them all is one of the city's nicest restaurateurs, Omar, himself, whose English is very good. You won't need a first course if you order the couscous (75F). The grilled beef and lamb (95F) are also excellent, as are some of the North African wines. *47 rue de Bretagne, 3e, tel. 01–42–72–36–26. Métro: Arts et Métiers. No lunch Sun.*

The Studio. You might almost think you were at a Texas saloon except for the fact that this place is in a magnificent 17th-century stone-paved courtyard, filled with candlelit tables in good weather. Early evenings bring the sounds of music and clomping feet from the dance school upstairs . . . another sure sign you're not in the Wild West. You'll find good ole American spareribs (90F), as well as a hickory-smoked beef sandwich plate with coleslaw, green beans, and fries (70F). Otherwise, the food is completely Tex-Mex, as in *huevos rancheros* (eggs with tortillas and salsa; 75F) served at the popular weekend brunch. *41 rue du Temple, 4e, tel. 01–42–74–10–38. Métro: Rambuteau. No lunch weekdays.*

MONTMARTRE

The first rule of eating in Montmartre is: Don't buy anything near the tourist-infested Sacré-Coeur and place du Tertre, where you're sure to be overcharged. If you insist on being in the shadow of the Sacré-Coeur, try going behind it to **rue Lamarck** and **rue Caulaincourt** for relatively cheap French fare. Better yet, head down the stairs toward **rue Muller,** where the food is cheaper and more ethnic. For the most authentic African cuisine, go east to the area between **rue de la Goutte-d'Or** and **rue Doudeauville.** Homey little restaurants and fresh produce shops abound on **rue des Abbesses,** but if you want something a bit different, try exploring along **rue des Trois-Frères.**

UNDER 40F • La Pignatta. This Italian pizzeria and deli sells fresh pastas and panini with eggplant (16F–28F), some non-Italian items like hummus and tabbouleh (70F per kilo), and loaves of poppyseed bread (4F). You can also get a passable pizza for 30F. *2 rue des Abbesses, 18e, tel. 01–42–55–82–05. Métro: Abbesses. Cash only.*

UNDER 60F • Au Grain de Folie. Although hardcore vegetarians may find some of the choices bland and somewhat pricey, this restaurant's redeeming dish is the *au grain de folie,* a refreshing and filling grain concoction accompanied by fresh veggies and topped with warm goat cheese. You can get soup and a tart for 60F; à la carte items run 45F–65F. Refuel with the 15F organic apple juice, because no matter where you're going in Montmartre, it's usually uphill. *24 rue de la Vieuville, 18e, tel. 01–42–58–15–57. Métro: Abbesses.*

Le Fouta Toro. Get a whole day's worth of food for 50F. Some of the Senegalese dishes are terrific, like the *mafé au poulet* (chicken in peanut sauce) for 47F, but the seafood dishes could stand improvement. Warm, cheery surroundings, jolly service, and huge portions make it a great dinner spot, packed with locals of northern Montmartre. *3 rue du Nord, 18e, tel. 01–42–55–42–73. Métro: Marcadet-Poisson-niers. Closed Tues.*

Rayons de Santé. The menu here is entirely vegetarian, featuring 20F–30F appetizers like vegetable pâté and artichoke mousse. Main courses (30F–35F) include spicy couscous with vegetables and soy sausage or vegetarian goulash. You can also choose between a 48F menu or a three-course (dessert included) 63F menu. Mornings, come for an omelet (30F) and then check out the mini health-food store in front. *8 pl. Charles-Dullin, 18e, tel. 01–42–59–64–81. Métro: Abbesses. Cash only. Closed Sat. No dinner Fri.*

UNDER 80F • Au Virage Lepic. At a bend in one of Montmartre's steep and winding streets, Au Virage Lepic seems to belong to the last century—one can easily imagine Balzac's *ouvriers* (workers) huddling over some wine in the cozy dining room. The food is great, and the atmosphere casual and decidedly untouristed—the kind of place where today's Parisians come to talk art and politics over dinner. The *pavé au poivre* (beef-steak with pepper) is 65F, or you can get a delicious soupe à l'oignon for 35F. *61 rue Lepic, 18e, tel. 01–42–52–46–79. Métro: Abbesses.*

UNDER 100F • Au Refuge des Fondus. Just when you think there's not enough oxygen in the room to support another body, the jovial proprietor asks you to scoot over so he can seat another dozen. You're sure to know your neighbors by the time you leave. The waiter simply asks *"viande ou fromage?"* (meat or cheese?) and *"rouge ou blanc?"* (red or white wine?), then sets you up with an aperitif, appetizers, fondue, dessert, and wine for 87F. You'll probably feel stupid drinking wine out of a baby bottle (no joke), but you'll also eat heaps of food and have a hell of a good time. Reservations are essential. *17 rue des Trois-Frères, 18e, tel. 01–42–55–22–65. Métro: Abbesses.*

According to one shopworn legend, the word "bistrot" dates back to the early 19th century after the fall of Napoléon, when the Russian soldiers occupying Paris supposedly banged on zinc-topped café bars yelling "buistra"—"hurry" in Russian.

La Bouche du Roi. The "Mouth of the King" is a self-proclaimed Franco-Benin enterprise that blends West African cuisine with traditional French cooking. Colorful tapestry seats and mellow African tunes will help you forget the mob scene at the Sacré-Coeur. Weekday nights often feature live music; Friday nights an African *conteuse* (storyteller) weaves her tales. But the real reason to come is the food: a 55F lunch menu (80F at dinner) with specialties like *maffé* (beef in seasoned peanut sauce) and *tale tale* (fried bananas). Try the chicken cooked with plantains and coconut milk (60F) for a real treat. *4 rue Lamarck, 18e, tel. 01–42–62–55–41. Métro: Abbesses or Château-Rouge. Closed Mon.*

L'Eté en Pente Douce. This unassuming spot at the foot of the stairs leading up to the Sacré-Coeur sees regulars filing in for fantastic dinners. The asymmetrical dining room feels like a country house, and outdoor tables are great for gazing at the nearby park. Large salads cost 45F–60F, meat dishes 60F–80F, and a delicious pear dessert with nuts is 30F. Reserve for dinner or come for lunch, when things are considerably calmer. *23 rue Muller, 18e, tel. 01–42–64–02–67. Métro: Château-Rouge.*

Le Kezako. This self-proclaimed hangout of Montmartre "professors, plumbers, and engineers" is among Paris's best tapas joints. Sophie and Miguel serve cheap Spanish food and good sangria (65F per liter) in tiny, oddly mirrored rooms. A glass of sangria and a small tapa (22F) make a perfect snack, and a collection of four larger tapas (68F) makes a filling meal. The 85F menu includes paella, sangria, and coffee. *12 rue Véron, 18e, tel. 01–42–58–22–20. Métro: Abbesses.*

Le Moulin à Vin. The atmosphere and the crowd at this popular wine bar recall postwar Paris as depicted by photographers like Doisneau and Boubat. Danielle, the welcoming owner, once worked in a bank, but has never looked back since she traded in her calculator for a corkscrew. A fascinating mix of locals come for excellent cheese trays (60F), salads (50F), and delicious dishes like rabbit in mustard sauce (75F) or quiche Lorraine (60F). Wines by the glass run from 14F–25F. *6 rue Burq, 18e, tel. 01–42–52–81–27. Métro: Abbesses. Closed Mon., Sun. No lunch Tues., Fri., or Sat.*

A FULL LOAD OF COURSES

You'll hear mixed reviews of the university cafeteria-style restaurants, but you can't beat the price: For about 15F you can get a three-course meal. If you've been gnawing on bread and Brie for a week, this is nirvana. They're supposed to ask to see a student ID card (if you don't have one, the price gets jacked up 10F), but they often don't. Tickets come in sets of 10; if you only want one meal it'll cost 30F (just buy a ticket off a nice French student for the 15F deal). Lunch hours hover around 11:30–2; dinner is served 6:30–10. The "Resto-U" at 115 boulevard St-Michel (RER Luxembourg) doles out all-you-can-eat couscous or lentils with meat, vegetables, salad, and bread.

For a complete list of university restaurants, stop by CROUS (39 av. Georges-Bernanos, 5e, tel. 01–40–51–37–17, RER Port-Royal). Otherwise, try one of the following: 10 rue Jean-Calvin, 5e, métro Censier-Daubenton; 3 rue Mabillon, 6e, métro Mabillon; 45 blvd. Diderot, 12e, métro Gare de Lyon; 156 rue de Vaugirard, 15e, métro Pasteur; av. de Pologne, 16e, métro Porte Dauphine.

MONTPARNASSE

Boulevard du Montparnasse, which separates bourgeois St-Germain-des-Prés from the middle-class district of Montparnasse, was once one of the great Bohemian hangouts of Europe. Today it's rather out of fashion, and the cafés where Hemingway and Man Ray once dawdled over a glass of wine are filled with tourists drinking Cognac. Despite some traumatic urban renewal during the seventies, this is a real-people neighborhood, which means plenty of good, cheap places to eat if you poke around. If your budget is tight, you can always get a good Breton crepe around **rue d'Odessa** or **rue Daguerre;** the area was the original settling ground for Breton migrants looking for work in Paris at the turn of the century.

UNDER 60F • Chez Papa. Rowdy waitresses serve southwestern French food at this crowded place across from the cemetery. Mongo salads packed with potatoes, ham, cheese, and tomato are known as *boyardes* and cost a piddling 35F. Escargots "Papa" (49F) come piping hot in a bright orange pot. The prix-fixe menu goes for 50F day and night until 1 AM. At breakfast opt for an *omelette paysanne* (34F), filled with tomatoes, bacon, potatoes, and mushrooms. *6 rue Gassendi, 14e, tel. 01–43–22–41–19. Métro: Denfert-Rochereau. Other location: 206 rue La Fayette, 10e, tel. 01–42–09–53–87. Métro: Louis Blanc.*

Mustang Café. This is the most popular of the many Tex-Mex café-bars in Montparnasse, drawing foreign students and young Parisians. You won't be soaking up French culture, but you can have a decent meal at almost any hour—they're open daily 9 AM–5 AM. Taco salads cost 49F, quesadillas 39F, enchiladas 59F, and Dos Equis 30F. Weekdays 4–7 margaritas and cocktails are half-price. Expect it dark, loud, and cramped. *84 blvd. du Montparnasse, 14e, tel. 01–43–35–36–12. Métro: Montparnasse.*

UNDER 80F • Aux Artistes. This restaurant is as artsy as its name suggests: worn, covered in paint and posters from top to bottom, and inhabited by cool people who were born halfway through a cigarette. The food is French, and the chicken dishes are especially good. For 75F you can choose among 29 appetizers, 35 main dishes, and several cheeses or simple desserts. Get a bottle of house wine (32F) to top it all off. *63 rue Falguière, 15e, tel. 01–43–22–05–39. Métro: Pasteur. Closed Sun. No lunch Sat.*

Pont Aven–Chez Mélanie. Of the legions of crêperies below boulevard du Montparnasse, this one is among the best. Lively crowds of neighborhood students come for the *galette du jour* (buckwheat crepe), plus salad and cider for 44F. A la carte galettes go for 15F–50F, dessert crepes for 15F–40F. The lunch menu (64F) includes an appetizer, galette, and crepe; the dinner menu (76F) has a salad, galette, and cider. *54 rue du Montparnasse, 14e, tel. 01–43–22–23–74. Métro: Vavin.*

NEAR THE EIFFEL TOWER/RODIN MUSEUM

Though the restaurants in this aristocratic part of town cater primarily to diplomats and politicians, along with stray tourists and countesses, there are a surprisingly large number of good, inexpensive places tucked away among the well-buttoned-up streets. **Rue de Sèvres,** which attracts the shopping crowd, is a promising walk for a good lunch, and you might poke around the side streets near the **rue Cler** market. The cafés, haphazardly filled with students from nearby campuses, are also pleasant.

UNDER 100F • Au Babylone. The proprietress hustles her family around the tables of this lunch-only restaurant, serving grilled specials to everyone from political bigwigs to students, all under the watchful gaze of ceramic Pope plates. The four-course 90F menu includes cheese and wine. Appetizers (try the 20F pâté Basque) are inexpensive, and main courses, like a creamy veal stew or a plate of sausages, are about 50F. The best deal is the wine: 18F for a half-bottle of house red. *13 rue de Babylone, 7e, tel. 01–45–48–72–13. Métro: Sèvres-Baby-lone. Cash only. Closed Sun. and Aug.*

Au Pied du Fouet. A favorite canteen of André Gide and Jean Cocteau, this minuscule restaurant retains a Paris-in-the-fifties feel, right down to vintage plastic napkin dispensers. Popular with well-heeled locals who also frequent three-star spots but like the cozy, homey atmosphere here, this place serves solid, modestly priced home-cooking. Don't expect fine service: You sit elbow to elbow and are served briskly to make way for other hungry diners. The hot cabbage and bacon salad (35F) and baby scallops (65F) are typical of the ever-changing menu. Instead of coffee at the crowded bar, walk down the street to the tearoom of the lovely **La Pagode** cinema (No. 57)—it also serve good brownies. *45 rue de Babylone, 7e, tel. 01–47–05–12–27. Métro: Vaneau. Cash only. Closed Sun. No dinner Sat.*

If you can't stomach a deadly shot of espresso, swallow your pride and ask for a "café allongé." Waiters will smirk as they bring what's sometimes referred to as a "café américain": an espresso poured into a bigger cup and watered down.

Bar de la Maison de l'Amérique Latine. Walk through the brightly lit gallery of Latin American art and past the expensive restaurant to this cultural center's cool and dark café-bar. A la carte dishes include Mexican quesadillas (64F) and Guatemalan stuffed peppers (60F), with appetizers like Argentinean empanadas (28F). Wash it all down with a 25F Corona. Although the bar fills up at mealtimes with handsome but snobby art enthusiasts and diplomatic attachés, it's a quiet place in the morning or late afternoon. *217 blvd. St-Germain, 7e, tel. 01–45–49–33–23. Métro: Rue du Bac. No dinner Oct.–Apr. Closed weekends and Aug.*

Chez l'Ami Jean. If you're smitten with Basque food, the ebullient Jean and his family will dish you up some pâté *de campagne* (country-style pâté; 25F) and then treat you with specialties like *truite* (trout) meunière (55F) or Basque chicken (with tomatoes and red peppers, also 55F). Equally tempting desserts run 25F–40F. This is the meeting place for the North American Basque Organization, or NABO. *27 rue Malar, 7e, tel. 01–47–05–86–89. Métro: La Tour–Maubourg. Closed Sun.*

SPLURGE • Au Bon Acceuil. As soon as you hit town, make reservations at this bustling little bistro, just a few steps from the Eiffel Tower. Join the well-heeled crowd dining on the 120F menu—a deal for such great food. Depending on the season and what struck the chef's fancy when he went to market, you'll get to sample such skillfully cooked dishes as baked Saint Marcellin cheese on salad, tender veal fillet in a lemon-caper sauce, or pot-au-feu. *14 rue de Monttessuy, 7e, tel. 01–47–05–46–11. Métro: Ecole Militaire. Closed Sun.*

QUARTIER LATIN

The Quartier Latin has a slew of reasonable restaurants that keep its student population (and tourists) well fed. Competition is high among French, Greek, and Tunisian eateries on **rue de la Huchette.** For more upscale dining, try the area behind **square René-Viviani.** And, if you're really hard up, don't forget that you can always survive rather nicely on bread, wine, and cheese. Otherwise, try **rue Mouffetard** for a mean 13F crepe at one of the stands; you'll also find many French, Greek, and Mexican places offering a full meal for 50F–70F.

UNDER 40F • Al Dar. The deli side of this otherwise expensive Lebanese restaurant offers delicious sandwiches (24F) and small plates (30F) of falafel and spicy chicken sausage. A variety of goodies costs 65F if you eat at the picnic tables outside, 60F if it's packed to go. The lack of a menu and hurried counterpeople can make it difficult to order, but pointing should do the trick. *8–10 rue Frédéric-Sauton, 5e, tel. 01–43–25–17–15. Métro: Maubert-Mutualité.*

UNDER 60F • Le Boute Grill. Some Maghrebian expats feel this Tunisian restaurant has the best couscous in Paris. The servings are enormous and come with a choice of—count 'em—14 combinations of meat, including one with tripe stuffed with herbs (52F). A three-course menu at 72F includes wine, but even the ravenous men hunched over their plates shudder at the thought of finishing it all. *12 rue Boutebrie, 5e, tel. 01–43–54–03–30. Métro: Cluny–La Sorbonne. Cash only. Closed Sun.*

Cousin Cousine. This spacious, airy crêperie picks up on the French fetish for old flicks, with galettes named *L'Ange Bleu* (walnuts, blue cheese, crème fraîche; 35F) and *Mad Max* (ground beef, cheese, ratatouille; 41F). Simpler galettes start at 14F; the usual sundaes and flambéed crepes are 30F–35F. A *bolée* (bowl) of cider starts at 14F. *36 rue Mouffetard, 5e, tel. 01–47–07–73–83. Métro: Monge. Cash only under 150F.*

Le Jardin des Pâtes. The "Garden of Pasta" serves freshly made, organic-grain pastas (46F–73F) lavished with sauces like mixed vegetables with ginger and tofu; carnivores can sink their teeth into a smoked duck sauce with cream and nutmeg. Entrées, like the avocado paired with melon sorbet, are about 25F. The granola folk who own the restaurant have even found additive-free beers (24F). *4 rue Lacépède, 5e, tel. 01–43–31–50–71. Métro: Monge. Closed Mon.*

La Petite Légume. This small restaurant near the Jardin des Plantes takes its vegetarianism seriously—most dishes use no dairy products, and several of the desserts are fat-free. Portions are generous, tasty, and relatively cheap: Grains with mixed vegetables cost 35F–40F, miso soup 30F, the vegetarian platter (tofu galette, vegetables, rice, and dried fruits) 60F. You can buy pastries (16F–32F) and whole-grain breads during the day. *36 rue des Boulangers, 5e, tel. 01–40–46–06–85. Métro: Cardinal Lemoine. Closed Sun.*

UNDER 80F • L'Apostrophe. Early diners get a deal at this romantic, country-style nook near the Panthéon. The 65F two-course menu (add 10F for dessert), served only until 8 PM, features appetizers like leek vinaigrette soup, main courses like pepper steak or shish kebabs, and banana flambé to finish it all off. Huge candles in bottles ensure a campy setting. *34 rue de la Montagne-Ste-Geneviève, 5e, tel. 01–43–54–10–93. Métro: Maubert-Mutualité.*

UNDER 100F • Mirama. This bustling Chinese noodle shop is extremely popular with local students and academics, who come for big steaming bowls of noodles in broth garnished with roast pork, shrimp, vegetables, or other choices. The roast ducks hanging in the window are tasty, too, as are the pork spareribs in black bean sauce. *17 rue St-Jacques, 5e, tel. 01–43–54–71–11. Métro: St-Michel.*

Surma. Regulars fill the small dining room of this Indian restaurant across from the south wall of La Mosquée. The three-course menu is 98F (59F lunch with fewer choices), but you may do better ordering à la carte from among the 11 tandooris and 21 curries, priced 48F and up. Other highlights include *begun barta* (spicy roasted eggplant spread; 30F) and the fluffy cheese nan bread (19F). Top it off with a tiny pitcher of *citron lassi* (lemon yogurt drink; 20F). *5 rue Daubenton, 5e, tel. 01–43–36–31–75. Métro: Censier-Daubenton.*

SPLURGE • Chantairelle. Dig deep into your bag for a few more francs and come here for a really fantastic meal. The young team who runs this place hail from the Forez, in the south-central Auvergne, and they've created an ambience that makes you feel like you're there: old doors, an old well, and even little bottles of oil scented with the characteristic odors of the region (hay, etc.). The big portions of delicious hearty food—stuffed cabbage (65F), and *potée* (pork, potatoes, and vegetables poached in bouillon; 75F)—will fill you up. Order the Châteauguy (70F), a big-boned native red, to go with your meal. *17 rue Laplace, 5e, tel. 01–46–33–18–59. Métro: Maubert-Mutualité. Closed Mon.*

Chez Joel D–Bistrot de l'Huître. If you've been yearning for oysters but are worried about the expense, head to this cozy little place in the quietest part of the 5th. The oysters come from all along the French Atlantic coast, and depending upon which grade and type you choose, you can scarf down a dozen for about 120F. If you're really feeling extravagant, follow up with the chocolate mousse (30F). *285 rue St-Jacques, 5e, tel. 01–43–54–71–70. RER Port-Royal, Luxembourg. Closed Sun.*

ST-GERMAIN-DES-PRES

Beyond the chichi galleries and boutiques of St-Germain are plenty of substantial dining options. **Rue Monsieur-le-Prince** is one of the best restaurant streets in the city; here you can find Asian spots with three-course menus for as little as 50F. **Rue des Canettes** (try **La Crêpe Canettes**) and the surrounding small streets are best for crepes and other fast eats; the classic French fare here often falls flat (let the crowds inside the restaurant be your guide). **Rue de Seine** and **rue de Buci** are lined with food shops, most of which have prepared items to go and are open until 7 or 7:30.

UNDER 40F • Au Plaisir des Pains. They pack pita pockets with fillings of your choice (grilled red peppers, tomato, mozzarella, and lettuce for 25F, other combinations 20F–30F), throw them on the grill, and then pack it up picnic-style for you (napkins and all). A good thing, considering the 10F charge to sit down and the Jardin du Luxembourg nearby. *62 rue de Vaugirard, 6e, tel. 01–45–48–40–45. Métro: Rennes. Cash only. Closed Sun.*

UNDER 60F • Cosi. The opera-loving New Zealander who owns this fancy sandwich shop can often be seen at the stone oven in back baking his trademark focaccia bread. You choose the ingredients—such as chèvre, spinach, smoked salmon, mozzarella, tomatoes, or curried turkey (30F–50F)—or you can just munch on the slightly salty bread for 9F. Add to this a glass of wine (14F), modern wood decor with photos of opera greats, a changing selection of opera music, and voilà: French deli. *54 rue de Seine, 6e, tel. 01–46–33–35–36. Métro: Odéon. Cash only.*

Orestias. This restaurant is fine if you're in the mood for a boisterous meal; otherwise, the haphazard service may drive you nuts. It's owned by a Greek family that communicates by shouting: They shout at you to take a seat and then shout your order to the kitchen. Meals are typically a three-course affair (44F; two-course lunch menu, 37F) featuring a variety of grilled meats and desserts like baklava. Vegetarians may not enjoy the animal heads on the wall glowering down at patrons. *4 rue Grégoire-de-Tours, 6e, tel. 01–43–54–62–01. Métro: Odéon. Closed Sun.*

UNDER 80F • Le Coffee Parisien. This popular but tiny spot, frequented by St-Germain's young leisure class, serves brunch all day at the diner-style counter or at tables. We're talking real brunch, like eggs Benedict (70F), pancakes (50F), and eggs Florentine (70F). The 40F spinach salad is quite good. *5 rue Perronet, 7e, tel. 01–40–49–08–08. Métro: St-Germain-des-Prés.*

Restaurant des Beaux-Arts. Students and professors painted the frescoes on the walls and regularly fill up this lively, old-time establishment near the Ecole des Beaux-Arts. The three-course 75F menu with wine is extensive, including daily specials like fondue, rabbit, steak, or lamb. A budget tourist's favorite. *11 rue Bonaparte, 6e, tel. 01–43–26–92–64. Métro: St-Germain-des-Prés. Cash only.*

UNDER 100F • Chassagne Restaurant. With a meaty three-course 85F menu (lunch 65F) with grilled specialties, this could be one of the best deals for a classic French meal. Locals linger in Chassagne's dark, rustic interior. Servers may even attempt timid English translations if you look perplexed enough. *38 rue Monsieur-le-Prince, 6e, tel. 01–43–26–54–14. Métro: Odéon. RER: Luxembourg. Closed Sun.*

Les Jardins de St-Germain. This traditional restaurant near the Eglise St-Germain-des-Prés fills up at lunch with well-dressed professionals and students from the nearby business school. The 68F lunch menu (79F at dinner) includes a generously garnished main course, your choice of veggies, and dessert. The same owners run **La Ferme St-Germain** across the street; the two restaurants open alternately on Sundays. *14 rue du Dragon, 6e, tel. 01–45–44–72–82. Métro: St-Germain-des-Prés. Closed every other Sun.*

Le Petit Mabillon. In a section of St-Germain where restaurants are generally expensive, this friendly Italian spot puts them all to shame with a delicious, filling, three-course menu (77F). In good weather, sit outside and watch the crowds going to the market across the street. Pastas made fresh daily cost 55F à la carte. *6 rue Mabillon, 6e, tel. 01–43–54–08–41. Métro: Mabillon. Closed Sun. No lunch Mon.*

Village Bulgare. Tucked into a quiet side street near the Pont Neuf, this restaurant was started by a Bulgarian dancer and his wife, who used to cook for homesick dance-troupe members. Sample Bulgarian specialties like *kebabtcheta* (a grilled meat roll; 52F) and *banitza* (a baked pastry filled with cheese; 35F); the three-course menu costs 85F. Their flyers deem it "Une cuisine qui chante" (cooking that sings). *8 rue de Nevers, 6e, tel. 01–43–25–08–75. Métro: Pont-Neuf. Cash only. No dinner Sun., no lunch Mon.*

SPLURGE • Le Bistrot d'Opio. This restaurant serves delicious Provençal cuisine on a street packed with standard French restaurants. The 119F menu allows you to choose almost any entrée, main course, and dessert on the menu. Try the salmon baked on a bed of sea salt, or the duck prepared with honey and 19 spices, including anise and cloves. The chocolate fondant for dessert is a chocoholic's dream come true. *9 rue Guisarde, 6e, tel. 01–43–29–01–84. Métro: Mabillon.*

BISTROS AND WINE BARS

There's a subtle difference between *bistrots à vins* (wine bistros) and their often sometimes more expensive counterparts, *bars à vin* (wine bars). Bistros, a quintessentially Parisian institution, are earthy places that are all about wine—sold by the bottle or by the glass—and snacks like cheese and meat plates, although many of them are just as proud of their cuisine as they are of their wine. They often specialize in obscure regional vintages and sometimes buy grapes from the vineyards, which they blend themselves. Many wine bars, though not all, are run by British; these are pricier, more upscale places with generally broad and sophisticated wine lists.

Le Baron Rouge. Refreshingly mellow, the Red Baron has enough varieties of cheap wine—patrons draw straight from the barrel—to keep its young crowd happy. Wine starts at 7F, meat plates at 35F, and smoked duck is 18F. The decor, like the crowd, is low-key and casual, with sawdust-covered floors and wooden tables. About twice a week a live rock or blues band takes over, forcing some patrons out onto barrels set up on the sidewalk. *1 rue Théophile-Roussel, near pl. d'Aligre, 12e, tel. 01–43–43–14–32. Métro: Ledru-Rollin. Cash only. Closed Mon. No dinner Sun.*

Bistrot des Augustins. The Augustins, the best of several bistros along the Seine in St-Germain, has a worn wood-and-brass bar, speckled mirrors, and shelves cluttered with dried flowers. When the weather is nice, the front doors open onto the street. Join the devoted clientele drinking quality wine by the glass (15F and up) and munching on goat cheese salads (40F) or liver terrine (32F). *39 quai des Grands-Augustins, 6e, tel. 01–43–54–41–65. Métro: St-Michel. Cash only under 100F.*

Bistrot–Cave des Envierges. A cozy room and a few scattered sidewalk tables mark this old, casual bistro just above the Parc de Belleville. Ten wines—five whites and five reds—are offered daily at 8F–22F a glass, and the list always features at least a couple of Loires. Snacks like gazpacho cost 30F, meat or cheese plates go for 45F. A cool, hang-loose crowd—not that there's ever much of one—makes this a great place to unwind. *11 rue des Envierges, 20e, tel. 01–46–36–47–84. Métro: Pyrénées. Cash only. Closed Mon. and Tues.*

Le Bouchon du Marais. For a quieter meal at this bistro, grab a table downstairs. For something more boisterous, reserve ahead for a table *à l'étage* (on the second floor). The patron specializes in Touraine wines and has a wide selection by the glass (30F–40F). Otherwise, 70F gets you a glass of wine, a main dish, and dessert. In winter, you can also have the raclette (cheese melted over potatoes) menu (115F), a perfect meal to have in the cozy, chalet-like upstairs. The walls are full of snapshots of the patron and his friends, all conspicuously drunk. *15 rue François-Miron, 4e, tel. 01–48–87–44–13. Métro: St-Paul. Closed Sun.*

Le Brin de Zinc. A relaxed crowd of locals gathers at tables on the sidewalk of this busy market street for an afternoon glass of wine (25F). Indoors, mingle with suited regulars munching on platters of cheese (50F) or meats (65F) with a bottle of wine (90F and up) from the well-stocked cellar. More substantial food, such as the blanquette de veau, is expensive (about 90F) but excellent—or stick to the cheap and delicious quiche Lorraine (25F). *50 rue Montorgueil, 2e, tel. 01–42–21–10–80. Métro: Etienne Marcel. Closed Sun.*

Le Coude Fou. Yet another mellow Marais institution where you're bound to meet some cool people if you hang around long enough. Avoid the artsy, expensive food (70F–90F) and get a bottle of wine (90F and up) or a beer (20F); then join the regulars (including a fair number of Anglophones) hunkered around tables made from wine crates. *12 rue du Bourg-Tibourg, 4e, tel. 01–42–77–15–16. Métro: Hôtel de Ville or St-Paul. No lunch Sun.*

Jacques Mélac. Since 1938 Jacques Mélac, one of the great hams of Paris, has been turning out reliably good wine, which has won this friendly little place global renown. Jacques offers a large selection of labels, but definitely try his own award-winning 1981 wines (bottles start at 70F). The bar and dining room are packed with locals who aren't afraid to serve themselves when the waiters are a little slow.

Omelets (20F–50F) and plates of meats and cheese (20F–60F) may accompany the wine, but the waiters refuse to serve water with the food. In mid-September, when the grapes on the vines outside Jacques Mélac's windows ripen, he closes off the street and holds his own private harvest festival. Everyone picks, the young'uns stomp, and the drinking goes on through the night. *42 rue Léon-Frot, 11e, tel. 01–43–70–59–27. Métro: Charonne. Closed weekends and Aug.*

Le Relais du Vin. M. Beaugendre's 18-wine-long list starts with a 65F bottle of Château Coquille 1992 rosé and winds up at a 1,400F Château Margaux 1976 Premier Grand Cru Classé; glasses of the less expensive stuff go for 12F–21F. For 40F you can compare small glasses of three different Burgundies. The menu runs 65F for two courses and a drink, 85F for three courses; lighter dishes such as spinach salad topped with raisins and cheese (40F) are served until past midnight. *85 rue St-Denis, at rue des Prêcheurs, 1er, tel. 01–45–08–41–08. Métro: Les Halles. Closed Sun.*

La Robe et le Palais. Owned by two, young French guys, this low-key wine bar near Les Halles is a good place to sample wines from all over France—120 to be exact—served *au compteur* (according to the quantity consumed). Have a glass, then order one of the creative takes on classic dishes on the 70F and 85F lunch menus or à la carte (85F–100F) at dinner. *13 rue des Lavandières-Ste-Opportune, 1er, tel. 01–45–08–07–41. Métro: Châtelet. Closed Sun. No lunch Sat.*

Le Rouge Gorge. You won't find boisterous, glass-clinking guzzlers at this sophisticated Marais wine bar. The rustic and homey rooms give it the feel of an isolated country house, a good place to take that edition of *War and Peace* and mull over life and a glass of white (from 15F) or red (from 12F) wine from Corsica. You can get a decent plate of *figatelli* (spinach and polenta; 62F) or desserts and cheeses (around 30F). *8 rue St-Paul, 4e, tel. 01–48–04–75–89. Métro: Sully-Morland. Closed Sun. and Aug.*

If you're wandering around and need to find a bathroom, one of the ubiquitous cafés may be your best bet. Not only are they on almost every street corner, but proprietors are required by law to let anyone use their bathrooms, whether patrons or not.

CAFES

Along with air, water, and the three-course meal, the café remains one of the basic necessities of life in Paris. Though they continue to close in the face of changing work and eating habits, cafés can still be found on almost every corner. Many of them look alike—the unfortunate result of '60s and '70s renovations—and only if you stick around long enough and become a regular (or write entire books, as Simone de Beauvoir did) will you discover their true intrigue. Those on the *grands boulevards* (such as boulevard St-Michel, boulevard St-Germain, and the Champs-Elysées) and in the big tourist spots (near the Louvre, the Opéra, and the Eiffel Tower, for example) will almost always be the most expensive and the least interesting. The more modest establishments (look for nonchalant locals) will give you a cheaper cup of coffee and a feeling of what real French café life is like.

Cafés are required to post a *tarif des consommations,* a list that includes prices for the basics: *café* (espresso), *café crème* (the same with hot milk), *chocolat chaud* (hot chocolate), *bière à la pression* (beer on tap), *vin rouge* (red wine), *kir* (white wine flavored with crème de cassis), and *citron* or orange *pressé* (fresh-squeezed lemonade or orange juice). They list two prices, *au comptoir* (at the counter) and *à terrasse* or *à salle* (seated at a table). Below we give the seated prices. If you just need a quick cup of coffee, have it at the counter and save yourself money. If you have a rendezvous, sit at a table: Remember you're paying rent on that little piece of wood, and hang out as long as you like. Cafés are usually open until midnight or later and charge about 5F more per drink after 10 PM or so.

L'Allée Thorigny. A bright, simple café a few steps from the Musée Picasso provides everything you need: temporary shelter or a seat outside, a cup of coffee (9F), newspapers and magazines (from the newsstand on the corner), chessboards, and self-serve candy (14F for 100g). *2 pl. Thorigny, 3e, tel. 01–42–77–32–05. Métro: St-Paul or Chemin Vert. Closed Tues.*

Amnesia Café. The music is just loud enough to keep conversations private at this dimly lit, predominantly gay café with big, comfy chairs. In fact, the atmosphere is so mellow, it might reconcile you with the preppy types that frequent it. Their scrumptious salad plates (45F–65F) offer more greenery than most cows could consume. A café costs 9F, café crème 14F, and a jumbo crème 18F; beers run

LEFT BANK
LITERARY CAFES

If you really want to sink a lot of money into an a cup of café crème, stop by one of the cafés made famous by their artsy patrons of the 19th and early 20th centuries. On place St-Germain-des-Prés is Les Deux Magots, named after the Chinese figures inside. Still milking its reputation as one of the Left Bank's prime meeting places for the intelligentsia, Deux Magots charges 21F for a cup of coffee. Past patrons include Verlaine, Rimbaud, Gide, Picasso, and Breton. Sartre and de Beauvoir supposedly met here, but spent more time two doors down at the Café de Flore, hanging with his fellow angst-ridden friend Camus.

Perhaps the most famous bastion of Left Bank café culture (and certainly one of the most expensive, having become a pricey bar-restaurant), La Closerie des Lilas (171 blvd. du Montparnasse) marks its bar seats with plaques indicating who once sat there. Buy an expensive drink and you can rest where Baudelaire, Apollinaire, and Hemingway once sat. Le Procope (13 rue de l'Ancienne Comédie), the self-proclaimed "first café in the world," was founded in 1689 and supplied coffee and booze to Rousseau, Balzac, Hugo, Voltaire, Napoléon, Robespierre, Ben Franklin, and Oscar Wilde. Now it's a stuffy restaurant.

20F–30F. Nightfall ups both the prices and the crowd. *42 rue Vieille-du-Temple, 4e, tel. 01–42–72–16–94. Métro: St-Paul or Hôtel de Ville.*

Au Soleil de la Butte. Here you'll find the rare commodity of a good cup of coffee in an untouristy café near the Sacré-Coeur. A sparse local crowd hangs out on the covered terrace sipping café (10F) and beer (10F–15F). The menu is long and includes salads from 30F. This café has the dear idiosyncrasy of also serving meals at off-times. *32 rue Muller, 18e, tel. 01–46–06–18–24. Métro: Château Rouge.*

Brûlerie de l'Odéon. When you enter this old-fashioned coffee brewery specializing in teas, the friendly proprietress might engage you in conversation about the weather, even if you don't speak French. The decor (teak tables and coffee paraphernalia) is as low-key as the service. Café is 10F–11F, café crème 15F, and pastries 13F–20F. *6 rue Crébillon, 6e, tel. 01–43–26–39–32. Métro: Odéon. Cash only. Closed Sun.*

Le Café. The subdued name says it all. A young, goateed crowd and cool, low-key tunes keep the atmosphere about as mellow and unpretentious as it gets in Paris. Bring a book and munch on a zucchini and cheddar tart (45F) or a *croque monsieur* (grilled ham-and-cheese sandwich) with a side-salad (40F). Or bring a friend and sip kir (20F) while you play one of the backgammon, chess, or domino games they've got in back. *62 rue Tiquetonne, 2e, tel. 01–40–39–08–00. Métro: Etienne Marcel. Cash only. Closed Sun. morning.*

Café Beaubourg. Style alert: The crowd here looks like it's just back from Ibiza or Saint-Tropez. Yet despite the intimidatingly slick exterior, the waiters are actually friendly and used to tourists. Best of all are the bookshelves filled with French titles that you can browse while you lounge in the shadow of the Centre Georges Pompidou. Tackle a large salad (45F–50F), but beware of the pricey drinks. *100 rue St-Martin, 4e, tel. 01–48–87–63–96. Cash only. Métro: Rambuteau.*

Café de l'Industrie. This place is so cool that it doesn't even bother to open on Saturdays. Every twenty-something in town flocks to the large, smoky rooms where modern art hangs from the walls. This is a great place for a light dinner and drink before hitting the Bastille scene. Sink into one of the corner cushy seats and hide out all day, or come later to schmooze with the French night owls at the bar. Beers are 16F. *16 rue St-Sabin, 11e, tel. 01–47–00–13–53. Métro: Bastille or Bréguet-Sabin. Closed Sat.*

Café Marly. This flamboyant and unabashedly sophisticated café overlooks the Cour Marly in the Louvre's Richelieu wing. The stunning view, name-dropping clientele, and reputation might justify paying 16F for a café or 35F for a chocolate tart, at least once. The extra-long hours (from 8 AM to 2 AM) are an added bonus. *Cour Napoléon, 1er, tel. 01–49–26–06–60. Métro: Palais Royal–Musée du Louvre.*

Café au Petit Suisse. At the edge of the Quartier Latin and across the street from the Jardin du Luxembourg, this place is full of students, starving writers, and other locals. Sit in the cozy little room when the weather is rotten and, when it isn't, on the sunny terrace. With private booths and an indoor balcony, the Petit Suisse draws you in without being flashy or touristy. *9 rue Corneille, at rue de Vaugirard, 6e, no phone. Métro: Odéon. RER: Luxembourg. Cash only. Closed weekends.*

Le Café du Trésor. Although it's tucked in a little side street off rue Vieille-du-Temple, this bright café is definitely an attention grabber. The blue, yellow, red, and green tables are inscribed with bits of conversation (lest you run out of ideas), and the plush seats indoors accent the modern art on the walls. The handsome gay waiters will promptly equip you with beer (16F–28F) or *kir royal* (champagne with black currant liqueur; 40F). *5–7 rue du Trésor, 4e, tel. 01–44–78–06–60. Métro: St-Paul. Cash only.*

Feast your eyes on the goods at Fauchon (26 pl. de la Madeleine, 8e, tel. 01–47–42–60–11, métro Madeleine) and Hédiard (21 pl. de la Madeleine, 8e, tel. 01–42–66–44–36, métro Madeleine), world-famous, fine French food shops.

Café Wah-Wah. Here's a grungy Bastille café with decor that was lifted straight from San Francisco's Haight district or London's Camden Town. Don't be intimidated by the multiply pierced, tattooed regulars; the bar folk are really nice and the music is just loud enough to mask your bad French accent. Café is 6F, a pression 12F, and kirs 15F. *11 rue Daval, 11e, tel. 01–47–00–08–48. Métro: Bastille. Cash only.*

Chez Camille. The outdoor terrace is only slightly larger than a balcony, and the cramped inside is painted a pale yellow. The patrons are young, hip, and mostly male Montmartrois, who come regularly to enjoy the soft jazz and the cheap beer (10F–15F). *8 rue Ravignan, 18e, tel. 01–46–06–05–78. Métro: Abbesses. Cash only. Closed Mon.*

Les Colonies du Paradis. Okay, so the name (the Colonies of Paradise) is cheesy, and so is the Mariah Carey–style pop music they play. But this sunny, two-floor café is gorgeous and right off place de la Bastille. More importantly, their weekday happy hour (5 PM–8 PM) lets you sip tropical cocktails for only 20F. *3 rue du Faubourg St-Antoine, 11e, tel. 01–43–44–01–00. Métro: Bastille.*

La Palette. Have a café crème (12F) or wine (20F) while contemplating the splotched palettes of local artists and beaux-arts students at this old, muted café amidst rue de Seine's galleries. The waiters are talkative and the clientele nocturnal—it's a good place for late-night socializing. Come on balmy evenings when everyone crowds the tables outside under the cherry trees. *43 rue de Seine, 6e, tel. 01–43–26–68–15. Métro: Mabillon. Cash only. Closed Sun.*

Pâtisserie Viennoise. A scaled-down version of its Austrian counterparts, this cramped local institution keeps aspiring doctors from the nearby Ecole de Médecine caffeinated. Pastries are made in the kitchen downstairs, including several variations on the chocolate torte (15F), each named for a famous composer; lesser pastries start at 5F. *8 rue de l'Ecole-de-Médecine, 6e, tel. 01–43–26–60–48. Métro: Odéon. Cash only. Closed weekends and Aug.*

La Pause. This smoky Bastille café (but what isn't smoky in Paris?) has an outdoor terrace overlooking the rue de Charonne, loaded with art galleries and music stores. Coffee is a reasonable 8F, crème 12F. If you're hungry, dig into the succulent salmon quiche (42F). A trendy, relaxed French crowd, with a significant but not overwhelming contingent of motorcyclists, packs it all day. *41 rue de Charonne, 11e, tel. 01–48–06–80–33. Métro: Bastille or Ledru-Rollin. Cash only.*

Sydney Coffee Shop. After you hike up a small 30° incline, a tiny counter and two tables welcome you to this low-key, Australian Internet café. Foster's is 40F a pint, Melbourne bitter 30F. Check your e-mail for 1F a minute while you munch, since 35F specials make this a great lunch spot as well. *27 rue Lacépède, 5e, tel. 01–43–36–70–46. Métro: Monge or Cardinal Lemoine. Cash only. Closed Sun.–Mon.*

SALONS DE THÉ

French cafés tend to appeal to chain-smoking crowds of chattering French people, but *salons de thé* (tea rooms) are mellower institutions that no longer cater only to fussy matronly ladies. Regularly filled with students and artists seeking portions generous enough to share, the salons specialize in *tartes salées* (savory tarts with cheese and vegetables), *tartes sucrées* (dessert tarts), and, of course, tea. In the Marais they pop up on every corner, and gay proprietors can be less intimidating sources of information about gay life in the neighborhood than a bartender. That said, you'll see more women than men in salons de thé, and they're often alone, making these places a great refuge for single women travelers. They tend to be open in the afternoons, seeming to beckon just as your feet are rebelling against a day of marble-floored museums and cobblestone streets.

A Priori Thé. This small salon serves up large pots of tea (22F) in its comfortably worn room in the galerie Vivienne, an elegant renovated passage near the Place des Victoires. Tables line the old glass-roofed galleria, making the place feel like a sidewalk café, only without the traffic and gloomy weather. Older women come here to sip on exotic teas (mango, mint, and almond are a few of the 25F options) and nibble on divine, although expensive, pastries (30F). It's the perfect place to catch up on your letter writing—there's even a funky postcard shop right next door. *35–37 galerie Vivienne, at 66 rue Vivienne, 2e, tel. 01–42–97–48–75. Métro: Bourse. Cash only.*

La Charlotte de l'Isle. This minute salon de thé should really be called a *salon de chocolat*; birds and fish made of chocolate-dipped orange peels peer curiously out the front window, and they melt real chocolate bars for the sumptuous hot chocolates (20F). An ample selection of teas is available in bulk or by the cup (15F), and there's always an inventive selection of dessert tarts (15F–20F). Wednesday afternoons the friendly owner hosts reservation-only marionette shows. *24 rue St-Louis-en-l'Ile, 4e, tel. 01–43–54–25–83. Métro: Pont-Marie. Cash only. Closed Mon.–Wed. and July–Aug.*

Les Enfants Gâtés. A few blocks to the east you have the beautiful place des Vosges, in the other direction bars and restaurants—and in the middle of it all a café with low lights, tattered leather chairs, ceiling fans, and old movie posters. Coffee costs 15F and loose-leaf flavored teas 25F. Get a drink and stay as long as you like—the welcoming manager may even hand you a magazine from his huge stack. *43 rue des Francs-Bourgeois, 4e, tel. 01–42–77–07–63. Métro: St-Paul. Cash only.*

Mariage Frères. This is the most reputable teahouse in Paris; the shop up front sells hundreds of varieties of loose leaves by the gram, as well as every device imaginable in which to brew them. A pot of tea in the chic salon at the back will run you 45F, desserts 45F–55F. Don't forget to visit their tea museum upstairs. Avoid the bland, overpriced brunch. *30 rue du Bourg-Tibourg, 4e, tel. 01–42–72–28–11. Métro: Hôtel de Ville or St-Paul. Closed Mon. Other location: 13 rue des Grands Augustins, 6e, tel. 01–40–51–82–50. Métro: Mabillon. Closed Tues.*

La Mosquée. Inside Paris's main mosque, this salon de thé has an intricately tiled interior, Moroccan wood carvings, and tapestried benches. Let the Middle Eastern music lull you, and then visit the Turkish baths next door for pure decadence (*see* box, Turkish Delights, *in* Chapter 2). Coffee or a teeny (but potent) glass of sweet mint tea is 10F; baklava and other pastries cost 11F–15F. *19–39 rue Geoffroy-St-Hilaire, 5e, tel. 01–43–31–18–14. Métro: Censier-Daubenton. Cash only.*

Muscade. Tucked away inside the western arcade of the Palais Royal, this tearoom is one of the prettiest and calmest in Paris. Choose from a broad selection of teas from local purveyor Betjeman & Barton (25F a pot), along with a delicious pastry or dessert (40F). If you're hungrier, opt for one of the large salads (50F). In summer, consider coming here for a light supper when you can sit outside and have the gardens almost to yourself. *36 rue de Montpensier, 1er, tel. 01–42–97–51–36. Métro: Palais-Royal.*

MARKETS AND SPECIALTY SHOPS

Three-course meals are fantastic, but sometimes there is nothing finer (or cheaper) than picnic of a baguette, *fromage* (cheese), and a tomato *sur l'herbe* (on the grass)—or on a bridge or a bench. As well as many open-air markets, Paris has a medley of specialty shops—including boulangeries (which not only sell bread but also inexpensive sandwiches), fromageries, *charcuteries* (butcher selling cold cuts), and *épiceries* (the French equivalent of a deli), and late-hour markets. For a change from the ubiquitous baguette, **P. L. Poujaran** (20 rue Jean-Nicot, 7e, tel. 01–47–05–80–88, métro La Tour–Maubourg) has delicious black-olive and whole grain breads, and **Poilâne** (*see above*) sells great sourdough. No picnic in Paris is complete without a good bottle of wine: *See* Wine *in* Chapter 6 for a list of good-priced wine shops. Drinking in public is allowed, as long as you are picnicking (not walking around) and are in a spot that does not obstruct traffic (i.e., not in the middle of a busy square).

Monoprix and **Prisunic** both house low-priced *supermarchés* (supermarkets), but you usually have to weave through clothing and perfume departments to reach the food. Monoprix is all over and usually open until 8 or 9; the Prisunic just off the Champs-Elysées (109 rue de La Boétie, 8e, tel. 01–42–25–10–27) is open Monday–Saturday until midnight. On most side streets, especially in budget lodging areas, look for *alimentations générales*—small grocery stores that offer standard snack items at steep prices. They're generally open until 9 or 10 PM.

A lifesaver for anyone on a budget, **Ed l'Epicier** is the cheapest supermarket in Paris. Although the selection varies, you can always find the basics (pasta, rice, beans, meat, cheese, wine, chocolate) for way less than anywhere else. Bring your own grocery bags. *84 rue Notre-Dame-des-Champs, 6e, métro Notre-Dame des Champs; 80 rue de Rivoli, 4e, métro Hôtel de Ville; 123 rue de Charonne, 11e, métro Bastille.*

OPEN-AIR MARKETS

There is no better way to experience the "real" Paris than by joining the haggling, pushing, pointing, and shouting that takes place at Paris's 84 open-air markets. Don't be intimidated, because not much French is needed—shopping in markets merely requires a little body language. The best time to go is in the morning, when you'll get the best selection and the merchants will be more patient with your halting French.

Most boulangeries in Paris aren't allowed to make their own bread because you need a special permit to own an oven. To have a real loaf of bread baked by real Parisian boulangers, look for a blue and yellow sign in front saying ARTISAN BOULANGER.

Many are only open until 1:30 PM. Unless you see a sign saying "Libre Service" (self-service), the grocer chooses your items for you. You can, however, object to anything she chooses or tell her which ones you prefer. Pointing should do the trick if you don't speak any French.

The list "Les Marchés de Paris" at the tourist office will give you a detailed plan of all the markets; otherwise, pick and choose from the following. The cheapest market is on **place d'Aligre** (12e, métro Ledru-Rollin, open daily). Here you'll find fresh fruit, veggies, cheese, pastries, kosher butchers, coffee, clothing, flowers, and cooking utensils. The market at **place Monge** (5e, métro Monge, open Wed., Thurs., and Sun.) is another well-known cheapie. Paris's biggest outdoor market is held on **boulevard de Reuilly** between rue de Charenton and place Félix-Eboué (12e, métro Dugommier, open Tues. and Fri.). More permanent covered markets take place on **rue Mabillon** (6e, métro Mabillon) and **rue de Bretagne** (3e, métro Filles-Calvaire). Hours for these markets are Monday–Saturday 8–1 and 3–7, Sunday 8–1. For organic food, head to the **Marché Biologique** (6e, métro Rennes, open Sun.), on boulevard Raspail between rue du Cherche-Midi and rue de Rennes.

One of the most enjoyable market streets is **rue Montorgueil**. For Chinese, Vietnamese, and Thai food, check out the excellent daily **Chinese market** near Paris's Chinese district in the 13th arrondissement; take the métro to Porte de Choisy and you can't miss it. If you're still not satisfied, try the south end of **rue Mouffetard** (5e, métro Monge), **rue de Buci** (6e, métro Odéon) near St-Germain, **rue Daguerre** (14e, métro Denfert-Rochereau) in Montparnasse, and **rue Lepic** (18e, métro Blanche or Abbesses) in Montmartre, all with astounding arrays of produce, cheeses, meats, breads, candies, and flowers.

NON-FRENCH FOODS

At larger supermarkets it's easy to become frustrated by the limited range of non-French foods they tend to offer. Luckily, most French people fulfill these needs in specialty stores. American and British goods are most common in neighborhoods like St-Germain and the Marais, kosher food is common in the Marais (4e), and Asian and Middle Eastern supplies are plentiful around Belleville (19e), Chinatown (13e), and the 10th arrondissement.

La Grande Epicerie. Perhaps the best part of the department store Au Bon Marché (*see* Department Stores *in* Chapter 6) is the gourmet grocery on the bottom floor. Other than the finest brands and the highest prices on all your usual French supplies, this place has sections devoted to American, British, Italian, Indian, and kosher goods. The excellent produce section here, though pricey, has a much wider selection than the typical market. *38 rue de Sèvres, 7e, tel. 01–44–39–81–00. Métro: Sèvres-Babylone.*

Izraël. This small, packed shop in the Marais specializes in hard-to-find goods from all over the world, including huge bins of rices, grains, and olives, some prepared dishes, and shelves of prepackaged goods. Pick up anything from Indonesian soya sauce (15F) to barbecue sauce (50F) to Kraft marshmallow spread (30F). *30 rue François-Miron, 4e, tel. 01–42–72–66–23. Métro: St-Paul. Open Tues.–Sat. 9:30–1 and 2:30–7.*

Mexi & Co. If you're tired of faux Mexican food, this specialty store sells your basic Mexican and Latin American goods at high prices: A can of refried beans costs 16F, a kilo of flour tortillas 36F. At several sidewalk tables or the inside bar you can sip on a Tecate (18F) while munching on the chicken burrito plate (29F) or free chips and salsa. *10 rue Dante, 5e, tel. 01–46–34–14–12. Métro: Maubert-Mutualité or Cluny–La Sorbonne. Closed weekends.*

Ste-Kioko. Come here for fresh and packaged Japanese foods. *46 rue des Petits-Champs, 2e, tel. 01–42–61–33–66. Métro: Pyramides. Closed Sun.*

Supermarché Asia-France International. Everything you could possibly desire for Asian cuisine—dozens of different types of noodles, spicy sauces, and cheap produce—constitute the bulk of this supermarket's stock. *48 blvd. de Belleville, 20e, tel. 01–40–33–43–33. Métro: Couronnes. Closed Mon.*

Tang Frères. This chain of Chinese supermarkets (with a largely Vietnamese clientele) sells Asian produce and packaged items—anything from tea to preserved squid intestines. *168 av. de Choisy, 13e, tel. 01–44–24–06–72. Métro: Place d'Italie or Tolbiac. Closed Mon.*

Thanksgiving. Don't do major shopping here; it would be cheaper to have someone Fed Ex a care package from home. But when you gotta have Oreos, you can get 'em here for 50F. Other finds include Jell-O (12F), peanut butter (32F), Pop Tarts (35F), and a good selection of California wines. The restaurant upstairs sells "New York" bagels and cream cheese with lox (65F), or baked potatoes with cheddar or spinach (25F). *20 rue St-Paul, 4e, tel. 01–42–77–68–29. Métro: St-Paul.*

SWEETS

In Paris's fabulous boulangeries, patisseries, and *confiseries* (candy shops), luscious French desserts are everywhere, so it's important that you pick up some of the vocabulary: *chausson aux pommes* (an apple turnover); *religieuse* (a puff pastry filled with chocolate- or coffee-flavored whipped cream and drizzled with chocolate); *madeleines* (sponge-cake dipping cookies that are not quite as orgasmic as Proust implies); the *opéra* (a triple-decker chocolate-and-cream indulgence); *tartelettes* (minitarts); and *choux à la crème* (round, cream-filled pastries).

Chocolate fanatics should seek out **Léonidas** (7 rue des Innocents, 1er, tel. 01–42–36–11–92, métro Châtelet–Les Halles), or the oldest sweet shop (AD 1761) in Paris, **A la Mère de Famille** (35 rue du Faubourg-Montmartre, 9e, tel. 01–47–70–83–69, métro Rue Montmartre). Proving that the French can do chocolate cheaply is **Le Chocolatier de Paris** (71 rue de Tolbiac, 13e, tel. 01–45–86–38–39, métro Nationale), where a kilo (2.2 pounds) costs just 100F. Also worth a visit is **La Charlotte de l'Isle** (24 rue St-Louis-en-l'Ile, 4e, tel. 01–43–54–25–83, métro Pont Marie), which has sumptuous dark chocolate and a little tearoom where you can enjoy it; it's closed mornings and Monday and Tuesday. Across the street is **Berthillon** (31 rue St-Louis-en-l'Ile, 4e, métro Pont Marie, tel. 01–43–54–31–61), whose ice creams and sorbets are ambrosia for mere mortals; it's closed Monday and Tuesday.

REFERENCE LISTINGS

BY TYPE OF CUISINE

AMERICAN

Under 60F

Chicago Pizza Pie Factory (*Champs-Elysées*)

La Theière dans les Nuages (*Le Marais*)

Under 80F

Le Coffee Parisien (*St-Germain-des-Prés*)

Haynes (*Gare de l'Est and Gare du Nord*)

Under 100F

The Studio (*Le Marais*)

CHINESE/SOUTHEAST ASIAN

Under 40F

Lao Siam (*Belleville*)

Under 60F

Da Lat (*Belleville*)

Under 80F

Restaurant Tai-Yien (*Belleville*)

Under 100F

Mirama (*Quartier Latin*)

CRÊPERIES

Under 60F

Cousin Cousine (*Quartier Latin*)

Crêpes-Show (*Bastille*)

Modas (*Belleville*)

Under 80F

Pont Aven–Chez Mélanie (*Montparnasse*)

DELIS

Under 40F

Al Dar (*Quartier Latin*)

L'As du Fallafel (*Le Marais*)

Au Plaisir des Pains (*St-Germain-des-Prés*)

La Pignatta (*Montmartre*)

Sacha et Florence Finkelsztajn (*Le Marais*)

Under 60F

Barry's (*Champs-Elysées*)

Cosi (*St-Germain-des-Prés*)

Under 80F

Chez Marianne (*Le Marais*)

EASTERN EUROPEAN

Under 40F

Sacha et Florence Finkelsztajn (*Le Marais*)

Under 80F

Tokaj (*Bastille*)

Under 100F

A la Ville de Belgrade (*Gare de l'Est and Gare du Nord*)

Village Bulgare (*St-Germain-des-Prés*)

FRENCH

Under 60F

Le Bistrot du Peintre (*Bastille*)

Chez Papa (*Montparnasse/Gare de l'Est and Gare du Nord*)

Cousin Cousine (*Quartier Latin*)

La Crêpe Canettes (*St-Germain-des-Prés*)

Crêpes-Show (*Bastille*)

Dame Tartine (*Les Halles and Beaubourg*)

Modas (*Belleville*)

Le Petit Gavroche (*Le Marais*)

Restaurant Chartier (*Gare de l'Est and Gare du Nord*)

Under 80F

L'Apostrophe (*Quartier Latin*)

Au Petit Ramoneur (*Les Halles and Beaubourg*)

Au Pied de Fouet (*Near the Eiffel Tower*)

Au Virage Lepic (*Montmartre*)

Aux Artistes (*Montparnasse*)

Café de la Cité (*Les Halles and Beaubourg*)

Café Moderne (*Bastille*)

Chez Clement (*Champs-Elysées*)

Chez Joel D.–Bistrot de l'Huître (*Montparnasse*)

Le Gavroche (*Louvre to Opéra*)

L'Incroyable (*Louvre to Opéra*)

Le Palet (*Louvre to Opéra*)

Le Petit Keller (*Bastille*)

Pont Aven–Chez Mélanie (*Montparnasse*)

Restaurant des Beaux-Arts (*St-Germain-des-Prés*)

Le Temps des Cerises (*Bastille*)

Under 100F

Au Babylone (*Near the Eiffel Tower*)

Au Refuge des Fondus (*Montmartre*)

Au Rendez-vous des Chauffeurs (*Belleville*)

Baracane (*Le Marais*)

Chalet Maya (*Gare de l'Est and Gare du Nord*)

Chantairelle (*Quartier Latin*)

Chassagne Restaurant (*St-Germain-des-Prés*)

Chez l'Ami Jean (*Near the Eiffel Tower*)

Chez Clement (*Champs-Elysées*)

Chez Justine (*Belleville*)

Chez Max (*Les Halles*)

L'Eté en Pente Douce (*Montmartre*)

Les Jardins de St-Germain (*St-Germain-des-Prés*)

Le Moulin à Vin (*Montmartre*)

Le Petit Keller (*Bastille*)

Le Pic à Vin (*Montmartre*)

Splurge

A la Courtille (*Belleville*)

Au Bon Accueil (*Near the Eiffel Tower*)

Au Camelot (*Bastille*)

Au Petit Tonneau (*Near the Eiffel Tower*)

Le Bistrot d'Opio (*St-Germain-des-Prés*)

Chez Paul (*Bastille*)

Le Gamin de Paris (*Le Marais*)

Julien (*Gare de l'Est and Gare du Nord*)

GREEK

Under 60F

Orestias (*St-Germain-des-Prés*)

Under 80F

Le Vieux Byzantin (*Belleville*)

Zagros (*Bastille*)

INDIAN

Under 80F

Bhai Bhai Sweets (*Gare de l'Est and Gare du Nord*)

Under 100F

Naz Restaurant (*Bastille*)

Surma (*Quartier Latin*)

ITALIAN

Under 40F

La Pignatta (*Montmartre*)

Under 60F

Le Jardin des Pâtes (*Quartier Latin*)

Under 80F

Paparazzi (*Gare de l'Est and Gare du Nord*)

Under 100F

Le Petit Mabillon (*St-Germain-des-Prés*)

La Tavola Calda (*Les Halles*)

JAPANESE

Under 80F

Higuma (*Louvre to Opéra*)

Japanese Barbecue (*Les Halles and Beaubourg*)

Under 100F

Yamamoto (*Louvre to Opéra*)

Splurge

Foujita (*Louvre to Opéra*)

LATIN AMERICAN/TEX MEX

Under 60F

Jip's (*Les Halles and Beaubourg*)

Mustang Café (*Montparnasse*)

Under 100F

Bar de la Maison de l'Amérique Latine (*Near the Eiffel Tower*)

SPANISH

Under 100F

Le Kezako (*Montmartre*)

TURKISH/MIDDLE EASTERN/NORTH AFRICAN

Under 40F

Al Dar (*Quartier Latin*)

L'As du Fallafel (*Le Marais*)

Under 60F

Le Boute Grill (*Quartier Latin*)

Chez Rami & Hanna (*Le Marais*)

Van Gölu (*Gare de l'Est and Gare du Nord*)

Under 80F

Café Moderne (*Bastille*)

Chez Marianne (*Le Marais*)

Restaurant Sarah (*Bastille*)

Le Vieux Byzantin (*Belleville*)

Zagros (*Bastille*)

VEGETARIAN

Under 60F

Au Grain de Folie (*Montmartre*)

La Petite Légume (*Quartier Latin*)

Rayons de Santé (*Montmartre*)

Under 80F

Country Life (*Louvre to Opéra*)

Under 100F

Chez Omar (*Le Marais*)

Entre Ciel et Terre (*Les Halles and Beaubourg*)

WEST AFRICAN

Under 60F

Le Fouta Toro (*Montmartre*)

Under 100F

La Bouche du Roi (*Montmartre*)

SPECIAL FEATURES

DINNER AND ENTERTAINMENT

Under 60F

Van Gölu (*Gare de l'Est and Gare du Nord*)

Under 80F

Haynes (*Gare de l'Est and Gare du Nord*)

Under 100F

La Bouche du Roi (*Montmartre*)

OUTDOOR DINING

Under 40F

Al Dar (*Quartier Latin*)

Under 60F

Le Bistrot du Peintre (*Bastille*)

Dame Tartine (*Les Halles and Beaubourg*)

Under 80F

Au Petit Ramoneur (*Les Halles and Beaubourg*)

L'Incroyable (*Louvre to Opéra*)

Under 100F

L'Eté en Pente Douce *(Montmartre)*

Le Petit Mabillon *(St-Germain-des-Prés)*

The Studio *(Le Marais)*

Splurge

A la Courtille *(Belleville)*

TAKE-OUT

Al Dar *(Quartier Latin)*

L'As du Fallafel *(Le Marais)*

Au Plaisir des Pains *(St-Germain-des-Prés)*

Barry's *(Champs-Elysées)*

Chez Marianne *(Le Marais)*

Chez Rami & Hanna *(Le Marais)*

Country Life *(Louvre to Opéra)*

La Pignatta *(Montmartre)*

Sacha et Florence Finkelsztajn *(Le Marais)*

5

AFTER DARK

UPDATED BY IAN PHILLIPS

W hether you're a jazz fiend or a dance freak, a patron of the arts or a lounge lizard seeking refuge in a dark smoky bar, Paris's streets provide ample destinations for nocturnal creatures. From opulent opera houses to low-key bars, dance floors in 17th-century cellars, or just a stroll along the light-splintered Seine—you can find it all in Paris after dark.

There are a million tempting ways to blow money if you happen to have it: theaters, discos, concert halls, films, legendary cabarets, or one of the 40F Bateaux-Mouches that cruise along the river (*see* Boat Travel *in* Chapter 1). The jazz and world music scene add even more sparks to the city's nightlife. For events and information, consult the ubiquitous advertisement boards or check in the weekly entertainment bibles, *Pariscope* (3F) or *L'Officiel des Spectacles* (2F). Both have comprehensive listings of what's happening around town and run from Wednesday to Tuesday. *Pariscope* has the added advantage of having a small English-language section. For more alternative events, you should check out the selective listings in the hip monthly *Nova Magazine* (10F).

A night out doesn't have to be expensive to be fun. Grab a bottle of wine and hang out on the Pont des Arts among doting couples, drummers, and rollerbladers to watch the sunset and listen to amateur musicians. Another great place is on the banks of the Seine on the Ile St-Louis; before national holidays, this little island is thronged with musicians, students, and anyone else who doesn't have to get up in the morning. In the summer, place des Vosges, place St-Catherine, and the front of the Centre Pompidou are all home to impromptu guitar, jazz, and accordion music as well. Come nightfall, La Défense becomes an enormous illuminated skateboarder haven. The esplanade looks much more eerie and futuristic when the sleek high-rises are bathed in orange city lights. For information on the many free classical concerts performed in the city's churches, concert halls, and museums, *see* Opera, Classical Music, and Dance, *below.*

Gay life has its geographic base in the Marais, though it's not the raging scene that American urban dwellers might be used to. During the afternoons and early evenings, many Marais cafés cater to mixed crowds. Lesbian life is less visible. Contact the **Maison des Femmes** (8 cité Prost, 11e, tel. 01–43–48–24–91, métro Faidherb-Chaligny), a feminist-lesbian resource center and cafeteria, or the **Centre Gai et Lesbien** (3 rue Keller, 11e, tel. 01–43–57–21–47, métro Ledru-Rollin) for information on events. The free monthly *Illico,* found in gay bars and cafés, has a calendar of gay events, including tea dances, lectures, and concerts, as well as topical essays. *Café* (10F), a more serious gay magazine, also lists

Paris events; **Double-Face,** a monthly aimed primarily at men, lists gay and gay-friendly bars, clubs, and pick-up spots. It's free at **Les Mots à la Bouche** (*see* Bookstores *in* Chapter 6) and some bars.

BARS

Most Parisian bars (at least the ones that aren't open as cafés earlier in the day) open around 6 PM and close at 2 AM, even on weekends. Cafés, bars, and *boîtes* (dance clubs) in Paris tend to mutate over the course of an evening—something that was a restaurant at lunch could become a bar at 8 PM and then a dance club until sunrise. This means that a place we call a café (*see* Cafés *in* Chapter 4) could wind up being a great place to have a drink after dinner or to listen to live music on certain nights. If you want a relatively quiet place, try hitting bars during the *apéritif* (around 6 PM). That's when Parisians congregate to decide where they want to meet up later.

Law requires that prices be posted, and in most bars, you will find two different tariffs—*au comptoir* (cheaper prices if you stand with your drink at the bar) and *à salle* (more expensive rates if you sit down at a table). In many places, prices are increased by a few francs after 10 PM. In general, expect to pay 15F–30F for a draft beer, referred to as *une pression, une demi-pression,* or simply *une demi* (all mean a half-pint on tap).

The following suggestions are, on the whole, the most popular bars of the moment. As such, they are not necessarily the cheapest. If your budget is really tight, you would be best off hanging out with the locals at more anonymous joints. As a general rule, the further you move away from the center, the cheaper the prices.

BASTILLE

About five years ago, the Bastille was the hottest nightlife area in town. Though the scene for those in-the-know has moved to Belleville (*see below*), the Bastille still remains very popular for a night out on the town. The block-long **rue de Lappe** has more bars per meter than any other street in Paris, and **rue de la Roquette** starts off crowded at place de la Bastille and grows desolate to the north. Side streets like **rue de Charonne** harbor low-key joints and a generally local scene. **Rue Keller** also has a number of gay hangouts. You might want to drop by **Dame Pipi** (9 rue de Charonne, 11e, tel. 01–48–05–05–83, métro Ledru-Rollin) and lounge on their fuschia seats. **La Galoche d'Aurillac** (41 rue de Lappe, 11e, tel. 01–47–00–77–15, métro Bastille, Ledru-Rollin) is much more homey; go there to mingle with the grandmothers at the bar and check out the clogs hanging from the ceiling.

Bar des Ferrailleurs. This bar can immediately be identified by the weird, rusty iron things hanging from its windows and the friendly, unpretentious crowd inside. Sink into the incredibly comfortable velvet seats in the back (you might have trouble standing up again), or stand in the more lively area around the bar. Sip 14F beers or a 45F Long Island iced tea to a steady stream of jazz. *18 rue de Lappe, 11e, tel. 01–48–07–89–12. Métro: Bastille.*

Boca Chica. A little courtyard filled with metal tables and chairs and potted plants leads you into this popular, colorful tapas bar. Take a high stool and stare up at the bull's head staring down at you from behind the bar as you order tapas (15F–40F) and a glass of beer (10F) or sangria (15F). Play a game of chess or backgammon, or enjoy one of the twice-weekly concerts with a distinctly Latin feel (Brazilian music, tango, and Latin jazz). *58 rue de Charonne, 11e, tel. 01–43–57–93–13. Métro: Ledru-Rollin.*

Café de l'Industrie. This lively café is a great place, night or day, for a light meal and a beer (or two). The walls are eclectically lined with guns, animal hides, and old black-and-white photos of French cinema stars. The cheapest draught beer is 19F. *16 rue St-Sabin, 11e, tel. 01–47–00–13–53. Métro: Bastille. Closed Sat.*

Le Lèche Vin. Jesus and Mary smile benevolently as you down draughts in this kitsch bar lined with Christmas-tree lights and religious paraphernalia. The scene is offbeat and fun, and reminiscent of a grungy Seattle bar, with a much less image-conscious crowd that in most of the Bastille. A demi-pression goes for 10F. *13 rue Daval, 11e, tel. 01–43–55–98–91. Métro: Bastille.*

Les Portes. If the madness of rue de Lappe and rue de la Roquette gets to be too much, head for this laid-back bar. Occasionally, there's jazz in the cellar (except in summer). Prices hover at about 20F for a kir and 22F for a draft beer; the best deal is the giant 30F kriek. Incredibly, prices don't go up during performances. Take a table outside and watch the drunken revelers stumble home from rue de Lappe.

FRUITY BREWSKI

Beer isn't always made exclusively from barley and hops. If the usual stuff triggers your gag reflex, try some of these other flavorful drink varieties.

BECASSE: a Belgian strawberry-flavored beer.

CALVADOS: an apple brandy.

CIDRE: cider, choose between doux (sweet) and sec (dry).

DIABOLO: tonic water flavored with grenadine.

KIR: white wine flavored with cassis.

KRIEK: black cherry–flavored beer.

MONACO: a light beer with grenadine syrup.

PANACHÉ: a mixture of half-beer and half-lemonade.

PÊCHERESSE: peach-flavored beer.

PELFORTH FRAMBOISE: dark beer with raspberry flavoring.

Performance schedules vary, so be sure to call ahead. *15 rue de Charonne, 11e, tel. 01–40–21–70–61. Métro: Bastille.*

Sans Sanz. This huge, two-story bar-restaurant is a favorite among those who are cool—and know it. After 10 PM, that means a lot of people. Downstairs, there is a different DJ each night, playing a selection of groove, soul, and hip-hop. On the more sophisticated second floor, you can eat fancy food and spy on the downstairs crowd via a huge video screen. Beer runs from 10F (19F after 10 PM). *49 rue du Faubourg-St-Antoine, 11e, tel. 01–44–75–78–78. Métro: Bastille.*

BELLEVILLE

This area, on and around **rue Oberkampf,** has become *the* hottest, hippest area over the past two years. Artists and fashion folk have moved into the multicultural, immigrant-rich Belleville, but many of the bars manage to avoid being over-pretentious. Many of them cater to a mixed crowd of artsy types, students, and locals.

Café Charbon. This beautifully restored 19th-century café once played host to the famous music-hall stars, Maurice Chevalier and Mistinguett. Nowadays, a trend-setting clientele schmoozes to the jazz playing in the background. The atmosphere gets even livelier at night when a DJ takes over (at 10 PM Tuesday–Sunday). *109 rue Oberkampf, 11e, tel. 01–43–57–55–13. Métro: St-Maur, Parmentier.*

Cannibale Café. With its large mirrors, old-fashioned chairs and tables, and long curved bar, this café-bar has a distinctly popular feel to it. Sip a demi (from 11F) and listen to a great selection of recorded world music. They also serve light meals at lunch and in the evenings (until 12:30 AM). At 6:30 PM on Sundays, there are live concerts, varying from acoustic guitar and lute music to gypsy, tango, and Celtic melodies. *93 rue Jean-Pierre Timbaud, 11e, tel. 01–49–29–95–59. Métro: Couronnes.*

Le Cithéa. This cool, youthful joint has a bar and a dance floor. Come for the jazz, acid-jazz, groove, soul, salsa, and funk concerts on Thursday, Friday, Saturday, and Monday or Tuesday; Wednesday is techno night. After the concerts are over, a DJ takes over until 5 AM. *112 rue Oberkampf, 11e, tel. 01–40–21–70–95. Métro: St-Maur, Parmentier.*

Les Couleurs. Chill out under a palm-tree mural and sip Cuban milkshakes (32F) or mango and tamarind juice (12F) while listening to a soothing mix of classical, jazz, and world music at this very laid-back bar. Every Saturday (10 PM–4 AM), join the crowd for tango, or come earlier in the evening for a concert of jazz or world music (6 PM–10 PM), held on Sunday night, too. *117 rue St-Maur, 11e, tel. 01–43–57–95–61. Métro: St-Maur, Parmentier.*

La Favela Chic. It's difficult to find a more trendy place than this small Brazilian-style bar. The terrace is usually packed with beautiful young things drinking *caipirinhas* (cachaça—a rum-like liquor—lime juice, cane sugar, and crushed ice) or *mojito* (rum, mint, cane sugar, lemon juice, and sparkling water), while the crowd inside chats against a background of Latin rhythms. *131 rue Oberkampf, 11e, tel. 01–43–57–15–47. Métro: Ménilmontant.*

Lou Pascalou. This low-key neighborhood joint has pool tables indoors and melancholy youth on the terrace. Cheap (11F) beers and the requisite jazz background music make this a good place to catch a glimpse of old Belleville life. *14 rue des Panoyaux, 20e, tel. 01–46–36–78–10. Métro: Ménilmontant.*

Le Soleil. Come here on sunny afternoons to enjoy a cold beer (from 10F) on the huge, crowded terrace. Regulars come daily and stay for hours. You'll soon notice that almost everybody seems to know each other. It's a good place to hang out if you made the trip to Paris to meet the city's unique breed of musicians and artists. *136 blvd. de Ménilmontant, 20e, tel. 01–46–36–47–44. Métro: Ménilmontant.*

CHAMPS-ELYSEES

The Champs-Elysées (Les Champs to the initiated) and the streets branching off from it are *not* the budget traveler's domain. Over the past few years, many glitzy bars have opened and quickly gained a reputation by inviting models and stars. After the first few weeks, however, the model count goes down and a nouveau riche crowd of businessmen with slicked-back hair, sharp suits, and mobile phones, and their beautiful companions move in. Many of these bars have strict door policies, so be prepared to be turned away if you don't fit in with the clientele mold. If some glamour is what you're after, the best place to try is the **Buddha Bar** (8 rue Boissy d'Anglas,

The prime gay pick-up joints in the Marais (4e, métro Hôtel de Ville) are Le Central (33 rue Vieille-du-Temple), Cox's (15 rue des Archives), and Le Quetzal (10 rue de la Verrerie), which even provides cards for you to write your number on.

8e, tel. 01–53–05–90–00, métro Concorde), which is worth a visit simply to see the huge statue of Buddha himself. Otherwise, push your way past the bouncers at **Barfly** (49 av. George V, 8e, tel. 01–53–67–84–60, métro George V), check out **Le Bash** (67 rue Pierre Charron, 8e, tel. 01–45–62–95–70, métro F. D. Roosevelt), or take in tennis star Yannick Noah's contribution to Parisian snobbery, **Doobies** (2 rue Robert Estienne, 8e, tel. 01–53–76–10–76, métro F. D. Roosevelt). If you're looking for fun rather than fashion points, check out **Chesterfield Café** (124 rue de la Boëtie, 8e, tel. 01–42–25–18–06, métro F. D. Roosevelt), which is popular with Americans. Happy hour goes from 4 PM–8 PM on weekdays and there are two dance floors for grooving to a selection of funk, rap, and rock. From Tuesday to Saturday, there are also rock and blues concerts at 11 PM (Keanu Reeves played here when he came to Paris with his group Dogstar).

LES HALLES

Though Les Halles is most frequented for its live-jazz bars, a number of watering holes cater to those who prefer to pay a reasonable price for beer and listen to a record instead. At night the area is almost as touristy as during the day, but it catches some gay nightlife from the nearby Marais and still lures a fair number of Parisians with relatively cheap drinks and plenty of late-night eateries. Unaccompanied women should be careful at night, especially around the deserted sex shops of northern Les Halles.

Banana Café. Gay waiters with big muscles serve 30F beers at this snazzy Les Halles bar. The interior is sleek and dim, and the terrace near the Fontaine des Innocents is prime people-watching territory. Most nights, the downstairs area becomes a small, sweaty boîte. *13 rue de la Ferronnerie, 1er, tel. 01–42–33–35–31. Métro: Châtelet.*

La Baraka. All bars should be like La Baraka: It's laid-back, friendly, and serves lots of cheap beer (9F50 before 10 PM, 13F after). A small place dotted with jazz memorabilia, La Baraka is the spot of choice for artsy types, thanks to the theater school next door. The charming couple who've been running the place for years give everyone a warm reception while pumping a steady stream of jazz, blues, and rock. They also serve great tapas (12F–29F a plate). *6 rue Marie Stuart, 2e, tel. 01–42–36–10–56. Métro: Etienne Marcel. Closed Mon.*

Comptoir. Facing the Jardin des Halles, this sleek, fashionable art deco bar with neon lights lining the ceiling will provide you with a kir (25F) or a frothy beer (23F–28F). Come early for a quiet drink, or around midnight if you prefer to see the place packed and happening. *37 rue Berger, 1er, tel. 01–40–26–26–66. Métro: Les Halles.*

L'Eustache. Loved by young Parisians without much cash, this tiny, classic café-bar has jazz concerts Thursday–Saturday 10:30 PM–4 AM and an accordionist on Sunday nights. Beers are 15F at the bar, 40F seated. *37 rue Berger, 1er, tel. 01–40–26–23–20. Métro: Les Halles.*

Frog & Rosbif. This English pub has everything you could want from a "local" spot. The beer is brewed on the premises (22F for a half-pint, 35F a pint, or 25F a pint during happy hour, 6 PM–7 PM weekdays) and there are darts and a giant-screen TV for watching rugby or soccer. Other activities include a magician on Thursday or Friday night, and a jazz brunch (12 PM–4 PM) and quiz night (9 PM) on Sunday. Food is served at lunch and baked potatoes only are served from 6 PM–10 PM. *116 rue St-Denis, 2e, tel. 01–42–36–34–73. Métro: Etienne Marcel.*

LE MARAIS

An artsy, gay neighborhood, the Marais is filled with all kinds of people and all kinds of nocturnal options. In the evenings, the bars and cafés overflow with a mixed crowd, but as the night settles in, most places turn exclusively gay. **Rue Vieille-du-Temple** and **rue Ste-Croix de la Bretonnerie** are the main drags. In addition to the bars listed below, check out the sprawling, cushy couches at the **Majestic Café** (34 rue Vieille-du-Temple, 4e, tel. 01–42–74–61–61, métro Hôtel de Ville), where a beer goes for 20F underneath a red light and tacky statues. At **Le Pick-Clops** (corner of rue Vieille-du-Temple and rue du Roi-de-Sicile, 4e, tel. 01–40–29–02–18, métro Hôtel de Ville), Rolling Stones posters surround a semipretentious but fun crowd downing 16F beers (19F after 10 PM).

Amnesia. This popular café-bar is the most mixed of all the gay establishments in the Marais. Day and night, a cool crowd sinks into the deep armchairs, surrounded by plants, mosaic tiles, and ceiling fans. Beers cost 14F–22F; prices go up 5F after 10 PM. *42 rue Vieille-du-Temple, 4e, tel. 01–42–72–16–94. Métro: Hôtel de Ville.*

L'Apparemment Café. Dim lights, soft music, comfortable seats, and a strong coffee (12F) or cocktails (50F)—all you need after trekking around the Marais all day. Flip through a magazine or play a board game to collect your energy before hitting the bars. *18 rue des Coutures-St-Gervais, 3e, tel. 01–48–87–12–22. Métro: Filles du Calvaire.*

Bar d'Arts/Le Duplex. Art exhibits and alternative music characterize the dim atmosphere of this gay men's bar full of sexy, young, tortured-artist types. Women are welcome but are usually few and far between. A pression costs around 22F. *25 rue Michel-Le-Comte, 3e, tel. 01–42–72–80–86. Métro: Rambuteau.*

La Chaise au Plafond. A heterosexual haven in the Marais, this bar has a nice old Parisian feel. Never overcrowded, it is the perfect place to meet friends. Have a beer (17F) or an excellent glass of wine (around 20F), and even a light meal (20F–60F). Even though the bar is called "the chair (*chaise*) on the ceiling (*plafond*)," you'll actually see Hertfordlike spots when you look up. Be sure to check out the futuristic metal toilets downstairs. *10 rue du Trésor, 4e, tel. 01–42–76–03–22. Métro: Hôtel de Ville.*

Les Scandaleuses. This bar has quickly established itself as one of the hippest lesbian hangouts in Paris. Men are welcome (in small numbers) as long as they are accompanied by a number of "scandalous women." A beer will set you back 20F. During happy hour (6 PM–8 PM), you get two for the price of one. *8 rue des Ecouffes, 4e, tel. 01–48–87–39–26. Métro: St-Paul.*

MONTMARTRE AND PIGALLE

Montmartre nightlife consists of neighborhood bars and pubs filled with locals (and tourists eager to join the scene), but Pigalle, famed for its abundance of sex shops, strip shows, and prostitution has a little more, uh, action. To avoid the worst, steer clear of **rue Pigalle** and stay north of **boulevard de Clichy.** For the more wholesome Montmartre scene, head up streets like **rue Lepic** and **rue Caulaincourt.** Insomniacs and those who have missed the last métro can find refuge at **Le Dépanneur** (27 rue Fontaine, 9e, tel. 01–40–16–40–20, métro Blanche) for a '50s-style diner meal anytime, day or night.

Club-Club. This fun Pigalle bar is often packed with artsy types and students. There are slightly anarchic poetry readings on Tuesday, and on Wednesday everyone brings along three records of their choice to the bar party. A DJ livens up the place from 10:30 PM–2 AM on Friday and Saturday and the beer is reasonably cheap (20F for a demi, 20F for two demis 8 PM–9 PM weekdays). *3 rue André Antoine, 18e, tel. 01–42–54–38–38. Métro: Pigalle.*

Le Moloko. Cool people and those merely aspiring to be so fill this *branché* (hip) bar-boîte until 6 AM. The three rooms include a dance floor, a smoky, plush sitting room, and a lounging "salon." Admission is free, so splurge on a Molokococktail (55F–65F), or sip a 35F beer. During happy hour, 9:30 PM–midnight, Monday–Thursday, and 9:30 PM–11 PM, Friday–Saturday, beers are only 20F. *26 rue Fontaine, 9e, tel. 01–48–74–50–26. Métro: Pigalle.*

Le Sancerre. A nightly gathering of jovial Montmartrois fills up this established neighborhood bar. During the day, young artist types sun themselves outside and roll their eyes at the passing tourists. The 10F50 pression goes up to 18F after 10 PM. *35 rue des Abbesses, 18e, tel. 01–42–58–08–20. Métro: Abbesses.*

QUARTIER LATIN

Though most spots near the river are intolerably touristy and expensive, there are some mellow bars up the hill from **boulevard St-Germain,** near **place Maubert,** and on **rue Mouffetard,** where beers are affordable. English-speaking folks tend to hang out in bars around here. So it's a good place to meet Brits, Aussies, Canadians, or—if you've had any trouble finding them—Americans.

If you actually go to clubs to hear the music and dance, try to find a club featuring a guest (and preferably foreign) DJ. Otherwise, you might be subjected to badly remixed techno all night.

Café Oz. A bunch of Aussies runs this small, convivial bar where Foster's on tap is 35F a pint. The sign outside claims ON PARLE FRANÇAIS (We speak French), but they must not get much practice: Young Americans have taken over, along with foreigners from other countries who adopt the place from semester to semester. *184 rue St-Jacques, 5e, tel. 01–43–54–30–48. Métro: Cluny–La Sorbonne. RER: Luxembourg. Other location: 18 rue St-Denis, 2e, tel. 01–40–39–00–18. Métro: Les Halles.*

Connolly's Corner. Come to this friendly Irish bar near rue Mouffetard to play darts and have a demi (17F) or a pint of Guinness (35F). Don't wear a tie or it will snipped off and stuck on the wall (though you'll be compensated with a free pint). Pints are only 28F during happy hour Monday–Friday 6–8 PM, and there's traditional Irish music on Tuesday, Thursday, and Sunday. *12 rue Mirbel, 5e, tel. 01–43–31–94–22. Métro: Place Monge, Censier-Daubenton.*

Finnegan's Wake. A mixed Franco-British crowd hangs out here drinking Guinness on tap (35F) and listening to Irish music. There's dancing in the vaulted cellar on Thursday night. *9 rue des Boulangers, 5e, tel. 01–46–34–23–65. Métro: Jussieu.*

Le Piano Vache. University students come here in groups to rest heavy elbows on the tables, chain-smoke, and solve the world's problems. The bar is sufficiently dark and the music sufficiently angst-inspiring to keep you from getting too optimistic. Beer is 30F (40F after 10 PM). On Tuesdays, pastis is a mere 10F, making this a great introduction to the anise-flavored drink. Most afternoons there's a drink *du jour* for 15F and most evenings a happy hour from 6 PM–9 PM. *8 rue Laplace, 5e, tel. 01–46–33–75–03. Métro: Cardinal Lemoine. Closed before 6 PM during university vacations.*

ST-GERMAIN-DES-PRES

For what used to be the swingingest quartier around, St-Germain's nightlife has fallen pretty flat. Most of the jazz bars have tried unsuccessfully to go upscale, and the bars are overrun by foreigners about 20 years behind the times. The spots that have managed to keep a low profile have done the best, holding on to a loyal clientele and almost justifying the 30F and up that you'll pay for your beer. Most of the good bets are between **boulevard St-Germain** and the **Jardin du Luxembourg.**

Chez Georges. As the nostalgic decor suggests, this upstairs bar has been serving glasses of red wine, pastis, and beer (20F–30F) to older men in work clothes for the past 60-odd years. Down in the basement, young folks crowd around tiny tables. Don't be intimidated if the place looks packed—there's always room to squeeze in somewhere, and the regulars are more than willing to make new friends. *11 rue des Canettes, 6e, tel. 01–43–26–79–15. Métro: Mabillon. Closed Sun., Mon., and mid-July–mid-Aug.*

THE LITTLE SPARROW

Born in Belleville in 1915 (and abandoned on someone's doorstep shortly thereafter), Edith Piaf began singing in cafés and on the streets of Paris by age 15. Often called "the Little Sparrow," Piaf soon became famous for her expressive, tremulous voice. But one look at a photo of this waifish, saucer-eyed singer, and you'll know that life was not all song and dance; Piaf's career was filled with tragic relationships and drug addiction. After a serious illness, she made a comeback in 1961, but died two years later. The songs she made famous—including "La vie en rose" and "Je ne regrette rien"—are likely to pop up in any cabaret show.

La Paillotte. Nurse a cocktail (56F) until the early hours in this dark, smoky joint, which is decorated like a beach hut with fake grass roofing. The owner stations himself at the bar to greet you and keeps a close eye on the turntable—he has one of the best classic jazz collections in Paris. Beers are 30F at the bar, 38F seated. *45 rue Monsieur-le-Prince, 6e, tel. 01–43–26–45–69. Métro: Odéon. Closed Sun.*

CABARET

Cabaret is enjoying a bit of a revival these days, but it isn't necessarily the type with showgirls and feathers. The more famous and traditional cabarets in the city, such as **Le Moulin Rouge** (pl. Blanche, 9e, tel. 01–46–06–00–19, métro Blanche), the **Lido** (116 bis av. des Champs-Elysées, 8e, tel. 01–40–76–56–10, métro George V), and **Le Paradis Latin** (26 rue Cardinal-Lemoine, 5e, tel. 01–43–25–28–28, métro Cardinal-Lemoine) are now almost entirely the domain of foreign business people and wealthy tourists who pay 500F–800F a pop. At the world-famous **Folies Bergères** (32 rue Richer, 9e, tel. 01–44–79–98–98, métro Cadet), cabarets are no longer performed, only musical revues and plays. Parisians are, however, falling over themselves to see Berlin-style cabaret with singers, magicians, and trapeze artists. Spanish dance star Blanca Li regularly organizes cabaret-style **fiestas** in clubs around Pigalle (check *Pariscope* for dates and locations) and the club, **Les Etoiles** (61 rue du Château d'Eau, 10e, tel. 01–47–70–60–56, métro Château d'Eau, République), hosts a cabaret evening every Monday. Other, more traditional Maurice Chevalier–style cabarets and trendy spots include the following.

Au Lapin Agile. This venue on Montmartre's back side has been around since 1860, including a stint under the ownership of Aristide Bruant, the famous Parisian cabaret balladeer. Today it's still serving up classic French oldies—largely to French tourists—in a dark, close room. Any evening sees solo pianists, singers, and other musicians, who rotate from 9 PM to 2 AM. Entrance with one drink is 110F; second drinks go down to around 30F. *22 rue des Saules, 18e, tel. 01–46–06–85–87. Métro: Lamarck-Caulaincourt. Closed Mon.*

Au Pied de la Butte. It has everything you ever hoped for from a Paris cabaret, including glittery, flashy numbers interspersed with Edith Piaf favorites. Though the focus is on singers, you'll also see comedians, magicians, balloon artists, and more. The entrance fee of 180F includes two drinks. Additional drinks are an extra 90F. *62 blvd. Rochechouart, 18e, tel. 01–46–06–02–86. Métro: Anvers.*

Le Cabaret. Princess Caroline, Liza Minelli, and Naomi Campbell have all been spotted at this hot spot for the rich and famous, just off the Champs-Elysées. It was once an erotic cabaret and red velvet still dominates. Admission is free, but drinks are a steep 70F. This does, however, give you the chance to groove to hip-hop, soul, R&B, funk, and see cabaret acts, between 12:30 PM and 2 AM, with all the beautiful people. *68 rue Pierre Charron, 8e, tel. 01–42–89–44–14. Métro: F. D. Roosevelt.*

DANCE CLUBS

Hefty covers, discriminatory door policies, and a scrambling crowd of rich, spoiled teens—how you perceive Paris's *boîte de nuit* (nightclub) scene depends on how keen you are to mix with territorial regulars. In any case, nobody could fairly claim that it is really happening and you won't be spoilt for choice. New clubs rarely pop up, but two of the latest are at Pigalle—**Le Temple** (9 pl. Pigalle, 9e, tel. 01–48–74–27–17, métro Pigalle) and **Le Magic** (78 blvd. de Clichy, 18e, tel. 01–53–41–84–84, métro Trinité), an erotic cabaret during the week, with a mixed crowd clubbing on Friday and Saturday. The techno scene is almost nonexistent and you're much more likely to find yourself dancing to seventies disco or house music. Paris's boîtes do, however, offer incredible people-watching opportunities and a good lesson in how to dish out French attitude.

If your face doesn't grace the cover of *Vogue,* it's hard to get around the usual 60F–150F cover charge. Your best bet is to hook up with someone who has a pass; fickle staff members hand out passes inside the clubs to those deemed cool enough to be invited back. Once you plunge into this scene, make sure you have a lot of stamina, since clubs generally don't really get going until about 1:30 AM and don't wind down until about 6 AM. Many clubs also host weekly afternoon "tea dances," gatherings where couples dance the swing and more traditional steps. Tea dances are often men- or women-only; check *Pariscope* for listings.

In gaining admission, women have an advantage over men; at heterosexual places, guys are better off finding one or two women to accompany them. However, at the hippest club in town, **Le Queen** (*see below*), which caters mainly to a gay crowd, women will have trouble getting in unless they are with at least two men. Following these guidelines will also up your chances: (1) Dress well. This means sleek and sophisticated for Champs-Elysées clubs, outrageous and scantily clad for Pigalle haunts, and funky and retro for the Bastille. (2) Arrive early (between the 11 PM opening time and midnight). Until you become known at a particular disco door, this little trick greatly improves your shot at getting in—and at getting in free. (3) Avoid going in big same-sex groups (except, of course, to gay clubs). Most places prefer mixed groups and couples. Two big-name clubs to avoid are **La Locomotive** (90 blvd. de Clichy, 18e, tel. 01–53–41–88–88, métro Blanche) and **La Scala** (188 bis rue de Rivoli, 1er, tel. 01–42–60–45–64, métro Palais Royal–Musée du Louvre), which play mostly mainstream house music for young and pouty crowds bathed in cheesy laser-light effects.

Montmartre's Studio 28 (10 rue Tholozée, 18e) is not a late-night venue, but it did gain notoriety for being brave enough to show avant-garde pieces such as Buñuel's "Un Chien Andalou" and François Truffaut's early films.

Les Bains. This former Turkish bath has been the chosen nightspot for the private parties of models and stars for the past 15 years. On ordinary nights, however, it generally attracts middle-age businessmen with wads of money looking for younger women, and pretty young women looking for men with wads of money. Recently, the interior has been redecorated and the club is now attracting a younger, trendier crowd. Stars still pop by on a regular basis. You'll have to get past the choosy doorwoman and then fork out 100F if you want to spot them. Things go late—until 10 AM on Friday and Saturday and 6 AM other nights. *7 rue du Bourg-l'Abbé, 3e, tel. 01–48–87–01–80. Métro: Etienne Marcel.*

Le Bus Palladium. "Le Bus" was the hottest nightspot in Paris in the '60s—the Beatles came here when they were in town. A fashionable, but relaxed crowd now comes to dance to rock, funk, and disco. On Tuesday, women get free admission and free drinks. Every other Wednesday, the place turns to erotica with a strip show at 1 AM. There's no cover on Wednesday and Thursday, and it's 100F (with a drink) for men on Tuesday and for everyone on the weekend. *6 rue Fontaine, 9e, tel. 01–53–21–07–33. Métro: Pigalle. Closed Sun.*

L'Elysée Montmartre. Normally a concert venue, the Elysée Montmartre holds extremely popular *bals* (balls) every other Saturday (80F). The music runs the gamut of hits from the forties to the eighties—from accordion music to rock 'n roll, disco, reggae, and punk. The DJ is backed up by a 10-piece orchestra, and cakes and sweets are given out free. Drinks run 20F–60F. *72 blvd. de Rochechouart, 18e, tel. 01–44–92–45–49. Métro: Pigalle.*

L'Entr'acte. Paris has a serious dearth of lesbian clubs, but L'Entr'acte is the most happening place at the moment for gay women. Music ranges from house and techno to groove and rock, with free tapas and sangria on Friday. The cover is 50F (with a drink) on the weekend. After that, you can count on 50F for each additional beer. *25 blvd. Poissonière, 2e, tel. 01–40–26–01–93. Métro: Bonne-Nouvelle. Closed Mon.–Wed.*

Les Folies Pigalle. Decorated like a 1930s bordello, this small club plays techno and hip-hop for a crowd crammed onto the two-level dance floor. Frequent drag shows might spotlight a faux Cher, Barbra Streisand, or Boy George, and weekends feature giddy theme nights. Lately they've been trying to bring in more women with male strip shows (for women only) on Friday nights (9 PM–11 PM). Admission is free during the week, 100F on the weekend, and 150F for shows. Drinks are 50F. *11 pl. Pigalle, 9e, tel. 01–48–78–25–56. Métro: Pigalle.*

Keur Samba. The richer and more stylish you look, the better your chances of gaining entry into this super-sleek club near the Champs-Elysées. The music ranges from reggae to African soukous, American hip-hop, and house. Dress up and bring generous funds for the 120F entrance and first drink; don't even think about buying another (100F) unless you can convince one of the rich-kid regulars to spring for it. *79 rue de la Boëtie, 8e, tel. 01–43–59–03–10. Métro: St-Philippe du Roule.*

Le Queen. This high-profile, super-cool gay nightclub on the Champs might admit a woman if she's accompanied by at least two men. Thursday nights are strictly men-only. Everyone gyrates to house music on the vast dance floor (Monday is '70s night), and the whole scene is outrageous and definitely very image-conscious. The cover is free during the week (except on Mondays, when it's 50F with a drink) and 100F on the weekend (with a drink). Dress hot, bright, tight, and gay. *102 av. des Champs-Elysées, 8e, tel. 01–53–89–08–90. Métro: George V.*

Rex Club. With its huge red billboard screaming at you from three blocks away, the Rex is no hidden secret. Inside, the decor is high '70s, with a roller-rink dance floor and mirrored backdrop. The club now devotes itself almost exclusively to techno and house music. There is also a special jungle night on Tuesdays. The cover varies from 50F to 100F. Beer is always 30F. *5 blvd. Poissonnière, 2e, tel. 01–42–36–83–98. Métro: Bonne-Nouvelle. Closed Sun.–Tues.*

FILM

On any given night, the range of films screening in Paris is phenomenal. That obscure documentary that only lasted a week at your local art-cinema back home might play here on a regular basis, even if the attendance rarely hits double digits. You'll also find low-budget films in a dozen or so languages.

Most foreign films are shown in the *version originale* (original language) with French subtitles, marked "v.o." in listings; the abbreviation "v.f." (*version française*) means a foreign film is dubbed in French. Both of Paris's entertainment weeklies, *L'Officiel des Spectacles* and *Pariscope*, have comprehensive film listings—prices normally run 35F–55F with some discounts for students. Nearly all theaters offer the reduced rate to everyone on either Monday or Wednesday. UGC also sells four-film and six-film passes (132F and 195F respectively), which can be used at any of their theaters; Gaumont has a five-film pass (175F).

The small, funky cinemas where you'll find independent and classic films are mostly clustered in and around the Quartier Latin. Many have a system of stamping a card every time you attend a film; you then get the sixth film for free. Often they have limited but obscure collections and show the same 40 or 50 films over and over, or they have festivals dedicated to a director (i.e., Bergman, Fassbinder, Wenders, Hitchcock, Allen, etc.) or actor (i.e., Marlon Brando, Audrey Hepburn, etc.). Two of the best art-house cinemas are **Champol** (51 rue des Ecoles, 5e, tel. 01–43–54–51–60, métro Cluny–La Sorbonne) and **Quartier Latin** (9 rue Champollion, 5e, tel. 01–43–26–84–65, métro Odéon, Cluny–La Sorbonne).

Paris also has big, flashy cinemas with plush seats, good sound, and blockbuster films. One of the most modern is the 15-screen **UGC Ciné Cité** in the Forum des Halles (pl. de la Rotonde, Nouveau Forum des Halles, 1er, tel. 01–40–26–12–12, métro Châtelet–Les Halles), which also has an Internet café. Another big cinema is the new **14 Juillet-sur-Seine** complex at La Villette (14 quai de la Seine, 19e, tel. 08–36–68–47–07, métro Stalingrad). Two of the biggest theaters are **Gaumont Grand Ecran** (30 pl. d'Italie, 13e, tel. 01–45–80–77–00, métro Place d'Italie) and **Max Linder Panorama** (24 blvd. Poissonnière, 9e, tel. 01–48–24–88–88, métro Bonne-Nouvelle). Both have immense screens and seat hundreds of people; Max Linder tends to carry cult and classic films. France is very proud of its technological movie wonders, which include the **Dôme Imax** (La Défense, tel. 08–36–67–06–06, métro or RER La Défense), showing 3-D flicks, and **La Géode** (26 av. Corentin-Cariou, 19e, tel. 01–40–05–12–

12, métro Corentin-Cariou), which has the largest movie screen anywhere, ever (*see* Museums, Cité des Sciences et de l'Industrie *in* Chapter 2).

In February, cinemas in the city organize **18 Heures/18F** during which you pay only 18F for 6 PM shows. At the end of June, during the one-day **Fête du Cinéma,** theaters across Paris let you see all the movies you want for 10F after you pay for the first film. The city of Paris subsidizes **Août au Ciné** (August at the Movies) when all those under 25 pay only 25F per film. Throughout July and August, classics and more recent, popular films are shown on the huge screen at La Villette; admission is free. Chairs can be rented (30F) if you don't want to sit on the grass.

Cinéma Gaumont La Pagode. Although the selection of first-run French and international films is pretty standard here, you've probably never seen another theater like this one. In 1896, the wife of the owner of Au Bon Marché (*see* Department Stores *in* Chapter 6) built this Pagoda-style building for what was to become the most fashionable salon in Paris; it became a theater in 1931, and filmmaker Louis Malle rescued it from wreckers 40 years later. The silk-and-gilt Salle Japonaise is the best place to watch a film. A tiny café takes over the garden in summer. Tickets are 45F–47F, and 38F on Wednesday. *57 bis rue de Babylone, 7e, tel. 08–36–68–75–07. Métro: St-François Xavier.*

Cinémathèque Française. Founded in 1936 by Henri Langlois, this is a world-famous cinephile heaven, where different classic French and international films are shown Tuesday–Sunday. Film schedules often pay homage to a certain filmmaker, with a few unrelated pieces thrown in for variety. Tickets are 28F, and 30F for afternoon films at the Faubourg-du-Temple address. The Chaillot location also has a tiny film museum. *Palais de Chaillot at Trocadéro, 16e, tel. 01–47–04–24–24. Métro: Trocadéro. Other location: 18 rue du Faubourg-du-Temple, 11e, tel. 01–47–02–24–24. Métro: République.*

The Lumière brothers, inventors of the "Cinématographe" (a precursor to the movie projector), showed their first film—the first public showing of any projected film ever—in 1895 in a café at 14 boulevard des Capucines.

L'Entrepôt. This all-in-one cinema, café, bar, restaurant, and bookstore is a must for film lovers. The three cinemas host a variety of festivals and show some great art and international films. Hang around the bar with other types who are suffering for their art and maybe an independent filmmaker will discover you. Film tickets are 35F. *7 rue Francis-de-Pressensé, 14e, tel. 01–45–43–41–63. Métro: Pernety.*

Le Lucernaire. This multimedia supercenter has two stages, three cinemas, occasional concerts, art exhibitions, a restaurant, and a café. The film selection is eclectic. Shows are 41F, and 30F on Monday and Wednesday. On one of the stages, *Le Petit Prince* has been running for 10 years; shows cost 118F–140F, and less if you spring for a 100F membership card. *53 rue Notre-Dame-des-Champs, 6e, tel. 01–45–44–57–34. Métro: Notre-Dame-des-Champs.*

Vidéothèque. Though hard-core moviegoers may scoff at the idea of videotapes, the Vidéothèque is one of Paris's most important resources for moving images. It has over 5,400 films, either filmed in Paris or with the city as the subject. A full day of audiovisual stimulation costs just 30F; the daily program can vary from a score of avant-garde shorts to a handful of feature-length films from the 1930s, all screened either in an immaculate projection room or on private consoles. The auditorium is also a forum for symposia and lectures, drawing international critics and filmmakers eager to argue about the meaning of the tracking shot. *2 Grande Galerie, Forum des Halles, 1er, tel. 01–40–26–34–30. Métro: Les Halles. Closed Mon.*

LIVE MUSIC

Paris has loved jazz for as long as jazz has been around. American artists flocked here during the post–World War II boom and fostered an appreciative and innovative atmosphere for their music making. There's still some fine music being played in Paris, but while young French groups try earnestly to catch the beat, these days it's hard to find truly jazzy dives. For some time now African, Caribbean, and South American music has been moving in, spicing up the club circuit; many "jazz" joints have a weekly *zouk* (Caribbean dance music) or salsa night.

Most jazz clubs are in **Les Halles, St-Germain,** or the **Quartier Latin.** You can usually stay all night for the price of a drink—a 50F–100F drink, that is. For cheaper shows, keep an eye on some of the museums and cultural centers around town (the Institut du Monde Arabe, for example); they occasionally host free or almost-free concerts. The free monthly *Paris Boum-Boum* (available at *boulangeries,* or bakeries) has a section on world-music shows around town.

If jazz sounds about as exciting to you as staring at a brick wall, there are plenty of places where you can mosh to your heart's content with a bunch of hot and sweaty punkers. Rock and punk are alive and well in Paris—and usually cheaper to hear than jazz. For most thrash and punk shows, look to the Pigalle area. The **Elysées Montmartre** (72 blvd. de Rochechouart, 18e, tel. 01–44–92–45–49, métro Barbès-Rochechouart) is one of the better venues for alternative bands, as well as for reggae and heavy metal bands. **Le Bataclan** (50 blvd. Voltaire, 11e, tel. 01–47–00–30–12, métro Oberkampf) is good for international pop. **Le Divan du Monde** (75 rue des Martyrs, 18e, tel. 01–44–92–77–66, métro Pigalle) presents great if not hyper-famous bands of all kinds in a smaller setting; the cover runs 60F–80F. **Hot Brass** (211 av. Jean-Jaurès, 19e, tel. 01–42–00–14–14, métro Jean-Jaurès) is the place for jazz and some of the best Latin jazz and funk bands in Paris.

The **Théâtre de l'Olympia** (22 rue Caumartin, 9e, tel. 01–47–42–25–49, métro Opéra, Havre-Caumartin) is the temple of *la chanson française* (French songs); it also welcomes older French acts and middle-of-the-road international stars. Top international rock and pop acts like Céline Dion, Bruce Springsteen, and Mariah Carey generally perform at either **Palais Omnisports Paris Bercy** (8 blvd. Bercy, 12e, tel. 01–44–68–44–68, métro Bercy) or **Le Zénith** (211 blvd. Jean-Jaurès, 19e, no phone, métro Jean-Jaurès). You can reserve tickets in advance at **Virgin Megastore** or **FNAC** (*see* Chapter 6). For information on future concerts, either check out the boards at FNAC or keep an eye on the billboards in the métro.

Au Duc des Lombards. Quality European blues and jazz acts regularly fill up this Les Halles club for 10 PM shows. Admission varies between 50F and 80F and beers only cost 24F (12F before 10 PM). A potentially hefty cover charge might apply if the band is especially good and/or famous. The restaurant upstairs serves passable meals for around 100F until 1 AM every night except Sunday and Monday. *42 rue des Lombards, 1er, tel. 01–42–33–22–88. Métro: Châtelet.*

Le Baiser Salé. This bar's small, potentially hot upstairs room is the perfect venue for small, potentially hot ensembles. Sit back on your velvety turquoise seat and listen to music ranging from blues to fusion to Afro-jazz. There are concerts nightly at 8 PM and 10:30 PM, and the cover varies between 30F and 90F. Beers cost about 25F. *58 rue des Lombards, 1er, tel. 01–42–33–37–71. Métro: Châtelet.*

Le Caveau de la Huchette. This classic *caveau* (underground club) has been serving up swing and Dixieland to hepcats since the 1950s. The young, wholesome crowd still swing-dance here like it's going out of style. Cover is 60F, 70F on weekends. Drinks start at 22F. *5 rue de la Huchette, 5e, tel. 01–43–26–65–05. Métro: St-Michel.*

La Cigale. This old-style theater–turned–concert hall is just the right size for a good mosh pit. Big names (as well as small ones) make frequent appearances, churning out loud, fast rock and indie music for a chain-smoking audience. A small bar in the basement keeps you fueled with 25F beers. The cover charge runs 80F–150F; for the really popular groups, buy your tickets in advance at FNAC or Virgin Megastore. *120 blvd. Rochechouart, 18e, tel. 01–49–25–81–75. Métro: Pigalle.*

Gibus. In the past, the Police, the Clash, the Pretenders, the Stray Cats, and Deep Purple all appeared here. More recently, the Gibus has become a temple of techno music, with special hardcore, jungle, and trans-goa evenings. A live band begins most evenings. A DJ then takes over at the turntable. There is also a funk night on Tuesday. Admission ranges 20F–80F (free for women before midnight on Friday and Saturday). Beers are 50F. *18 rue Faubourg-du-Temple, 11e, tel. 01–47–00–78–88. Métro: République. Closed Mon.*

La Java. Parisians hooked on Latin rhythm give La Java the thumbs up, and with good reason. The city's best salsa and samba bands frequently animate the place, and the enthusiastic crowd has as many experts as novices. Most importantly, male patrons are there to dance, not grope their partners. Cover is 50F–100F with one drink. Salsa plays on Friday, samba and a tea dance (2 PM–7 PM) on Sunday. *105 rue Faubourg-du-Temple, 10e, tel. 01–42–02–20–52. Métro: Belleville. Closed Mon., Tues.*

New Morning. This is Paris's big-time jazz club. All the greats have sweated on its stage at one time or another: Archie Shepp, Dizzy Gillespie, Miles Davis, and Celia Cruz, among them. The quality and reputation remain exceptional, and the repertoire now includes reggae, salsa, and Latin jazz. Cover for the dark, 600-seat club is 110F–130F. Drinks are 30F. Concerts start at about 9 PM; check *Pariscope* to see who's playing. *7–9 rue des Petites-Ecuries, 10e, tel. 01–45–23–51–41. Métro: Château d'Eau.*

L'Opus Café. Run by a bunch of young French hipsters, this place is a cool hangout for twentysome-things who look like they were born smoking in the back of a blues bar. Tables are scattered downstairs and in an upstairs loft, with no seat more than 20 feet from the stage. Traditional jazz ensembles perform on Tuesday and Wednesday from 9 PM onward. The cover is 50F. *167 Quai de Valmy, 10e, tel. 01–40–34–70–00. Métro: Louis Blanc.*

OPERA, CLASSICAL MUSIC, AND DANCE

The performing arts scene in Paris is overwhelming, with two of the world's greatest opera houses, more than 150 theaters, and a daily dose of at least a dozen classical concerts. There are opportunities for everyone, whether in the form of costly tickets to snooty musical societies, modern dance performances, free concerts in churches and cathedrals, or flute sonatas on the banks of the Seine. If you're looking for dance, generally more avant-garde or up-and-coming choreographers are found in the smaller spaces around the Bastille and the Marais and in theaters in the nearby suburbs. Classical ballet can be found in places as varied as the opera house and the sports stadium. Full listings of all kinds of performances can be found in both *Pariscope* and *L'Officiel des Spectacles*. Look out for the magic words *entrée gratuite* or *entrée libre* ("free-bie," in other words). The posters and notices pasted on the walls of métro stations are also good ways to keep up with the calendar.

Every June 21, France comes alive with free music in celebration of the summer solstice. During this Fête de la Musique, Paris's churches, clubs, parks, and squares fill with musicians and onlookers. You owe it to yourself to stay out all night.

There is plenty of free music in Paris. **Eglise de la Madeleine** (pl. de la Madeleine, 8e, métro Madeleine) has free concerts on Sunday at 4 PM; **Eglise St-Merri** (78 rue St-Martin, 4e, tel. 01–42–71–93–93, métro Châtelet) has free classical concerts Saturday at 9 PM and Sunday at 4 PM; and **L'Eglise Américaine** (65 quai d'Orsay, 7e, tel. 01–47–05–07–99, métro Invalides) has choral and organ music Sunday at 6 PM. The **Conservatoire National Supérieur de Musique et de Danse** (209 av. Jean-Jaurès, 19e, tel. 01–40–40–46–47, métro Jean-Jaurès) has student concerts practically every day at 12:30 PM and 7 PM, as does the **Ecole Normale de Musique** (78 rue Cardinet, 17e, tel. 01–47–63–85–72, métro Malesherbes) on Tuesday and Thursday at 12:30 PM. The **Conservatoire Paul Dukas** (45 rue de Picpus, 12e, tel. 01–43–47–17–66, métro Picpus) has free concerts on Tuesday at 7 PM. Another venue worth checking for free concerts is the **Maison de Radio France** (*see below*). Inexpensive concerts are held at the **Louvre** (*see* Major Attractions *in* Chapter 2; tel. 01–40–20–52–99 for information; 40F–60F) at 12:45 PM on Thursday and at the **Musée d'Orsay** (*see* Major Attractions *in* Chapter 2; tel. 01–40–49–49–66 for information; 35F–70F) on Tuesday and Thursday.

Tickets to major performances are not impossible to get if you use a little foresight. At most venues, the box office starts selling tickets two weeks before a performance, though a limited number are available one month in advance if you charge by phone. Discounts and day-of-performance tickets are often available for students age 25 or under; depending on the show, you should arrive 15–90 minutes early to try for any leftover tickets—sometimes excellent seats can be had for as little as 10% of the original price. You can always get tickets by phone from **FNAC** (tel. 01–40–41–40–00) or **Virgin Megastore** (tel. 01–44–68–44–08), though you'll pay a service charge and availability may be limited.

Centre Georges Pompidou–IRCAM. One of the four divisions within the Centre Georges Pompidou (*see* Major Attractions *in* Chapter 2), IRCAM (Institut de Recherche et Coordination de l'Acoustique et de la Musique) takes care of the "gestural" arts. Performances at the institute's multipurpose hall, under the place Igor-Stravinsky, include contemporary music, computer-generated videos, dance, drama, lectures, philosophy seminars, and debates. The center's médiathèque is open to the public and specializes in the latest technological innovations. *31 rue St-Merri, on pl. Igor-Stravinsky, 4e, tel. 01–42–17–12–33. Métro: Rambuteau/Hôtel de Ville. Tickets sold at the counter on the ground floor. Closed weekends.*

Cité de la Musique. Two concert halls are housed in this quirky, postmodern building at La Villette. The program is generally varied and refreshingly original. Pierre Boulez's Ensemble Intercontemporain performs regularly and concerts (35F–200F) range from individual recitals to world music to special cre-

QUEL GUIGNOL!

In French slang, to be a "guignol" means to be a clown, and to "faire le guignol" (act like a guignol) means to act silly. This is a pretty good indication of what to expect from a guignol show. These traditional puppet farces have entertained French children for centuries, and they continue to do so to this day (along with their parents, who might not want to admit they enjoy the skits as much as their kids). Here are a few good places to catch a show:

GUIGNOL DE PARIS. Set outdoors in the Parc des Buttes-Chaumont, these puppets attract kiddies daily at 3 PM. Parc des Buttes-Chaumont, between av. Bolivar and rue Botzaris, 19e, tel. 01-43-64-24-29. Métro: Buttes-Chaumont.

MARIONNETTES DES CHAMPS-ELYSÉES. This theater specializes in guignol classics. Shows happen daily at 3 PM, 4 PM, and 5 PM. Rond Point des Champs-Elysées, between av. Matignon and av. Gabriel, 8e, tel. 01-40-35-47-20. Métro: Champs-Elysées–Clemenceau.

MARIONNETTES DU CHAMP DE MARS. You can catch a show daily at 3:15 PM and 4:15 PM. Champ de Mars, 7e, tel. 01-48-56-01-44. Métro: Ecole Militaire.

ations mixing music with dance and circus. Make sure to check out the excellent **Musée Musique** (Music Museum), which traces the history of music using 900 instruments from 2500 BC to the present and interactive headsets. Concerts of original or replicas of medieval and baroque instruments are given in the museum's auditorium. The Cité also organizes master classes and forums and some rehearsals are open to the public. *221 av. Jean Jaurès, 19e, tel. 01-44-84-44-84 for reservations and information. Métro: Porte de Pantin.*

Maison de Radio France. The government's broadcasting center until the privatization of the airwaves, this vast complex is now home to countless radio and TV stations. In addition to studios, meeting halls, and a small museum devoted to the entire establishment (tours in French are 18F), the complex includes the smallish, modern Salle Olivier Messiaen, home to the **Orchestre National de France,** which also performs regularly at larger venues. Seats are available one month before a show, or turn your radio dial to 81.7 or 92.1 FM (France Musique) to hear the concert for free. There are also free orchestra soloist concerts and 30F jazz and traditional music concerts. The box office is open Monday–Saturday 11–6. *116 av. du Président Kennedy, 16e, tel. 01-42-30-15-16. Métro: Ranelagh or Bir-Hakeim. RER: Maison de Radio France.*

Opéra Bastille. In his quest to join the likes of Louis XIV and Napoléon III as one of the grand builders of Paris, Mitterrand had the Opéra Bastille built on place de la Bastille to replace the renowned Opéra Garnier (*see below*). Mitterrand's three-billion-franc project was the city's second redefinition of the opera house and an ambitious attempt to become (once again) the center of European opera. Designed by Uruguayan-born Canadian architect Carlos Ott and inaugurated on July 13, 1989 in commemoration of the Revolution, the Bastille received resoundingly negative criticism and was unflatteringly compared to a sports arena. The quality of the operatic productions has also since consistently been panned. The building was meant to offer "democratic" opera, but with many seats hovering around the 500F mark, they are well out-of-range of the ordinary wallet (seats range from 60F–600F). Taking part in all the excitement and controversy requires minimal planning. Tickets go on sale at the box offices two weeks before any given show or a month ahead by phone. Schedules and tickets are available at either Bastille or Garnier. Seats for concerts go for 45F–230F. Rush tickets are on sale just before a performance.

Bring a book and get in line a couple of hours in advance if you want a chance. The box office is open Monday–Saturday 11–6. *120 rue de Lyon, 12e, tel. 01–44–73–13–99 (information) or 01–44–73–13–00 (reservations). Métro: Bastille.*

Opéra Comique. The seasons are shorter, the director is less flamboyant, and the late-19th-century building is less grandiose than the Opéra Bastille or the Opéra Garnier. But the Opéra Comique stages a dozen operas and concerts each season in a more intimate setting than the other major theaters can offer. Prices for operas run 50F–490F. The box office is open Monday–Saturday, 11–7. *5 rue Favart, 2e, tel. 01–42–44–45–46. Métro: Richelieu-Drouot.*

Opéra Garnier. The most pompous of all Parisian buildings, the Opéra was built by Charles Garnier after he won an architectural competition in 1861. Unable to settle upon any one style, Garnier chose them all: a Renaissance-inspired detail here, a rococo frill there, Greek shields put up at random. The regal lobby, with a grand stairway and a mirrored ballroom, is as big as the auditorium; together they cover more than 3 acres. The hall itself is rich, velvety, and gaudy, with an extraordinary number of gilt statuettes and a ceiling repainted by Marc Chagall in 1964. The Opéra is home to France's finest ballet company and classical ballets alternate with operas and programs by modern choreographers. Tickets (30F–610F) go on sale roughly a month in advance over the phone or two weeks in advance in person. Call or stop by to reserve seats, but you must go in person for the 30F–60F cheapies. You can also try to get rush tickets sold 15 minutes before a performance. During the day, you can climb the ornate stairway and check out the plush auditorium for the 30F visitors' fee. A small museum features Degas's simple portrait of Wagner. The box office is open 11–6:30 daily. *8 rue Scribe, 9e, tel. 01–44–73–13–00 (reservations), 01–40–01–22–63 (information on visits). Métro: Opéra.*

In 1994, French designer Christian de Portzamparc was awarded the Pritzker Prize, the world's most prestigious honor for an architect. Evaluate his sinuous forms yourself by checking out the Cité de la Musique or the Café Beaubourg.

Sainte-Chapelle. The intimate size and utter exquisiteness of this building make seeing a concert at Sainte-Chapelle (*see* Major Attractions *in* Chapter 2) worth the cost and hassle of getting a ticket. Most seats start at 120F, and the concerts, mainly small classical ensembles, often sell out early. For tickets, come as soon as they're put on sale and expect to wait in line. *4 blvd. du Palais, 1er, tel. 01–42–05–25–23. Métro: Cité.*

Salle Gaveau. This high-quality concert venue named after the famous French piano makers has an Old World atmosphere. The program includes chamber music, and piano and singing recitals by a whole host of international stars and young prizewinners. Seats go for between 95F and 500F. *45 rue la Boëtie, 8e, tel. 01–49–53–05–07. Métro: Miromesnil.*

Salle Pleyel. Another grand old hall, this one has the unique distinction of having hosted Chopin's last public performance. These days it's the main stomping ground of the Orchestre de Paris. The hall also sees some dance and jazz, including regular stops by the Golden Gate Quartet. Tickets are sold on a looser schedule than at other theaters; call about specific shows. The box office is open Monday–Saturday, 11–6. *252 rue du Faubourg St-Honoré, 8e, tel. 01–45–61–53–00. Métro: George V, Ternes.*

Théâtre des Champs-Elysées. Once home to the Ballets Russes and Josephine Baker, this large, fancy musical theater now stages a bit of everything—operatic soloists, ballets, orchestras, marionette shows, and jazz acts. Tickets generally run 60F–290F. The box office is open Monday–Saturday, 11–7. *15 av. Montaigne, 8e, tel. 01–49–52–50–50. Métro: Franklin D. Roosevelt.*

Théâtre Musical de Paris. Ideally located on the place du Châtelet by the Seine, the Théâtre Musical is less self-important than its famous cousins, the Opéra Bastille and the Opéra Garnier. The excellence of the theater's opera productions tends to draw a devoted crowd and the theater is also second home to William Forsythe's astounding Ballett Frankfurt. Tickets cost 77F and up. The theater continues its "Midis Musicaux" (Musical Noons) series, with concerts in the foyer on Monday, Wednesday, and Friday starting at 12:45; seats cost 50F. The "Dimanches Musicaux" (Musical Sundays) start at 11:30 and cost 80F. The box office is open daily 11–7. *1 pl. du Châtelet, 1er, tel. 01–40–28–28–40 (reservations, 12F supplement per seat). Métro: Châtelet.*

Théâtre de la Ville. The fraternal twin of the Beaux-Arts Châtelet across the way, the Théâtre de la Ville is the main Parisian venue for contemporary dance. It regularly welcomes top-notch choreographers such as Pina Bausch, Trisha Brown, and Anne-Teresa de Keersmaeker. In 1899, legendary French actress Sarah Bernhardt bought the theater, named it after herself, and began performing regularly.

When the city took over, it naturally renamed it after itself. Bernhardt memorabilia can, however, still be seen in a room off the right-hand staircase. As well as dance, the theater also puts on a few plays each season and organizes an annual series of world music concerts. Tickets for most shows cost 90F–140F and can be purchased two weeks in advance. The box office is open Monday–Saturday, 9–8 (Monday until 6). *2 pl. du Châtelet, 4e, tel. 01–42–74–22–77 (reservations). Métro: Châtelet. Other location: 31 rue des Abbesses, 18e. Métro: Abbesses.*

THEATER

The Parisian theatrical scene goes back to 17th-century French playwrights like Corneille, Racine, and Molière. If this nearly 400-year-old tradition intimidates you a bit, note that Paris has also been a center for great 20th-century experimental theater; Antonin Artaud, Samuel Beckett, Jean Genet, and Jean-Paul Sartre all staged works here in the 1930s, '40s, and '50s. The legacy of the absurdists lives on, for example, at the stubborn Théâtre de la Huchette, which has been playing Ionesco's *La Leçon* and *La Cantatrice Chauve* for years.

If you're in search of discount tickets and have the patience to wait in line, check out the discount kiosks at the **gare Montparnasse** (pl. Raoul Dautry, 15e, métro Montparnasse-Bienvenue) and at **La Madeleine** (15 pl. de la Madeleine, 8e, métro Madeleine), both open Tuesday–Saturday 12:30–8 and Sunday 12:30–4. They sell tickets for same-day performances at up to half the original price. If you're a student or under 26, go to the **Kiosk Paris-Jeunes** (25 blvd. Bourdon, 4e, métro Bastille) for youth discount tickets. A number of private theaters (e.g., Essaïon, Main d'Or-Belle de Mai, Petits-Mathurins, Studio des Champs-Elysées, Poche-Montparnasse) sell half-price tickets for *avant-premières* (previews) between seven and 14 days before opening. Details can be found in *L'Officiel des Spectacles* and *Pariscope,* or at the theaters themselves.

As well as the theaters listed below, high-quality productions can also be caught at a number of excellent theaters in the suburbs. Some of the best are **MC 93** (1 blvd. Lénine, tel. 01–41–60–72–72, métro Bobigny-Pablo) in Bobigny; **Théâtre des Amandiers** (7 av. Pablo-Picasso, tel. 01–46–14–70–00, RER Line A to Nanterre Préfecture, then shuttle bus to theater) in Nanterre; and the **Théâtre Gérard Philippe** (59 blvd. Jules-Guesde, tel. 01–48–13–70–00, RER D to St-Denis, then follow signs) in St-Denis.

Les Bouffes du Nord. This theater was founded by British theater man Peter Brook, whose influence ensures a repertoire of out-of-the-ordinary productions and eccentric comedies. Performances in its beautifully decrepit decor feel otherworldly. Tickets are cheap: 60F–140F. *37 bis blvd. de la Chapelle, 10e, tel. 01–46–07–34–50. Métro: La Chapelle.*

Chaillot. Founded by Jean Vilar in post–World War II Paris as part of the movement to revive live theater, France's first *théâtre national* (national theater) stages highly regarded theatrical and musical productions in its two halls under the terrace of the Trocadéro. Those produced by resident director Jérôme Savary tend to be particularly eye-opening. Tickets run 80F–160F, depending on the show and your status. The box office is open Monday–Saturday 11–7, and Sunday 11–5. *1 pl. du Trocadéro, 16e, tel. 01–47–27–81–15. Métro: Trocadéro.*

Comédie Française–Salle Richelieu. The Comédie Française traces its origins to 1680, when Louis XIV merged Molière's acting company with other troupes, establishing the first completely French theater. The group lost its lease in 1770, but Louis XV saved it by ordering the construction of the Odéon; four years later the troupe was brought under even tighter royal control with the construction of the Théâtre Français (now called the Salle Richelieu) in the Palais Royal. Since then, this stage has been the permanent playground for the ghosts of Great French Theater. The Comédie-Française has a reputation as a bastion of traditionalism; the fact that the lobby holds the chair in which Molière collapsed and died after a performance in 1673 only reinforces this myth. The company, however, doesn't always produce Racine and Molière; sometimes they branch out to Camus and Sartre. Tickets run 35F–185F. The box office is open daily 11–6. *2 rue de Richelieu, 1er, tel. 01–44–58–15–15. Métro: Palais-Royal–Musée du Louvre.*

Odéon Théâtre de l'Europe. Under the direction of Lluís Pasqual, the Odéon has made pan-European theater its primary focus. Tickets run 30F–150F, with half-price rush tickets available 50 minutes before curtain time. If you're a student or under 26 and a regular theatergoer, consider buying the Carte Complice Jeune for 100F. It gives you 25% off all seats. The basement holds the experimental Petit Odéon, where all seats run 50F–70F. The box office is open Monday–Saturday 11–6:30. *1 pl. de l'Odéon, 6e, tel. 01–44–41–36–36. Métro: Odéon.*

Théâtre de la Huchette. It was at La Huchette that Eugène Ionesco founded and developed a theatrical and philosophical style that came to be known as Theater of the Absurd. Parisians, while somewhat confused by Ionesco's surreal story lines, were so smitten by his words that *La Cantatrice Chauve* (The Bald Primadonna) has been performed every night here since its premiere in 1950. Both it and Ionesco's 1951 play *La Leçon* (The Lesson) have played at La Huchette for years, although plays by Tennessee Williams have been creeping in. Tickets are generally 100F. The box office is open Monday–Saturday 5–9. *23 rue de la Huchette, 5e, tel. 01–43–26–38–99. Métro: St-Michel.*

CAFE THEATER

This subgenre of Paris theater is devoted to low-budget and potentially subversive productions. Unless your French is pretty good, you'll have a hard time understanding, but it's still worth it—these little shows often present funny views and critiques of French society and culture. Despite the name, most *café-théâtres* do not sell refreshments. Some well-known and popular venues include **Au Bec Fin** (6 rue Thérèse, 1er, tel. 01–42–96–29–35, métro Palais-Royal, Pyramides), which has fairly large-scale productions, and **Le Point Virgule** (7 rue Ste-Croix-de-la-Bretonnerie, 4e, tel. 01–42–78–67–03, métro Hôtel de Ville), which specializes in comedy.

Café d'Edgar. Tongue-in-cheek skits are the specialty at this small, red-benched café-théâtre in Montparnasse. Three shows are performed nightly except Sunday, and the price is 80F a show. *58 blvd. Edgar-Quinet, 14e, tel. 01–42–79–97–97. Métro: Edgar Quinet. Closed Sun.*

Café de la Gare. A happy crowd piles onto wooden benches to catch the comedies at this popular theater where the young Gérard Depardieu and Miou-Miou once performed. On stage are two quality 90-minute shows per night with tickets between 50F and 120F each. *41 rue du Temple, 4e, tel. 01–42–78–52–51. Métro: Hôtel de Ville.*

ENGLISH-LANGUAGE THEATER

Theater enthusiasts who aren't quite ready to brave the French language should keep an eye out for Paris-based English-language troupes such as **Dear Conjunction** and the **On Stage Theater Company.** Larger troupes like the **Royal Shakespeare Company** also occasionally pass through town.

Théâtre de Ménilmontant. The English-language company **American Conservatory Theater** (ACT, tel. 01–40–33–64–02) is based here and puts on a diverse range of productions. Tickets are 50F–90F. *15 rue du Retrait, 20e. Métro: Gambetta. Call ACT for reservations.*

Théâtre de Nesle. Although not exclusively English-language, this theater frequently hosts the On Stage Theater Company with modern plays by the likes of Harold Pinter and Bertolt Brecht. Tickets run 80F–90F. The box office is open Tuesday–Saturday 11–7. *8 rue de Nesle, 6e, tel. 01–46–34–61–04. Métro: Odéon.*

SHOPPING

UPDATED BY SUZANNE ROWAN KELLEHER

Paris is a paradise for fashion victims, but it can terrorize those of us who fear well-coiffed ladies brandishing tiny, manicured dogs. It's not uncommon to see speedwalking Parisians slow to a crawl as their eyes lock on an attractive *vitrine* (shop window). Truth is, shopping here can be contagious, and if you don't buy something—a book, shoes, lingerie (this *is* Paris)—you're missing out on a truly Parisian experience. Luckily, shopping in Paris doesn't have to leave you franc-less: There *are* shops where you can get a good deal on items from Kookaï T-shirts to Hermès scarves. Window-shopping—what the French call *lécher les vitrines* (literally, licking the windows)—is also fun, and you won't have to part with one centime.

If you have decided to treat yourself to a Dior tie or a bottle of L'Air du Temps, do yourself a favor and check prices at home before coming. The dreaded 20.6% French sales tax (known as the TVA or *détaxe*) often means that items are cheaper in the mall back home. If you're a serious shopper, come during either of Paris's two main sale months, January and July, when the streets are lined with the word *soldes* (sale) and the average discount is 30%–50%.

There is only one way around the TVA. If you're a non-European resident, aged 15 and over, and staying in the EU for fewer than six months, you can reclaim part of the tax. But there's a catch: To qualify, your purchases in a single shop must total at least 1,700 francs. The amount of the refund varies from shop to shop but usually hovers between 13% and 16%. The major department stores have simplified the process with special *détaxe* desks where the *bordereaux* (export sales invoices) are prepared, and all paperwork must be presented to French customs when you leave the country. There is no refund for food, wine, or tobacco.

Whenever possible, use credit cards over cash. You'll be billed at a better exchange rate than what foreign exchange windows and *cambios* (money-changing booths) offer for your dollars, pounds, or punts. Even the corner newsstand or flea-market salesperson is likely to honor plastic for purchases over 100 francs. Visa is by far the most preferred card, followed closely by MasterCard/EuroCard. American Express, Diners Club, and Access tend to be accepted only by the larger international stores.

When shopping for clothes, keep in mind that returns are virtually unheard of (though exchanges are usually okay). Most stores in Paris stay open until 6 or 7 PM and close on Sundays, and many take a lunch break sometime between noon and 2 PM.

SHOPPING BY NEIGHBORHOOD

BASTILLE

Welcome to the epicenter of hip Parisian street fashion. This gentrified neighborhood is the antithesis of the quintessential Parisian style. Instead, you'll find its youthful denizens sporting tattoos, body-piercings, and the sort of cutting-edge fashion you find in New York's East Village. Scores of up-and-coming designers have followed Jean-Paul Gaultier here, forming a nice complement to the art galleries, furniture stores, and bars. The area also has plenty of self-consciously cool shops that sell trendy clothes. **Rue de la Roquette** is the main shopping drag.

CHAMPS-ELYSEES AND SURROUNDINGS

The city's most celebrated avenue—and most touristy—is active 24 hours a day with nightclubs, cinemas, and fast-food joints. Four ritzy 20th-century arcade malls (Galerie du Lido, Le Rond-Point, Le Claridge, and Elysées 26) capture most of the retail action. The surrounding streets are the shopping ground of the rich Parisian elite. All of fashion's big names are here—from Chanel and Dior to Hermès and Valentino—with prices as sinful as you'd imagine. Even if you can't afford a thing, it's fun to window-shop along **avenue Montaigne** and **rue du Faubourg-St-Honoré** while chanting "thousands of francs, thousands of francs," so you don't accidentally fall in love with anything.

Key lingo: "soldes" or "promotion" (sale); "dégriffé" or "stock" (discounted designer labels); "braderie" or "fin de série" (clearance); "occasions," "fripes," "dépôts-ventes," "troc" or "brocante" (secondhand); "nouveautés" (new arrivals).

LES HALLES AND BEAUBOURG

Most of the narrow pedestrian streets on the former site of Paris's main food market are lined with fast-food joints, sex shops, jeans outlets, and garish souvenir stands, but **rue du Jour** is the exception (MaxMara, Agnès B., and Junior Gaultier are all here). In the middle of the action is the **Forum des Halles**, a modern, multilevel, underground shopping mall (some say eyesore) containing a few decent French chain stores and a cinema complex (with a cybercafé). Frequent fashion shows are given by 50 young designers in the **Forum des Créateurs** (call 01–44–76–96–56 for information). On Saturday, the place is crazy.

LOUVRE

Below the staid, elegant Louvre lurks **Le Carrousel du Louvre** (99 rue de Rivoli), open 10 AM–8 PM every day except Tuesday. This big, fancy mall jammed under the Louvre contains over 30 big-name stores (among them Virgin Megastore and Esprit), as well as a restaurant court. This is all worth a look if only to see the inverted glass pyramid that plunges into its center; the design is by the inimitable I. M. Pei, the architect responsible for the pyramid at the Louvre's entrance.

LE MARAIS

Among the pre-Revolution mansions of the Marais are many an artsy clothing boutique and gift shop. It's a bit more expensive and elegant than the Bastille and Les Halles, but cheaper than just about everywhere else. A key advantage: It's the only neighborhood with shops open on Sunday afternoons. Good streets for browsing are **rue des Francs-Bourgeois, rue Ste-Croix-de-la-Bretonnerie,** and **rue Vieille-du-Temple. Rue des Rosiers** and **rue Pavée** are known for their kosher delis and Jewish-interest bookstores.

MONTMARTRE

Somehow, Montmartre manages to combine a small town's intimate atmosphere with a big city's cosmopolitan panache. **Rue des Abbesses** is a perfect place to stroll among fruit stands, wine shops, fishmongers, and a few small clothing stores. Stay away from the area right around the Sacré-Coeur and the sleazy area near place Pigalle unless, of course, you like that sort of thing.

MONTPARNASSE

Need proof that bargains do exist in Paris? The proliferation of *boutiques stocks*—outlets where top designers sell last year's collections at a discount—makes **rue d'Alésia** the city's best for bargain hunting. Leave the charmless commercial center in the Tour Montparnasse to those who don't know any better.

QUARTIER LATIN

Shops here cater to the local student population, so you'll find many stores selling cheap clothes at cheap prices. Although **boulevard St-Michel** is schlocky and crowded, the smaller streets around **place Maubert** in the 5th arrondissement are lined with tiny music stores with excellent collections of rare and/or used vinyl, as well as buckets of CDS and K7s (French shorthand for cassettes—get it?) and good-to-browse bookstores (*see* Specialty Shops, Bookstores, *below*). **Rue Mouffetard** is better for wandering than shopping, especially if you head all the way downhill to the open-air produce market at the bottom.

ST-GERMAIN-DES-PRES

Like the Marais, this immensely walkable neighborhood is best known for its one-of-a-kind boutiques, though an invasion of the big name brands (Kenzo, Louis Vuitton, Giorgio Armani, Thierry Mugler, Christian Dior Men, and Romeo Gigli) has sparked much local controversy. All the streets are good for shopping, but some of best are **boulevard St-Germain, rue de Rennes, place St-Sulpice** and the streets off it, and **rue Bonaparte**. No trip to Paris is complete without an afternoon of browsing here.

DEPARTMENT STORES

For an overview of Parisian *mode* (fashion), visit the *grands magasins,* Paris's monolithic department stores. Generally they are more expensive than their American counterparts, though big sales can make things affordable (well, almost). Visit to gawk at the ornate architecture, scoff at prices, and marvel at the historical value of it all; some of the stores have been around since 1869. Most department stores are open Monday through Saturday from about 9:30 AM to 7 PM; note that a couple host free fashion shows.

Au Bon Marché (22 rue de Sèvres, 7e, tel. 01–44–39–80–00, métro Sèvres-Babylone), the world's oldest grand magasin, is most notable for its gourmet grocery—one of the largest in Paris—stocked with French wines, chocolates, foie gras, and cheeses.

Au Printemps (64 blvd. Haussmann, 9e, tel. 01–42–82–50–00, métro Havre-Caumartin, Opéra, or Auber) has three floors of women's fashion featuring top designers like Helmut Lang and Dolce & Gabbana. Free fashion shows are held on Tuesday (all year) and Friday (March–October) at 10 AM under the cupola on the seventh floor of La Mode, the building dedicated to women's and children's fashion. The three-store complex also includes Brummel, a six-floor emporium of menswear.

Bazar de l'Hôtel de Ville (52–64 rue de Rivoli, 4e, tel. 01–42–74–90–00, métro Hôtel de Ville), or BHV, has minimal fashion pickings but is noteworthy for household goods, art supplies, and its huge hardware department in the basement.

Galeries Lafayette (40 blvd. Haussmann, 9e, tel. 01–42–82–34–56, métro Chaussée d'Antin, Opéra, or Havre-Caumartin; Centre Commercial Montparnasse, 15e, tel. 01–45–38–52–87, métro Montparnasse-Bienvenue) carries nearly 80,000 fashion labels under its stained-glass dome, including rising stars like Marion Chanet, Ann Demeulemeester, and Marcel Marongiou. Free fashion shows are held every Wednesday at 11 AM (tel. 01–48–74–02–30, for reservations).

Marks & Spencer (35 blvd. Haussmann, 9e, tel. 01–47–42–42–91, métro Havre-Caumartin, Auber, or Opéra; 88 rue de Rivoli, 4e, tel. 01–44–61–08–00, métro Hôtel de Ville) stocks well-priced basics like underwear and socks. For inexpensive take-out sandwiches and salads, stop into the popular English grocery (ground floor of the Haussmann store, basement of Rivoli branch).

La Samaritaine (19 rue de la Monnaie, 1er, tel. 01–40–41–20–20, métro Pont-Neuf or Châtelet), a sprawling five-store complex, carries everything from designer fashions to cuckoo clocks. But it is most notable for its rooftop café in Building 2, which has one of the best views of Paris.

BARGAIN BASEMENT

Most Parisians dash into their local **Monoprix** or **Prisunic**—the French equivalent of Kmart, with branches throughout the city—several times a week. Come here if you run out of toothpaste, shampoo, batteries, pantyhose, or other essentials. Both chains carry inexpensive children's clothes of surprisingly good quality.

Tati (central location at 140 rue de Rennes, 6e, tel. 01–45–48–68–31, métro St-Placide; 4 blvd. de Rochechouart, 18e, tel. 01–42–55–13–09; 13 pl. de la République, 3e, tel. 01–48–87–72–81; 106

rue du Faubourg-du-Temple, 11e, tel. 01–43–57–92–80) has bargain-basement prices and hectic, jumbled sales floors. Shop carefully, as goods—from clothes to kitchen utensils—vary in quality. The store's trendy "La Rue Est à Nous" line is good for that one, cheap, fashionable item that you'll probably only wear this year.

SHOPPING ARCADES

Paris's 19th-century commercial arcades, called *passages,* were the forerunners of the modern shopping mall. Glass roofs, decorative pillars, and mosaic floors give them an old-fashioned air. With some patient browsing, you can find all sorts of shops tucked into the alleys, with such items as clothing, jewelry, rare stamps, secondhand books, and even antique canes.

The major arcades are in the 1st and 2nd arrondissements and include **Galerie Véro-Dodat** (19 rue Jean-Jacques Rousseau, 1er, métro Les Halles); **Galerie Vivienne** (4 rue des Petits-Champs, 2e, métro Bourse), home to a range of interesting shops, including Gaultier and Yukii Tori, as well as an excellent tearoom and a top-quality wine shop, Cave Legrand; **Passage des Panoramas** (11 blvd. Montmartre, 2e, métro Montmartre), which opened in 1800 and is the oldest of them all; **Passage des Pavillons** (6 rue de Beaujolais, 1er, métro Palais-Royal); and **Passage des Princes** (97 rue de Richelieu, 2e, métro Richelieu-Drouot). **Passage Jouffroy** (12 blvd. Montmartre, 9e, métro Montmartre) is full of shops selling toys, postcards, antique canes, perfumes, original cosmetics, and dried flowers: Try Pain d'Epices (No. 29) and Au Bonheur des Dames (No. 39). **Passage Verdeau** (12 blvd. Montmartre, 9e, métro Montmartre), across the street from Passage Jouffroy, has shops selling antique cameras, toy soldiers, and rare gemstones.

SPECIALTY SHOPS

ART SUPPLIES

Art supplies in Paris can be pretty reasonable if you nose around enough. Prices may seem high, but don't forget—this is where the masters at the Ecole des Beaux-Arts in St-Germain seek out their burnt sienna. Also try gallery districts like the Bastille.

FNAC (*see* Bookstores, *below*) is primarily a book and music store, but it also has a good selection of reasonably priced photo equipment and stationery.

Gibert Joseph Papeterie (30 blvd. St-Michel, 5e, tel. 01–44–41–88–66, métro St-Michel) has its own discount line of notebooks and stationery.

Graphigro (133 rue de Rennes, 6e, tel. 01–42–22–51–80, métro Rennes) is popular with Beaux-Arts students for its huge selection of paints, papers, and easels, as well as for its frequent sales.

BOOKSTORES

Bookstores of all shapes and subjects are spread throughout Paris, but those specializing in art, literature, economics, politics, language, and gastronomy are most abundant on the Left Bank. The best place to look for lit crit and philosophy texts is in the areas that spawn them, specifically **boulevard St-Michel** near the Ecole Normale Supérieure, **place de la Sorbonne,** and all of those little streets tucked in between. Gibert Joseph, Presses Universitaires, and the FNAC in Les Halles are also good places to try. Finally, be sure to check out the *bouquinistes* (booksellers) along the Seine, particularly between **boulevard du Palais** and the **Pont au Double** (*see* box, *below*), for inexpensive secondhand books, prints, and old postcards.

A Tire-d'Ailes (81 rue St-Louis-en-l'Ile, 4e, tel. 01–40–46–89–37, métro Pont Marie), a little bookshop on Ile St-Louis, has an international selection of poetry and might sell you just the thing to woo that scornful Parisienne.

FNAC (1 rue Pierre-Lescot, 1er, tel. 01–40–41–40–00, métro Châtelet; 136 rue de Rennes, 6e, tel. 01–49–54–30–00, métro St-Placide; 26–30 av. des Ternes, 8e, tel. 01–44–09–18–00, métro Ternes; 4 pl. de la Bastille, 12e, tel. 01–43–42–04–04, métro Bastille), a multistory chain with four

LES BOUQUINISTES

They crowd around the river like green flies, hawking plastic Eiffel Towers and other tourist paraphernalia, or so it seems at first glance. Truth is, many bouquinistes are bona fide bibliophiles—careful collectors who have spent a lifetime dealing in classics, as well as posters (30F–100F), comic books (35F), magazines, postcards, poetry and literature (10F–30F), pocket books (15F), and sometimes even sheet music. They open shop Monday through Saturday at 10 AM (more or less) and pack up around 6, but much depends upon their mood, the weather, and the crowds.

major locations in the city, sells a great deal more than mere books—like music, computer software, photo equipment, videos, and concert tickets, all for reasonable prices—by French standards.

Gibert Jeune (2–10 pl. St-Michel and 27 quai St-Michel, 6e, tel. 01–43–25–70–07, métro St-Michel) sells heaps of new and used books—not only scholarly ones, but also colorful, hardback art books. Some of the stores have specialties like science, religion, or fiction, so consult the yellow awnings in front of the several branches clustered on place St-Michel. The selection of English literature at the 10 place St-Michel site is terribly classical, but if you're determined to work your way through Dickens, titles go for 10F–15F less here than at other English-language bookstores.

Gibert Joseph (26 blvd. St-Michel, 6e, tel. 01–44–41–88–88, métro Cluny–La Sorbonne) sells moderately priced books that run from the general (tourism, language aids) to the very specific (particularly in economics, politics, literature, and anthropology).

La Hune (170 blvd. St-Germain, 6e, tel. 01–45–48–35–85, métro St-Germain des Prés), across the street from the Café de Flore and Les Deux Magots, is a landmark for intellectuals. Belles lettres are downstairs, but the main attraction is the comprehensive collection of books on art and architecture upstairs. Stay here until midnight with all the other genius-insomniacs.

Librairie Gallimard (15 blvd. Raspail, 7e, tel. 01–45–48–24–84, métro Rue du Bac) buys and sells new (and some used) literature and literary criticism in French; it's open Mon.–Sat. 10–7.

ENGLISH-LANGUAGE BOOKSTORES

Paris has several English-language bookstores, including **Brentano's** (37 av. de l'Opéra, 2e, tel. 01–42–61–52–50, métro Opéra), **Galignani** (224 rue de Rivoli, 1e, tel. 01–42–60–76–07, métro Tuileries), and **W. H. Smith** (248 rue de Rivoli, 1er, tel. 01–44–78–88–89, métro Concorde), carrying fiction, travel, language books, and magazines. Note, though, that new books in English cost about twice as much as they do back home.

Shakespeare & Company (37 rue de la Bûcherie, 5e, no phone, métro St-Michel) specializes in expatriate literature. The daring founder of the original institution, Sylvia Beach, published Joyce's *Ulysses* in 1922 after it was deemed obscene and turned down by other publishers. The current owner, George Whitman, claims Walt as an ancestor and will say anything to capitalize on the reputation of Beach's salon; he adopted the name years after the first Shakespeare and Company closed. The staff can be pretentious, but the shelves of secondhand books often hold bargains. Poets often give readings upstairs.

Tea & Tattered Pages (24 rue Mayet, 6e, tel. 01–40–65–94–35, métro Duroc) is best of all for cheap, secondhand paperbacks, plus new books (publishers' overstock) at low prices. Tea and brownies are served, and browsing is encouraged.

Village Voice (6 rue Princesse, 6e, tel. 01–46–33–36–47, métro Mabillon), known for its selection of contemporary authors, hosts regular literary readings.

SPECIALTY BOOKSTORES

Attica (64 rue de la Folie-Méricourt, 11e, tel. 01–48–06–17–00, métro Oberkampf) has all you need to learn a language, including children's grammar books and corny language tapes.

Aux Films du Temps (8 rue St-Martin, 4e, tel. 01–42–71–93–48, métro Châtelet, Hôtel de Ville) is heaven for film buffs, with technical books on filmmaking and film history, as well as big, glossy posters and movie stills.

La Fourmi Ailée (8 rue du Fouarre, 5e, tel. 01–43–29–40–99, métro St-Michel) has a large selection of literary works by or about women. The refined tearoom in back serves pots of tea and scones.

L'Harmattan (16–21 rue des Ecoles, 5e, tel. 01–46–34–13–71, métro Maubert-Mutualité), an impressive bookstore-publisher, likes to describe itself as "Au carrefour des cultures" (at the crossroads of cultures): They specialize in African, Arabic, Spanish, Portuguese, Latin American, and Asian literature.

L'Introuvable (23 rue Juliette-Dodu, 10e, tel. 01–42–00–61–43, métro Colonel Fabien) is the place for para-literature: spy novels, science fiction, mysteries, and westerns. The English-speaking shop owner carries nothing but first-run editions, mostly in French.

La Librairie des Femmes (74 rue de Seine, 6e, tel. 01–43–29–50–75, métro Mabillon) is strong on theoretical feminist texts, many of which it publishes. The English section includes translations of French women writers like Colette and Anaïs Nin.

La Librairie Gourmande (4 rue Dante, 5e, tel. 01–43–54–37–27, métro St-Michel) sells precious and pricey antique cookbooks. Other books of equal gastronomic caliber, however, are offered for less, as are a delicious collection of reproductions of old food advertisements.

La Librairie Publico (145 rue Amelot, 11e, tel. 01–48–05–34–08, métro Filles du Calvaire), Paris's main anarchist bookstore, is pretty low-key.

Les Mots à la Bouche (6 rue Ste-Croix-de-la-Bretonnerie, 4e, tel. 01–42–78–88–30, métro Hôtel de Ville), Paris's only overtly gay bookstore, features magazines, art, photography, novels, and poetry in French and English. Come here to pick up gay and lesbian guidebooks to France, and to find out what's going on around town.

CLOTHING AND ACCESSORIES

DISCOUNT SHOPS

If you can't leave this city without buying something with a designer label, the *boutiques stocks* or *magasins de dégriffés* (discounted designer label shops) are your best bet. These shops are packed with good stuff—last year's collections and slightly damaged goods at big discounts. Unfortunately, this doesn't mean they're always a steal—even so, given the original prices, a bargain is in the eye of the beholder.

A one-stop mecca for 40%–50% reductions on well-known labels in the boutiques stocks is **rue d'Alésia** (14e, métro Alésia). Some of the best are Cacharel Stock (No. 114), Chipie Stock (No. 82), Dorothée bis Stock (No. 74), Diapositive Stock (No. 14), and Majestic by Chevignon (No. 12). SR Store (No. 64) slices 50% off last year's prices on Sonia Rykiel fashions for the whole family, then manages to chop another 20%–30% off during the January and July sales.

Alaïa (18 rue de la Verrerie, 4e, tel. 01–42–72–19–19, métro Hôtel de Ville), selling the boutique stock of Azzedine Alaïa, is hidden away in a courtyard in the Marais. Look for last year's (and previous years') summer and winter collections, all mixed together and priced 50% below retail.

Anna Lowe (35 av. Matignon, 8e, tel. 01–43–59–96–61, métro Miromesnil) is a treasure trove for women who adore classic designer names (Valentino, Armani, Givenchy, Lacroix, Montana). Though still expensive, the savings are substantial on new ready-to-wear designer labels and one-of-a-kind haute couture gowns. Unlike most discounters, this shop will do alterations.

Comptoirs du Trocadéro (17 av. Raymond Poincaré, 16e, tel. 01–53–65–75–75, métro Trocadéro) is Paris's very first factory outlet emporium. Inside, you'll find 20 quality brands (including Cottonade, Blanc Bleu, and Le Monde du Bagage) and a huge choice of home decorations, linens, leather goods, and clothing. Everything costs 20% to 50% less than retail.

Et Vous Stock (17 rue de Turbigo, 2e, tel. 01–40–13–04–12, métro Etienne-Marcel) chops 50% off the price of last year's collections from Et Vous. Both women's and men's fashions are sold here.

Mendès (65 rue Montmartre, 2e, tel. 01–42–36–83–32, métro Sentier) sells last season's Yves Saint Laurent Rive Gauche, Christian Lacroix, and Variations lines at half price.

Le Mouton à Cinq Pattes (18 rue St-Placide, 6e, tel. 01–45–48–86–26, métro Sèvres-Babylone; 15 rue Vieille-du-Temple, 4e, tel. 01–42–71–86–30, métro Hôtel de Ville; 19 rue Grégoire-de-Tours, 6e, tel. 01–43–29–73–56, métro Odéon) is Paris's best-known boutique de dégriffé. The shop cuts off the *griffés* (labels) from last year's big-name collections (you'll find more Italians and Germans than French), then sells everything at a huge reduction—sometimes as much as 70% below retail.

Stock Kookaï (82 rue Réaumur, 2e, tel. 01–45–08–93–69, métro Réaumur-Sébastopol) is the place to find big savings on end-of-series items in the Kookaï line. There are some good steals here.

Studio Lolita (2 rue des Rosiers, 4e, tel. 01–48–87–09–67, métro St-Paul) sells last season's Lolita Lempicka line—sharp suits and whimsical dresses—for half price. Lolita bis, the junior line, is sold in a separate shop across the street.

JEWELRY

The best square in Paris for gawking is **place Vendôme,** home of the Ritz hotel and the world's most famous jewelers—Cartier, Chaumet, Van Cleef & Arpels, to name just three. Their little trinkets are obscenely gorgeous and the prices are just plain obscene. For us regular folk, there are some alternatives.

Agatha (97 rue de Rennes, 6e, tel. 01–45–48–81–30, métro St-Sulpice; 12–14 av. Champs-Elysées, 8e, tel. 01–43–59–68–68, métro Franklin D. Roosevelt) has trendy but moderately priced seasonal collections.

La Droguerie (9 rue du Jour, 1er, tel. 01–45–08–93–27, métro Les Halles) is a do-it-yourselfer's paradise, with jars and jars of all the beads, bangles, baubles, ribbons, strings, and clasps you need to make your own fashion statement.

KIDS' CLOTHES

Bonpoint (82 rue de Grenelle, 7e, tel. 01–45–48–05–45, métro Rue du Bac) is one of *the* clothing lines for precious Parisian *enfants* (children). This store sells Bonpoint at savings of 40% off items from last year's collection—and even more if you come during the supersales in January and June.

Du Pareil Au Même (15 and 23 rue des Mathurins, 8e, tel. 01–42–66–93–80, métro Havre-Caumartin; 7 rue St-Placide, 6e, tel. 01–40–49–00–33, métro St-Placide; 135 av. Emile Zola, 15e, tel. 01–40–59–48–82, métro Emile Zola) is an affordable alternative to Jacadi, Tartine et Chocolat, and other makers of exquisite but scandalously priced French kids' clothes. This chain sells well-made basics in soft, brightly colored jersey and cotton for newborns to young teens.

LINGERIE

Allende (28 rue Bergère, 9e, tel. 01–48–00-93–19, métro Rue Montmartre) gets their affordable inventory directly from an Austrian factory. There's a wide selection of undergarments, ranging in style from sweet, embroidered cottons to racy silk numbers.

Diva (161 rue St-Charles, 15e, tel. 01–45–54–50–72, métro Boucicaut) practically gives away *fin-de-séries* (end of series) items from top French lingerie lines—Prestige, Boléro, Lou, Aubade, Chantelle, and Lejaby—for prices 50% to 70% off retail. In summer, Livia bathing suits go for half price.

MAKEUP AND PERFUME

Parisian women (and the French fashion bible, *Elle* magazine) swear by the two beloved French dimestores, **Monoprix** and **Prisunic,** for inexpensive, good-quality cosmetics. (The Prisunic branch at 109 rue de la Boétie, 8e, is the best-stocked.) Look for the brand names Arancil and Bourjois, whose products are made in the Chanel factories.

Catherine (5 rue Castiglione, 1er, tel. 01–42–61–02–89, métro Concorde) typically offers reductions of 30% off the retail price of all the big name perfumes.

Les Halles Montmartre (85 rue Montmartre, 2e, tel. 01–42–33–11–13, métro Bourse) routinely discounts its wide range of perfumes and cosmetics by 30%–40%.

Make Up For Ever (5 rue de la Boétie, 8e, tel. 01–42–65–48–57, métro St-Augustin) is a must-stop for makeup artists, models (Kate Moss is a regular), and actresses (Madonna has dropped in, too). The selection, spanning 40 shades of foundation, 100 eye shadows, 24 glittering powders, and scores of fake eyelashes, may not help you be a model, but it can help you look like one.

Michel Swiss (16 rue de la Paix, 2nd Floor, 2e, tel. 01–42–61–61–11, métro Opéra; 24 av. de l'Opéra, 1er, tel. 01–47–03–49–11, métro Pyramides) is the place to save up to 25% on perfumes, designer jewelry, and fashion accessories. There's no storefront window; enter the courtyard and take the elevator upstairs.

RESALE CLOTHING

Catherine Baril (14 and 25 rue de la Tour, 16e, tel. 01–45–20–95–21, métro Passy) sells one-of-a-kind, barely worn designer haute couture and ready-to-wear. No. 25 is devoted to menswear.

Réciproque (89, 92, 95, 97, 101, and 123 rue de la Pompe, 16e, tel. 01–47–04–30–28, métro Rue de la Pompe) is Paris's largest and most exclusive swap shop. There's not much in the way of service or space, but savings on all the big names—Nina Ricci, Dior, Chanel, Yves Saint Laurent, Thierry Mugler, Alaïa—are significant. The newest shop, at No. 92, specializes in leather goods. Réciproque is closed Sundays and Mondays and from the end of July through August.

SCARVES AND BAGS

Accessoires à Soie (21 rue des Acacias, 17e, tel. 01–42–27–78–77, métro Argentine) scores with shopping-savvy Parisians who must have their scarves. The wide selection of silk scarves in all shapes and sizes includes many big-name designers, and everything costs about half of what you'd pay retail.

Didier Ludot (23 galerie Montpensier, 1er, tel. 01–42–96–06–56, métro Palais-Royal), under the arcades of the Palais Royal, sells secondhand accessories in impeccable condition by Hermès and Chanel. Much-coveted Hermès's Kelly bags start at 4,000F—still pricey, but thousands of francs below retail. Hermès silk scarves start at 600F, or about 50% off the original price. Chanel shoes and jewelry are also reduced.

Maroquinerie Vaugirard (86 rue de Vaugirard, 6e, tel. 01–40–49–08–80, métro St-Placide) sells marked-down luggage and leather goods made by the likes of Delsey, Enny, and Longchamp.

SHOES

Try the **rue de Rivoli** (1er), **boulevard St-Michel** (5e), **avenue du Général-Leclerc** (14e), and **rue Grégoire de Tours** (6e) for inexpensive shoe chains like André and Ormond. In addition, the **Forum des Halles** (1er) houses about a dozen shoe shops selling fashionable, but cheap footwear.

Girod (59 rue St-Antoine, 4e, tel. 01–42–72–10–26, métro Bastille) has an impressive range of reasonably priced vintage women's shoes from the sixties and seventies.

Mi-Prix (27 blvd. Victor, 15e, tel. 01–48–28–42–48, métro Porte-de-Versailles) is an unruly jumble of end-of-series designer footwear and accessories from the likes of Maud Frizon, Philippe Model, Walter Steiger, and Lacroix, priced at up to 60% below retail.

Orcel Diffusion (7 rue Meslay, 3e, tel. 01–48–87–72–98, métro République) sells a wide selection of classic styles for women, with excellent discounts at the back of the shop. Men have a more limited selection.

TRENDSETTERS

Forum des Jeunes Créteurs (Level -1, Forum des Halles, 1er, no phone, métro Châtelet) promotes 50 rising-star designers—some zany, some sophisticated—and sells their creations at wholesale prices. The pickings are slimmer in the men's collections.

Le Shop (3 rue d'Argout, 2e, tel. 01–40–26–21–45, métro Sentier) is a two-story emporium housing 20 hip designers who bring—gasp—Technicolor to Paris's still predominately neutral-color fashion landscape. You'll find groovy retro clubwear and chunky platform shoes as well as sporty casual labels like Brittany Kana Beach. Nothing is outrageously expensive, not much is *noir,* and the basement Internet café is a great place for a coffee break.

VINTAGE CLOTHING

Around Les Halles you'll find fun and trashy used clothes; try **rue St-Martin** and **rue St-Merri. Rue de la Grande-Truanderie** is home to the best collection of 50F Hawaiian shirts in all of Paris. The lower part of **rue St-Denis** has a slew of stores selling used leather jackets. You can also try the flea markets (*see* Markets, *below*) or the **Salvation Army** (12 rue Cantagrel, 13e, tel. 01–43–83–54–40, RER Blvd. Masséna); it's not necessarily the height of fashion, but it's cheap and you never know what you'll find—it's also a Le Corbusier masterpiece.

GIFTS AND HOUSEWARES

Rue de Paradis (10e, métro Gare de l'Est) is lined with discount china and crystal showrooms. You'll find serious savings on fine Limoges porcelain—hardcore collectors come armed with style numbers, pocket calculators, and lists of comparison prices. Arts-Céramiques (No. 15) has special sales in its back room. La Tisanière (No. 21) sells china seconds.

Argenterie des Francs-Bourgeois (17 rue des Francs-Bourgeois, 4e, tel. 01–42–72–04–00, métro St-Paul), a quirky secondhand shop, sells old-fashioned silver settings from estates and grand hotels by the kilo. You can pick up a beautiful bracelet fashioned from a Victorian silver spoon or fork for under 100F.

La Vaissellerie (80 blvd. Haussmann, 8e, tel. 01–45–22–32–47, métro Havre-Caumartin; 85 rue de Rennes, 6e, tel. 01–42–22–61–49, métro Rennes; 92 rue St-Antoine, 4e, tel. 01–42–72–76–66, métro St-Paul) is chock-a-block with the sort of ingenious kitchen gadgets that the French love, priced below what you would pay for such creativity back home.

PHARMACIES

While American drugstores (and British chemists) stock everything from vitamins to pulp novels to batteries, French pharmacies are meccas for quality skin and hair care. Favorite finds include Roger & Gallet perfumed bath foams and shower gels, the Klorane plant-based line of shampoos, and Phyto 7, a leave-in hair moisturizer that jetsetting models and actresses swear by. You'll find aspirin and other medicines, adhesive bandages, and saline solution for contact lenses (*solution rinçage*) in pharmacies rather than in supermarkets.

Some with English-speaking staff include **Pharmacie Dérhy** (84 av. des Champs-Elysées, 8e, tel. 01–45–62–02–41, métro Georges V), open 24 hours a day, 365 days a year; **Pharmacie Anglo-Américaine** (6 rue Castiglione, 1er, tel. 01–42–60–72–96, métro Palais-Royal), stocking foreign medicines and open daily 9–7:30; and **Pharmacie Européenne de la Place Clichy** (6 pl. Clichy, 9e, tel. 01–48–74–65–18, métro Place Clichy), open 24 hours a day, seven days a week.

RECORDS, CDS, AND CASSETTES

Record shops may abound in Paris, but music doesn't come cheap: Expect a new CD to run you 100F minimum. If you can afford it, some branches of **FNAC** (*see* Bookstores, *above*) sell new music plus concert tickets. The **Virgin Megastore** (52–60 av. des Champs-Elysées, 8e, tel. 01–49–53–50–00, métro Franklin-D.-Roosevelt; Carrousel du Louvre mall, 99 rue de Rivoli, 1er, tel. 01–49–53–52–90, métro Palais-Royal) is just that—a megalith with a megaselection, a million listening stations, and some great prices on new albums. Concert tickets are sold at the Virgin *billeterie* (ticket counter). If you're looking for alternative music and lesser-known bands that FNAC ignores, go to the Carrousel du Louvre location.

ALTERNATIVE AND PUNK

Parallèles (47 rue St-Honoré, 1er, tel. 01–42–33–62–70, métro Châtelet) attracts a hip crowd for its good selection of used indie CDs (25F and up). New CDs start at 65F. They've also got vinyl and a big collection of rock anthologies (many in English).

Rough Trade (30 rue de Charonne, 11e, tel. 01–40–21–61–62, métro Ledru-Rollin or Bastille) primarily sells imports, including indie, techno, house, and ambient music. This is the first place to look for information on bands passing through Paris—and to buy tickets. You can listen before you buy, and the staff is very helpful (and often speaks English).

Le Silence de la Rue (8 rue de la Fontaine-du-But, 18e, tel. 01–42–55–61–34, métro Lamarck-Caulaincourt) is a tiny shop whose flaming red exterior heralds the latest deals in indie, garage, punk, noise, and all things alternative. There's a big vinyl collection, and you can ask to hear something before buying, provided it's not on sale.

JAZZ AND WORLD MUSIC

Paris Jazz Corner (5 rue de Navarre, 5e, tel. 01–43–36–78–92, métro Monge) is staffed by people who know all about the jazz, blues, and world music they have on vinyl and CD, both new (80F–100F) and used (25F–50F). For African music and salsa, try the specialty record stores **Afric' Music** (3 rue des Plantes, 14e, tel. 01–45–42–43–52, métro Alésia) or **Anvers Musique** (35 blvd. de Rochechouart, 9e, tel. 01–42–80–18–56, métro Barbès-Rochechouart).

Crocodisc (40–42 rue des Ecoles, 5e, tel. 01–43–54–33–22, métro Maubert-Mutualité) is a knowledgable dealer trading in vinyl, cassettes, and CDs. At No. 42, look for international rock; No. 40 is given over to funk, dance, techno, and World Music.

CrocoJazz (64 rue de la Montagne-Ste-Geneviève, 5e, tel. 01–46–34–78–38, métro Maubert-Mutualité) is a great resource for secondhand jazz, blues, Cajun, and gospel. Count on 70F–120F for CDs, 40F for cassettes (or three for 100F).

WINE AND CHOCOLATE

To come to France and not purchase a bottle of wine or a piece of fine chocolate is a punishable offense. Good (if not famous) wines can be found for as little as 14F at the local supermarket, or turn to **Nicolas,** Paris's favorite purveyor of reliable, inexpensive wines. There's a branch on seemingly every street corner.

A la Mère de Famille (35 rue du Faubourg-Montmartre, 9e, tel. 01–47–70–83–69, métro Cadet) is an enchanting shop well versed in mouthwatering chocolates and old-fashioned bonbons, sugar candy, and more.

Le Cave Augé (116 blvd. Haussmann, 8e, tel. 01–45–22–16–97, métro St-Augustin), circa 1850, is one of the best wine shops in Paris. Ask the congenial, English-speaking owner, Marc Sibard, to recommend a good, inexpensive bottle. He won't disappoint.

Juveniles (47 rue de Richelieu, 1er, tel. 01–42–97–46–49, métro Palais Royal–Musée du Louvre), a restaurant–cum–wine-bar-cum–wine shop, has a British owner and many French fans. Not only can you try a dozen vintages by the glass (12F–40F), but you can buy wines from around the world for exceptional prices.

La Maison du Chocolat (52 rue François 1er, 8e, tel. 01–47–23–38–25, métro Franklin-D.-Roosevelt; 8 bd. de la Madeleine, 9e, tel. 01–47–42–86–52, métro Madeleine; 225 rue du Faubourg St-Honoré, 8e, tel. 01–42–27–39–44, métro Ternes) is heaven for cocoa purists. Take home chocolates, ice cream, and other treats, or meet a friend in the tearoom on rue François 1er for sinfully rich hot chocolates and chocolate-mousse frappés.

MARKETS

Parisian *marchés aux puces* (flea markets) sell old treasures, vintage clothing, handmade fashions, shoes, appliances, and (you will soon discover) a lot of junk. Don't ever pay the asking price, and keep haggling, or you'll wonder why you paid 600F for a pair of pink plastic shoes. Keep a close eye (and firm hand) on your wallet; pickpockets thrive in the crowded conditions.

Paris also has several specialized outdoor markets, including a **stamp market** at the corner of avenue de Marigny and avenue Gabriel (8e, métro Champs-Elysées–Clemenceau) on Thursdays, Saturdays, and Sundays. Three **flower markets** brighten the city streets Tuesday–Sunday from 8 AM until about 7; the main one, at **place Louis-Lépine** (4e, métro Cité) on the Ile de la Cité, turns into a bird and pet market on Sundays; the markets at **place de la Madeleine** (8e, métro Madeleine) and **place des Ternes** (8e, métro Ternes) stick to flowers and such. For information about outdoor **food markets,** *see* Chapter 4.

MARCHE AUX PUCES ST-OUEN

This sprawling flea market on Paris's northern boundary (18e, métro Porte de Clignancourt) still attracts crowds on weekends and Monday, even though its prices aren't as low as they used to be. You can find used clothing and cheap, junky clothing, as well as excellent finds in the bins of old prints and vintage advertisements. The little shops that mushroom around the various markets tend to deal in vintage leather, African crafts, and records. For lunch, stop for mussels and fries in one of the rough-and-ready cafés.

MARCHE AUX PUCES MONTREUIL

This market (20e, métro Porte de Montreuil) is smaller and funkier than St-Ouen. Asian and African trinkets abound but, above all, it is best for secondhand and vintage clothing. It's open all weekend, but less crowded on Monday mornings.

7 ILE-DE-FRANCE

UPDATED BY SIMON HEWITT

nless you were born in a café, there comes a point when you need a short escape from the city. With its rural pace, peaceful villages, and impressive châteaux, the Ile-de-France is an ideal getaway (and you can easily zip back to Paris if you need an urban fix). The Ile-de-France completely surrounds Paris, so it's fairly easy to spend a morning in a Paris museum and an afternoon walking through the Forest of Fontainebleau, gawking at the cathedral at Chartres, or biking in Compiègne. At the other end of the spectrum are the region's hardcore tourist sites: The palace at Versailles, the controversial Disneyland Paris, and Parc Astérix, all of which have their share of outrageous prices, heavy crowds, and bad food.

Although not exactly an *île* (island), the Ile-de-France is cordoned off from the rest of the country by three rivers: the Seine, the Marne, and the Oise. These and the region's many brooks and streams have long stood to defend the area and keep it lush, two factors that once attracted royalty with a get-away-from-the-masses mind-set. Forests stocked with easily catchable animals were also a big draw, enticing rich hunters who, presumably, needed all the help they could get. Today, the region's châteaux stand as monuments to the wealth, power, and aim of the French monarchy.

On summer weekends, Parisians flock to the forests and small towns of the Ile-de-France, while tourists make their way to its châteaux and palaces, driving prices for food and lodging turret-high. The only way to eat without plunking down serious cash is to picnic; luckily, this is one of the best ways to enjoy the countryside, and markets are plentiful. Budget lodging is even easier, thanks either to youth hostels (in towns like Chartres, Vernon, and Compiègne) or a good supply of inexpensive hotels. As a general rule, well-touristed towns make their *fermeture hebdomadaire* (weekly closing) on Tuesday, so museums and markets may be closed—call ahead if in doubt.

VERSAILLES

Louis XIII originally built the château in Versailles as a rustic hunting lodge in 1631, but when Louis "Sun King" XIV converted it from a weekend retreat to the headquarters of his government, he didn't cut any corners. Architect Louis Le Vau restored and added to the original lodge, while Charles Le Brun handled the interior decoration. Jules Hardouin-Mansart later remodeled the whole thing, expanding on Le Vau's improvements. They began in 1661 and spent the next 50 years designing everything his royal acquis-itiveness could want, including a throne room dedicated to Apollo, the king's mythological hero. Jacques-Ange Gabriel later added an opera house so Louis XV could be entertained at home without troubling himself to mingle with the common folk. Reconstruction efforts aimed at bringing the entire estate back to how it looked when the Sun King lived here will continue for the next couple of decades; billboards provide updates on what's currently being worked on.

Your best strategy at Versailles is to look beyond the overflowing trash bins and cigarette-butt-littered cobblestones and imagine what life was like here during the two centuries that it served as the home of French royalty. Picture France's overdressed nobility promenading through the gardens plotting dan-gerous liaisons, perhaps fawning over the king and queen in the dazzling **Galerie des Glaces** (Hall of Mirrors). Imagine Louis XVI and Marie-Antoinette entertaining in the **Grands Appartements,** decorated with sumptuous marble, gilded bronzes, and ceiling paintings of mythological figures. Now imagine the day in 1789 when a revolutionary mob marched the 24 km (15 mi) from Paris to Versailles to protest the bread shortage, only to find Louis lounging in this pleasure palace. No wonder they forced the king to leave Versailles and go to Paris so they could keep an eye on him.

BASICS

There are three **Offices de Tourisme** locations in Versailles. The branch (tel. 01–39–53–31–63) opposite the Gare Rive Gauche train station in Les Manèges, a shopping mall, is closed on Mondays. Another office (tel. 01–39–50–36–22), just north of the château next to the auto entrance at 7 rue des Réservoirs, is closed on Sundays. May through September, a third, constantly crowded office sets up Tuesday–Sunday at the château's main gate. All three locations have loads of brochures and helpful English-speaking employees, and all are open until around 6 PM.

Rent bikes in Petite Venise, at the head of the Grand Canal, directly behind the château. Bikes cost 30F an hour, and you must leave an ID as a deposit. The dirt trails lead you into the forest or to the farthest end of the canal.

COMING AND GOING

The best way to reach the Château de Versailles from Paris is via the **yellow RER Line C** to Ver-sailles–Rive Gauche (35 minutes, 13F). Otherwise, frequent SNCF trains from Paris's Gare Montpar-nasse stop at Gare des Chantiers (rue des Etats-Généraux) south of the château (13–27 minutes, 13F); trains from Paris's Gare St-Lazare head via La Défense to the Gare Rive Droite (35 minutes, 17F50), close to the town museum and the market halls on place du Marché de Notre-Dame. All three stations are within walking distance of the château.

FOOD

Picnicking is the cheapest and easiest way to eat here. If you don't bring your own food, be prepared to work up an appetite walking to the nearest sandwich shop **Classe Croûte,** in the Les Manèges shopping mall just across from the Gare Rive Gauche; the decent sandwiches cost 18F–30F. Otherwise, there's a **Monoprix** supermarket on the corner of avenue de l'Europe and avenue de St-Cloud, five minutes to your right as you exit the Gare Rive Gauche. If you're not hot on the picnic idea, try one of the small restaurants behind place du Marché-Notre-Dame (about 200 yards on from Monoprix), or one of the brasseries overlooking the place d'Armes in front of the château. Of course, the farther you get from the château, the better luck you'll have finding something that isn't priced for tourists with a capital T. If you have time, walk five blocks southeast of the château to the St-Louis district (beyond the cathedral) and stand in line with the locals for a freshly made sandwich (12F–20F) at **Traiteur Philippe Joly** (62 rue d'Anjou, tel. 01–39–50–28–46).

WORTH SEEING

It's hard to tell which is larger—the tremendous château that housed Louis XIV and 20,000 of his courtiers, or the line of 20,000 visitors standing in front of it. You may be able to avoid the hour-and-a-half wait for a tour if you arrive here at 9 AM sharp, when the château opens. The hard part is figuring out where you're supposed to go once you arrive: There are different lines depending on tour, physical ability, and group status. Frequent guided tours in English visit the private royal apartments. More detailed hour-long tours (also in English) explore the opera house or Marie-Antoinette's private parlors; call the day before to check times. The opera house is especially interesting because the architect, wanting the acoustics of a violin, built the hall entirely of wood, and then had it all painted to resemble

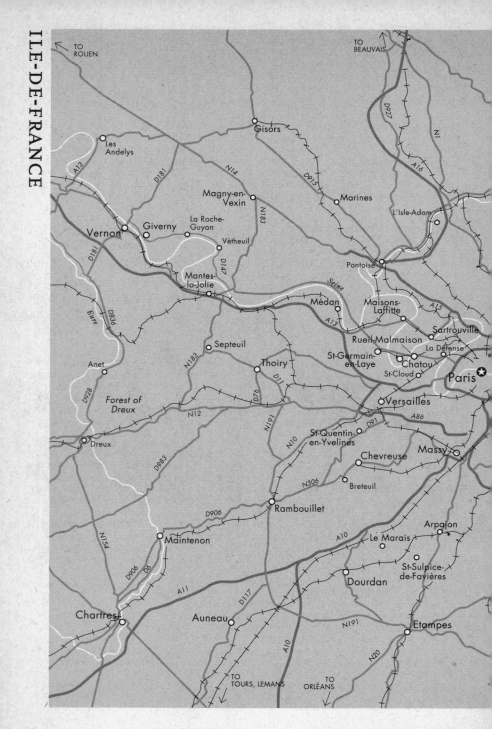

ILE-DE-FRANCE

TO
ROUEN

TO
BEAUVAIS

D927

N1

A16

Gisors

Les
Andelys

A13

D181

N14

D915

Magny-en-
Vexin

Marines

L'Isle-Adam

Giverny

La Roche-
Guyon

N183

Vernon

Vétheuil

D181

D147

Pontoise

Mantes-
la-Jolie

Seine

Médan

Maisons-
Laffitte

A15

D836

Eure

A13

Rueil-Malmaison

Sartrouville

Septeuil

N183

Thoiry

La Défense

St-Germain-
en-Laye

Chatou

Anet

D928

D76

D11

St-Cloud

Paris ★

Forest of
Dreux

N12

Versailles

A86

Dreux

N191

D91

D983

N10

St-Quentin-
en-Yvelines

Massy

Chevreuse

N306

Breteuil

Rambouillet

D906

Arpajon

Maintenon

A10

Le Marais

St-Sulpice-
de-Favières

N154

D906

D6

Dourdan

A11

Chartres

D117

Auneau

N191

Etampes

A10

N20

TO
TOURS, LEMANS

TO
ORLÉANS

162

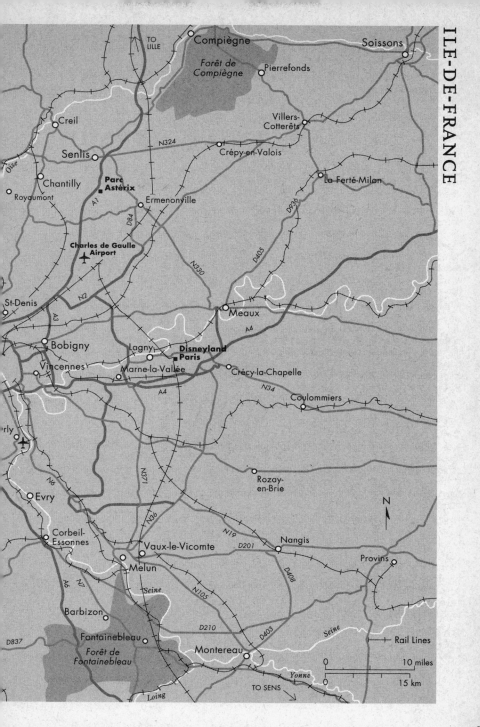

TO LILLE

Compiègne

Soissons

Forêt de Compiègne

Pierrefonds

Creil

Villers-Cotterêts

N324

Crépy-en-Valois

Senlis

La Ferté-Milon

Chantilly

Parc Astérix

Royaumont

A1

Ermenonville

D936

D84

Charles de Gaulle Airport

N330

D405

St-Denis

N2

A3

Meaux

A4

Bobigny

Lagny

Disneyland Paris

Vincennes

Marne-la-Vallée

Crécy-la-Chapelle

A4

N34

Coulommiers

rly

N6

N371

Rozay-en-Brie

N

Evry

N36

Corbeil-Essonnes

N19

Nangis

Vaux-le-Vicomte

D201

Provins

A6

N7

Melun

D408

Seine

N105

Barbizon

D210

D403

Seine

Rail Lines

D837

Fontainebleau

Montereau

0   10 miles

Forêt de Fontainebleau

Yonne

0   15 km

Loing

TO SENS

marble. You can go through a few rooms, including the Hall of Mirrors, without a tour—by means of yet another line. To figure out the system, pick up a brochure at the information tent at the gates of the château, or consult the information desk at the ticket center. *Tel. 01–30–84–76–18. Admission 45F, 35F Sun. Tours 25F–50F. Open Tues.–Sun. 9–6:30 (Oct.–Apr. until 5:30).*

If you don't feel like hassling with crowds and lines, or if you don't have any money left but still want to say that you've been to Versailles, check out the free **gardens.** This is where you'll find Versailles's hundreds of famous fountains. If you're wondering why they don't work—well, they do, but you'll have to come on a Sunday and shell out 25F to see them in action. For a real spectacle, come on one of several Saturdays in summer for the **Fêtes de Nuit,** when the fountains come to life with music and fireworks. Ask at a tourist office for dates and ticket prices (70F–185F). Otherwise, lose the tourists huddled around the fountains and discover 250 acres of gardens a little further away from the château. Tourist brochures ask that you not picnic on the lawns, but they don't say anything about the grottoes, groves, and grassy areas scattered throughout the woods. Chances are good that you won't run into a gendarme if you stay away from the main attractions. *Gardens open daily 7–sunset, weather permitting.*

A guide written by Louis XIV himself, *Manière de montrer les jardins de Versailles* (How to Show the Versailles Gardens), is being consulted as the gardens are returned to their Sun King days. Le Nôtre's gardens are brimming with walkways, pools, viewpoints, woods, velvet lawns, a **Colonnade** of 24 marble columns, an **Orangery** and tons of statuary. Perhaps most impressive are sculpture groupings emerging from two pools: the **Bassin de Neptune** (Neptune's Basin) sea god with dragons and cherubs and the **Bassin d'Apollo** (Apollo's Basin) sun god in his chariot emerging amid sea monsters to bring light to the world. Beyond the Apollo Basin is the **Grand Canal,** which Louis XIV equipped with brightly colored gondolas. Today a boat ride down it costs 25F.

In the northwest corner of the gardens are the smaller châteaux, the **Grand Trianon** and the **Petit Trianon,** used as guest houses for everyone from Napoléon I to Richard Nixon. Although you can go inside, the visit is anticlimactic if you've just toured the big château. Behind the Petit Trianon is the **Hameau de la Reine** (Queen's Village), a collection of cottages where Marie-Antoinette came to play peasant among the real-life versions who were recruited to fill her wonderland. You can reach this corner of the gardens on a tram (29F) that leaves every 35 minutes from the north side of the château, but walking is cheaper. *Admission: Grand Trianon 25F, 15F Sun.; Petit Trianon 15F, 10F Sun. Both open May–Sept., daily 10–6:30; Oct.–Apr., Tues.–Fri. 9–12:30 and 2–5:30, weekends 10–5:30.*

CHARTRES

Make your way to Chartres to see the **Notre-Dame de Chartres** cathedral and you will be following in the footsteps of religious pilgrims over 1,000 years ago: In the late 9th century, King Charles the Bald presented Chartres with the *sacra camisia* (sacred tunic) of the Virgin Mary, turning the city into a hot spot for the Christian faithful. The magnificent Gothic cathedral here was built in the 12th and 13th centuries, in appreciation of the miraculously unsinged state of Mary's tunic after the original church burned to the ground in 1194.

Like the cathedral, the old part of town has been preserved in its cloak of mellowing old stone. The signposted **route touristique** behind the cathedral takes you along cobblestone streets past riverbanks dotted with old wash houses, stone buildings, and a bridge all but demolished by World War II bombing. But stray from the path and you'll be slapped by modern apartment buildings and whizzing traffic. (Sometimes old pieces of buildings have been reworked into new ones—keep an eye out to see through the modern exterior and into the past.) If you prefer a ride to walking, take the **Promotrain** (30F), which passes by all of Chartres's major sights and leaves from place de la Cathédrale mid-March–October between 10 and 7. However, the cathedral is most striking after you've wandered around the town's narrow passages and then suddenly come upon it looming above.

BASICS

The **Office de Tourisme** is well stocked with information about the cathedral, town, and special events in the region. Hotel reservations cost 10F. *Pl. de la Cathédrale, tel. 02–37–21–50–00. Open weekdays 9:30–6:30, Sat. 9:30–6, Sun. 10:30–12:30 and 2:30–5:30.*

COMING AND GOING

Hourly trains make the 50- to 70-minute, 140F round-trip from Paris's Gare Montparnasse to Chartres's **train station** (pl. Pierre Sémard, tel. 02–37–28–50–50), which puts you within walking distance of the cathedral; a map in the station shows you exactly where to go. You can check your bags from 8 AM to 7:30 PM for an extortionate 20F, or put them in equally expensive lockers.

WHERE TO SLEEP

The **Auberge de Jeunesse** is the only affordable place to crash in Chartres. Its ugly exterior doesn't reflect the clean, comfortable, quiet interior. Each room has two to eight beds, a sink, and plenty of storage space. The hostel is toward the bottom of the old town, across the river from the cathedral— a well-marked 20-minute walk from the train station or a five-minute trip on Bus 3. Beds are 70F, including breakfast; sheets are 16F. *23 av. Neigre, tel. 02–37–34–27–64, fax 02–37–35–75–85. 70 beds. Reception open noon–10. Check-in from 3 PM. Curfew 11:30 PM. Laundry. Closed last 3 wks in Dec.*

FOOD

The cheapest area to eat is the old town south of the cathedral—**rue Noël-Ballay, rue du Cygne,** and **rue du Bois-Merrain-Marceau** are good bets for grocery stores and inexpensive restaurants. **Feu Follet** (21 pl. du Cygne, tel. 02–37–21–24–06) is the place for cheap hamburgers (12F) and crepes. For more substantial meals, head for the restaurants on **rue de Porte Morard. Au P'tit Morard** (25 rue de la Porte-Morard, tel. 02–37–34–15–89) has 80F and 100F menus. Or explore narrow **rue au Lait** near the cathedral. **Le Caveau de la Cathérale** (12 rue au Lait, tel. 02–37–34–91–64) has a vaulted 12th-century ceiling and a three-course lunch menu for 60F. **Le Buisson Ardent** (10 rue au Lait, tel. 02–37–34–04–66) serves a more sophisticated 120F menu (including quail salad) in its second-floor, wood-beamed dining room.

WORTH SEEING

NOTRE-DAME DE CHARTRES • Notre-Dame de Chartres cathedral has over 21,500 square feet of glass, including 38-foot-high stained-glass windows, some of which date from 1210. The oldest window is *Notre Dame de la Belle Verrière* (Our Lady of the Beautiful Window), in the south choir. Note the smaller windows depicting the guilds that sponsored the artwork—a good indication of commercial enterprise in the so-called Dark Ages. Also noteworthy are the mismatched towers, the result of lightning striking the north tower in the 16th century, decapitating its spire. Don't spend all your time looking up, though; the black and white pattern on the floor of the nave is one of the few to have survived from the Middle Ages. The faithful were expected to travel along its entire length (nearly 1,000 feet) on their knees. Malcolm Miller, who looks like he stepped right out of an Addams Family episode, gives fabulous tours in English daily at noon and 2:45 PM, providing information on the narrative stained glass and his own travels for 30F. Otherwise, you can head out the cathedral's south door to the crypt across the street and rent a Walkman and a (vastly inferior) tape-recorded tour in English (30F). For an additional 20F that might be better spent elsewhere, you can climb the north tower for a view of the city. Organ recitals are given July–October on Sunday at 4:45 PM free of charge, though definitely not free of crowds. Show up early to stake out a seat. *Open daily 7:30–7:30.*

CENTRE INTERNATIONAL DU VITRAIL • The International Stained Glass Center has temporary exhibits of stained-glass works from the Middle Ages to the present. The exhibition shop in the same complex has beautiful pictures and gift items of old and new glass works. Admission to the shop is free, but that doesn't mean you'll escape with your wallet unscathed. *5 rue du Cardinal-Pie, tel. 02–37–21–65–72. Admission 20F. Open daily 9:30–12:30 and 1:30–6 (weekends from 10).*

MUSÉE DES BEAUX-ARTS • The Fine Arts Museum, behind the cathedral, is in the former bishop's palace. The collection of drawings, tapestries, and archaeological finds will be interesting only to those who have a real fascination with Chartres's history. If anything interesting is unearthed during the excavation of the medieval convent in front of the cathedral, the museum may get a needed infusion of artifacts. Check the sign in front of the museum to see if the changing contemporary exhibit is truly worth 20F. *29 cloître Notre-Dame, tel. 02–37–36–41–39. Open Apr.–Oct., Wed.–Mon. 10–1 and 2–6; Nov.–Mar., Wed.–Mon. 10–noon and 2–5, Sun. 2–5.*

GIVERNY

From 1883 until his death in 1926, Claude Monet painted some of his most famous works in (and of) the gardens at Giverny, 80 km (50 mi) northwest of Paris. The gardens themselves are a work of art that Monet spent several years perfecting before he began re-creating them on canvas. He planted colorful checkerboard gardens, installed a water lily pond, put up a Japanese bridge, and finally decorated the interior of his house to match it all. Ultimately, he would paint the same scene in different seasons, weather conditions, and times of day, thus developing innovative techniques for capturing light, water, and reflections on canvas.

The 156F round-trip train-and-bus ride (the train to Vernon and then the local bus) may sound extravagant for a day trip, but it's worth it if you're a fan of impressionism. For the full effect, come midweek in the morning to avoid the crush. The colors radiate best on sunny days, especially in late spring. Don't limit yourself to the gardens, though; Monet's large collection of Japanese prints, a great source of inspiration to French impressionists, cover the walls of his house and are worth seeing if the crowds have not reached asphyxiating numbers. Otherwise, the few rooms are sparsely furnished and decorated only with Monet reproductions and his family's (limited) artistic efforts. *Tel. 02–32–51–28–21. Admission: gardens 25F; gardens and house 35F. Open Apr.–Oct., Tues.–Sun. 10–6.*

If you want to see "real" paintings, walk down the street to the **Musée Américain,** with its excellent collection of American impressionist works influenced by Monet. Founded in 1992, the museum handsomely houses Sargents and Cassatts as well as lesser-known painters, along with an expensive restaurant and a beautiful garden "quoting" some of Monet's plant combinations. It makes an elegant respite from the hordes up the street. *99 rue Claude-Monet, tel. 02–32–51–94–65. Admission 35F. Open Apr.–Oct., Tues.–Sun. 10–6.*

BASICS

The **Office de Tourisme** near the church in nearby Vernon has brochures on Monet's time at Giverny. There's enough information at the train station if you're just planning a short trip, but if you want to go hiking or biking in the surrounding forest, be sure to stop at the office for trail maps. *36 rue Carnot, tel. 02–32–51–39–60. Open Tues.–Sat. 9:30–noon and 2:30–6:30, Sun. and Mon. 10–noon.*

COMING AND GOING

Trains leave every couple of hours from Paris's Gare St-Lazare for the 50-minute, 66F ride to Vernon; buses meet the trains and whisk you away to Giverny for 12F more. The last bus back to Vernon from Giverny leaves around 5 PM, so check with the driver before you settle down for a late afternoon pastis. If you have the time and energy, the 6-km (3½-mi) stretch from Vernon to Giverny is nice and flat with a slight incline at the end: If you want a bike for the ride to Giverny and around town, rent one at the train station in Vernon for 55F a day (plus a 1,000F or credit-card deposit); bikes must be back by 8:30 PM. From the train station, walk (or bike) through town along rue d'Albuféra to the river, cross the bridge, and hang a right on the road to Giverny; the footpath is off to the left of the main road. Food is ridiculously expensive in Giverny itself, so bring a picnic from Paris or stock up at the numerous grocers and patisseries lining rue d'Albuféra.

WHERE TO SLEEP

If you decide that Giverny deserves more than a day trip, you can try the only hotel there—**La Musardière** (123 rue Claude-Monet, tel. 02–32–21–03–18). In a converted mansion near Monet's house, this hotel has a garden, a veranda, and spacious rooms for 300F–350F. There are also two *chambres d'hôte* (bed-and-breakfasts) in Giverny: **Marie-Claire Boscher's** (1 rue Colombier, tel. 02–32–51–39–70) for 240F a night, and **Eric Carrière's** (6 rue Juifs, tel. 02–32–51–02–96) for 260F–300F a night. Book at least 6 weeks ahead in summer. There's another chambre d'hôte by the river in nearby Vernon; **Le Moulin St-Jean** (rue Pierre-Bonard, tel. 02–32–51–59–49) looks out over a pretty garden and is particularly suitable for families or a group of friends. A room for four costs 440F, including a copious breakfast.

HOSTEL • Also in Vernon is the Auberge de Jeunesse, a clean, spacious hostel. A bed is 50F a night, sheets are 18F, and breakfast is 20F. The sprightly man who runs the place advises you on how best to spend your time in Giverny. The big garden doesn't quite rival Monet's, but it connects the hostel to a great 20-site campground with kitchen and laundry facilities and hot showers, all for 30F a night. Reservations are advised for all the facilities. *28 av. de l'Ile-de-France, tel. 02–32–51–66–48. From Vernon train station, walk 2 km (1¼ mi) on road marked PARIS. 16 beds. Reception open 8–10 and 6:30–8:30.*

OUTDOOR ACTIVITIES

The rolling hills and tree-lined river meandering between Vernon and Giverny have many trails that are ideal for hiking and biking. About 20 trails climb up hills or run alongside the shady river; to find the best of them, pick up the hiking guide from the tourist office. You can also get information about *gîtes d'é-tape* (rural dorms) and chambres d'hôte (*see above*) in the area. If you plan to bike the rougher trails, you'll need a *VTT* (mountain bike); **Martin Cycles** in Vernon (84 rue Carnôt, tel. 02–32–21–24–08) rents them for 100F a day, 150F for Saturday through Monday (4,000F or credit-card deposit required, reservation recommended).

CHANTILLY

An impressive Renaissance castle, immense stables, and a famous horse-racing track combine to make this quaint, tranquil little town 45 km (30 mi) north of Paris worth a visit. Hop off the train, ponder the sights, refuel at a café, and you'll be rested and ready to leave by early evening. Which is a good thing, since there aren't many cheap places to sleep.

If spending the day at the track is your cup of tea, note that Chantilly's only official horse races are held in June, with the major international events on the first and second Sundays and smaller races on various weekdays. However, it's not uncommon to see low-key races throughout the year, so don't be deterred from coming in spring or fall. You can enter the stands on the far side of the racing oval for 40F and bet the rest of your cash on a sure thing. Call the **S.E.C.F.** (tel. 03–49–10–20–39), which organizes the international events, for race information and schedules. Save yourself the racetrack admission by sitting on the grass next to the bleachers.

The Château de Chantilly had a reputation for fine cuisine in the 17th century and today remains the eponym for fresh whipped cream. Anything you order "à la chantilly" will come with the stuff.

BASICS

The **Office de Tourisme** is run by a bunch of locals who know the area like the back of their hand. They hand out brochures on horse races and the different combinations of tickets you can buy for the museums, château, and park. It also has the most confusing hours in all of France. *23 av. Maréchal Joffre, tel. 03–44–57–08–58. Open May–Sept., Mon. and Wed.–Sat. 9–12:30 and 2:15–6:15, Sun. 9–12:30; Oct.–Apr., Mon. and Wed.–Sat. 9–12:30 and 2:15–6:15 (Nov.–Feb., Sat. until 5:15).*

COMING AND GOING

You can reach Chantilly from Paris's Gare du Nord on RER Line D or on the regular train (both 40 minutes, 41F). From Chantilly's train station, head straight down rue des Otages, hang a shallow left when it ends, and head back through the wooded trails; a beautiful 15-minute walk across a field takes you to the stables. If there are races going on, you'll have to scoot around the outskirts of the field. Otherwise, you can just walk straight across (provided no one too official is watching). If you want to bus it, hop on any town bus passing in front of the station.

WHERE TO SLEEP AND EAT

The cheapest hotel in Chantilly is the **Lion d'Or** (44 rue du Connétable, tel. 03–44–57–03–19) where rooms (without toilets) start at 160F. The grocery store **Kandi** (55 rue du Connétable, tel. 03–44–57–01–47) has all you need for snacks on the lawns. **A la Renommée** (9 rue de Paris, tel. 03–44–57–01–13), a charcuterie near the tourist office, will custom-make sandwiches for 20F. Surprisingly, the snack carts at the entrance of the château won't completely rip you off. Restaurants around town tend to be pricey and not terribly exciting (serving your basic 90F menu or 40F salad). One exception is **La Calèche** (3 av. du Maréchal-Joffre, tel. 03–44–57–02–55), near many of the fancier restaurants but with a tasty plat du jour for 52F. Most town eateries also offer expensive desserts topped with mounds of *chantilly* (whipped cream).

WORTH SEEING

Chantilly's château came first and the stables and racetrack later, but older isn't always better—even in France. The spectacular stables, the **Grandes Ecuries,** which hold the **Musée Vivant du Cheval** (Living Museum of the Horse), house an elite cadre of racehorses in luxury (note the arched, molded ceilings).

Surprisingly, the stables aren't just for show; the horses in them are actual racehorses. In the rooms around the training courtyard is a huge collection of jockey uniforms, harnesses, bits, biological diagrams—everything imaginable to do with horses. The museum visit includes a casual show-off session for the horses. On Sunday afternoons at 3:15 and 4:45 the show goes upscale with costumes, music, and special tricks; admission, however, doubles. *Tel. 03–44–57–13–13. Admission 50F. Open Apr. and Sept.–Oct., Wed.–Mon. 10:30–5:30; May–June, daily 10:30–5:30; July–Aug., Wed.–Mon. 10:30–5:30, Tues. 2–5:30; Nov.–Mar., Wed.–Mon. 2–4:30, weekends and holidays until 5:30; closed 1st 2 wks of Dec.*

A visit to the actual château is just icing on the cake. Behind the stables and totally surrounded by water, the château contains a so-so collection of furniture and clothes, including Napoléon's hat. The **Musée Condé,** though, displays outstanding paintings by Raphael, Watteau, Ingres, and Corot, plus local porcelain and the *Très Riches Heures du Duc de Berry,* one of the most celebrated medieval illuminated manuscripts. Admission to the museum is included with château entrance, so you can judge for yourself whether it lives up to its self-styled billing as one of the "most beautiful museums in France." *Tel. 03–44–54–04–02. Admission 40F. Open Mar.–Oct., Wed.–Mon. 10–6; Nov.–Feb., Wed.–Mon. 10:30–12:45 and 2–5.*

Versailles landscape architect André Le Nôtre also created Chantilly's gardens. They stretch from either side of the grandiose fountains, encompassing bridge-linked canals, lily ponds, and clearings in manicured woods. Each section of the garden represents a period of history from the 17th to 19th century: **Le Jardin Français** (the French Garden), laid out in the 1600s, is the most formal and full of flowers; **Le Petit Parc** (the Little Park) and **Le Hameau** (the Hamlet), which inspired similar gardens at Versailles, are from the 18th century; and **Le Jardin Anglais** (the English Garden) is from the 19th century. As usual, you're not supposed to hang out on the grass of the formal gardens, but you're welcome to picnic on the lawns in front of the château. *Admission 18F, free with château visit. Open 10 AM–dusk when the château is open.*

CHEAP THRILLS

L'Aérophile is the world's largest helium balloon, and it hovers 450 feet in the air, providing fantastic views of Chantilly's château, stables, and gardens, not to mention neighboring towns and, on clear days, the Eiffel Tower. The balloon is attached to a cable right next to Le Hameau in the gardens, so you don't exactly feel as free as a bird, but a good breeze can make it pretty exciting. Real hot-air balloon rides cost over 1,200F, so enjoy the cable. *Admission 50F (after you've paid the 18F park fee). Open Apr.–Nov., weekdays 2–7, weekends 10–7.*

NEAR CHANTILLY

SENLIS

Just a short bus ride from Chantilly, the tiny, medieval, cobblestone passageways of well-preserved Senlis are worth a visit. Based on the Roman town of Augustomagus founded in AD 8, the village found God in the 4th century and was home to some of the first kings in France thereafter. Access to the park, where you can wander through the mossy ruins of the old château, is a mere 5F. Don't confuse this with the slightly bloodthirsty **Musée de la Venerie** (Hunting Museum, 14F), inside the park; hourly tours take you through three floors of hunting trophies, hunting scenes, and hunting costumes, all to the blare of hunting horns. The **Rendez-vous de Septembre,** held in odd-numbered years, turns the old town totally pedestrian and totally touristed (call ahead to avoid the exact weekend in September) as revelers eat, drink, listen to music, and parade around.

BASICS • Buses meet almost all trains to Chantilly for the 20-minute ride to Senlis's defunct brickwork train station (15F). The **Office de Tourisme** (pl. du Parvis-Notre-Dame, tel. 03–44–53–06–40) has plenty of information about Senlis and the surrounding area. *Open Wed.–Mon. 10–noon and 2:15–6:15; closed mid-Dec.–late Jan.*

WHERE TO SLEEP AND EAT • Senlis caters to well-heeled French tourists, so the cheapest hotel is the **Hôtel du Nord** (110 rue de la République, tel. 03–44–53–01–16), which gets you pretty and clean Munchkin-size rooms for 225F. A fun place for dinner is **Le Gril des Barbares** (19 rue de Châtel, tel. 03–44–53–12–00), with three-course meals in a 12th-century cave for 120F. You can pick up groceries at the **Prisunic** (rue de la République) and a sandwich on **place de la Halle,** just southeast of the ramparts, in one of the many "sandwicheries."

COMPIEGNE

It's possible to do Compiègne itself in an afternoon, but you'll have to move fast to see the château, the forest, and nearby Pierrefonds all in one swoop. You may be tempted to stay a little longer than you expect—biking the Oise Valley is a welcome change from fighting métro crowds, and tossing back cold beers with the students of the Université de Technologie de Compiègne (UTC) is a lot cheaper here than in Paris.

The real draw in Compiègne, however, is the surrounding forest, which is nice for hiking. The tourist office can give you information about free guided walking tours run by **Compiègne AVF Accueil** on the weekends. If you don't have a lot of time, rent a bike (*see* Outdoor Activities, *below*) to get you to the **Clarière de l'Armistice** and to **Pierrefonds** (*see* Near Compiègne, *below*) without dealing with infrequent buses. It's a straight shot to Pierrefonds, but once you enter the maze of trails, you'll get lost if you don't have a map—pick up a free one when you rent a bike, or buy the 15F **Circuits Pédestres** (Walking Tours) booklet at the tourist office. Penny-pinching souls with a poor sense of direction should note that all trail markers have a red dash in the direction of Compiègne. Once you enter the forest, it's flat, easy riding with gorgeous, varying scenery.

BASICS

The bustling **Office de Tourisme** next to the Gothic Hôtel de Ville is jam-packed with leaflets and brochures on Compiègne, the forest, and the castle at Pierrefonds. *Pl. de l'Hôtel de Ville, tel. 03–44–40–01–00. Open Mon.–Sat. 9:30–12:15 and 1:45–6:15, Sun. 9:30–12:30 and 2:30–5; Nov.–Easter, closed Sun.*

The last weekend in May, Compiègne hosts the Foire aux Fromages et aux Vins, a big wine-and-cheese fair complete with wandering minstrels and folks hell-bent on beating last year's record consumption of 58,000 bottles of wine and 17,000 pieces of cheese.

COMING AND GOING

Trains leave at least three times a day from Paris's Gare du Nord for the 68F, 50- to 70-minute trip to Compiègne. The train and bus station is across the river from the center of town—a five-minute walk, max. Just cross the bridge to the right of the station and continue straight on rue Solferino through to place de l'Hôtel de Ville. On the other side of the square, rue Solferino turns into rue Magenta. Head off to your left for the château and to your right for the cobblestone pedestrian zone. City Buses 1, 2, and 5 are free and run from the station into the center of town (except on Sundays).

WHERE TO SLEEP

Cheap options are few and far between, and all are a good deal less charming than the hostel at Pierrefonds (*see* Near Compiègne, *below*). Some of the best choices are the **Hôtel de France** (17 rue Eugène-Floquet, tel. 03–44–40–02–74), which is the epitome of French provincial and has creaky floors; rooms range from 160F–360F with bath (some are big enough for families); the **Hôtel de Flandre** (16 quai de la République, tel. 03–44–83–24–40), near the train station, which has spacious if characterless rooms starting at 270F; the **Hôtel du Lion d'Or** (4 rue Général Leclerc, tel. 03–44–23–32–17, fax 03–44–86–06–23) with cute, small singles for 120F and doubles for 150F; and the **Hôtel St-Antoine** (17 rue de Paris, tel. 03–44–86–17–18), with doubles for 95F–140F.

HOSTEL • The best budget option is the **Auberge de Jeunesse,** a conveniently located hostel with bunk-filled rooms for only 30F a night, plus 13F for sheets. The showers are hot and the rooms are clean, but the hostel has one big drawback: The woman who runs it would rather let you sleep in the streets than break her precious 10 PM curfew. *6 rue Pasteur, tel. 03–44–40–72–64. Reception open 7–10 AM and 5–10 PM. HI card required. Closed mid-Sept.–Mar.*

FOOD

Brasseries abound around **place Hôtel de Ville** and in the pedestrian area, but they're not cheap. Try **Le Songeons** (40 rue Solférino, tel. 03–44–40–23–98), one block down toward the river from the center, for a decent 50F plat du jour. **Stromboli's Pizzeria** (2 rue des Lombards, in passage la Potene, tel. 03–44–40–06–21), closed Sundays, is a local favorite, a fact that comes in handy when you're trying to find the passage. You may have to wait a while to be seated, but the crispy-crust pizzas and pungent pastas (37F–50F) are worth it. For picnic packers, the open-air **Marché Place du Change** behind the pedestrian zone, open until 12:30 PM on Wednesdays and Saturdays, will ready you for the road. Otherwise, **Djerba Market** (cours Guynemer, tel. 03–44–40–01–36), open daily 8–8, is an absolute treasure, with everything from trail mix to fresh Sicilian olives, homemade couscous, fruit, and vegetables. **Monoprix** (rue Solferino) has the cheapest bulk grocery supplies.

WORTH SEEING

Compiègne is a mix of ramshackle half-timber houses and modern stucco buildings that went up after World War I flattened parts of the town. In fact, the armistice ending the war was signed in a railway car just 6 km (3½ mi) away from the then wiped-out town. If you rent a bike (*see* Outdoor Activities, *below*), you can visit the railcar in a memorial park called the **Clarière de l'Armistice** (tel. 03–44–85–14–18) and pay 10F to look through the windows at memorabilia of the event. (No buses come here, and it's closed Tuesdays.)

CHÂTEAU DE COMPIÈGNE • Louis XV built this château in the 18th century. It's a grand estate like Fontainebleau, not a Sleeping Beauty–type structure. It saw some war action of its own, during the Revolution and World War I. Never one for futons and milk crates, Napoléon redid the whole thing in marble, gold, and silk, though all that's left is some old furniture and flaking gold paint. You can see everything during a drab one-hour guided visit. But you won't get much out of it if you don't speak French, and from the looks of the park and gardens behind the château, Compiègne's royalty must have spent most of their time in the backyard. The colorful English **garden** and wide expanse of grass and trees make one of the nicest hangouts in France, and it's free—the gate is right off place du Château. Admission to the château also gets you into two museums. At the **Musée de la Voiture** (Car Museum) in the north wing, follow the animated tour guide to get the lowdown on the cars. One looks like an early rendition of the Batmobile, but the others just look like ornate chariots. Old-fashioned bicycles sneak their way in, too. The ho-hum **Musée du Second Empire** is a mishmash of furniture, clothes, and art set up in stark rooms. *Tel. 03–44–38–47–00. Admission 32F. Open Wed.–Mon. 9:15–5:30 (Oct.–Mar. until 3:45).*

MUSÉE DE LA FIGURINE HISTORIQUE • Though it doesn't sound particularly exciting, the Doll History Museum, in the passage next to the tourist office, has a collection of superbly detailed dolls, fully decked out in costumes. *Tel. 03–44–40–72–55. Admission 12F. Open Tues.–Sat. 9–noon and 2–6, Sun. 2–6 (Nov.–Feb. until 5).*

AFTER DARK

Au Bureau (17 pl. de l'Hôtel de Ville, tel. 03–44–40–10–11) makes a good starting point for an evening out. In booths surrounded by English pub paraphernalia, you can enjoy a 45F pizza as you down your first cold one. Once you're ready, ease over to the bar to choose from over 100 beers from 20-odd countries or order a "meter" of beer. For a cozier, more youthful scene, try the **Sweet Home Pub** (corner rue St-Corneille and rue d'Austerlitz), where things get wild later in the evening as more and more 25F brews are consumed. For dancing, try **Le City Hall** (27 pl. Hôtel de Ville, tel. 03–44–40–80–40), where the young and studious get hot and sweaty.

OUTDOOR ACTIVITIES

Endless trails—paved, unpaved, and downright sloshy—wind through shady groves of birch, oak, and French broom in the **Forêt de Compiègne.** There are only a couple of steep trails, but you'll have plenty of opportunities for exploration and discovery. The man at **Picardie Forêts Vertes** (4 rue de la Gare, tel. 03–44–90–05–05) is terrific, but you need to call the day before you want a bike; he'll have it waiting for you at the station. Tell him what you want to explore and how steep a ride you want, and he'll give you a map with your own personalized route. His office is just to your right as you exit the train station, but he is seldom there; you'll have better luck on weekends and holidays, when you can find him at the Carrefour Royal by the campground. All of this pampering has a price, of course—120F per day.

NEAR COMPIEGNE

PIERREFONDS

Tucked away in the Forêt de Compiègne, the 12th-century **Château de Pierrefonds** has round towers with pointy tops, cannon notches in the walls, a moat—everything a proper château should have. The interior of the château is decorated with medieval memorabilia. Between the château and a lake, half-timbered houses and teardrop spires rise out of Pierrefonds' tiny village. Between April and September, get wet and wacky on the lake at Pierrefonds with a pedal boat (48F for two people) or rowboat (25F per person), each rented by the half hour. *Tel. 03-44-42-80-77. Admission 28F. Open May-Aug., daily 10-6; Sept.-Apr., daily 10-12:30 and 2-5.*

COMING AND GOING • Getting here from Compiègne is a beautiful and easy bike ride—a flat 14 km (8½ mi) through lush green forest—and the initial view of the château as you round the final curve is worth the effort. Buses from Compiègne only run three times daily (fewer on Sunday, none on holidays) from the station and charge 13F; if you get stranded in Pierrefonds, the taxi costs a whopping 180F.

WHERE TO SLEEP AND EAT • The **Château de Jonval** (2 rue Séverine, tel. 03-44-42-80-97) has been converted into a hostel with rooms for two to eight people. Ever wondered what it would be like to open the window of your own castle bedroom and gaze across a tiny valley at a majestic medieval château glistening in the morning light? Here's your chance to find out. For 75F (plus a 30F membership fee per room), you get a simple bed and breakfast, but the superb setting makes it worthwhile. Another option is the **Hôtel des Etrangers** (10 rue Beaudon, tel. 03-44-42-80-18), where some rooms (250F-350F) have views of the castle. The hotel also has the best restaurant in town, with menus for 80F (weekdays), 100F, and 150F. Cheap picnic food is difficult to come by, so stock up in Compiègne. Crepe fans should check out **Ty Breiz** (8 rue du Beaudon, tel. 03-44-42-86-62), where the oversize, delicious *galettes* (buckwheat pancakes; 25F-40F) put anything you get in Paris to shame.

FONTAINEBLEAU

If you love the sight of a richly decorated château but can't handle Versailles's crush of tourists, head for Fontainebleau, a quick 65 km (40 mi) south of Paris. Elaborate, garish, and even occasionally beautiful, Fontainebleau's castle technically dates back further than Louis XIV's palace at Versailles. And if the château's regimented gardens seem too uptight, forage in the thick forest nearby (*see* Outdoor Activities, *below*).

During the fall, many go mushroom hunting in the Fontainebleau forest. But don't even THINK about doing this yourself without taking your finds to a pharmacist to verify that they're NOT poisonous, as dangerous look-alikes abound.

BASICS

Those interested only in Fontainebleau's château can pick up everything they need at the main entrance. If the forest is calling, however, the **Office de Tourisme** has some crucial items, including a very detailed forest map (35F) and the schedules of irregular local buses. The hard part is finding the office. Hint: Look behind the carousel on the place du Napoléon Bonaparte. *31 pl. du Napoléon Bonaparte, tel. 01-64-22-25-68. Open weekdays 9:30-12:30 and 2-6:30, Sat. 9:30-6:30, Sun. 10-12:30 and 3-5:30; Oct.-Apr., closed Sun.*

COMING AND GOING

Trains leave every hour from Paris's Gare de Lyon and cost 46F for the 40-minute trip. The 3-km (2-mi) walk from the train station in Avon to the château takes about 30 uninteresting minutes along avenue Franklin Roosevelt, unless you stop to rent a bike (*see* Biking, *below*). Or take Bus A/B (every 15 minutes) from the station until you see the château. During high season, when the bus is crowded, most visitors slip on without a ticket; honest types buy the 9F ticket on board.

FOOD

At **Au Délice Impérial** (1 rue Grande, tel. 01-64-22-20-70), near the tourist office, large salads set you back only 38F. A few doors over, **La Taverne Alsacienne** (23 rue Grande, tel. 01-64-22-20-85) serves a 58F three-course menu with French specialties. Otherwise, there are a few mediocre crêperies (crêpe stands) on **rue Montebello,** where crepes go for 15F-35F, and several great specialty shops in the pedestrian zone around **rue des Sablons.** For general groceries there's a **Prisunic** a few blocks from the center toward Avon on rue Grande.

WORTH SEEING

The **gardens** of Fontainebleau, like the château, reflect a mix of styles. Designed in part by Versailles's landscape architect extraordinaire, André Le Nôtre, they don't quite achieve the same magnificence. Yet the nice thing about these gardens (and Fontainebleau in general) is that they are relatively untainted by tourists. Locals fish for salmon and carp in the Grand Canal and walk their dogs along Le Prairie, the grassy expanse on the edge of the sculptured gardens. If you have a burning desire to know more about Napoléon or French military history, there's always the **Musée Napoléonien d'Art et d'Histoire Militaire**

PUTTING THE PARIS IN DISNEYLAND PARIS

The following are quirks unique to Mickey's European pied-à-terre: Wine is served in the park (they changed their no-alcohol policy in 1993). Tombstone inscriptions at Phantom Manor read: "Jasper Jones, loyal manservant, kept the master happy; Anna Jones, faithful chambermaid, kept the master happier." No Mickey walking around—he was too mobbed by kiddies, so he stays in one spot, and you have to line up to see him. Cast members look like they need a cigarette. If you sit on the lawn, "happy" Disney characters lose the grin and use the whistle.

(88 rue St-Honoré, north of rue de France; open Tues.–Sat. 2–5), which claims to be the third-biggest military museum in France. Whoopee.

CHATEAU DE FONTAINEBLEAU • In 1528, King François I had license to kill just about anything he wanted, so no one complained when he commissioned this upscale hunting lodge—and we're talking way upscale. The château has been used as both a hunting lodge and an official residence for nearly eight centuries by more than 30 sovereigns. Each king who lived here left his mark—a tower here, a staircase there—with additions that reflect the style of his period. Because of these hundreds of years of architectural influences, Napoléon I called Fontainebleau "La Maison des Siècles" (The House of Centuries).

Pay up and you can see the **Grands Appartements** and the **Salles Renaissances,** the fully furnished living quarters of François I, Napoléon III, and all the royalty in between. The same ticket admits you to the **Musée Napoléon I** (15 rooms filled with arms, guns, hats, uniforms, and other relics of Napoléon's life) and the **Musée Chinois,** which holds the Empress Eugénie's private collection of Chinese goodies. An extra fee allows you into the kings' private rooms, the **Petits Appartements.** If you really have your heart set on seeing these smaller rooms, call ahead (tel. 01–60–71–50–70) to find out if tours are running that day. In addition, there are regular free concerts on the castle's organ in the **Chapelle de la Trinité;** call 01–64–22–68–43 for information. *Admission 35F; additional 15F for Petits Appartements. Open June–Oct., Wed.–Mon. 9:30–5; Nov.–May, Wed.–Mon. 9:30–12:30 and 2–5.*

OUTDOOR ACTIVITIES

The château's gardens back right onto 42,000 acres of the **Forêt de Fontainebleau,** one of the biggest national forests in France. If you want to play in the woods, don't come on a Monday, however, when most of the rental-equipment facilities are closed. The tourist office sells a 35F topo guide called *Guide des Sentiers de Promenades dans le Massif Forestier de Fontainebleau,* which covers paths throughout the forest. For a good view of the whole beech-, birch-, and pine-covered expanse, head up to the **Tour Denecourt** (Denecourt Tower), about 5 km (3 mi) northeast of the château.

BIKING • The trails here are a dream—endless and totally unrestricted. The tourist office has trail maps and guides, but you can easily explore the former hunting grounds on your own. **A la Petite Reine** (32 rue des Sablons, tel. 01–60–74–57–57) rents mountain bikes for 80F per weekday, 100F per weekend day, with a 2,000F or credit-card deposit. **Mountain Bike Folies** (246 Grande Rue, tel. 01–64–23–43–07) is another rental option with similar prices. Both have half-day rentals for 50F–80F. Most of the steeper trails are west of town, but ask the bike store people to point out the best places to ride on your map.

CLIMBING • Rock clusters and small gorges abound, but getting the gear and then both the gear and yourself to them is tricky. **Top Loisirs** (16 rue de Ferrare, tel. 01–60–74–08–50) rents gear in town but doesn't open until 10 AM, and if you're relying on buses to get here, the day will be over before you touch rock. Your best bet is to rent in Paris, then arrive in town early enough to stop at the tourist office to book one of the many guides. Once you've done that, you can check the bus schedules or walk the 5–8 km (3–5 mi) to your climbing spot.

DISNEYLAND PARIS

It's controversial, it's expensive, and it's a hell of a lot of fun. Though the park's chances of survival were shaky for a while—it lost almost $1 billion in 1993—attendance and, more importantly, length of stay, have been on the upswing. It's the money you spend on hotels, food, and felt hats with plastic ears that really brings in the bucks—and the longer you stay, the more felt hats with plastic ears you're likely to buy. Frequent cold, damp weather hasn't helped attendance either, but you'd think they'd have thought of that before they started construction. But no matter how you feel about the Disneyfication of Europe, it can be tempting to blow a month's pay on the spotless grounds, good rides, and long lines that characterize this meticulously conceived fantasy world. Basically, it's the best of the American Disney parks attractions rolled into one condensed version. **Star Tours, Captain Eo, Big Thunder Railroad, It's a Small World, Peter Pan** . . . they're all here, and more state-of-the-art than ever. Other rides include **Indiana Jones and the Temple of Peril,** with Disney's first-ever roller coaster loop, and the $120 million **Space Mountain,** the scariest Disney ride ever. Although Adventureland's **Middle Eastern Grand Bazaar** and **Fantasyland's Alsatian Village** give the park a bit of faux international flair, it's definitely more "Disneyland" than "Paris." The American Old West theme seems to find its way into everything, and the Roaring '20s are bigger here than they ever were in the States.

Although Disneyland Paris will never be a travel bargain, you can save money by timing your visit carefully. Rates do not simply rise with the temperature; they fluctuate with school and national holidays, weekends, and season. Most of June, for example, admission costs 175F, but in February and March (ski season) it jumps back up to 250F. Call ahead to verify prices for specific dates—going a day later could make a big difference. Lines within the park are usually ridiculous on weekends, but apparently everyone rushes to get here first thing in the morning, then poops out by early afternoon. *Tel. 01–60–30–60–30. Take RER Line A to Marne-la-Vallée/Chessy (38F). Admission 175F–400F depending on season and no. of days. Open daily 9–7 (until 11 in summer).*

WHERE TO SLEEP

It's so expensive to stay here that it's no wonder hardly anyone spends the night. The least expensive hotels within the resort, the **Hotel Santa Fe** and **Hotel Cheyenne,** have rooms for up to four people at 300F–650F, and April through September the **Davy Crockett Ranch** has cabins for up to six people from 475F. Hotel/park admission packages can make a night here slightly more attractive. *Tel. 01–49–41–49–10 for reservations; 407/W–DISNEY from the U.S.; 0171/753–2900 from the U.K.*

FOOD

Although most budget visitors just smuggle food into the park, a few restaurants inside actually have menus that won't break your bank, including the **Café Hyperion** (inside Videopolis in Discoveryland), with a menu from 40F; the **Pizzerria Bella Notte** (Fantasyland), with a menu from 50F; and the **Cowboy Cookout Barbeque** (Frontierland), also with a menu from 40F. The restaurants serve mostly American-style food.

ELSEWHERE NEAR PARIS

PARC ASTERIX

All French kids know comic book hero Astérix and his loyal, larger sidekick, Obélix. In the year 50 BC, these stubby Gauls beat up invading (and usually pretty idiotic) Romans trying to attack their village in Brittany. A swig of magic potion makes Astérix invincible in battle, and menhir-toting Obélix fell into a vat of the stuff as a child and was permanently fortified. Read one of the comic books before you go, to get the most out of this cartoon world.

If you think you know amusement parks, this French-style one could be a real eye-opener. You learn about French history on your way from one attraction to the next (only in Paris would they lump an amusement park with a historical lesson), from a Gaul village with printmakers and potters, to a little Roman village, to a miniaturized version of Paris complete with a Dixieland band. Most of the attractions are glorified versions of carnival rides, spinning and twirling you around until your lunch makes an encore appearance. There are some fun ones, though, like the ultra-loopy **Goudurix roller coaster** and **Grand Splatch,** which will get you soaked. Be warned that some attractions close on weekdays—call ahead if you have your heart set on any ride in particular—and that the park can be really empty and depressing during the week. *Tel. 01–44–62–34–04. Admission 160F. Open mid-Apr.–mid-Oct., weekends 10–6 (until 7 PM on peak days); also open weekdays July–Aug.; for other weekdays, call ahead.*

COMING AND GOING

From Paris, take RER Line B3 to the Charles de Gaulle/Roissy terminus (46F), where you can catch an 18F shuttle (20 minutes) that runs to the park (9:30–1:30) and back (4:30–park closing) every half hour.

PROVINS

If you've never seen a fortified medieval town, visiting Provins is a must. Built mostly in the 12th and 13th centuries, the *ville haute* (upper village) is entirely surrounded by stone ramparts and has all kinds of medieval stuff to explore. See the tower where they used to keep criminals; an enormous church with imposing wooden doors and a big, black dome; an executioner's house; subterranean passages running under the whole town; tiny, flowered, cobblestone streets; and, of more recent origin, a beer garden where locals come to hear live music. From the train station, walk across the bridge, through the commercial center, and up the hill, following the signs that say ITINÉRAIRE PIÉTON (pedestrian route).

The ramparts and medieval building are courtesy of the Count of Champagne, who brought money, people, and ideas to Provins in the early 13th century, turning it into a major commercial center. People came to buy, sell, and trade their goods, paying taxes to the count, who, in turn, offered them protection. Apparently the system worked; the count made enough money to build the town and the convent in the neighboring forest. Everything was running smoothly until river transportation became all the rage in Europe, and Provins found itself high and dry. Eight centuries later, without its superpower status, it's merely a great day trip from Paris. If you hit Provins in late May or early June, you'll find the **Fête Médiévale,** when the whole town dresses up, acts like barbarians from the Middle Ages, and eats a lot of junk food. Entrance is 30F, but it's free if you happen to be wearing a medieval costume.

BASICS

The hour-long train ride from Paris will set you back 73F. Take one of the three morning trains from Paris's Gare de l'Est; the only afternoon train is at 4 PM and won't leave you enough time to return to the city. If you miss the last train to Paris, the nightlife isn't exactly kicking in Provins, but you can find cheap hostel-like housing at **Le Chalet** (3 pl. Honoré de Balzac, tel. 01–64–00–02–27) for 50F–80F. For a bit more luxury, check out the beautifully converted farmhouse at **La Ferme du Châtel** (5 rue de la Chapelle St-Jean, tel. 01–64–00–10–73), where fancy doubles are 260F. As for food, it's all cutesy, overpriced meals in the walled village, but there's a **Monoprix** market on your walk from the train station, where you can stock up on cheap grub.

ST-GERMAIN-EN-LAYE

Scale down Versailles, take away 95% of its tourists, plop it down on a terrace overlooking the Seine, and you have the **Château de St-Germain-en-Laye.** The original château, the first palace built by French royalty outside Paris, was started by Louis VI, known as Le Gros (the Fat), in the early 12th century as a defensive stronghold. François I and his successors transformed St-Germain from a fortress to a royal residence. Louis XIV then called in Hardouin-Mansart and Le Nôtre to make additions and improvements. Never satisfied, he finally abandoned the château entirely and built Versailles.

Thanks to Napoléon III, the château now houses the **Musée des Antiquités Nationales** (admission 22F; open Wed.–Mon. 9–5:15), an archaeological collection from paleolithic times to the Middle Ages. If that's not your thing, you can enjoy an unobstructed view of the Seine and the distant Paris skyline from the **Petite Terrasse** in front of the château. Protected from the forest by the château walls, the **Grande Terrasse** has a 4-km (2½-mi) loop for joggers and serious promenaders. The gardens are free, open until 9:30 PM, and stretch into the endless **Forêt de St-Germain,** which is dotted with picnic tables. The tourist office can give you maps for trails as long as 18 km (11 mi) in this dense but relatively flat forest.

BASICS

All this serenity is just a 20-minute RER ride from Paris. Take the Red Line A1 from La Défense for 11F, or buy a ticket good from the center of Paris for 17F50. The **Office du Tourisme** is set up in Claude Debussy's house and can give you minimal information on the few museums in the area, as well as surrounding places of interest. *38 rue au Pain, tel. 01–34–51–05–12. From the RER station, head right, past the church; rue au Pain is on left. Open Tues.–Fri. 9:15–12:30 and 2–6:30, Sat. 9:15–6:30; also Mar.–Oct., Sun. 10–1.*

FRENCH GLOSSARY

The French are not known for being tolerant of foreigners who butcher their language. But, even if you haven't spent a few years mastering the language's uvular r's and labial u's, a good phrase book, a small dose of humility, and a great deal of *politesse* should help. Remember to use "Madame" and "Monsieur" when addressing people you don't know. Living Language™ cassettes, CDs, phrase books, and dictionaries make it easy to learn the essentials. If you can't find them at your local bookstore, call 800/733–3000.

PRONUNCIATION

French is not an easy language for English speakers to pronounce. The vowel and nasal sounds are difficult; consonants at the end of words are usually not pronounced; and, when a word ending in a consonant is followed by a word beginning with a vowel, the two words are often run together (this is called *liaison*). At least you can almost always count on the stress being on the last syllable. Here's a little guide to get you started:

a like the **a** in saw
e like the **ea** in earth
é and *è* like the **ay** in hay
eu and *œ* like the **oo** in hoof
i like the **i** in magazine

o like the **o** in no
ou like the **oo** in zoo
u like **oo** with your lips pursed
ui a short "wee" sound
oi a short "wah" sound

NASAL SOUNDS

Nasal sounds in French are much less pronounced than they are in English. They aren't easy to develop an ear for, but there are really only three of them: the nasal in *faim* (hungry) or *vin* (wine), the nasal in *bon* (good), and the nasal in *an* (year).

CONSONANTS

Consonants resemble English a lot more closely than the vowels, with a few exceptions: **s** is often pronounced **z** as in "rose"; **ch** is always **sh** like "shoe"; **j** has a soft **zhuh** sound, **ll** is often like the **y** in yam; and **th** is always **t**.

French	Pronunciation	English
BASICS		
Bonjour	Bohn-zhoor	Hello
Bonsoir	Bohn-swahr	Good evening
Bonne nuit	Bun-wee	Good night (before going to bed)
Comment allez-vous?	Cummunt-allay-voo	How are you?
Je vais bien	Zhuh-vay-bee-en	I'm fine
Ça va?	Sah-vah?	How's it going?

Ça va	Sah-vah	It's going fine
D'accord	Dah-core	Okay
Au revoir	Oh-vwahr	Goodbye
Excusez-moi	Ex-cuze-ay-mwah	Excuse me
Parlez-vous anglais?	Par-lay-voo-zang-lay	Do you speak English?
Je ne parle pas français	Zhun-parl-pah-frawn-say	I don't speak French
Je suis américain(e)	Zhuh-sweez-ahm-air-ee-can(nuh)	I'm American
Je suis australien(ne)	Zhuh-sweez-oh-stray-lee-en(nuh)	I'm Australian
Je suis canadien(ne)	Zhuh-swee-cah-nah-dee-en(nuh)	I'm Canadian
Je suis anglais(e)	Zhuh-sweez-ahn-glay(glezz)	I'm English
Je suis écossais(e)	Zhuh-sweez-ay-coss-ay(ezz)	I'm Scottish
Je suis irlandais(e)	Zhuh-sweez-eer-lahn-day(dezz)	I'm Irish
Etudiant(e)	Ay-too-dyahn(tuh)	Student
Je ne comprends pas	Zhuh-nuh-cum-prond-pah	I don't understand
Pardon	Pahr-dohn	Sorry/excuse me
Je ne sais pas	Zhun-say-pah	I don't know
S'il vous plaît	See-voo-play	Please
Merci	Mehr-see	Thank you
De rien	Duh-ree-en	You're welcome
Non	Noh	No
Oui	Wee	Yes
Où est/sont . . .	Oo-ay/sohn	Where is/are . . .
Les toilettes	Lay-twah-lett	Bathroom
La poste	Lah-pust	Post office
La laverie	Lah-lahv-ree	Laundromat
La banque	Lah-bonk	Bank
Ça coûte combien?	Sah-coot-cohm-bee-en	How much does this cost?
Avez-vous...	Ah-vay-voo	Do you have...
Fermeture annuelle	Fair-muh-toohr-ahn-yoo-ell	Annual closure
En vacances	On-va-cons	On vacation
Jour ferié	Zhoor-fehr-ee-ay	Holiday
Ouvert(e)	Oo-vehr	Open
Fermé(e)	Fair-may	Closed
Que sont vos horaires?	Keuh-sohn-vohs-orr-air	What are your hours?
A quelle heure...?	ah-kell-uhr	At what time..?.
Entrée	Ohn-tray	Entrance
Sortie	Sore-tee	Exit
Hôtel de ville	Oh-tell-duh-veel	City hall
Rez-de-chaussée	Ray-duh-shoh-say	Ground floor
Sous-sol	Soo-sull	Basement
Zone piétonne	Zunn-pee-ay-tunn	Pedestrian zone
Quartier	Car-tee-ay	District

EMERGENCIES AND MEDICAL AID

La police	La-poh-lees	Police
Arrêtez!	Ah-reh-tay	Stop!
Aidez-moi!	Ay-day-mwah	Help me!
Au secours!	Oh-suh-coor	Help!
En cas d'urgence	Ohn-cah-doohr-zhonce	In case of emergency
Fichez-moi la paix!	Fee-shay-mwah-lah-pay	Leave me alone!
Je suis malade	Zhuh-swee-mah-lahd	I'm sick
Appelez un médecin	Ah-pul-lay-uh-medd-sahn	Call a doctor
J'ai mal à la tête	Zhay-mall-ah-lah-tett	I have a headache
J'ai mal à l'estomac	Zhay-mall-ah-less-tum-ock	I have a stomach ache
L'hôpital	Loh-pee-tall	Hospital

La pharmacie	Lah-farm-ah-see	Drugstore
Ordonnance	Orr-dunn-ons	Prescription
Un médicament	Uh-may-dee-cah-mon	Medicine
Une aspirine	Oon-ass-pee-reen	Aspirin
Un préservatif	Uh-pray-zurve-ah-teef	Condom

COMING AND GOING

Aller-simple	Ah-lay-sam-pluh	One-way
Aller-retour	Ah-lay-ruh-toor	Round-trip
A pied	Ah-pee-ay	On foot
Assurance	Ah-soor-ohns	Insurance
Auto-stop	Oh-toe-stop	Hitchhiking
La banlieue	Lah-bahn-lee-yeuh	Suburbs
Consigne	Kohn-seen-yuh	Luggage storage
Correspondance	Kor-eh-spohn-dawnse	Connection
La fin de la ligne	Lah-fahn-duh-lah-leen-yuh	The end of the line
Vente de billets	Vahnt-duh-bee-yay	Ticket office
Un billet pour . . .	Uh-bee-yay-poor	A ticket for . . .
Composter votre billet	Com-poh-stay-votra-bee-yay	Validate your ticket
Circule tous les jours	Seer-cool-too-lay-zhoor	Runs every day
Sauf dimanche	Soaf-dee-mansh	Except Sundays
Combien de kilomètres?	Com-bee-en-duh-kee-loh-met	How many kilometers?
Je vais à . . .	Zhuh-vay-ah	I'm going to . . .
Je voudrais descendre à . . .	Zhuh-voo-dray-day-son-drah-ah	I want to get off at . . .
Le train part à quelle heure?	Luh-trahn-pahr-ah-kel-euhr	What time does the train leave?
Un plan de la ville	Uh-plohn-duh-lah-veel	City plan/map
Une carte routière	Oon-cart-roo-tee-air	Road map
L'aéroport	Lay-roh-por	Airport
La gare	Lah-gar	Train station
Chemins de fer	Shuh-man-duh-fair	Train tracks
Quai	Kay	Platform
Couchette .	Coo-shett	Sleeping compartment
La gare routière	Lah-gar-roo-tee-air	Bus station
Car	Cahr	Tourist bus
Arrêt	Ah-ray	Bus stop
Location de voitures	Loh-cah-see-ohn-duh-vwah-toor	Car rental agency
Essence	Ess-onse	Gas
Un pneu	Uh-puh-nuh	Tire
Feu rouge/vert	Fuh-roozh/vayr	Red/green stoplight
Une motocycle	Oon-moe-toe-see-cluh	Motorcycle
Autoroute	Oh-toe-root	Highway
La route pour . . .	Lah-root-poor	The road to . . .
Pont	Pohn	Bridge
Station de métro	Stah-see-ohn-duh-may-tro	Subway station
Tarif	Tah-reef	Fare
Ticket journalier	Tee-kett-zhoor-nall-ee-ay	One-day pass
Traverser	Tra-vayr-say	To cross
Un vélo	Uh-vay-loh	Bicycle

WHERE TO SLEEP

Une auberge de jeunesse	Oon-oh-bayrge-duh-zhoo-ness	Youth hostel
Une gîte d'étape	Oon-zheet-day-top	Rural hostel
Un refuge	Uh-ruh-fyooge	Mountain shelter
Un camping	Uh-camm-ping	Campground
Un emplacement	Un-omm-plass-mont	Campsite

Une chambre	Oon-shahm-bruh	Room
Une chambre pour deux personnes	Oon-shahm-bruh-poor-duh-pair-sunn	Double room
Je peux la voir?	Zhuh-puh-lah-vwarr	Can I see it?
On reste pour . . . jours	Ohn-rest-poor . . . zhoor	We're staying for . . . days
Avec	Ah-veck	With
Sans	Sahn	Without
Une douche	Oon-doosh	Shower
Un lavabo	Uh-lah-vah-boe	Sink
Draps	Drah	Sheets
Calme	Call-muh	Quiet
Le petit déjeuner	Luh-puh-tee-day-zhuh-nay	Breakfast
Compris	Cum-pree	Included

FOOD

Alimentation	Ah-lee-moan-tah-see-ohn	Food
Boulangerie	Boo-lahn-zhuh-ree	Bakery
Supermarché	Soo-pehr-mar-shay	Supermarket
J'ai faim	Zhay-fah	I'm hungry
Je voudrais . . .	Zhuh-voo-dray	I'd like . . .
Est-ce que service est compris?	Ess-kuh-sayr-veese-ay-com-pree	Is the tip included?
Je ne peux pas manger de . . .	Zhuh-nuh-puh-pah-mon-zhay-duh	I cannot eat . . .
Je suis végétarien(ne)	Zhuh-swee-vay-zhay-tay-ree-en	I'm a vegetarian
Le plat du jour	Luh-plah-doo-zhoor	Dish of the day
Une bouteille de . . .	Oon-boo-tay-duh	A bottle of . . .
Un verre de . . .	Uh-vayr-duh	A glass of . . .
L'addition	Lah-dee-see-ohn	Bill/check
Pain	Pah	Bread
Agneau	Awn-yoe	Lamb
Beurre	Buhr	Butter
Bifteck	Beef-tek	Beef steak
Champignons	Shahm-peen-yohn	Mushrooms
Chocolat	Sho-coh-lah	Chocolate
Confiture	Coh-fee-toohr	Jam
Eau gazeuse	Oh-gahz-uzz	Sparkling water
Fromage	Fro-mawzh	Cheese
Fruits de mer	Fweed-mehr	Shellfish
Jambon	Zham-bohn	Ham
Jus	Zhoo	Juice
Lait	Lay	Milk
Lapin	Lah-pah	Rabbit
Marrons	Mah-rohn	Chestnuts
Miel	Mee-ell	Honey
Moutarde	Moo-tard	Mustard
Oeuf	Uff	Egg
Poivre	Pwah-vruh	Pepper
Poisson	Pwah-sohn	Fish
Pomme	Pohm	Apple
Pommes de terre	Pohm-deuh-tehr	Potatoes
Porc	Pohr	Pork
Poulet	Poo-lay	Chicken
Rôti	Roh-tee	Roast
Sel	Sell	Salt
Sucre	Soo-cruh	Sugar
Viande	Vee-ahnd	Meat
Vin (rouge/blanc)	Vahn-(roo-zhuh/blahn)	Red/white wine

Vinaigre	Veen-ay-gruh	Vinegar
Yaourt	Yah-oort	Yogurt
Une assiette	Oon-ah-syet	Plate
Une fourchette	Oon-for-shet	Fork
Une cuillère	Oon-kwee-yay	Spoon
Un couteau	Uh-coo-toe	Knife
Une serviette	Oon-sehr-vee-et	Napkin
A point	Ah-pwah	Medium rare
Bien cuit	Bee-en-coo-ee	Well-done
Saignant	Senn-yahn	Rare (literally, bleeding)
A Emporter	Ah-ohm-poor-tay	Take-out

NUMBERS

Un/une	Uh/Oon	One
Deux	Duh	Two
Trois	Twah	Three
Quatre	Cat-ruh	Four
Cinq	Sank	Five
Six	Sees	Six
Sept	Sett	Seven
Huit	Weet	Eight
Neuf	Nuff	Nine
Dix	Deece	Ten
Onze	Ohn-zuh	Eleven
Douze	Dooz	Twelve
Treize	Trehz	Thirteen
Quatorze	Ka-torz	Fourteen
Quinze	Kanz	Fifteen
Seize	Sez	Sixteen
Dix-sept	Deece-set	Seventeen
Dix-huit	Dee-zweet	Eighteen
Dix-neuf	Deece-nuff	Nineteen
Vingt	Vahnt	Twenty
Trente	Tront	Thirty
Quarante	Cahr-ont	Forty
Cinquante	Sank-ont	Fifty
Soixante	Swah-sont	Sixty
Soixante-dix	Swah-sont-deece	Seventy
Quatre-vingts	Cat-ruh-vahnt	Eighty
Quatre-vingt-dix	Cat-ruh-vahnt-deece	Ninety
Cent	Sohnt	One hundred
Mille	Meal	One thousand

DAYS AND MONTHS

Dimanche	Dee-monsh	Sunday
Lundi	Lun-dee	Monday
Mardi	Mar-dee	Tuesday
Mercredi	Mehr-cruh-dee	Wednesday
Jeudi	Zheuh-dee	Thursday
Vendredi	Vohn-druh-dee	Friday
Samedi	Sam-dee	Saturday
Janvier	Zhahn-vee-ay	January
Fevrier	Feh-vree-ay	February
Mars	Mahss	March
Avril	Ah-vreel	April
Mai	May	May
Juin	Zhoo-wahn	June
Juillet	Zhwee-ay	July

Août	Oot	August
Septembre	Sep-tohm-bruh	September
Octobre	Ok-toh-bruh	October
Novembre	No-vohm-bruh	November
Decembre	Deh-sohm-bruh	December

INDEX